Introduction to Visual Basic.NET 2008 Programming

CCADCIM Technologies

525 St. Andrews Drive
Schererville, IN 46375
USA
(www.cadcim.com)

Contributing Author
Sham Tickoo
Professor
Purdue University Calumet
Hammond, Indiana
USA

CADCIM Technologies

Introduction to Visual Basic.NET 2008 Programming
CADCIM/TICKOO Publication

Published by CADCIM Technologies, 525 St Andrews Drive, Schererville, IN 46375 USA.

ISBN 978-1-942689-30-0

www.cadcim.com

DEDICATION

*To teachers, who make it possible to disseminate knowledge
to enlighten the young and curious minds
of our future generations*

*To students, who are dedicated to learning new technologies
and making the world a better place to live*

THANKS

To staff of CADCIM Technologies for their valuable help

Online Training Program Offered by CADCIM Technologies

CADCIM Technologies provides effective and affordable virtual online training on various software packages including Computer Aided Design and Manufacturing (CAD/CAM), computer programming languages, animation, architecture, and GIS. The training is delivered 'live' via Internet at any time, any place, and at any pace to individuals as well as the students of colleges, universities, and CAD/CAM training centers. The main features of this program are:

Training for Students and Companies in a Classroom Setting

Highly experienced instructors and qualified engineers at CADCIM Technologies conduct the classes under the guidance of Prof. Sham Tickoo of Purdue University Calumet, USA. This team has authored several textbooks that are rated "one of the best" in their categories and are used in various colleges, universities, and training centers in North America, Europe, and in other parts of the world.

Training for Individuals

CADCIM Technologies with its cost effective and time saving initiative strives to deliver the training in the comfort of your home or work place, thereby relieving you from the hassles of traveling to training centers.

Training Offered on Software Packages

CADCIM provides basic and advanced training on the following software packages:

***CAD/CAM/CAE**: CATIA, Pro/ENGINEER Wildfire, PTC Creo Parametric, Creo Direct, SOLIDWORKS, Autodesk Inventor, Solid Edge, NX, AutoCAD, AutoCAD LT, AutoCAD Plant 3D, Customizing AutoCAD, EdgeCAM, and ANSYS*

***Architecture and GIS**: Autodesk Revit Architecture, AutoCAD Civil 3D, Autodesk Revit Structure, AutoCAD Map 3D, Revit MEP, Navisworks, Primavera, and Bentley STAAD Pro*

***Animation and Styling**: Autodesk 3ds Max, Autodesk Maya, Autodesk Alias, The Foundry NukeX, MAXON CINEMA 4D, Adobe Flash, and Adobe Premiere*

***Computer Programming**: C++, VB.NET, Oracle, AJAX, and Java*

*For more information, please visit the following link: **http://www.cadcim.com***

Note
If you are a faculty member, you can register by clicking on the following link to access the teaching resources: ***www.cadcim.com/Registration.aspx***. The student resources are available at ***www.cadcim.com***. We also provide **Live Virtual Online Training** on various software packages. For more information, write us at ***sales@cadcim.com***.

Table of Contents

Chapter 3: Control and Loop Structures

Chapter 4: Arrays and Procedures

Chapter 5: Loop Structures

Chapter 6: Containers, Menus, and, Toolbars

Chapter 7: Components

Chapter 8: Working with MDI, In-built Dialogs, and Printing Controls

Chapter 9: Concepts of Object-oriented Programming

Chapter 10: Working with Database

Chapter 11: Introduction to Web Forms

Preface

VISUAL BASIC .NET 2008

Welcome to Learning Visual Basic.NET 2008, an example based textbook, written to cater to the needs of programmers who wish to understand the concepts of the language. The textbook highlights Visual Basic.NET (VB.NET) as the easiest and most productive tool for creating .NET applications, including Windows applications and Web applications.

VB.NET is an object-oriented computer language that has evolved from Microsoft's Visual Basic (VB). Like all .NET languages, programs written in VB.NET require the .NET framework to execute. While providing the traditional ease-of-use of Visual Basic development, Visual Basic .NET also allows optional use of new language features such as inheritance, method overloading, and structured exception handling. All these features make Visual Basic a powerful tool for learning object-oriented programming. Visual Basic .NET fully integrates with the .NET Framework and the Common Language Runtime, which together provide language interoperability, simplified deployment, enhanced security, and improved versioning support.

The highlight of the textbook is that each concept introduced in it has been exemplified by an application to clarify and facilitate better understanding. Also, the line-by-line explanation of source code of each application ensures that the user can master the programming techniques and concepts, and use them with flexibility while designing applications.

The main features of the book are as follows:

Programming Approach: This textbook introduces the key ideas of object-oriented programming in an innovative way. The concepts are illustrated through best programming examples, covering all aspects of VB.NET.

Notes: Additional information is provided to the users in the form of notes.

Illustrations: There is an extensive use of examples, schematic representations, tables, screen capture images, and applications.

Learning Objectives: The first page of every chapter summarizes the topics that are covered in it.

Self-Evaluation Test, Review Questions, and Exercises: Each chapter ends with a Self- Evaluation Test so that the users can assess their knowledge. The answers of the Self-Evaluation test are given at the end of the chapter. Also, the Review Questions and Exercises are given at the end of each chapter that can be used by the Instructors as test questions and exercises.

If you face any problem in accessing these files, please contact the publisher at *sales@cadcim.com* or the author at *stickoo@purduecal.edu* or *tickoo525@gmail.com*.

Stay Connected

You can now stay connected with us through Facebook and Twitter to get the latest information about our textbooks, videos, and teaching/learning resources. To stay informed of such updates, follow us on Facebook *(www.facebook.com/cadcim)* and Twitter (*@cadcimtech*). You can also subscribe to our YouTube channel *(www.youtube.com/cadcimtech)* to get the information about our latest video tutorials.

Chapter 1

Overview of the .NET Framework

Learning Objectives

After completing this chapter, you will be able to understand:

- *The concept of .NET.*
- *The components of .NET.*
- *The concept of Visual Studio .NET.*
- *The concept of IDE components.*

INTRODUCTION TO THE .NET FRAMEWORK

The .NET Framework is a collection of tools, technologies, and languages. It is a platform or an environment in which web applications are created. These applications can be used by the client machines anywhere in the world. The .NET is a platform-dependent and language-independent framework that can support multiple languages such as VB.NET, C#, Jscript, VBScript, and Managed C++. Also, applications created in the .NET environment can be executed on different platforms such as Linux, Unix, and so on.

The Framework includes the following objectives:

1. It provides a code execution environment that minimizes software exploitation and versioning conflicts.

2. It provides an environment that can successfully execute the code created by an unknown user.

3. It provides an environment that can be used to execute both window based and web-based applications.

4. It provides facilities to enable all applications to communicate with each other.

Figure 1-1 shows an overview of the .NET Framework structure.

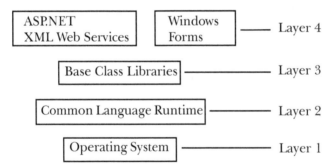

Figure 1-1 *The .NET Framework structure*

The layers of the .NET Framework are discussed next.

Operating System

The first layer of the framework is the operating system. An operating system is a set of programs, which is used as an interface between the user and the hardware. The operating systems supported by the .NET Framework are as follows:

1. Windows 98/Me
2. Windows 2000 Service Pack 3
3. Windows XP Service Pack 2
4. Windows 2000 Server
5. Windows 2003 Server

Common Language Runtime

The second layer is the Common Language Runtime (CLR). The runtime environment manages the execution of the code of the applications that are executed in the .NET environment. This layer provides services such as memory management, security, database support, and exception management.

Base Class Libraries

The Base Class Libraries is the third layer of the .NET Framework. A library is a collection of prewritten code known as classes. These classes contain the functions that are required for developing a .NET application.

ASP.NET and Windows Forms

The last layer of the Framework consists of ASP.NET and windows forms. A windows forms application can executes only on the local server, whereas an ASP.NET application can execute on both local and remote servers.

COMPONENTS OF .NET

The .NET Framework is divided into the following two main components:

1. The .NET Framework Class Library
2. Common Language Runtime

The .NET Framework Class Library

As mentioned above, the base class library is a collection of prewritten code known as classes. These classes contain the functions that are required to develop a .NET application. For example, ASP.NET classes are used to create web forms applications, and windows forms classes are used to create windows forms applications. The library also contains some other classes that are used to work with databases, managing security, and accessing files.

The classes in the .NET Framework are organized into certain groups called namespaces (discussed later in this chapter). To support a particular function, each namespace contains a particular class. For example, the namespace used for creating forms is known as **System. Windows.Forms**. Some of these classes are discussed below:

Windows Forms Application

The windows forms application is a window application that executes on user's PC. This application provides an interface that enables the user interaction. For the designing mode of an application, windows application uses the windows forms controls that are part of the user interface. These controls include textboxes, labels, and so on.

Web Forms Application

The web forms application executes on a web server. This application also provides a user interface. A web forms application uses the web forms controls that are similar to windows forms controls, except that the web forms controls are meant only for the web forms.

Common Language Runtime

The Common Language Runtime (CLR) provides the user with necessary services required to execute an application developed by any language supported by .NET. In the .NET Framework, the CLR is used to manage the execution of the code and provide access to numerous services, which in turn, simplify the development process of applications.

The code that executes within the CLR is known as the Managed Code. The CLR provides the Common Type System (CTS) to define the data types that are used by all .NET languages. Besides containing the common language specification for defining a basic subset followed by all programming languages, the CLR also provides interoperability between languages.

Managed Code Compilation

A programmer always writes the code of a program in such a way that it is readable by the user. This code is called as the source code. In .NET, the source code for any language is translated into the Microsoft Intermediate Language (MSIL). The MSIL is a CPU-independent set of instructions that can be easily compiled to a managed code. The term CPU-independent means that the MSIL can be moved from one computer to another. This MSIL is further compiled by the JIT (just-in-time) compiler and then converted into the machine code or the native code.

JIT Compiler

There may be one or more JIT compilers in the .NET Framework. The first time when an application is executed, the JIT compilers translate the MSIL code into the machine code.

For example, when you start developing your first ASP.NET page, it will be translated into the MSIL (also known as Intermediate Language, IL). The next time when you type the Universal Resource Locator (URL) of the page in the address bar of the browser, there will be a delay in the proceedings for a few seconds. This is because during this time the computer calls the IL code and converts it into the machine code using the JIT compiler. This is a one-time process that occurs when a page is requested for the first time. The next time when there is a request for this page, it will be displayed immediately because the CLR knows that the JIT compiler has already translated the page. The CLR retrieves the output of the page from the memory. If you edit and then execute this page, the CLR will detect the changes in the original file. It will then use the JIT compiler once again to translate the MSIL code into the machine code. Figure 1-2 shows the flow of the entire process.

Garbage Collection

Garbage collection is a method that is used to search the objects that are no longer in use, and then destroys them to release the memory. In the languages such as C++, the programmers have to keep a track of the useless objects and destroy them regularly to release the memory whereas, in .NET Framework, this work is done automatically. In .NET, there are two methods of garbage collection, which are discussed next.

Finalize-Runtime Garbage Collector

Finalize is the implicit method of garbage collection. This method of garbage collection keeps a track of the objects created by an application. It can track the unmanaged resources of an object, but it does not have the information on how the resources can be destroyed in

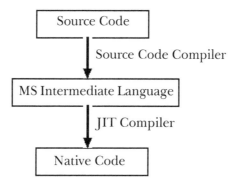

Figure 1-2 *The managed code compilation*

order to release the memory. For this purpose, different languages provide different methods of releasing the memory. For example, C# provides destructors, C++ provides managed extensions, and other languages, including the .NET Framework, provide the Finalize method.

In this method, the garbage collector does not delete the unmanaged resources, but adds them to a list called the Finalization list. Before adding it to the list, the Finalize method converts the unmanaged resources to the managed ones. For example, consider a resource, which is no longer in use but has a communication with another resource. In such case, this method will first break the communication and then add the resource to the finalization list. The resources that are not needed anymore will be removed from the list. This method is called at the runtime. When the garbage collector is executed next time, these resources are deleted and the memory is released.

Dispose
It is the explicit method of garbage collection in which the cleaning is done by the user, as per the requirement. This method is used to close or release the unmanaged resources and free the resources used by an object.

When you use this method, the object releases the resources held by it. For example, if the object X allocates another object Y, which further allocates Z, then the Dispose implementation of X must call Dispose on Y, which in turn will call Dispose on Z. This method does not delete the object or make it unusable. It only releases some resources used by the object. If reused, the object can reallocate the required resources.

ASSEMBLIES
An assembly is a unit of deployment (*.exe* or *.dll*). It is considered as the building block of programming. An assembly consists of a Dynamic Link Library (*.dll*), an executable file (*.exe*) or an HTML file (*.htm*), if it has more than one file. An assembly is divided into two parts, **Manifest** and **Modules**.

Manifest
This part of the assembly contains the information about the contents of the assembly. It also contains the version number of the assembly and ensures that the application always uses the correct version. The version numbers in assemblies are structured in the following sequence:

<major version>.<minor version>.<build number>.<revision>.

Figure 1-3 shows the screen display of the assemblies in .NET.

```
Object Browser | Form1.vb [Design] | Form1.vb | AssemblyInfo.vb |
Ⅱ\ (General)                                                  ▼  Ⅱ\ (Declarations)

    Imports System
    Imports System.Reflection
    Imports System.Runtime.InteropServices


⊟  ' General Information about an assembly is controlled through the following
   '  set of attributes. Change these attribute values to modify the information
   '  associated with an assembly.

└  '  Review the values of the assembly attributes

   <Assembly: AssemblyTitle("")>
   <Assembly: AssemblyDescription("")>
   <Assembly: AssemblyCompany("")>
   <Assembly: AssemblyProduct("")>
   <Assembly: AssemblyCopyright("")>
   <Assembly: AssemblyTrademark("")>
   <Assembly: CLSCompliant(True)>

   'The following GUID is for the ID of the typelib if this project is exposed to COM
   <Assembly: Guid("545103C8-5561-4991-872B-38B386000E3B")>

⊟  ' Version information for an assembly consists of the following four values:
   '
   '       Major Version
   '       Minor Version
   '       Build Number
   '       Revision
   '
   ' You can specify all the values or you can default the Build and Revision Numbers
└  ' by using the '*' as shown below:
```

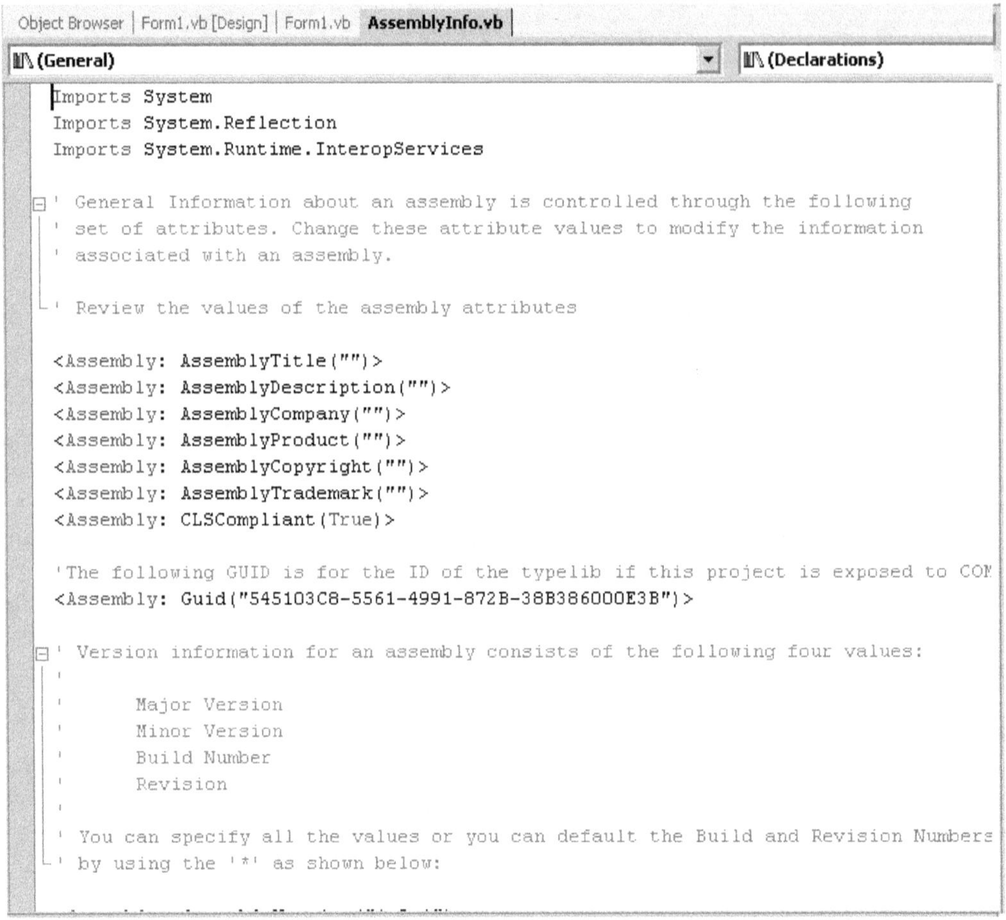

Figure 1-3 *The screen display of the assemblies in .NET*

Modules

This part of the assembly contains the internal files of the Intermediate Language (IL) that are ready to be executed.

Some of the functions performed by the assemblies are as follows:

1. The Microsoft Intermediate Language cannot be executed in a portable executable (PE) file without an associated assembly manifest.

2. Assemblies play an important role in security. In a way, an assembly is the unit where permission is requested and granted by the code of the application.

The assemblies are of the following two types:

1. Private Assemblies
2. Shared Assemblies

Private Assemblies

As the name suggests, these assemblies are only used within the application that contains them. In other words, every application has its own private assemblies, which are not accessible by any other application. Therefore, there is no risk of name collision because one application cannot use the private assemblies of the other application. Also, one application cannot overwrite, modify, or accidentally load the private assemblies of the another software.

Shared Assemblies

Shared assemblies are also known as common libraries. These assemblies can be used by more than one application. Therefore, unlike the private assemblies, there is a risk of name collision in shared assemblies. There is also a risk of an assembly being overwritten by the other versions of the same assembly.

To avoid the risk of an assembly being overwritten, the shared assemblies in .NET are placed in a special directory known as the global assembly cache (GAC). These assemblies cannot be used by simply copying them into a folder. Instead, they need to be installed into the cache.

To avoid the risk of name collision, VB.NET has the concept of strong name. According to this concept, the shared assemblies are given a name consisting of an assembly identity, which is based on public key cryptography. Cryptography is the science of coding messages so that they cannot be read by any person other than the intended recipient. It means when a message is sent from one computer to another, it is not in a readable form. To make it readable, a simple network-monitoring tool is used to expose the entire message in a graphical way. The conversion of a message consists of the following two processes:

1. Encryption
2. Decryption

Encryption
The message that needs to be secured is known as plaintext. This plaintext has to be converted into a coding form, which is known as ciphertext. The conversion of the plaintext to the ciphertext is known as encryption.

Decryption
When the coded message reaches its desired location, the ciphertext is reconverted into the plaintext. This reconversion is known as decryption.

Figure 1-4 shows the graphical representation of conversion of a message.

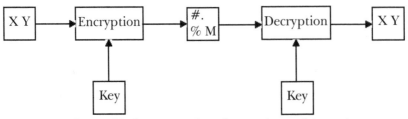

Figure 1-4 *The graphical representation of encrypting and decrypting a message*

In the above figure, X Y denotes the plaintext, which is converted into the ciphertext and then reconverted into the plaintext. The plaintext is encrypted using a key and the ciphertext is decrypted using the same key.

NAMESPACE

The .NET has a large number of classes, which are used by almost all the applications programmed in .NET. The number of these classes is so large that it is not easy to maintain them. The .NET Framework arranges them into a structure or a logical group called namespace. The base namespace in the .NET Framework is **System**.

When an application is created in the .NET Framework, some of the namespaces are automatically imported into the application. For example, if a windows forms application is created, then the following namespaces will be automatically added to the application:

> System
> System.Data
> System.Drawing
> System.Web
> System.XML

VISUAL STUDIO .NET

Before working on VB .NET, you must understand the environments that support this language. VB.NET is used to build applications in a special environment known as Visual Studio .NET.

Visual Studio .NET has the following features:

1. It provides an integrated environment for building, testing, and debugging different applications such as windows applications, web applications, console applications, and so on.

2. It is a group of products that include four programming languages: Visual Basic .NET, Visual C#.NET, Visual J#.NET, and Visual C++ .NET.

3. It also provides the tools that are used to develop a connection with the databases.

4. It checks the objects, retrieves the required data, and also stores it in the classes that can be used in any other language.

GETTING STARTED WITH VB.NET

To start Visual Studio, choose **Start > Programs > Microsoft Visual Studio 2008 > Microsoft Visual Studio 2008**, as shown in Figure 1-5 (this option depends upon the version of Visual Studio .Net you are using).

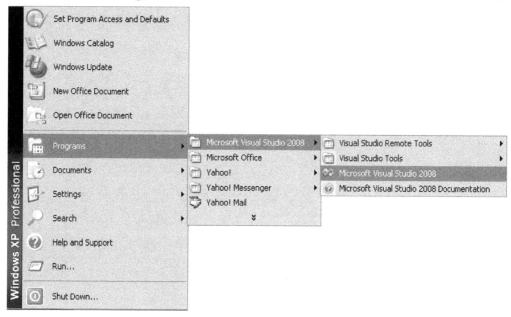

Figure 1-5 *Launching* **Microsoft Visual Studio 2008**

The steps required to create a VB.NET application are given next.

Step 1
Select the **Microsoft Visual Studio .NET 2008** option; the **Start Page** window will be displayed, as shown in Figure 1-6.

Step 2
Choose the link in front of the **Create** option from the **Recent Projects** area in the **Start Page** window; the **New Project** window will be displayed, as shown in Figure 1-7.

Step 3
To open a windows form, select the **Windows** option from the **Project types** area and the **Windows Forms Application** option from the **Templates** area. Enter the name that you want to assign to your application in the **Name** edit box. The default name, in case of windows forms, is **WindowsApplication1**. You can also select the location where you want to save this application using the **Location** drop-down list. Alternatively, you can choose the **Browse** button from the **New Project** dialog box, the **Project Location** dialog box will be displayed. Select the desired location to save your project and then choose the **OK** button from the **Project Location** dialog box. Next, choose the **OK** button from the **New Projec**t dialog box; the windows form will be displayed, as shown in Figure 1-8.

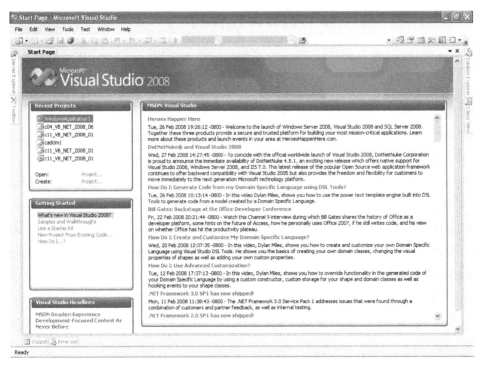

Figure 1-6 *The **Start Page** window*

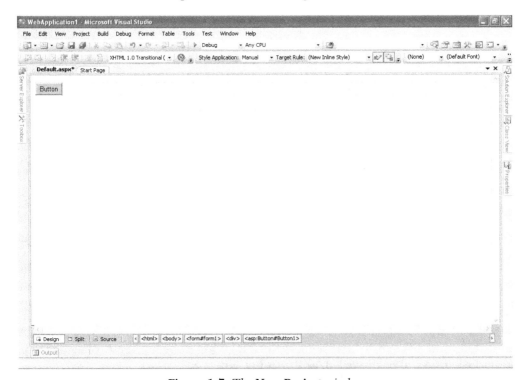

Figure 1-7 *The **New Project** window*

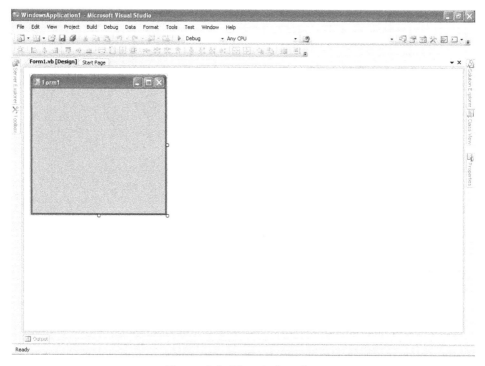

Figure 1-8 *The windows form*

IDE (INTEGRATED DEVELOPMENT ENVIRONMENT) COMPONENTS

IDE is a programming environment integrated into an application in order to provide a graphical user interface (GUI) builder, code editor, compiler, and debugger. The process of building an application is divided into the following parts:

Toolbox

The first step to create an application is designing. The toolbox contains all the controls that are needed for designing an application. You need to add the controls that will be displayed on the form at runtime. To add the controls, drag any controls from the toolbox and drop them on the form, or you can also double-click on them. For example, to add a **Button** control, drag it from the toolbox and drop it on the form. Alternatively, you can double-click on the **Button** control in the toolbox; it will be added to the form. Next, position the **Button** control on the form according to your requirement. In case the toolbox is not displayed, move the cursor on the **Toolbox** tab on the left of the form; the toolbox will be displayed, as shown in Figure 1-9. All controls are organized in different tabs. For example, if you are creating a windows application, then the controls in the **Windows Forms** tab will be used. However, when you create a web application, the web controls will be used and the **Windows Forms** tab will be disabled.

The different sections of the toolbox are discussed next.

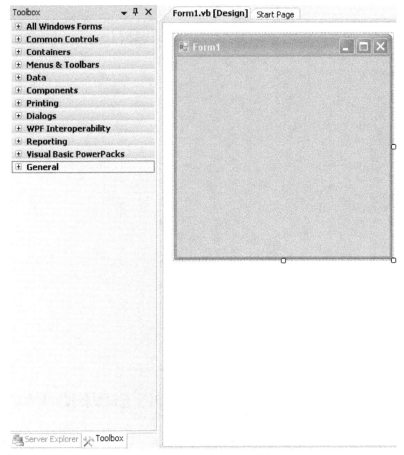

Figure 1-9 The Toolbox

All Windows Forms

The **All Windows Forms** section contains all the controls available in VB.NET environment.

Common Controls

The **Common Controls** section contains all the controls that are commonly used such as **Button** control, **CheckBox** control, **Label** control, and so on, as shown in Figure 1-10.

Containers

The **Containers** section contains the controls that can be used as the containers for other controls. In other words, you can place other controls within the controls under the **Containers** section. The **Container** section is shown in Figure 1-11.

Menus & Toolbars

The **Menus & Toolbars** section contains the controls that are used to create menus and toolbars, as shown in to Figure 1-12.

Figure 1-10 *The **Common Controls** section*   *Figure 1-11* *The **Containers** section*

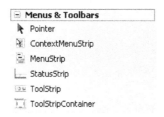

Figure 1-12 *The **Menus & Toolbars** section*

Data

The **Data** section contains all the controls that are used to communicate with the databases. The **Data** section is shown in Figure 1-13.

Figure 1-13 *The **Data** section*

Components

The **Components** section contains the controls that will mostly work in the background of an application such as **BackgroundWorker**, **Timer**, and so on, as shown in Figure 1-14.

Printing

The **Printing** section contains all the controls that can be used to set the printing details, preview the document, and so on. The **Printing** section is shown in Figure 1-15.

Dialogs

The **Dialogs** section contains all the dialog controls such as **ColorDialog** control, **FontDialog** control, and so on, as shown in Figure 1-16.

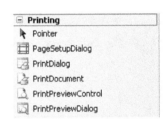

*Figure 1-14 The **Components** section*   *Figure 1-15 The **Printing** section*

*Figure 1-16 The **Dialogs** section*

Solution Explorer Window

The **Solution Explorer** window is located on the right of the windows form, as shown in Figure 1-17. The list of items displayed in the **Solution Explorer** window is as follows:

1. Solution name of the project
2. Project name
3. My Project
4. Windows form name

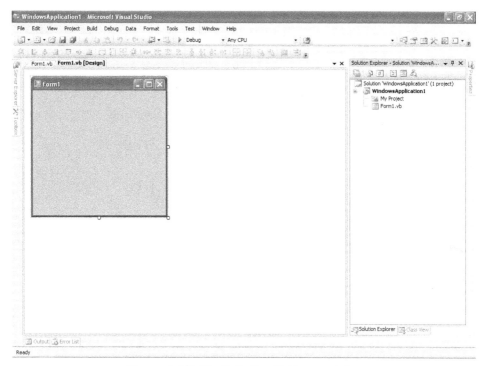

*Figure 1-17 The **Solution Explorer** window*

Right-click on the project name in the **Solution Explorer** window; the context menu will be displayed. Select the **Properties** option from the context menu; different options will be displayed, as shown in Figure 1-18. Alternatively, you can double-click on the **My Project** option from the **Solution Explorer** window. By default, the **Application** option is selected. In the **Application** option, you can set the values for the **Assembly name**, **Root namespace**, **Application type**, **Icon**, and **Startup form**, as shown in Figure 1-18. Choose the **Assembly Information** button; the **Assembly Information** dialog box will be displayed, as shown in Figure 1-19. Moreover, if you choose the **View UAC Setting** button, you can view the application manifest, as shown in Figure 1-20.

In the project properties window of the **My Project**, select the **Compile** option; various options will be displayed. You can set the path for the exe file of your application in the **Build output path**. Also, you can set the values for **Option explicit** in this window, as shown in Figure 1-21. The other commonly used option in the **My Project** window is the **References** option. It contains all the references and namespaces used in the application, as shown in Figure 1-22.

Properties Window

This window displays all the properties of a control. The **Properties** tab is located on the right of the design window. To display the **Properties** window, move the cursor over the **Properties** tab. Alternatively, you can right-click on any control and choose the **Properties** option from the context menu. By default, the properties of the form will be displayed in the **Properties** window, as shown in Figure 1-23.

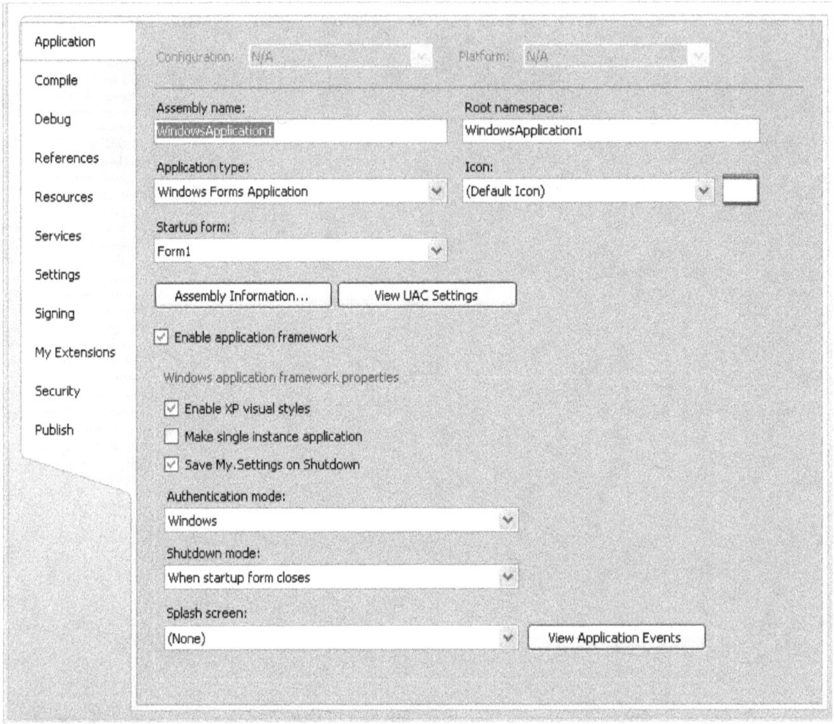

Figure 1-18 My Project properties window with Application option

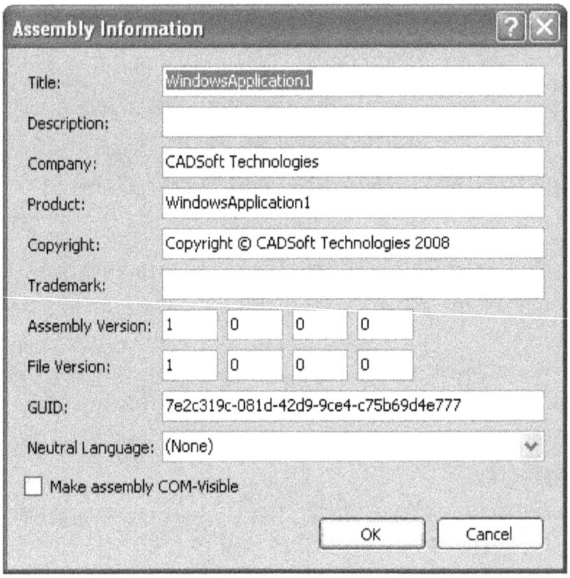

Figure 1-19 The Assembly Information dialog box

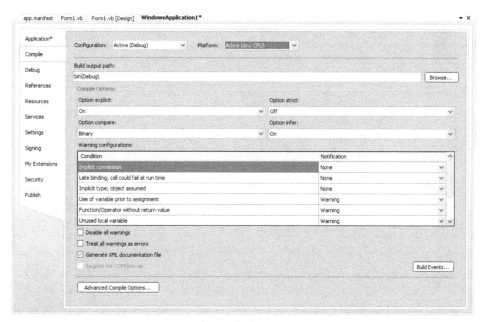

Figure 1-20 *The application manifest*

Figure 1-21 *Window with the* **Compile** *option selected*

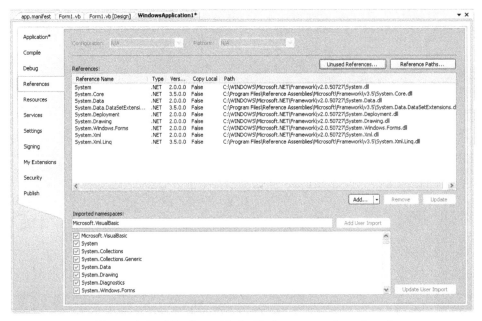

Figure 1-22 Window with the **References** option selected

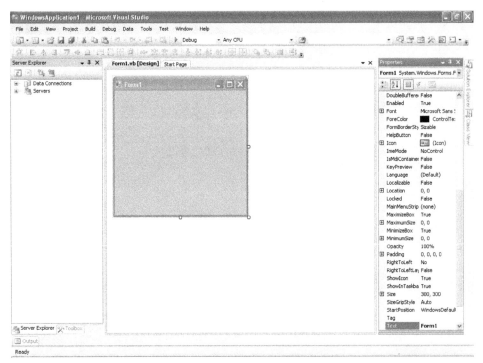

Figure 1-23 Screen display of the **Server Explorer** window and the **Properties** window

You will notice a drop-down list on the top of the **Properties** window. This drop-down list contains all the controls used in the application.

Server Explorer Window

The **Server Explorer** window is used for the database connection and it also contains the list of servers. The **Server Explorer** window is located on the left of the design window, as shown in Figure 1-23. You can drag and drop all the items from the **Server Explorer** window on the windows forms or web forms. For example, you can drag and drop any database table from the **Server Explorer** window on the form and VB.NET will automatically connect the table to the form.

Adding Controls to the Windows Forms Application

You can add the controls to a windows form by using any one of the following two methods:

1. Drag the control from the toolbox and drop it on the form.

2. Double-click on the required control; it will be added to the form.

For example, if you want to add a **Button** control to the form, then double-click on the **Button** control in the toolbox; it will be added to the upper left corner of the form, as shown in Figure 1-24. You can adjust the location of the **Button** control according to your requirements. To adjust the location, select the **Button** control and drag it to the desired location, refer to Figure 1-25. You can also modify the value of any property of the **Button** control using the **Properties** window, as shown in the Figure 1-26. You will note that the **Text** property of the **Button** control has been changed to **Show** in Figure 1-26. You can also change the color and size of the font of the text inside the control by changing the values of the **Forecolor** and **Font** properties in the **Properties** window. Similarly, you can set the other properties of the control.

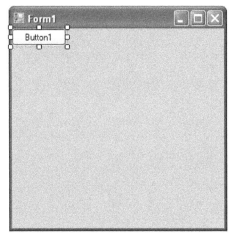 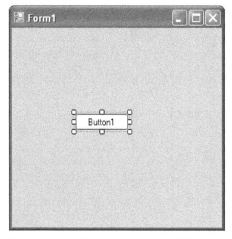

Figure 1-24 *The **Button** control added to the form*

Figure 1-25 *The new location of the **Button** control*

Adding Source Code to the Control

You can add the source code to any control in the code window. To do so, double-click on the control; the code window will be displayed. Alternatively, press the F7 key or right-click on the control and choose the **View Code** option; the code window will be displayed. If you want to add the code for the **Click** event of the **Button** control, then double-click on it; the code window will be displayed with the default event, as shown in Figure 1-27. Alternatively, you can select the **Click** event from the drop-down list located at the upper right corner of the code window. In the code window, you will notice two lines; you can enter the source code for the **Button** control between these lines, depending upon the action that you want the button to perform. For example, enter the following code between the two existing lines:

     MessageBox.Show("Hello")

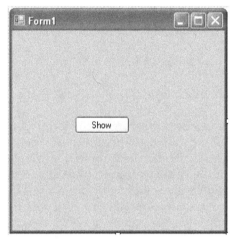

Figure 1-26 *The changed* ***Text*** *property of the* ***Button*** *control*

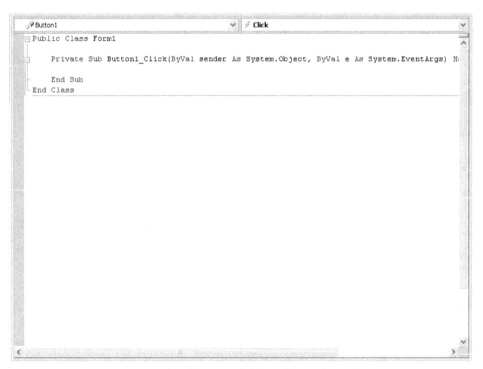

Figure 1-27 *The screen display of the code window*

Executing the Windows Application

To execute an application, choose **Debug > Start Debugging** form the menu bar. Alternatively, press the F5 key. The output of the code given on the previous page will be similar to Figure 1-28. Choose the **Show** button; a message box with the message **Hello** will be displayed, as shown in Figure 1-29.

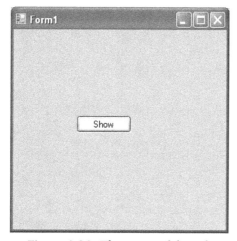

Figure 1-28 *The output of the code*

Figure 1-29 *The message box*

Creating Web Application

The following steps are required to create a web application:

1. Launch the **Microsoft Visual Studio 2008**. Select the **Web** node from the **Project types** area and the **ASP.NET Web Application** from the **Templates** area in the **New Project** dialog box.

2. The web form will be displayed, as shown in Figure 1-30.

You will notice three tabs, **Design**, **Split**, and **Source** at the lower left corner of the web form. The **Design** window is used to add the controls, refer to Figure 1-30. The **Source** window is used to enter the source code, as shown in Figure 1-31. The **Split** window splits the web form into the **Design** window and the **Source** window, as shown in Figure 1-32.

Adding Controls to the Web Forms

You can add controls to the web forms in the same way as you did in the windows forms. To add a control to the web form, double-click on the control in the toolbox; it will be added to the web form. Alternatively, you can drag the control from the toolbox and drop it on the web form. For example, if you want to add a **Button** control to the form, double-click on the **Button** control; it will be added to the web form, as shown in Figure 1-33.

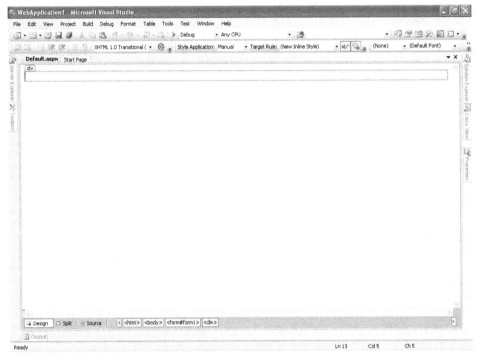

Figure 1-30 *The web form*

Figure 1-31 *The* **Source** *window*

Figure 1-32 *The **Split** window*

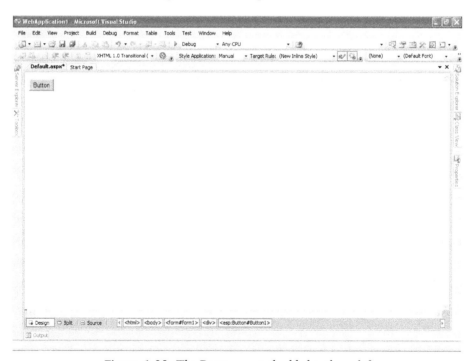

Figure 1-33 *The **Button** control added to the web form*

Adding Source Code to the Application

To add the source code to the application, right-click on the control and choose the **View Code** option from the context menu; the code window will be displayed. You can view two lines of code in the code window, as shown in Figure 1-34. These lines are for the **Page_Load** event. For example, if you want to add the source code to the **Click** event of the **Button** control, then you need to select the control and the event from the drop-down lists given on the top of the code window. From the drop-down list located on the left, select the **Button** control, and from the drop-down list on the right, select the **Click** event; you will notice that two more lines of code are added in the code window, as shown in Figure 1-35. Enter the following source code for the **Click** event of the **Button** control:

   MsgBox("Hello")

Figure 1-34 *The code window with the page load event*

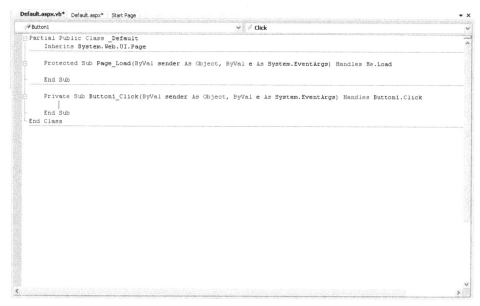

Figure 1-35 *The code window with **Click** event of the **Button** control*

Executing the Web Application

To execute the application, choose **Debug > Start Debugging** from the menu bar. Alternatively, press the F5 key. The output of the code entered in Figure 1-35 will be similar to Figure 1-36.

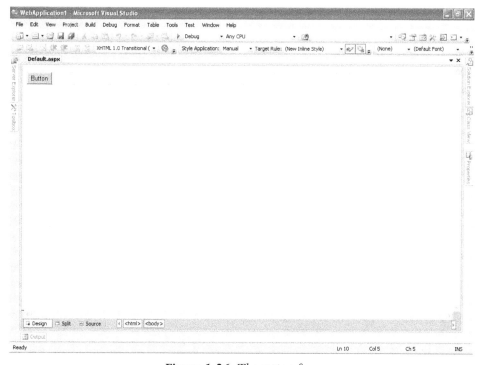

Figure 1-36 *The output form*

Choose the **Button** control; a message box with the message **Hello** will be displayed, as shown in Figure 1-37.

Figure 1-37 *The message box*

Self-Evaluation Test

Answer the following questions and then compare them to those given at the end of this chapter:

1. The .NET Framework is a _____ and _____ framework.

2. An operating system is a set of _____.

3. The base class library is a collection of _____ .

4. The code that runs within the CLR is called as _____.

5. Assemblies have two parts, _____ and _____.

Review Questions

Answer the following questions:

1. A **Button** control is a _____ shaped object.

2. GUI stands for _____.

3. There is a risk of _____ while using the private assemblies.

4. A program written in a user-readable form is called _____.

5. The .NET Framework supports multiple _____.

Answers to Self-Evaluation Test
1. platform-dependent, language-independent, **2.** programs, **3.** prewritten code, **4.** managed code, **5. manifest, module**

Chapter 2

Variables, Operators, and Constants

Learning Objectives

After completing this chapter, you will be able to:
- *Understand variables.*
- *Understand the types of variables.*
- *Understand the Strict option.*
- *Understand the data type conversion.*
- *Understand the concept of operators.*
- *Understand operator precedence.*
- *Understand the concept of constants.*
- *Format numbers.*

INTRODUCTION

In this chapter, you will learn about variables, constants, and operators used in VB.NET. The following topics will also be covered in this chapter:

1. Formatting numbers
2. Formatting a form

VARIABLES

During the executing a program, some information is stored temporarily and this storage location is known as variable. This location is associated with a specific address where a value can be stored and retrieved whenever required. A variable stores the data temporarily and it has a name, type, and value to store at runtime. The value stored in a variable can vary while the program is running. You can perform the following operations with the help of variables:

1. Copy and store the values in order to manipulate them.

2. Test values in order to determine whether they meet some criterion.

3. Perform arithmetic operations on the values.

Variable Naming Rules and Conventions

A variable name has to conform to VB.NET's naming rules, which are given below:

1. Variable names cannot contain periods or spaces.

2. Keywords such as **Dim**, **Sub**, **Private**, and so on cannot be used as variable names.

3. The first character of the variable name should be a letter or an underscore character.

4. After the first character, you can use digits, letters, or special characters.

The naming conventions for variables are discussed next.

1. Assign such names to the variables that indicate their purpose. For example, if a variable has to store the names of the customers, you may name it as **customer_name**.

2. Adopt a consistent style while naming a variable. For example, in a database named **order**, if the first column is named as **customer_name**, then the column for storing the quantity ordered by the customers should be **quantity_order**. Note that both the variable names have two words, beginning with small letters and separated by an underscore.

Data Types

A data type specifies the type of data that a variable can hold and also the amount of memory allocated to a particular variable. Table 2-1 lists the numeric data types used in VB.NET.

Data Type	Size	Range
Integer	4 bytes	-2,147, 483, 648 to 2,147, 483, 647
Short	2 bytes	-32,768 to 32,767
Long	8 bytes	Large value
Single	4 bytes	Negative numbers in the range of -340223E38 to -1.401298E-45 and positive in the range of 1.401298E-45 to 3.402823E38
Double	8 bytes	Negative numbers in the range of -1.79769313486232E308 to -4.94065645841247E-324 and positive numbers in the range of 4.94065645841247E-324 to 1.79769313486232E308
Decimal	16 bytes	These are integer and floating-point numbers and are scaled by a factor in the range of 0 to 28
String	10 bytes + (2 * string length)	0 to approximately two billion Unicode characters
Char	2 bytes	0 to 65535 (unsigned)
Boolean	4 bytes	True or False

Table 2-1 *Fundamental data types with their size and ranges*

The above mentioned data types are discussed next.

Integer

An integer data type is used to store only numeric values without any decimal point such as natural numbers, whole numbers, and so on. Integers can be stored using three different types of variables depending on their range. Integers can be of long, short, and integer data types. A long data type has a size of 8 bytes, so it can hold large values. A short data type has a size of 2 bytes, so it can store only small values. An integer data type has a size of 4 bytes and it can store the values that cannot to be stored by the short integer.

Single and Double

Single data type represents a single-precision floating-point number. Double data type variables are stored internally and have a greater accuracy and precision as compared to single data type variables. Consider the following example:

$$22/7 = 3.14285714..........$$

In cases like this, the value after the decimal will be infinite and will exceed the range allowed for double type variables. Therefore, the result will be truncated and the fractional values cannot always be represented accurately in the computer memory.

Decimal

Decimal data type variables are stored internally as integers in 16 bytes and are scaled by a power of ten. The scaling power is any integer value from 0 to 28. It determines the number of decimals to the right of the floating-point. When the scaling power is 0, the value is multiplied by 10^0. When the scaling power is 28, the value is divided by 10^{28}.

Boolean

The boolean data type variable stores true/false values. The boolean variables are integers that take the value -1 for true and the value 0 for false. Boolean variables are also combined with the logical operators such as AND, OR, NOT, and XOR.

String

These data type variables can only store text.

Char

A character variable stores a single character in two bytes.

Declaration of Variables

A statement that helps a programming language to create a memory location for a variable is called a variable declaration statement. It is used to indicate the name given to that memory location and the type of information it holds. The syntax for declaring a variable is as follows:

Dim VariableName As Data Type

For example:

Dim Area As Integer

In the above example, the word **Dim** stands for dimension and it directs the compiler that a variable is being declared. The word **Area** is the name of the variable. The term **As Integer** is used to specify that the variable will hold an integer value.

You can declare multiple variables in a single statement. A comma separator is used to separate these variables from one another. The syntax for declaring multiple variables in a single statement is as follows:

Dim VariableName1, VariableName2, VariableNameN As Data Type

For example:

Dim Area, Perimeter As Integer

In the above example, **Area** and **Perimeter** variables are declared as **Integer** data type.

You can also declare multiple variables of the same or different data types within a single statement. The syntax for declaring multiple variables of different types is as follows:

Dim VariableName1 As Integer, VariableName2 As String

For example:

Dim Area As Integer, Name As String

In the above example, **Area** variable is declared as an **integer** data type and **Name** variable is declared as a **String** data type.

Initializing a Variable

Initializing a variable means assigning an initial value to a variable while declaring it. The syntax for initializing a variable is as follows:

Dim VariableName As Datatype = initial value

For example:

Dim Area As Integer = 254

In the above example, **254** is assigned as the initial value to the variable **Area**.

You can also initialize multiple variables of the same or different types within a single statement. The syntax for declaring multiple variables within a single statement is as follows:

Dim VariableName1 As Datatype = initial value, VariableName2 = initial value

For example:

Dim Area As Integer = 254, Name As String = "Smith"

In the above example, **254** is assigned as the initial value to the integer variable **Area** and **Smith** is assigned as the initial value to the variable **Name**.

The following application illustrates the use of variables:

Application 1

Create an application to display a greeting message concatenated with the name entered by the user.

This application will prompt the user to enter a greeting message and a name. The application will concatenate them and display the complete message on the form.

The following steps are required to create this application:

Step 1
Start a new project and save it as **c02_VB_NET_2008_01**.

Step 2
Add four **Label** controls, three **Button** controls, and two **TextBox** controls in the form.

Step 3
Change the values of the **Text** property of all controls as follows:

Label1 to **Enter your greetings**
Label2 to **Enter your name**
Label3 to **This is your complete message**
Button1 to **Show Message**
Button2 to **Clear**
Button3 to **Exit**, as shown in Figure 2-1.

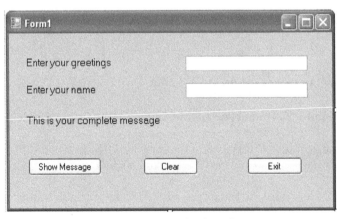

Figure 2-1 *Design mode of Application 1*

Step 4
Change the values of the **Name** property of the controls as follows:

Label1 to **lblgreetings**

Label2 to **lblname**
Label3 to **lblmessage**
Label4 to **lblDisplay**
Button1 to **btnShow**
Button2 to **btnClear**
Button3 to **btnExit**
TextBox1 to **txtgreetings**
TextBox2 to **txtname**

Step 5
The following is the source code for the **Show Message** button:

```
Private Sub btnShow_Click(ByVal sender As System.Object, _
ByVal e As System.EventArgs) Handles btnShow.Click
Dim Message As String
Message = txtgreetings.Text & " " & txtname.Text
lblmessage.Text = Message
End Sub
```

The following is the source code for the **Clear** button:

```
Private Sub btnClear_Click(ByVal sender As System.Object, _
ByVal e As System.EventArgs) Handles btnClear.Click
txtgreetings.Clear()
txtname.Clear()
Message.Text = ""
txtgreetings.Focus()
End Sub
```

The following is the source code for the **Exit** button:

```
Private Sub btnExit_Click(ByVal sender As System.Object, _
ByVal e As System.EventArgs) Handles btnExit.Click
End
End Sub
```

The source code for the application will be displayed on the screen as given next. The line numbers on the right are not a part of the program and are for reference only.

```
Public Class variables                                              1
Inherits System.Windows.Forms.Form                                  2
Private Sub btnShow_Click(ByVal sender As System.Object, _
ByVal e As System.EventArgs) Handles btnShow.Click                  3
Dim Message As String                                               4
Message = txtgreetings.Text & " " & txtname.Text                    5
lblDisplay.Text = Message                                           6
End Sub                                                             7
```

```
Private Sub btnClear_Click(ByVal sender As System.Object, _
ByVal e As System.EventArgs) Handles btnClear.Click        8
txtgreetings.Clear()                                       9
txtname.Clear()                                            10
lblDisplay.Text = ""                                       11
txtgreetings.Focus()                                       12
End Sub                                                     13
Private Sub btnExit_Click(ByVal sender As System.Object, _
ByVal e As System.EventArgs) Handles btnExit.Click         14
End                                                        15
End Sub                                                     16
End Class                                                   17
```

Line 1 and Line 17
Public Class variables
End Class
In Line 1, a class named **variables** is declared. The keyword **Public** specifies that this class can be accessed and used by any other class. In Line 17, the keyword **End Class** specifies the end of the class **variables**.

Line 2
Inherits System.Windows.Forms.Form
In this line, the namespace **System.Windows.Forms.Form** is used to provide classes to create and install windows forms applications.

Line 3 and Line 7
Private Sub btnShow_Click(ByVal sender As System.Object, _
ByVal e As System.EventArgs) Handles btnShow.Click
End Sub
The word **Sub** is the type of procedure. It means that the event procedure is a type of sub procedure. The word **Private** before the word **Sub** means that the procedure defined in this particular form is accessible throughout this form. The **btnShow_Click** is the click event that the procedure has to handle. It works whenever a user chooses the **Show** button control. In Line 7, **End Sub** marks the end of this procedure.

Line 4
Dim Message As String
In this line, the dimension for the variable **Message** is **String**. It means that the variable **Message** is declared as a **String** data type.

Line 5
Message = txtgreetings.Text & " " & txtname.Text
In this line, **txtgreetings.Text** specifies the text entered in the first textbox and **txtname. Text** specifies the text entered in the last textbox. The **&** operator is used to concatenate the values entered in the **Enter your greetings** textbox and the **Enter your name** textbox. After concatenation, the resultant value is assigned to the variable **Message** with the help of the assignment operator (**=**).

Line 6
lblDisplay.Text = Message
In this line, the value of the variable **Message** is assigned to the **Label** control named **lblDisplay**.

Line 8 and Line 13
Private Sub btnClear_Click(ByVal sender As System.Object, _
ByVal e As System.EventArgs) Handles btnClear.Click
End Sub
In Line 8, **btnClear** is the name of the **Button** control and **btnClear_Click** is the event that the procedure has to handle. It works whenever a user chooses the **Clear** button control. In Line 13, **End Sub** indicates the end of this procedure.

Lines 9-10
txtgreetings.Clear()
txtname.Clear()
In these lines, the **Clear()** method is used to clear all the text from **txtgreetings** and **txtname** textboxes.

Line 11
lblDisplay.Text = ""
In this line, "" represent an empty string that is assigned to the **Label** control named **lblDisplay**. This helps to clear the text of the **Label** control.

Line 12
txtgreetings.Focus()
In this line, the **Focus()** method is used to bring the cursor back to the **txtgreetings** textbox.

Line 14 and Line 16
Private Sub btnExit_Click(ByVal sender As System.Object, _
ByVal e As System.EventArgs) Handles btnExit.Click
End Sub
In Line 14, **btnExit** is the name of the **Button** control and **btnExit_Click** is the event that the procedure has to handle. It works whenever a user chooses the **Button** control. In Line 16, **End Sub** indicates the end of this procedure.

Line 15
End
In this line, **End** is used to exit from the current application.

Step 6
Press F5 on the keyboard to execute the application. After execution, the form will be displayed, as shown in Figure 2-2. Check the application by entering different values in the **TextBox** controls. For example, in the first **TextBox** control, enter **Good Morning**, and in the second **TextBox** control, enter **Smith**. You will get the message **Good Morning Smith** in the **Label** control, as shown in Figure 2-2. You can change the values, if required.

Figure 2-2 *Output of Application 1*

Option Explicit

In VB.NET, the default value of the **Option Explicit** is **On**. Therefore, if a variable is not declared before being used in the code of an application, then the code editor will underline the variable's name with a jagged blue line. This line is the indication of an error. If a user tries to use a variable that has not been declared earlier, then VB.NET throws an exception. So, when the **Option Explicit** is **On**, make sure that the variables have been declared before using them in the code.

By changing its value to **Off**, you can use the variables without declaring them. To change this default behavior, you need to enter the following statement at the beginning of an application:

        Option Explicit Off

The above statement specifies that the value of the **Option Explicit** option of the application is changed to **Off**.

Data Type Conversion

You can convert the data type of a variable from one type to another with the help of certain functions provided in VB.NET. The list of these functions is given in Table 2-2.

Function	Arguments Converted To
CChar	Character
CByte	Byte
CBool	Boolean
CDate	Date
CDec	Decimal
CInt	Integer (4 bytes)
CLng	Long (8 bytes)
CShort	Short (2 bytes)
CObj	Object
CStr	String
CDbl	Double
CSng	Single

Table 2-2 *Functions for data type conversion*

For example, if you want to convert an **integer** type variable **x** to a double type variable **y**, use the following source code:

```
Dim x As Integer
Dim y As Double
y = CDbl(x)
```

The function **CType** can also be used to convert a variable from one type to another. For example, a variable **x** has been declared as an integer type and the value **53** is assigned to it. The following statement is used to convert the value of variable **x** to double:

```
Dim x As Integer = 53
Dim y As Double
y = CType(x, Double)
```

VB.NET performs conversion of data types automatically, but it is not always the case. VB.NET provides two methods for data type conversion and these are given next.

1. Widening or implicit
2. Narrowing or explicit

These methods are explained below:

Widening or Implicit

The conversion of a data type with a smaller size to a greater size is known as Widening conversion. Suppose you have declared and initialized two variables, an **integer** and a decimal. Now, if you want to convert the **integer** variable to a decimal variable, then use the source code given below:

```
Dim acc_no As Integer = 23
Dim pi As Decimal = acc_no
```

In the above lines, an **integer** variable storing the value **23** is assigned to a decimal variable so that the value 23.0 is stored in the decimal variable. This conversion is possible only if the **Strict** option is switched to **Off**.

In case the **Strict** option is **On** and you want to assign the value of variable **pi** to the variable **acc_no**, you will get the following error message:

Option Strict disallows implicit conversion from Decimal to Integer

It means that a decimal data type cannot be converted to an **integer** data type because a **Decimal** data type has a greater magnitude than an **integer** data type.

Narrowing or Explicit

To convert a data type with a greater size to a smaller size, you can use the explicit method of conversion. For example, if you want to assign the value of variable **pi** to the variable **acc_no**, the statement for this conversion will be as follows:

```
acc_no = CInt(pi)
```

This type of conversion is known as Narrowing conversion.

The list of conversions that the VB.NET performs automatically is shown in Table 2-3.

Data Type	Wider Data Type
Integer	Double, Single, Long, Decimal
Char	String
Decimal	Single, Double
Double	No conversion
Single	Double
Short	Double, Single, Long, Decimal
Long	Double, Single, Decimal

Table 2-3 A list of conversions

Boxing and Unboxing

Boxing is a process in which an instance object is created and a value is copied to that instance. Boxing permits any value type to be implicitly converted to object type or reference type.

Unboxing is vice-versa of the boxing. It implicitly converts the object or the reference type to value type.

For example:

```
Dim Obj as Object
Dim Obj_Ins as Integer
Obj_Ins = 10

'Boxing
Obj=Obj_Ins

'Unboxing
Obj_Ins=Obj
```

In the above example, the variable **Obj** is declared as Object type. The variable **Obj_Ins** is declared as an integer. The value 10 is assigned to the variable **Obj_Ins**. In the Boxing process, the value of the variable **Obj_Ins** can be assigned to the variable **Obj**. In other words, the integer value type is implicitly converted to object type in Boxing process, and vice-versa in Unboxing process.

Static Local Variables

When a procedure is called more than once in an application, the value stored in the local variable is not preserved between the procedure calls. On the termination of the procedure, the local variables are destroyed. However, they get renovated when the procedure is called again.

For example:

```
Sub LocalDemo()                                          1
Dim i as Integer                                         2
MessageBox.Show(i)                                       3
i = 10                                                   4
End Sub                                                  5
```

In the above example, when **LocalDemo()** procedure is called, the variable **i** is automatically initialized to 0. In Line 4, the value 10 is assigned to the variable **i**. When this procedure gets terminated, the variable **i** is destroyed. When the procedure is called again, the variable **i** is recreated and initialized to 0.

Sometimes, you may need to preserve the value of a variable between the procedure calls. To do so, you need to declare the variable as a static local variable. The syntax for declaring a static local variable is as follows:

```
Static variable_name As DataType
```

In the above syntax, the keyword **Static** is used to declare the variable as a static local variable. The **variable_name** is a variable and the keyword **As** is used to declare the data type of the variable.

For example:

```
Sub StaticDemo()                                         1
Static i as Integer                                      2
MessageBox.Show(i)                                       3
i = 10                                                   4
End Sub                                                  5
```

In the above example, when **StaticDemo()** procedure is called, the variable **i** is automatically initialized to 0. In Line 4 (i = 10), the value of the variable **i** is set to 10. Note that when this procedure gets terminated, the variable **i** is not destroyed. When the procedure is called again, the variable **i** will have the value 10.

Scope of a Variable

There is a scope or visibility and lifetime of every variable. The scope of a variable is the part of the source code of an application where the variable is visible and can be accessed by other programming statements. The time period for which a variable exists in the memory of a computer is called its lifetime.

Local Scope

When a variable is declared within a procedure, the variable is accessible only to that particular procedure and such variables are said to have local scope. For example, if you write a procedure in which you want to calculate the sum of odd numbers in the range of 0 to 50 with the **Click** event of a button, the coding will be as follows:

```
Private Sub btnSum_Click(ByVal sender As System.Object, _
ByVal e As System.EventArgs) Handles btnSum.Click
Dim x As Integer
Dim S As Integer
For x = 0 To 50 Step 1
S = S + x
Next
MsgBox(" The sum is" & S)
End Sub
```

In this example, the variables **x** and **S** are local to the above procedure because they are declared within the above procedure and cannot be accessed from outside this scope.

These type of variables exist only till the procedure is executed. Once the procedure gets terminated, the memory allocated to these variables gets immediately deallocated.

Global Scope

If a variable can be accessed by the entire application, it is said to have a global scope. These types of variables can be declared only outside a procedure. These variables are common to the entire application procedure. If you use the access specifier **Public** instead of the keyword **Dim** with the variable, the variable becomes accessible to the entire application as well as all projects referencing the current project. This can be illustrated through an example using the code given below:

```
Public Glb_var As Integer
Public Glb_str As String

Private Sub btnSet_Click(ByVal sender As System.Object, _
ByVal e As System.EventArgs) Handles btnSet.Click
Glb_var = 20
Glb_str = "Twenty"
MsgBox(Glb_var.ToString & "" & Glb_str)
End Sub

Private Sub btnShow_Click(ByVal sender As System.Object, _
ByVal e As System.EventArgs) Handles btnShow.Click
Glb_var = 10
Glb_str = "Ten"
MsgBox(Glb_var.ToString & "" & Glb_str)
End Sub
```

In this source code, although the variables **Glb_var** and **Glb_str** are declared outside the procedures, yet both the procedures **btnSet_Click** and **btnShow_Click** can access these variables.

Lifetime of a Variable

Lifetime of a variable depends on the period for which a variable retains its value. For example, a global variable retains its value till the lifetime of an application, whereas a local variable retains its value as long as the particular procedure is running. Once the procedure gets terminated, the local variable loses its existence and the allocated memory is free. To call that procedure again, you need to initialize it once again and recreate the variable.

The following application illustrates the use of a static local variable:

Application 2

Create an application to display the message **John: Where are you going?**, using a static local variable.

This application will display the message **John: Where are you going?** in a **ListBox** control, using the static local variable.

The following steps are required to create this application:

Step 1
Start a new project and save it as **c02_VB_NET_2008_02**.

Step 2
Add a **ListBox** control and two **Button** controls to the form.

Step 3
Change the values of the **Text** property of the controls as follows:

Button1 to **Show**
Button2 to **Exit**

The form will appear, as shown in Figure 2-3.

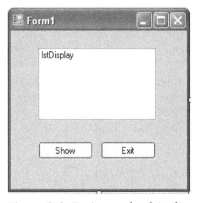

Figure 2-3 *Design mode of Application 2*

Step 4
Change the values of the **Name** property of the controls as follows:

ListBox1 to **lstDisplay**
Button1 to **btnShow**
Button2 to **btnExit**

Step 5
The following is the source code for the **Show** button:

```
Private Sub btnShow_Click(ByVal sender As System.Object, _       1
ByVal e As System.EventArgs) Handles btnShow.Click
lstDisplay.Items.Add("John: Where are you going?")               2
DisplayOutput()                                                  3
End Sub                                                           4
Sub DisplayOutput()                                              5
Static num As Integer                                            6
MessageBox.Show(num)                                             7
num += 1                                                         8
End Sub                                                           9
```

Explanation

In the above source code, the sub procedure **Sub DisplayOutput()** is declared. Within this procedure, **num** is declared as a static local variable. When this procedure is called for the first time, **num** will be initialized to 0. Its value will be displayed in a message box and the text, **John: Where are you going?** will be displayed in the **ListBox** control, as shown in Figure 2-4. The statement **num += 1** will add the value 1 to the variable **num**. When the procedure is called again, the value of the variable **num** will become 1 and the text **John: Where are you going?** will be displayed again in the **ListBox** control, as shown in Figure 2-5.

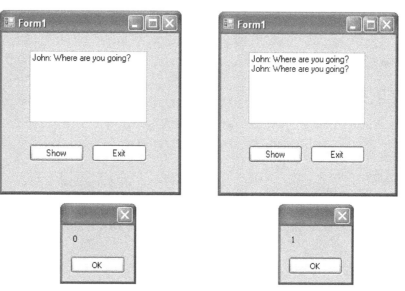

Figure 2-4 *The output of Application 2 with the initial value*

Figure 2-5 *The output of Application 2 with the value 1*

OPERATORS

Operators are defined as the symbols that are used when an operation is performed on the variables. In programming, some arithmetic operators are commonly used. The list of the commonly used arithmetic operators used in VB.NET is given in Table 2-4.

Operators	Operations
+	Addition
-	Subtraction
*	Multiplication
/	Division
^	Exponentiation

Table 2-4 List of operators

These operators can be used to perform some arithmetic operations. For example, the subtraction operator returns the result of the subtraction of two operands. Refer to the following statement where the operand 4 is subtracted from the operand 6 and the resultant value **2** is assigned to the variable **Diff**:

Diff = 6 - 4

You can also use variables as operands, as given below:

Volume = length * width * height

Square = side ^ 2

Average = points scored / total

There are two other special operators provided in VB.NET, integer division (\) and modulus (MOD).

\ Operator

The integer division (\) operator is used to divide two integer values. The resultant value is always an integer. If there is a fractional part in the output, it gets eliminated. For example, the following statement assigns the value **3** to the variable **Div**:

Div = 19 \ 5

In the above example, when 19 is divided by 5, the resultant value is 3.8. But only the value 3 will be assigned to the variable **Div**.

MOD Operator

This operator is known as the modulus operator. It also performs the division but returns the remainder and not the quotient. For example, the following statement assigns the value **4** to the variable **Var**:

Var = 19 MOD 5

In the above example, the value 4 is assigned to the variable **Var**, because when 19 is divided by 5, the quotient is 3 and the remainder is 4.

Operator Precedence

The operator precedence determines the order of execution of operators by the compiler. It means that an operator with a high precedence is executed before an operator with a low precedence. Several operators can be used in a single statement to create an expression, refer to the statement given below:

         Sum = z + 20 + x +7

In the above statement, the sum of operators **z**, **20**, **x**, and **7** is assigned to the variable **Sum**.

Different operators can also be used in an expression. Consider the following example:

         Result = 15 + 5 * 2

There are two methods for solving this expression, addition before multiplication and multiplication before addition.

Addition before multiplication
If the addition takes place before multiplication, the value assigned to the variable **Result** will be **40** (15 + 5 = 20, 20 * 2 = 40).

Multiplication before addition
If the multiplication takes place before addition, the value assigned to the variable **Result** will be **25** (15 + 10 = 25).

Note that the correct answer is **25** because the multiplication operator has a higher precedence over the addition operator.

Moreover, the arithmetic expressions are always evaluated from the left to the right. If an operand is between two operators, the operator with the higher precedence will be evaluated first. Division and multiplication have higher precedence over addition and subtraction.

The following is the list of precedence of arithmetic operators, from the lowest to the highest:

1. Addition (+) and Subtraction (-)

2. Modulus (MOD)

3. Integer division (\)

4. Multiplication (*) and division (/)

5. Exponentiation (^)

Note that the division and multiplication operators have the same precedence. Whenever there are two operators with the same precedence, the operator on the left will be evaluated first. Some of the examples are shown in Table 2-5.

Expression	Output
5 ^ 2 + 1	26
2 + 5 - 3 * 2	1
20 / 2 * 10	1
6 MOD 4 * 2	4

Table 2-5 Expressions with their output

Grouping within Parentheses

There are some operations that you may want to evaluate before other operations. You can group such operations within parentheses. For example, in the following statement, first the values **a**, **b**, and **c** are added, then the resultant value is divided by 5, and finally it is assigned to the variable **Grade**.

Grade = (a+b+c) / 5

If you remove the parentheses from the above statement, first the variable **c** will be divided by 5 and the resultant value will be added to the sum of variables **a** and **b**. Therefore, to get the desired result, you need to group a, b, and c within parentheses. Some of the examples showing the results using grouping within parentheses are given in Table 2-6.

Expression	Output
(7 + 4) * 2	22
18 / (8 - 2)	3
(5 - 2) / (2+1)	1

Table 2-6 Examples of grouping within parentheses

Compound Assignment Operators

In computer programming, an operation is performed on the value stored in a variable and the modified value is then assigned to the same variable. For this purpose, some special operators are used. These operators are called the compound assignment operators. The list of these operators is given in Table 2-7.

Assignment Operator	Example	Equivalent To
+ =	y += 5	y = y + 5
-=	y -= 7	y = y - 7
*=	y *= 9	y = y * 9
/=	y /= 3	y = y / 3
\=	y \= 2	y = y \ 2

Table 2-7 *Compound assignment operators*

For example:

y+=5

In the above example, the value **5** is added to the value of the variable **y** and then assigned to the variable **y**.

CONSTANTS

There are some variables whose values are fixed and cannot vary during execution. These variables are called constants. The syntax for declaring a constant is as follows:

Const constantname As type = value

For example, if you need to calculate the area and circumference of a circle as well as a cone with the same radius, then you can declare the value of the radius once in the program, as follows:

Const radius As Integer = 2.8796

You can now use this constant variable anywhere in the program.

For example:

area of a circle = 3.14159 * radius²
circumference of a circle =2 * 3.14159 * radius

In the above example, for calculating the area and circumference of a circle, there is no need to enter the value of the radius. Whenever you enter the constant value for variable **radius**, the compiler will replace it with the value (2.8796) declared in the beginning of the program.

The constants are preferred in programming for the following three reasons:

1.   You cannot change the value of a constant after its declaration.

2. The compiler processes the constants faster than the variables. The compiler replaces the constant names with their values and thus the program executes faster.

3. If you want to change the value of a constant, it can be changed in its declaration part. There is no need to make changes in the entire program.

Constants can be **Public** or **Private**. For example, you may want to use the constant **pi** that can be accessed by any procedure. The following statement is used to declare the constant **pi** as **Public**:

> Public Const pi As single = 3.14159

There are many constants used in VB.NET. They are grouped on the basis of their properties and each possible value of a property forms an enumeration. An enumeration is a set of user-defined integral constants. It is used when you want a property to take one value from a set of fixed values. Whenever you enter the name of a property, the enumeration list is displayed with all possible values of the given property. The editor knows which enumeration is to be applied and you can choose the required value from the list. A list of possible values of the **CheckAlign** property of a radio button is shown in Figure 2-6.

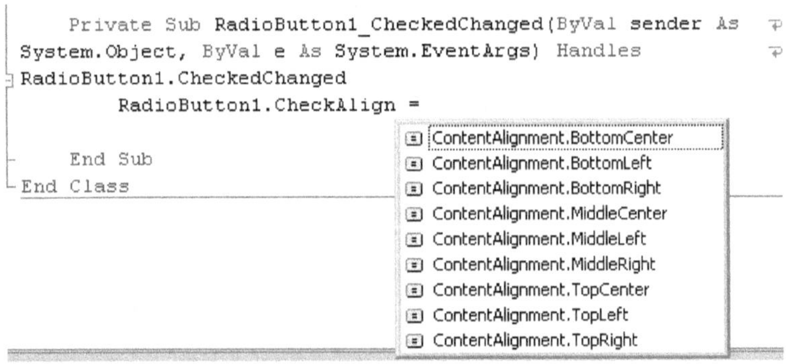

```
        Private Sub RadioButton1_CheckedChanged(ByVal sender As      ⇁
    System.Object, ByVal e As System.EventArgs) Handles              ⇁
    RadioButton1.CheckedChanged
            RadioButton1.CheckAlign =
                                    ☐ ContentAlignment.BottomCenter
        End Sub                     ☐ ContentAlignment.BottomLeft
    End Class                       ☐ ContentAlignment.BottomRight
                                    ☐ ContentAlignment.MiddleCenter
                                    ☐ ContentAlignment.MiddleLeft
                                    ☐ ContentAlignment.MiddleRight
                                    ☐ ContentAlignment.TopCenter
                                    ☐ ContentAlignment.TopLeft
                                    ☐ ContentAlignment.TopRight
```

Figure 2-6 *The possible values of the* **CheckAlign** *property*

FORMATTING NUMBERS

Formatting is the method of displaying a value in different ways. For example, a number 3570 can be displayed in many ways, as given below:

> 3570

> 3570.00

> 3570.0

There are several intrinsic functions which are provided by VB.NET to format numbers. The list of these functions is given in Table 2-8.

Function	Description
FormatNumber	Formats a specified number upto decimal points
FormatDateTime	Formats date, time, or both the expressions
FormatPercent	Formats a number as percent

Table 2-8 *Functions for formatting numbers*

FormatNumber

This function formats a number to two decimal places by default. For example, a number 3570 can be formatted as 3,570.00. The following code illustrates the usage of the **FormatNumber** function:

```
Dim func As Single
func = 3570.876
lblfunc.Text = FormatNumber (func)
```

The last statement assigns the value of variable **func** (3570.876) to the function **FormatNumber**. This function then returns the string "3570.88" to the **Text** property of **lblfunc**.

There is another way of using this function that will help you to format a number to more than two decimal places. The code to format a number to more than two decimal places is given below:

```
Label1.Text = FormatNumber (number, 3)
```

Consider a number 3570.8768768. If you want to format this number to three decimal places, the code will be as follows:

```
lblaverage.Text = FormatNumber (3570.8768768, 3)
```

where, **lblaverage** is the value assigned to the **Name** property of the **Label** control. The function returns the string 3,570.877 to the **Label** control. Note that all digits after .877 will be truncated.

FormatDateTime

This function is used to format the date expression. The syntax for **FormatDateTime** is as follows:

```
FormatDateTime (DateExpression [, Format])
```

In the above syntax, the first argument **DateExpression** specifies the date that is to be formatted. The second argument within the square brackets is optional. It specifies the method of formatting.

The following is the code for illustrating the usage of **FormatDateTime** function:

```
Dim day As Date
day = Today
lblDate.Text = FormatDateTime (day, DateFormat.LongDate)
```

In the second line, the keyword **Today** is used to retrieve the current date from the system and save the value in the variable **day**. In the third line, the value of the variable **day** is formatted to a long date format such as, "Tuesday, July 4, 2006", and then assigned to the **Text** property of **lblDate**.

Whenever you write the third line, a list of values will be displayed as soon as you enter comma after the variable **day**, as shown in Figure 2-7.

Figure 2-7 The list of values of the FormatDateTime property

The list of these values with their description is given next.

DateFormat.LongDate
This value is used to format a date in the **Long** format. It contains the day of the week, month, date, and year. For example, **Saturday, May 12, 2007**.

DateFormat.ShortDate
This value is used to format a date in the **Short** format. It contains the month, date, and year. For example, **5/12/2006**.

DateFormat.GeneralDate
This value of argument works in the same way as **DateFormat.ShortDate**.

DateFormat.LongTime
This value is used to format a time in the **Long** format. It contains hour, minute, second, and the indicators, **AM** or **PM**. For example, **07:20:12 AM**.

DateFormat.ShortTime
This value is used to format time in the **Short** format. It contains two digits for the hour and two digits for the minute and follows the 24 hours format. For example, **19:20**.

FormatPercent

This function is used to format its numeric arguments to percent by multiplying the argument by 100. Then, it rounds the argument to two decimal places and also adds a percentage sign (%). For example, to format .50 to 50.00%, the code will be as follows:

```
Dim x As Single
x = 0.5
lblpercent.Text = FormatPercent(x)
```

In the last statement, **lblpercent.Text = FormatPercent(x)**, the variable **x** is passed as an argument to the function **FormatPercent**. This function returns the value **50.00%**, which is assigned to the **Text** property of the **Label** control **lblpercent**.

As mentioned above, the function **FormatPercent** formats a number to two decimal places by default. But, you can also use this function to format a number to more than two decimal places. Fox example, to format .50 to four decimal places, the code will be as follows:

```
Dim x As Single
x = 0.5
lblpercent.Text = FormatPercent(x, 4)
```

The last statement will multiply the value of x (0.5) by 100 and then round the output to four decimal places (50.000%). The resultant value will be assigned to the **Text** property of the **Label** control.

Self-Evaluation Test

Answer the following questions and then compare them to those given at the end of this chapter:

1. The storage location used for holding some information in the computer's memory is known as _____.

2. Variables are used to copy and store the values in order to _____ them.

3. The red line under a variable is the indication of an _____.

4. If the scope of the variable is limited to a procedure, it is called as _____ scope.

5. VB.NET executes the statements within a procedure in a _____ order.

Review Questions

Answer the following questions:

1. If a variable can be accessed by the entire application, it is called _____.

2. _____ of a variable depends on the period for which a variable retains its value.

3. Once a procedure is over, the _____ variable loses its existence and the allocated memory gets free.

4. The variables that do not change values are called as _____.

5. The compiler processes the constants faster than the _____.

Exercises

Exercise 1

Create an application that accepts points scored in five subjects from the user and calculates their percentage. The output of the application should be similar to Figure 2-8.

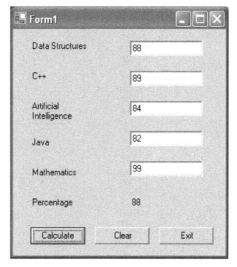

Figure 2-8 *Output of Exercise 1*

Exercise 2

Create an application that displays the message **God Bless You.......** concatenated with **My son**. The output of the application should be similar to Figure 2-9.

Figure 2-9 *Output of Exercise 2*

Answers to Self-Evaluation Test
1. variable, **2.** manipulate, **3.** error, **4.** local, **5.** sequential

Chapter 3

Control and Loop Structures

Learning Objectives

After completing this chapter, you will be able to:
- *Learn about If-Then statement.*
- *Learn about If-Then-ElseIf statement.*
- *Learn about nested If-Then statement.*
- *Learn about Select Case statement.*
- *Understand logical operators.*
- *Understand sub procedures.*
- *Understand static local variables.*
- *Understand functions.*
- *Understand arrays.*
- *Learn about For Each-Next statement.*
- *Understand parallel arrays.*
- *Understand multidimensional arrays.*

INTRODUCTION

In this chapter, you will learn about control structures and how to compare different values using logical operators. You will also learn to create radio buttons and check boxes.

CONTROL STRUCTURES

In the applications given in the previous chapter, you must have observed that the event procedures execute the statements sequentially. This means that the execution of statements one after the other depends on the order in which they appear in the application. Sometimes an application may require execution or skipping of some statements based on the result of a particular condition. Such requirements can be fulfilled by using the control structures. The control structures are of the following three types:

a. Sequential Control Structure
b. Decision Control Structure
c. Loop Control Structure

Sequential Control Structure

In a sequential control structure, the program statements are executed one after the other.

Decision Control Structure

The decision control statements are used to alter the flow of control in a program. An action is performed only when a particular condition exists in a program. Otherwise, no action is performed. There are three different types of decision control statements, which are as follows:

a. If-Then statement
b. If-Then-Else statement
c. Select Case statement

If-Then Statement

The **If-Then** statement is a single path statement, which means it executes a statement or a block of statements only if the condition is true. To execute a single statement, the syntax is as follows:

> If condition Then statement

In the above syntax, the **condition** can be evaluated as true or false. If the **condition** evaluates to true, the program will execute the statement that follows the condition. Otherwise, the next executable statement will get executed.

You can also define multiple statements in an **If-Then** block, where each statement is separated from the other by a colon (:). The syntax for the **If-Then** block is given next.

> If condition Then statement_1: statement_2: statement_3: .... statement_n
>   or
> If condition Then

statements
End If

In the above syntax, if the **condition** within the body of the **If-Then** statement evaluates to true, all the statements from 1 to n will be executed.

There are certain operators that are used to specify a condition that is tested by an **If-Then** statement. They are known as relational operators. These operators are discussed next.

Relational Operators

The relational operators are used to determine whether a particular relationship exists between two values. For example, the **Not equal to (<>)** operator is used to determine whether the operand on the left of the operator is equal to the operand on its right. Table 3-1 represents a list of relational operators used in VB.NET.

Operators	Meaning
<	Less than
>	Greater than
=	Equal to
>=	Greater than or equal to
<=	Less than or equal to
<>	Not equal to

Table 3-1 Relational operators

Relational operators always use two operands. Therefore, they are also called as binary operators. For example, the expression for the **Not equal to** operator is given below:

$$X <> Y$$

The above expression ($X <> Y$) determines whether **X** is equal to or not equal to **Y**, where **X** and **Y** are variables. This expression is called as a relational expression. It can be evaluated only as true or false. Table 3-2 represents a list of relational expressions.

For example:

Next, by using any one of these relational operators, you can write the **If-Then** statement as follows:

If selling > 100000 Then
profit = True
End If

Operators	Meaning	Output
x < y	If x is less than y	True
x > y	If x is greater than y	True
x = y	If x is equal to y	True
x >= y	If x is greater than or equal to y	True
x <= y	If x is less than or equal to y	True
x <> y	If x is equal to y	False

Table 3-2 Relational expressions with the output

In the above example, the greater than operator (>) is used to determine whether the value of the variable **selling** is greater than the value 100000. If it is, then the variable **profit** will be set to true.

The following application illustrates the use of the **If-Then** statement:

Application 1

Create an application to display the result of division of two numbers using the **If-Then** statement.

This application will prompt the user to enter two numbers. It will also display the resultant value on the form.

The following steps are required to create this application:

Step 1
Start a new project and save it as **c03_VB_NET_2008_01**.

Step 2
Add a **GroupBox** control, a **Label** control, and three **Button** controls to the form.

Step 3
Add four **Label** controls and two **TextBox** controls to the **GroupBox** control.

Step 4
Change the values of the **Text** property of the controls as follows:

Form1 to **If-Then_demo**
GroupBox1 to **Division**
Label1 to **Number 1**
Label2 to **Number 2**
Label3 to **Result**

Button1 to **Division**
Button2 to **Clear**
Button3 to **Exit**

Step 5
Delete the default values from the **Text** property
of **Label4** and **Label5**.

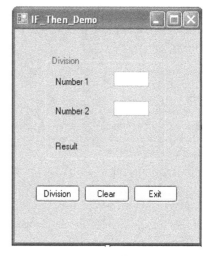

The resultant form will appear as shown in
Figure 3-1.

Step 6
Change the values of the **Name** property of the
controls as follows:

Label1 to **lblnum1**
Label2 to **lblnum2**
Label4 to **lbldivision**
Label5 to **lblmessage**
Button1 to **btnDivision**
Button2 to **btnClear**
Button3 to **btnExit**
TextBox1 to **txtnum1**
TextBox2 to **txtnum2**

Figure 3-1 *Design mode of Application 1*

Step 7
To add the code for the **Division** button, double-click on it and write the following source
code in the code window:

```
Dim number1, number2, result As Single
number1 = (txtnum1.Text)
number2 = (txtnum2.Text)
result = (number1 / number2)
lbldivision.Text = FormatNumber(result)
If number2 = 0 Then
lblmessage.Text = "Enter a valid number"
End If
```

Step 8
Next, double-click on the **Clear** button and write the following source code in the code window:
```
txtnum1.Clear()
txtnum2.Clear()
lbldivision.Text = ""
lblmessage.Text = ""
txtnum1.Focus()
```

Step 9
Similarly, double-click on the **Exit** button and write the following source code in the code window:

End

The source code that will be displayed in the code window is given next. The line numbers on the right are not a part of the program and are for reference only.

```
Public Class Form1                                                          1
Inherits System.Windows.Forms.Form                                          2
Private Sub btnDivision_Click(ByVal sender As System.Object, _
ByVal e As System.EventArgs) Handles btnDivision.Click                      3
Dim number1, number2, result As Single                                      4
number1 = (txtnum1.Text)                                                    5
number2 = (txtnum2.Text)                                                    6
result = (number1 / number2)                                               7
lbldivision.Text = FormatNumber(result)                                    8
If number2 = 0 Then                                                         9
lblmessage.Text = "Enter a valid number"                                   10
End If                                                                     11
End Sub                                                                    12
Private Sub btnClear_Click(ByVal sender As System.Object, _
ByVal e As System.EventArgs)   Handles btnClear.Click                      13
txtnum1.Clear()                                                            14
txtnum2.Clear()                                                            15
lbldivision.Text = ""                                                      16
lblmessage.Text = ""                                                       17
txtnum1.Focus()                                                            18
End Sub                                                                    19
Private Sub btnExit_Click(ByVal sender As System.Object, _
ByVal e As System.EventArgs) Handles btnExit.Click                         20
End                                                                        21
End Sub                                                                    22
End Class                                                                  23
```

Explanation
The line-by-line explanation of the above given source code is as follows:

Line 4
Dim number1, number2, result As Single
In the above line, **number1**, **number2**, and **result** are declared as single data type variables.

Line 5
number1 = (txtnum1.Text)
In this line, the value inside the parentheses (**txtnum1.Text**) specifies the value of the **Text** property of the associated **TextBox** control. The numeric value entered by the user in **TextBox** control is assigned to the variable **number1** with the help of the equal to (**=**) operator.

Line 6
number2 = (txtnum2.Text)
Its working is the same as that of Line 5.

Line 7
result = (number1 / number2)
In the above line, the value of the variable **number1** is divided by the value of the variable **number2**. After the division, the resultant value is assigned to the variable **result**.

Line 8
lbldivision.Text = FormatNumber(result)
In the above line, the value of the variable **result** is passed as an argument to the function **FormatNumber**. This function formats the value of the variable **result** up to two decimal places. Then, the resultant value is assigned to the **Text** property of **lbldivision**.

Line 9
If number2 = 0 Then
Here, the **If-Then** statement is used to check whether the value of the variable **number2** is equal to 0 or not. If it is 0, then the control will be transferred to Line 10.

Line 10
lblmessage.Text = "Enter a valid number"
In this line, the value **Enter a valid number** is assigned to the **Text** property of the **Label** control named **lblmessage** and the above message is also displayed on the form.

Line 11
End If
This line indicates the end of the **If-Then** statement.

Lines 14-15
txtnum1.Clear()
txtnum2.Clear()
In this line, the method **Clear** will delete the value of the **Text** property of the **txtnum1** and **txtnum2** textboxes.

Line 16
lbldivision.Text = ""
In this line, null value will be assigned to the **Text** property of the **lbldivision** label.

Line 18
txtnum1.Focus()
In this line, the **Focus** method is used to bring the focus to the **Number 1** textbox. It means each time a user executes the application, the cursor will be at **Number 1** textbox.

Step 10
Press F5 to execute the application. Enter the value **100** in the **Number 1** textbox and the value **3** in the **Number 2** textbox. Choose the **Division** button; the result of the division (33.33) will be displayed in the **Label** control, as shown in Figure 3-2.

Step 11
Choose the **Clear** button on the **IF_Then_Demo** form to clear the values from it. Enter the values **25** and **0** in the **txtnum1** and **txtnum2** textboxes, respectively. Then, choose the **Division** button. In this case, the result of the division will be **Infinity** and the message **Enter a valid number** will be displayed on the form, as shown in Figure 3-3.
Step 12

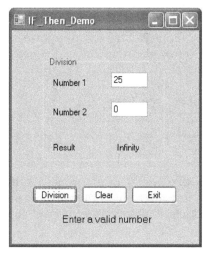

Figure 3-2 *Output of Application 1 with first set of values*

Figure 3-3 *Output of Application 1 with second set of values*

To exit from the **IF_Then_Demo** form, choose the **Exit** button. The application will return to its designing mode, refer to Figure 3-1.

If-Then-Else Statement

The **If-Then-Else** statement is a dual path statement, which means, if the condition given within the **If-Then** statement is true, then the statements associated with the **If-Then** block will be executed. Otherwise, the statements associated with the **Else** block will be executed. The syntax of the **If-Then-Else** statement is as follows:

```
If condition Then
statement_1
```

```
Else
    statement_2
End If
```

In the above syntax, if the given condition is true, then the **statement_1** will be executed and the **Else** block will be skipped. Otherwise, the **If-Then** block will be skipped and **statement_2** associated with the **Else** block will be executed.
For example:

```
If x Mod 2 = 0 Then
    lblmessage.Text = "Number is even"
Else
    lblmessage.Text = "Number is odd"
End If
```

In the above example, if the result of the modulus operation of the expression **x Mod 2** is 0, then the text string **Number is even** will be assigned to the **Text** property of the **lblmessage** label. Otherwise, the statement associated with the **Else** block will be executed and the string **Number is odd** will be assigned to the **Text** property of the **lblmessage** label.

The following application illustrates the use of the **If-Then-Else** statement:

Application 2

Create an application to check whether a number entered by the user is odd or even, using the **If-Then-Else** statement.

This application will prompt the user to enter a number, check whether the number is odd or even, and then display the result on the form.

The following steps are required to create this application:

Step 1
Start a new project and save it as **c03_VB_NET_2008_02**.

Step 2
Add a **GroupBox** control and three **Button** controls to the form.

Step 3
Add two **Label** controls and a **TextBox** control to the **GroupBox** control.

Step 4
Change the values of the **Text** property of the controls as given next. The form will appear as shown in Figure 3-4.

Form1 to **If-Then-Else**
GroupBox1 to **Even or Odd**

Label1 to **Number**
Button1 to **Show**
Button2 to **Clear**
Button3 to **Exit**

Step 5
Change the values of the **Name** property of the
controls as follows:
Button1 to **btnShow**
Button2 to **btnClear**
Button3 to **btnExit**
Label1 to **lblnum**
Label2 to **lblDisplay**
TextBox1 to **txtnum**

Figure 3-4 *Design mode of Application 2*

Step 6
Double-click on the **Show** button and add the following source code:

```
Dim Number As Integer
Number = txtnum.Text
If Number Mod 2 = 0 Then
lblDisplay.Text = "Number is even"
Else
lblDisplay.Text = "Number is odd"
End If
```

Step 7
To add the source code for the **Clear** button, double-click on it; the code window will be
displayed. You need to enter the following source code in the code window:

```
txtnum.Clear()
lblDisplay.Text = ""
txtnum.Focus()
```

Step 8
Similarly, add the following source code for the **Exit** button:

```
End
```

The following source code will be displayed in the code window:

```
Public Class Form1                                                      1
Inherits System.Windows.Forms.Form                                      2
Private Sub btnShow_Click(ByVal sender As System.Object, _
ByVal e As System.EventArgs) Handles btnShow.Click                      3
Dim Number As Integer                                                   4
Number = txtnum.Text                                                    5
```

If Number Mod 2 = 0 Then	6
lblDisplay.Text = "Number is even"	7
Else	8
lblDisplay.Text = "Number is odd"	9
End If	10
End Sub	11
Private Sub btnClear_Click(ByVal sender As System.Object, _	
ByVal e As System.EventArgs) Handles btnClear.Click	12
txtnum.Clear()	13
lblDisplay.Text = ""	14
txtnum.Focus()	15
End Sub	16
Private Sub btnExit_Click(ByVal sender As System.Object, _	
ByVal e As System.EventArgs) Handles btnExit.Click	17
End	18
End Sub	19
End Class	20

Explanation

Line 4

Dim Number As Integer

In the above line, **Number** is declared as an integer data type variable.

Line 5

Number = txtnum.Text

In this line, the text value of the **txtnum** textbox is assigned to the variable **Number** with the help of the assignment operator.

Line 6

If Number Mod 2 = 0 Then

In the above line, the **If-Then** statement is used to check the remainder of the expression **Number Mod 2**. If it evaluates to 0, then the message associated with the **If-Then** statement will be executed. Otherwise, the control will be transferred to Line 8.

Line 7

lblDisplay.Text = "Number is even"

In the above line, the value **Number is even** is assigned to the **Text** property of the **Label** control named **lblDisplay** and the message given above is also displayed on the form.

Line 8

Else

The **Else** block will be executed only if the condition given in the **If-Then** statement is false. Otherwise, the **Else** block will be skipped.

Line 9
lblDisplay.Text = "Number is odd"
In this line, the value **Number is odd** is assigned to the **Text** property of the **Label** control
named **lblDisplay** and the above message will also be displayed on the form.

Line 10
End If
This line indicates the end of the **If-Then-Else** statement.

Step 9
Press F5 to execute the application. Enter the value **20** in the **Number** textbox and choose the
Show button; a message **Number is even** will be displayed on the form, as shown in Figure 3-5.

Step 10
Choose the **Clear** button to clear the value in the **Number** textbox. Next, enter the value **23**
in this textbox. Again, choose the **Show** button; a message **Number is odd** will be displayed
on the form, as shown in Figure 3-6.
Step 11

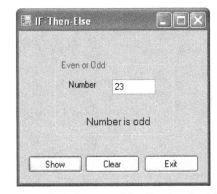

Figure 3-5 Output of Application 2 with
an even value

Figure 3-6 Output of Application 2 with
an odd value

Choose the **Exit** button to exit the **If-Then-Else** form.

If-Then-ElseIf Statement
The **If-Then-ElseIf** statement is a conditional statement used to check more than one
condition. The syntax of the **If-Then-ElseIf** statement is as follows:

```
If condition_1 Then
statement_1
ElseIf condition_2 Then
statement_2
ElseIf condition_3 Then
```

statement_3

|

ElseIf condition n Then
statement n
Else
statement
End If

In this syntax, the condition given within the **If-Then** statement is checked and if the condition evaluates to true, then **statement_1** will be executed. Otherwise, the condition given in the **ElseIf** statement will be checked. If it evaluates to true, then **statement_2** will be executed. If it evaluates to false, then the control will transfer to the next **ElseIf** statement and so on.

For example:

```
If score >= 90 Then
lblDisplay.Text = "Grade A"
ElseIf score >= 80 And score < 90 Then
lblDisplay.Text = "Grade B"
ElseIf score >= 70 And score < 80 Then
lblDisplay.Text = "Grade C"
Else
lblDisplay.text = "Poor Performance"
End If
```

The following application illustrates the use of the nested **If-Then-ElseIf** statement:

Application 3

Create an application to display the average of the points scored by a student in three different subjects, using the nested **If-Then-ElseIf** statement. The application should also display the resultant grade.

This application will prompt the user to enter the points scored by a student in three subjects. It will display the average of the points scored in the subjects and also the resultant grade on the form.

The following steps are required to create this application:

Step 1
Start a new project and save it as **c03_VB_NET_2008_03**.

Step 2
Add a **GroupBox** control and three **Button** controls to the form.

Step 3
Add six **Label** controls and five **TextBox** controls to the **GroupBox** control.

Step 4
Change the values of the **Text** property of the controls as follows:

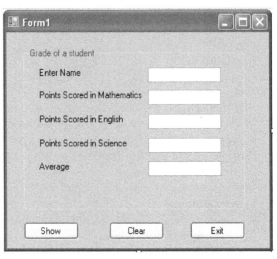

GroupBox1 to **Grade of a student**
Label1 to **Enter Name**
Label2 to **Points Scored in Mathematics**
Label3 to **Points Scored in English**
Label4 to **Points Scored in Science**
Label5 to **Average**
Button1 to **Show**
Button2 to **Clear**
Button3 to **Exit**

The resultant form will appear as shown in Figure 3-7.

Figure 3-7 Design mode of Application 3

Step 5
Change the values of the **Name** property of the controls as follows:

Label1 to **lblname**
Label2 to **lblmth**
Label3 to **lbleng**
Label4 to **lblscn**
Label5 to **lblavg**
Label6 to **lblDisplay**
TextBox1 to **txtname**
TextBox2 to **txtmth**
TextBox3 to **txteng**
TextBox4 to **txtscn**
TextBox5 to **txtavg**
Button1 to **btnShow**
Button2 to **btnClear**
Button3 to **btnExit**

Step 6
Double-click on the **Show** button and enter the following source code in the code window:

```
Dim Mathematics, English, Science As Integer          1
Dim Name As String                                    2
Dim score As Integer                                  3
Name = txtname.Text                                   4
Mathematics = txtmth.Text                             5
```

English = txteng.Text	6
Science = txtscn.Text	7
score = (Mathematics + English + Science) / 3	8
txtavg.Text = score.ToString	9
If score >= 90 Then	10
lblDisplay.Text = "Grade A"	11
ElseIf score >= 80 And score < 90 Then	12
lblDisplay.Text = "Grade B"	13
ElseIf score >= 70 And score < 80 Then	14
lblDisplay.Text = "Grade C"	15
Else	16
If score < 70 Then	17
lblDisplay.Text = "Try Again"	18
End If	19
End If	20

The source code for the **Clear** and **Exit** buttons is the same as discussed earlier in this chapter.

Explanation

Line 10

If score >= 90 Then

In this line, the relational expression **score >= 90** within the **If-Then** statement is checked. If it evaluates to true, the statement associated with the **If-Then** statement, **lblDisplay.Text = "Grade A"** will be executed and all other statements will be skipped. If the condition evaluates to false, then the control will be transferred to the **ElseIf** statement.

Line 11

lblDisplay.Text = "Grade A"

In this line, the text **Grade A** is assigned to the **Label** control named **lblDisplay** and this text will also be displayed on the form.

Line 12

ElseIf score >= 80 And score < 90 Then

This line will be executed if the condition given in the **If-Then** statement evaluates to false. In this line, the condition **score >= 80 And score < 90** is checked. If it evaluates to true, then the statement, **lblDisplay.Text = "Grade A"** associated with this **ElseIf** will be displayed. Otherwise, the control will be transferred to the next **ElseIf** statement.

Line 16

Else

If all the conditions from Line 10 to Line 14 evaluate to false, then the control will be transferred to this line and the statement, **Try Again** will be displayed.

Step 7

Press F5 to execute the application. Enter the following values in the respective **TextBox** controls:

Enter Name: **Mary**
Points scored in Mathematics: **98**
Points scored in English: **97**
Points scored in Science: **97**

Choose the **Show** button on the form; the output will be displayed, as shown in Figure 3-8.

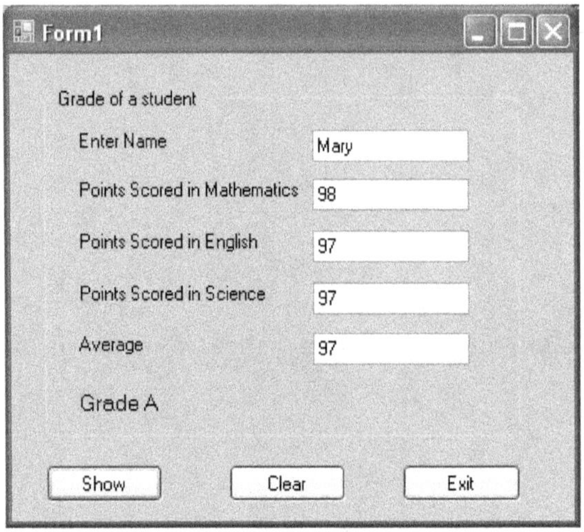

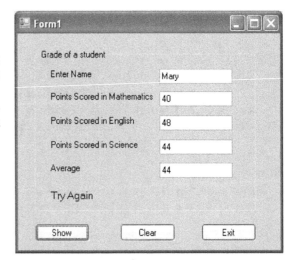

Figure 3-8 Output of Application 3 with the message **Grade A**

Next, choose the **Clear** button and enter the following values in the respective **TextBox** controls:

Enter Name: **Mary**
Points scored in Mathematics: **40**
Points scored in English: **48**
Points scored in Science: **44**

Choose the **Show** button on the form; the output will be displayed, as shown in Figure 3-9.

You can also try some other values to check the results.

Figure 3-9 Output of Application 3 with the message **Try Again**

Nested If-Then Statement

An **If-Then** statement which is used within another **If-Then** statement is known as a nested **If-Then** statement. In this structure, the last **Else** statement is always associated with the **If-Then** block that precedes it. The syntax of the nested **If-Then** statement is as follows:

```
If condition_1 Then
If condition_2 Then
statement_1
End If
Else
statement_2
End If
```

In the above syntax, if the condition 1 given within the first **If-Then** statement is true, then the control will be transferred to the next **If-Then** statement. If the condition 2 is true, then the statement 1 will be executed. However, if the condition 2 is false, then the control will be transferred to the **Else** block and the statement 2 will be executed.

For example:

```
If a > b Then
If a > c Then
lblDisplay.Text = "a is greater"
Else
End If
lblDisplay.Text = "c is greater"
End If
```

In the above example, if the condition **a > b** within the outer **If-Then** statement is true, then the control will be transferred to the inner **If-Then** statement. If the condition **a > c** is true, then the message **a is greater** will be displayed. Otherwise, the message associated with the **Else** block **c is greater** will be displayed.

The following application illustrates the use of the nested **If-Then** statement:

Application 4

Create an application to evaluate the qualification and experience of a candidate for two different posts in the computer department, using the nested **If-Then** statement.

This application will prompt the user to specify his qualification as well as enter the number of years of his experience, and then display the result on the form.

The following steps are required to create this application:

Step 1
Start a new project and save it as **c03_VB_NET_2008_04**.

Step 2
Add a **GroupBox** control and three **Button** controls to the form.

Step 3
Add a **ComboBox** control, three **Label** controls, and a **TextBox** control to the **GroupBox** control.

Step 4
Change the values of the **Text** property of the controls as follows:

GroupBox1 to **Job Requirement**
Label1 to **Qualification**
Label2 to **Experience**
Button1 to **Show**
Button2 to **Clear**
Button3 to **Exit**

The form will be displayed as shown in Figure 3-10.

Figure 3-10 *Design mode of Application 4*

Step 5
Change the values of the **Name** property of the controls as follows:

Label1 to **lblqul**
Label2 to **lblexp**
Label3 to **lblDisplay**
Button1 to **btnShow**
Button2 to **btnClear**
Button3 to **btnExit**

Step 6
Select the **Items** property of the **ComboBox** control. Choose the ellipses button on the right; the **String Collection Editor** dialog box will be displayed. Add the items **Computer Engineer**, **Electronics Engineer**, **Mechanical Engineer**, and **Textile Engineer** to the **String Collection Editor** dialog box. Choose the **OK** button.

Step 7
To add the code for the **Show** button, double-click on it and write the following source code:

```
Dim qualification As String                                          1
Dim experience As Integer                                            2
experience = TextBox1.Text                                           3
qualification = ComboBox1.Text                                       4
If experience >= 2 Then                                              5
If qualification = "Computer Engineer" Or _                          6
qualification = "Electronics Engineer" Then                          7
```

lblDisplay.Text = "You are eligible for the designation: Team Leader"	8
Else	9
lblDisplay.Text = "You are not eligible for the designation: Team Leader"	10
End If	11
Else	12
If qualification = "Mechanical Engineer" Or _	13
qualification = "Textile Engineer" Then	14
lblDisplay.Text = "You are not eligible for the designation: Trainee"	15
Else	16
lblDisplay.Text = "You are eligible for the designation: Trainee"	17
End If	18
End If	19

The source code for the **Clear** and **Exit** buttons is the same as discussed earlier in this chapter.

Explanation
Line 1
Dim qualification As String
In this line, **qualification** is declared as a string data type variable.

Line 2
Dim experience As Integer
In this line, **experience** is declared as an integer data type variable.

Line 3
experience = (TextBox1.Text)
In this line, the text value of the **TextBox1** textbox is assigned to the variable **experience** with the help of the assignment operator.

Line 4
qualification = ComboBox1.Text
In this line, **ComboBox1** contains the list of some qualifications in the **Items** property. The item selected by the user from the list is assigned to the variable **qualification**.

Line 5
If experience >= 2 Then
This line is the outer **If-Then** statement. In this line, the **If-Then** statement is used to check whether the value of the variable **experience** is greater than 2. If the condition associated with the **If-Then** statement is true, then the control will be transferred to Line 6. Otherwise, the control will be transferred to Line 12, which is the outer **Else** block.

Line 6 and Line 7
If qualification = "Computer Engineer" Or _
qualification = "Electronics Engineer" Then
In these lines, the **If-Then** statement is used to compare the value of the variable **qualification** with the values specified in the above statements. If any of the above two conditions is true, the message **You are eligible for the designation: Team Leader**, as given in Line 8, will be

displayed. Otherwise, the message **You are not eligible for the designation: Team Leader** will be displayed.

Line 8
lblDisplay.Text = "You are eligible for the designation: Team Leader"
In this line, the value **You are eligible for the designation: Team Leader** will be assigned to the **Text** property of the **Label** control named **lblDisplay**. As a result, the above message will be displayed on the form.

Line 9
Else
This is the inner **Else** block. This block will be executed only if the conditions associated with the inner **If-Then** block (Lines 6 and 7) are false. Otherwise, it will be skipped and the control will be transferred to the outer **Else** block in Line 12.

Line 10
lblDisplay.Text = "You are not eligible for the designation: Team Leader"
In this line, the message **You are not eligible for the designation: Team Leader** will be assigned to the **Text** property of the **Label** control named **lblDisplay** and the above message will also be displayed on the form.

Line 11
End If
This indicates the end of the inner **If-Then** block.

Line 12
Else
This is the outer **Else** block. This block will be executed only if the conditions associated with the outer **If-Then** block are false. Otherwise, it will be skipped.

Line 13 and Line 14
If qualification = "Mechanical Engineer" Or _
qualification = "Textile Engineer" Then
These lines are associated with the outer **Else** block. In these lines, the **If-Then** statement is used to compare the value of the variable **qualification** with the values specified in the above statement. If any of the above two conditions is true, the message **You are not eligible for the designation: Trainee** will be displayed.

Line 16
Else
If the conditions in Line 13 and Line 14 are not satisfied, then the control will be transferred to the **Else** block and the message **You are eligible for the designation: Trainee** will be displayed.

Line 18
End If
This line indicates the end of the **If-Then** (Line 13) statement, which is preceded by the outer **Else** block.

Line 19
End If
This line indicates the end of the outer **If-Then** (Line 5) statement.

Step 8
Press F5 to execute the application. Select an option from the **Qualification** combo box such as **Computer Engineer** and enter the value **3** in the **Experience** textbox. Next, choose the **Show** button; you will get a message **You are eligible for the designation: Team Leader** on the form, as shown in Figure 3-11. But, if you select the values that do not satisfy the conditions mentioned in the source code, you will get a message **You are not eligible for the designation: Team Leader** on the form, as shown in Figure 3-12.

Figure 3-11 Output of Application 4 with valid set of values

Figure 3-12 Output of Application 4 with invalid set of values

Step 9
Now, try to execute the application with some other values in the **Experience** textbox. Select the **Computer Engineer** option from the **Qualification** combo box and enter the value **1** in the **Experience** textbox. Next, choose the **Show** button; the message **You are eligible for the designation: Trainee** will be displayed on the form, as shown in Figure 3-13. Choose the **Clear** button to clear the values from the form. Now, try the values that will satisfy the condition associated with the **Else** statement, refer to Lines 13 and 14. Select the **Mechanical Engineer** option from the **Qualification** combo box and enter the value **1** in the **Experience** textbox. Next, choose the **Show** button; the message **You are not eligible for the designation: Trainee** will be displayed on the form, as shown in Figure 3-14.

Figure 3-13 Output of Application 4 with another set of valid values

Figure 3-14 Output of Application 4 with another set of invalid values

Select Case Statement

The **Select Case** statement tests the value of an expression only once. The result of the test is used to determine the set of statements that are to be executed. The syntax of the **Select Case** statement is as follows:

```
Select Case variable
Case value_1
statement_1
Case value_2
statement_2



Case Else
statement_n
End Select
```

In the above syntax, the first line starts with the keyword **Select** followed by another keyword **Case**, which is in turn followed by a variable. This variable is called as the test expression. This test expression can be a numeric or a string. The value of this expression is compared to the values followed by the **Case** expressions (value 1, value 2, and so on). If the test expression finds a match, the statement or the block of statements associated with the **Case** expression will be executed. If no match is found, then the control will transfer to the **Case Else** statement and the statements associated with it will be executed.

The following application illustrates the use of the **Select Case** statement:

Application 5

Create an application to display the months of a year according to the user's choice, using the **Select Case** statement.

This application will prompt the user to enter any number from 1 to 12. It will then display the name of the corresponding month in a message box.

The following steps are required to create this application:

Step 1
Start a new project and save it as **c03_VB_NET_2008_05**.

Step 2
Add a **GroupBox** control to the form.

Step 3
Add a **Label** control, a **TextBox** control, and three **Button** controls to the **GroupBox** control.

Step 4
Change the values of the **Text** property of the controls as follows:

Form1 to **Select Case**
GroupBox1 to **Months of the year**
Label1 to **Enter your choice**
Button1 to **Show**
Button2 to **Clear**
Button3 to **Exit**

The resultant form will appear as shown in Figure 3-15.

Figure 3-15 *Design mode of Application 5*

Step 5
Change the values of the **Name** property of the controls as follows:

Button1 to **btnShow**
Button2 to **btnClear**
Button3 to **btnExit**

Step 6
The following is the source code for the **Show** button:

```
Private Sub btnShow_Click(ByVal sender As System.Object, _
ByVal e As System.EventArgs) Handles btnShow.Click          1
Dim choice As Integer                                       2
choice = Convert.ToInt16(TextBox1.Text)                     3
Select Case choice                                          4
Case 1                                                      5
MessageBox.Show("January")                                  6
Case 2                                                      7
MessageBox.Show("February")                                 8
Case 3                                                      9
```

MessageBox.Show("March")	10
Case 4	11
MessageBox.Show("April")	12
Case 5	13
MessageBox.Show("May")	14
Case 6	15
MessageBox.Show("June")	16
Case 7	17
MessageBox.Show("July")	18
Case 8	19
MessageBox.Show("August")	20
Case 9	21
MessageBox.Show("September")	22
Case 10	23
MessageBox.Show("October")	24
Case 11	25
MessageBox.Show("November")	26
Case 12	27
MessageBox.Show("December")	28
Case Else	29
MessageBox.Show("Incorrect Value")	30
End Select	31
End Sub	32

The source code for the **Clear** and **Exit** buttons is the same as discussed in Application 1.

Explanation
Line 4
Select Case choice
This line represents the start of the **Select** statement followed by the keyword **Case**, which is inturn followed by the test expression **choice**. The value of this test expression is matched with all case constants one-by-one with the help of the **Select** statement. If a match is found, then the control will be transferred to the statement associated with that particular case.

Line 5
Case 1
This line begins with the keyword **Case**, which is followed by an integer value (1). This value is matched with the value of the test expression (**choice**). If a match is found, then Line 6 will be executed. Otherwise, the control will be transferred to **Case 2**.

Line 6
MessageBox.Show("January")
In this line, a message box with the message **January** will be displayed on the **Select Case** form.

The working of Lines 7 to 28 is the same as those of Lines 5 and 6.

Line 29

Case Else

If no match is found while comparing with all the above cases, then the statement associated with the **Case Else** will be executed.

Line 30

MessageBox.Show("Incorrect Value")

In this line, a message box with the message **Incorrect Value** will be displayed.

Step 7

Press F5 to execute the application. If you want to display the month January, then enter 1 in the **TextBox** control. Choose the **Show** button on the form; the month **January** will be displayed in a message box, as shown in the Figure 3-16. If you enter the value 13 in the **TextBox** control, you will get the message **Incorrect Value** in a message box, as shown in Figure 3-17.

Select with Multiple Statements

The **Case** statement can have multiple expressions separated by commas. The syntax for

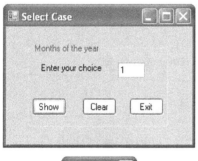

Figure 3-16 Output of Application 5 with valid value

Figure 3-17 Output of Application 5 with invalid value

the **Case** statement is as follows:

```
Select Case variable (test expression)
Case value_1, value_2, value_3
statement_1
Case value_4, value_5, value_6
statement_2
Case Else
|
statement_n
End Select
```

In the above syntax, the first line starts with the keyword **Select**, followed by the keyword **Case**, which is in turn followed by a variable. This variable is known as the test expression. In the previous topic, you have used only a single value with each **Case** keyword. In this case, you can use multiple values in a single **Case** statement, as shown in the following code:

```
Select Case choice
Case 1, 3, 5, 7, 9
MessageBox.Show("Odd number")
Case 2, 4, 6, 8, 10
MessageBox.Show("Even number")
Case Else
MessageBox.Show("Wrong entry")
End Select
```

In these lines, the variable **choice** is considered as an integer. Notice the multiple values with the keyword **Case**. If you enter 1, 3, 5, 7, or 9, you will get the message **Odd number**. If you enter 2, 4, 6, 8, or 10, you will get the message **Even number**.

You can also use multiple string values in a single **Case** statement. The following example illustrates the use of multiple string values with the keyword **Case**:

```
Select Case day
Case "Saturday", "Sunday"
MessageBox.Show("Holiday")
Case "Monday", "Tuesday", "Wednesday", "Thursday", "Friday"
MessageBox.Show("Working Day")
Case Else
MessageBox.Show("Invalid Value")
        End Select
```

You can also use relational operators in a **Case** statement. To do so, you need to use the keyword **Is** with the keyword **Case**. To determine whether the test expression falls within a particular range of values, use the keyword **To**. The following example illustrates the use of **Is** and **To** keywords in a **Case** statement:

```
Select Case score
Case Is >= 80
rank = "First Division"
Case 70 To 79
rank = "Second Division"
Case 60 To 69
rank = "Third Division"
Case 50 To 59
rank = "Poor Performance"
Case Else
MessageBox.Show("Invalid value")
End Select
```

In the above example, the keyword **Is** is used to check the relational expression (score >= 80).

The values that are on either sides of the **To** keyword are used to specify the given range. For example, the **Case** statement **Case 70 To 79** will not only compare the values 70, 79 but also compare the values that are between 70 and 79.

Loop Control Statements

In the previous section, you learned about the decision control statements, in which the flow of a program can be along two or more paths. Sometimes a program needs to repeat a particular statement or a block of statements one or more than one time. In such cases, the loop statements are used. The loop statements are used to repeat a particular block of code a certain number of times. The block of code is repeated until the given condition is true. If the condition becomes false, the loop ends and the control is transferred to the next statement immediately after the loop. There are three types of loop statements that are supported by VB.NET and they are discussed next.

1. Do While loop
2. Do Until loop
3. For Next loop

Do While Loop

This statement allows a program to execute a particular statement or block of statements as long as the specified condition is true. The **Do While** statement contains two parts. These are as follows:

a. A boolean expression.
b. A statement or a block of statements that will repeat as long as the given expression is true.

The syntax of the **Do While** loop is as follows:

```
Do While expression
statement/statements
Loop
```

In the above syntax, the **Do While** statement is the beginning of the loop and the **Loop** statement specifies its end. The statement or block of statements between the **Do While** and **Loop** statements are known as the body of the loop. When an application is executed, the expression associated with the **Do While** loop is tested. If the expression is true, the statement or statements associated with it will be executed. This process is repeated until the condition becomes false.

The following application illustrates the use of the **Do While** loop:

Application 6

Create an application to display the message **Welcome To Disney Land** five times, using the **Do While** loop.

This application will display the message **Welcome To Disney Land** five times in a **ListBox** control on a form.

The following steps are required to create this application:

Step 1
Start a new project and save it as **c03_VB_NET_2008_06**.

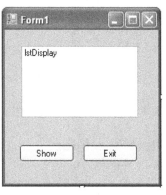

Step 2
Add a **ListBox** control and two **Button** controls to the form.

Step 3
Change the values of the **Text** property of the controls as follows:

Button1 to **Show**
Button2 to **Exit**

The resultant form will appear as shown in Figure 3-18.

Figure 3-18 Design mode of Application 6

Step 4
Change the values of the **Name** property of the controls as follows:

ListBox1 to **lstDisplay**
Button1 to **btnShow**
Button2 to **btnExit**

Step 5
The source code for the **Show** button is given next. The line numbers on the right are not a part of the code and are for reference only.

```
Dim a As Integer = 0                                        1
Do While a < 5                                              2
lstDisplay.Items.Add("Welcome To Disney Land")             3
a += 1                                                      4
Loop                                                        5
```

Explanation
The line-by-line explanation of the above given source code is given next.

Line 1
Dim a As Integer = 0
In this line, the variable **a** is declared as an integer type variable and is initialized with the value 0.

Line 2
Do While a < 5
In the above line, the **Do While** statement tests the value of the variable **a**. If the expression **a < 5** (a is less than 5) is true, then the statements within the body of this loop will be executed. Otherwise, the loop will be terminated and the control will be transferred to the statements following the **Loop** statement.

Line 3
lstDisplay.Items.Add("Welcome To Disney Land")
In the above line, **lstDisplay** represents a **ListBox** control. The **Items** property of the **ListBox** control is used to get the items from it and the **Add** function is used to add the items in the **ListBox** control. In this application, the item to be added to the **ListBox** control is **Welcome To Disney Land**.

Line 4
a += 1
In the above line, the combined assignment operator (**+=**) is used to increment the value of the variable **a** by one.

Line 5
Loop
This indicates the end of the body of the loop.

The following is the brief explanation of the working of the **Do While** statement in the given program:

In this source code, the variable **a** is initialized to 0. Next, the condition **a < 5** is checked. For the first time, it is true because a = 0 (0<5), so the message **Welcome To Disney Land** will be displayed in the list box. Next, with the help of the combined assignment operator (**+=**), the value of the variable **a** will be increased by 1 (0 + 1 =1). Again, the condition is true because a = 1 (1< 5). So, the message given above will be displayed again. This process will be repeated until the condition becomes false.

Step 6
Press F5 to execute the application. The output form will be displayed, as shown in Figure 3-19. Choose the **Show** button on the form; you will get the message **Welcome To Disney Land** five times in the **ListBox** control, as shown in Figure 3-20.

Figure 3-19 *Output form of Application 6*

Figure 3-20 *Output of Application 6*

There is another way of using the **Do While** loop. If you want to execute a statement once, even if the condition is false, you can use the following syntax of the **Do While** loop:

> Do
> statement
> Loop While expression

In the above syntax, the body of the loop will be executed first and then the expression will be evaluated.

The following part of the application illustrates another use of the **Do While** loop.

This part of the application will display the message **Welcome To Disney Land** once in the **ListBox** control on a form.

The following is the source code for this part of the application:

```
Dim a As Integer = 0
Do
lstDisplay.Items.Add("Welcome To Disney Land")
a += 1
Loop While a > 5
```

Explanation

In the above program, the variable **a** is declared as an integer type variable and it is initialized with the value 0. Next, the statement **Welcome To Disney Land** will be added to the **ListBox** control. Then the expression **a > 5** will be evaluated. In this case, the expression will be false because a = 1 (1 < 5), so the loop will get terminated. As the expression given in the above program is false, the statement will be executed only once, as shown in Figure 3-21.

Figure 3-21 *Output of Application 6
using the **Do While** loop*

Do Until Loop

Like the **Do While** loop, the **Do Until** loop also contains two parts but it continues to repeat the body of the loop until the given expression is true. This means that the **Do Until** loop is executed if the given condition is false. The syntax of the **Do Until** loop is as follows:

    Do Until expression
    statement/statements
    Loop

The following application illustrates the use of the **Do Until** loop.
Create an application to display the percentage of score obtained by a student in different

Application 7

subjects using the **Do Until** loop.

This application will prompt the user to first enter the total number of subjects and then the score obtained in each subject by a student. The application will also display the percentage of the score obtained.

The following steps are required to create this application:

Step 1
Start a new project and save it as **c03_VB_NET_2008_07**.

Step 2
Add a **GroupBox** control to the form.

Step 3
Add three **Label** controls and two **Button** controls to the **GroupBox** control.

Step 4
Change the values of the **Text** property of the controls as follows:

GroupBox1 to **Score**
Label1 to **Choose the Calculate button**
Label2 to **Percentage**
Button1 to **Calculate**
Button2 to **Exit**

Step 5
Change the values of the **Name** property of the
controls as follows:

Label1 to **lblcal**
Label2 to **lblpnt**
Label3 to **lblPercentage**
Button1 to **btnCalcAverage**
Button2 to **btnExit**

The resultant form will appear as shown in
Figure 3-22.

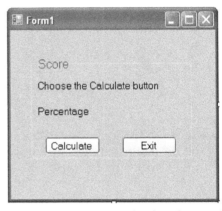

Figure 3-22 Design mode of Application 7

Step 6
The following is the source code for the
Calculate button:

```
Dim score_obtained As Single                                        1
Dim num As Integer                                                  2
Dim total_subjects As Single                                        3
Dim counter As Integer                                              4
Dim percentage As Single                                            5
Dim total_score As Single                                           6
total_subjects = InputBox("Enter the total number of subjects", _
"Number of subjects")                                               7
total_score = InputBox("Enter the total score", "Total Score")      8
num = total_subjects                                                9
score_obtained = 0                                                  10
counter = 1                                                         11
Do Until counter > num                                              12
total_subjects = InputBox("Enter the score of subjects " & _
counter.ToString, "Score Obtained")                                 13
score_obtained = score_obtained + total_subjects                    14
counter = counter + 1                                               15
Loop                                                                16
percentage = score_obtained / total_score * 100                     17
lblPercentage.Text = percentage                                     18
```

Explanation

The line-by-line explanation of the source code is as follows:

Line 1
Dim score_obtained As Single
In the above line, **score_obtained** is declared as a single data type variable. This variable will hold the value of the score obtained by the student.

Line 2
Dim num As Integer
In the above line, **num** is declared as an integer data type variable. This variable will hold the number of subjects entered by the user.

Line 3
Dim total_subjects As Single
In the above line, **total_subjects** is declared as a single data type variable. It will hold the value of the input from the user.

Line 4
Dim counter As Integer
In the above line, **counter** is declared as an integer data type variable. It is the counter variable for the loop.

Line 5
Dim percentage As Single
In this line, **percentage** is declared as a single data type variable. It will hold the value of the percentage of score obtained by a student.

Line 6
Dim total_score As Single
In the above line, **total_score** is declared as a single data type variable. It will hold the value of the total score obtained by a student.

Line 7
total_subjects = InputBox("Enter the total number of subjects", _
"Number of subjects")
In the above line, the **InputBox** is a function. Whenever this function is called, an input box is displayed. Here, the argument list contains two arguments, **Enter the total number of subjects** and **Number of subjects**. The first one will be displayed in the input box, which is used to prompt the user to enter a value. The value entered by the user is then assigned to the variable **total_subjects**. The second argument (**Number of subjects**) will be displayed in the title bar of the input box.

Line 8
total_score = InputBox("Total Score", "Enter the total score")
The argument list of the function **InputBox** contains two arguments, **Total Score** and **Enter the total score**. The first one will be displayed in the input box, which is used to prompt the

user to enter a value. The value entered by the user is then assigned to the variable **total_score**. The second argument will be displayed in the title bar of the input box.

Line 10
score_obtained = 0
In the above line, the value 0 is assigned to the variable **score_obtained**.

Line 11
counter = 1
In the above line, the value 1 is assigned to the variable **counter**. It is the counter variable for the loop.

Line 12
Do Until counter > num
In the above line, the **Do Until** loop repeats until the value of the variable **counter** is greater than **num**. This loop is used to read the value of **num** from the user and also to increment the **counter**.

The following is the brief explanation of working of the **Do Until** loop in the given source code:

The working of the **Do Until** loop is the same as the **Do While** loop except that the **Do Until** loop continues to repeat till the given condition is true. In the source code given in this application, the **Do Until** loop repeats until the value of the variable **counter** is greater than the value of the variable **num** (counter > num).

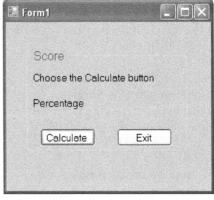

Step 7
Press F5 to execute the application; a form will be displayed, as shown in Figure 3-23.

Figure 3-23 Output form of Application 7

Step 8
Choose the **Calculate** button; the **Number of subjects** input box with the message **Enter the total number of subjects** will be displayed. Now, enter the value **5** in the input box, as shown in the Figure 3-24.

Step 9
Choose the **OK** button; the **Total Score** input box will be displayed. Enter the value **500** in the input box, as shown in the Figure 3-25.

Step 10

Again, choose the **OK** button; the **Score Obtained** input box with the message **Enter the score of subject 1** will be displayed. Enter the value **90** in the input box, as shown in Figure 3-26. This is the score obtained by the student in the first subject.

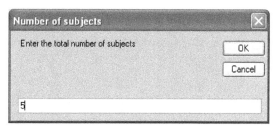

Figure 3-24 The **Number of subjects** *input box*

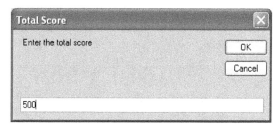

Figure 3-25 The **Total Score** *input box*

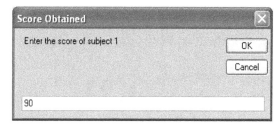

Figure 3-26 The **Score Obtained** *input box for subject 1*

Step 11

Choose the **OK** button; the **Score Obtained** input box with the message **Enter the score of subject 2** will be displayed. Enter the value **80** in the input box, as shown in Figure 3-27. This is the score obtained by the student in the second subject.

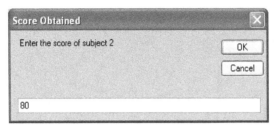

*Figure 3-27 The **Score Obtained** input box for subject 2*

Similarly, you will get the input boxes for subject 3, subject 4, and subject 5, as shown in Figures 3-28, 3-29, and 3-30, respectively.

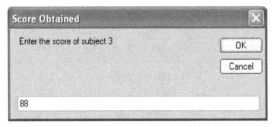

*Figure 3-28 The **Score Obtained** input box for subject 3*

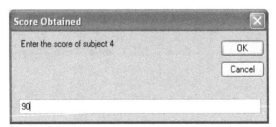

*Figure 3-29 The **Score Obtained** input box for subject 4*

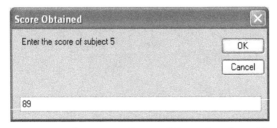

*Figure 3-30 The **Score Obtained** input box for subject 5*

Step 12

After entering the values of the scores obtained in all subjects, choose the **OK** button; the value 87.4 will be displayed as the **Percentage** on the form, as shown in the Figure 3-31.

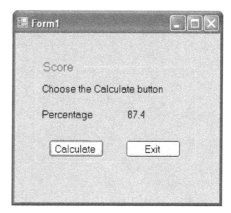

Figure 3-31 *Result of Application 7*

For Next Loop

The **For Next** loop is also used to execute a particular block of code for specific number of times. It is mostly used when you know the number of times the body of the loop needs to be executed. The syntax of the **For Next** loop is as follows:

> For counter = StartValue To EndValue [Step increment]
> statement/statements
> Next [counter]

In this syntax, the variable **counter** is the loop's counter and it must be numeric. The **StartValue** is the initial value assigned to the variable **counter** and the **EndValue** is the value that will be tested against the value of the variable **counter** before each repetition. The increment argument **Step increment** is optional. You can set any value for it. If the increment part is omitted, the **counter** variable is incremented by 1. The **Next** statement indicates the end of the **For** loop. It also increments the **counter** variable.

The following application illustrates the use of the **For Next** loop:

Application 8

Create an application to display the multiples of a number entered by the user.

This application will prompt the user to enter a number. It will also display the multiples of the number entered by the user in the **ListBox** control.

The following steps are required to create this application:

Step 1
Start a new project and save it as **c03_VB_NET_2008_08**.

Step 2
Add a **ListBox** control and three **Button** controls
to the form.

Step 3
Change the values of the **Text** property of the
controls as follows:

Button1 to **Show**
Button2 to **Clear**
Button3 to **Exit**

The resultant form will appear as shown in
Figure 3-32.

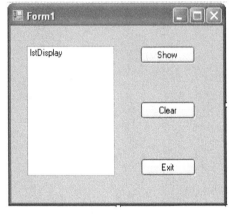

Figure 3-32 *Design mode of Application 8*

Step 4
Change the values of the **Name** property of the controls as follows:

Button1 to **btnShow**
Button2 to **btnClear**
Button3 to **btnExit**
ListBox1 to **lstDisplay**

Step 5
The following is the source code for the **Show** button:

```
Dim n, t As Integer                             1
Dim i As Integer                                2
n = InputBox("Enter a number", "Table")         3
For i = 1 To 10                                 4
t = i * n                                       5
lstDisplay.Items.Add(t)                         6
Next i                                          7
```

Explanation
Line 4
For i = 1 To 10
In the above line, the counter variable **i** is assigned the value 1, which is the **StartValue** and
then it is compared to the value 10, which is the **EndValue**. If the value of variable **i** is less
than or equal to 10, then the control will be transferred to the next line, **t = i * n**. Otherwise,
the loop will be terminated.

Line 5
t = i * n
In the above line, the result of the multiplication of the values of **n** and **i** will be assigned to the variable **t**.

Line 6
lstDisplay.Items.Add(t)
In the above line, the value of the variable **t** will be displayed in the list box for upto ten iterations.

Line 7
Next i
In the above line, the **Next** statement is used to increment the value of the counter variable **i** by one.

Step 6
Press F5 to execute the application; the form will be displayed, as shown in Figure 3-33

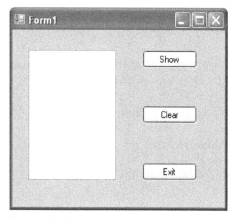

Figure 3-33 Output form of Application 8

Next, choose the **Show** button; the **Table** input box with the message **Enter a number** will be displayed. Enter the value **9** in the input box, as shown in Figure 3-34.

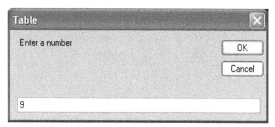

*Figure 3-34 The **Table** input box*

Step 7
Choose the **OK** button in the input box; the multiples of number 9 will be displayed in the list box, as shown in Figure 3-35.

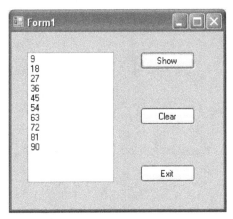

Figure 3-35 Output of Application 8 for number 9

Nested For Next Loop

A nested loop is a loop within the body of another loop. In the nested loop, the outer loop takes control over the inner loop. The syntax of the nested **For Next** loop is as follows:

    For counter 1 = StartValue To EndValue [Step increment] 'Outer Loop
    statement/statements
    For counter 2 = StartValue To EndValue [Step increment] 'Inner Loop
    statement/statements
    For counter 3 = StartValue To EndValue [Step increment] 'Innermost Loop
    statement/statements

    Next [counter 3]
    Next [counter 2]
    Next [counter 1]

In the above syntax, the innermost loop is repeated for each iteration of the outer loop and the inner loop. The inner loop is repeated for each iteration of the outer loop. It means when the execution begins, the application encounters the outer loop. If the condition in the outer loop is true, then the control is transferred to the inner loop. If the condition in the inner loop is true, the control is transferred to the innermost loop. This process is repeated until the outer loop ends.

Application 9

The following application illustrates another use of the nested **For Next** loop:

Create an application to display the numbers from 0 to 5 thrice in the **ListBox** control.

This application will display the numbers from 0 to 5 thrice in the **ListBox** control.

The following steps are required to create this application:

Step 1
Start a new project and save it as **c03_VB_ NET_2008_09**.

Step 2
Add a **ListBox** control and three **Button** controls to the form.

Step 3
Change the values of the **Text** property of the controls as follows:

Button1 to **Show**
Button2 to **Clear**
Button3 to **Exit**

The form will be displayed, as shown in Figure 3-36.

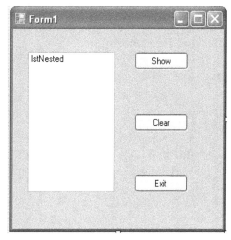

Figure 3-36 *Design mode of Application 9*

Step 4
Change the values of the **Name** property of the controls as follows:

ListBox1 to **lstNested**
Button1 to **btnShow**
Button2 to **btnClear**
Button3 to **btnExit**

Step 5
The following is the source code for the **Show** button:

```
Dim i, j As Integer                    1
For i = 0 To 2                         2
lstNested.Items.Add(i)                 3
For j = 0 To 5                         4
lstNested.Items.Add(j)                 5
Next j                                 6
Next i                                 7
```

Explanation
Line 1
Dim i, j As Integer
In the above line, **i** and **j** are declared as the integer data type variables.

Line 2
For i = 0 To 2
In the above line, the counter variable of the outer loop **i** is assigned the value 0, which is the **StartValue** and then it is compared to the value 2, which is the **EndValue**. If the value of the counter variable **i** is less than or equal to 2, then the control will be transferred to the next line **lstNested.Items.Add(i)**. Otherwise, the loop will be terminated.

Line 3
lstNested.Items.Add(i)
In the above line, the value of the variable **i** will be displayed in the **ListBox** control for upto three iterations.

Line 4
For j = 0 To 5
In the above line, the counter variable of the inner loop **j** is assigned the value 0, which is the **StartValue** and then it is compared to the value 5, which is the **EndValue**. This inner loop (For j = 0 To 5) will be repeated for each iteration of the outer loop (For i = 0 To 2).

It will work as follows:

First iteration   i = 0   j = 0
                                              1
                                              2
                                              3
                                              4
                                              5
                                              |
Second iteration   i = 1   j = 0

                                              5
                                              |
Third iteration   i = 2   j = 0

                                              5

Line 5
lstNested.Items.Add(j)
In the above line, the value of the variable **j** will be displayed in the **ListBox** control for upto six iterations of the inner loop.

Line 6
Next j
In the above line, the **Next** statement is used to increment the counter variable **j** by one.

Line 7
Next i
In the above line, the **Next** statement is used to increment the counter variable **i** by one.

Step 6
Press F5 to execute the application; the resultant form will be displayed.

Step 7
Choose the **Show** button; the output form will be displayed, as shown in Figure 3-37.

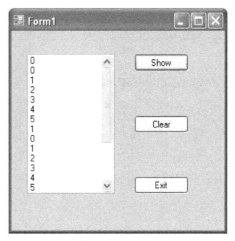

Figure 3-37 *Output of Application 9*

Notice the scroll bar in Figure 3-37. VB.NET provides the facility of adding a scroll bar to the **ListBox** control if it has more items than the visible range.

With-End With Loop

You can perform several operations on a single control, using the **With-End With** loop. The syntax of the **With-End With** loop is as follows:

> With ControlName
> statement/statements
> End With

In the above syntax, the **With** statement is used with the value of the **Name** property of a control. Next, **statement/statements** specify the operations that you want to perform on the control and the statement **End With** indicates the end of the **With** block.

The following application illustrates the use of the nested **With-End With** loop:

Application 10

Create an application to perform different operations on a **Button** control, using the **With-End With** loop.

This application will perform different operations on a **Button** control.

The following steps are required to create this application:

Step 1
Start a new project and save it as **c03_VB_NET_2008_10**.

Step 2
Add a **Button** control to the form. Delete the default value of the **Text** property of the **Button** control.

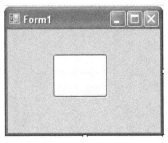

Step 3
Change the value of the **Name** property of the **Button** control to **btnDemo**.

The resultant form will appear, as shown in Figure 3-38.

Figure 3-38 Design mode of Application 10

Step 4
The following is the source code for the **Button** control:

```
With btnDemo                                   1
.Width = 50                                     2
.TextAlign = ContentAlignment.MiddleLeft        3
.Text = "Show"                                  4
End With                                        5
```

Explanation
Line 1
With btnDemo
In the above line, the **With** statement indicates the beginning of the **With** block. **btnDemo** is the value of the **Name** property of the **Button** control.

Line 2
.Width = 50
In the above line, **.Width = 50** is the property of the **Button** control. It will set the width of the **Button** control to the value 50 at runtime.

Line 3
.TextAlign = ContentAlignment.MiddleLeft
In the above line, the **TextAlign** property of the **Button** control is assigned the value **ContentAlignment.MiddleLeft**. It will align the text of the **Button** control to the left at runtime.

Line 4
.Text = "Show"
In the above line, the value **Show** will be assigned to the **Text** property of the **Button** control at runtime.
Line 5

End With
This line indicates the end of the **With** block.

Step 5
Press F5 to execute the application; the output form will appear, as shown in Figure 3-39.

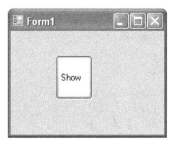

Figure 3-39 *Output of Application 10*

LOGICAL OPERATORS

The logical operators are used between two or more relational expressions in order to combine them. These operations can also reverse the logic of an expression. Table 3-3 shows a list of the logical operators.

Operators	Function
And	Combines two expressions. Both expressions must be true
Or	Combines two expressions. One or both the expressions must be true
Xor	Combines two expressions. One expression must be true
Not	Reverses the logic of an expression

Table 3-3 *The logical operators*

The And Operator

The **And** operator is used to combine two relational expressions. If both the expressions are true, only then the overall expression is evaluated to be true. The syntax of an **And** operator is as follows:

        If expression_1 And expression_2 Then
        statement
        End If

In the above syntax, two relational expressions are combined using the **And** operator. The statement associated with the **If-Then** statement will be executed only if both the expressions (expression_1 and expression_2) are true.

For example:

> **If x > 20 And y < 10 Then**
> **lblDisplay.Text = "Number is correct"**
> **End If**

In the above example, the statement **Number is correct** will be displayed only if the variable **x** is greater than 20 (x > 20) and the variable **y** is less than 10 (y < 10). If only one expression is true, then the statement will not be displayed.

The Or Operator

The **Or** operator is also used to combine two relational expressions. In this case, if one or both the expressions are true, only then the overall expression is evaluated to be true. Otherwise, it is evaluated to be false. The syntax of the **Or** operator is as follows:

> If expression_1 Or expression_2 Then
> statement
> End If

In the above syntax, two relational expressions are combined using the **Or** operator. The statement will be executed only if any one or both of the given expressions are true.

For example:

> **If x > 20 Or y < 10 Then**
> **lblDisplay.Text = "Number is correct"**
> **End If**

In the above example, the string **Number is correct** will be displayed only if the value of the variable **x** is greater than 20 or value of **y** is less than 10, or if both the expressions are true.

The Xor Operator

The **Xor** operator is used to combine two relational expressions. In this case, if any one of the two expressions is true, only then the overall expression is evaluated to be true. Otherwise, it is evaluated to be false. The syntax of the **Xor** operator is as follows:

> If expression_1 Xor expression_2 Then
> statement
> End If

In the above syntax, two relational expressions are combined using the **Xor** operator. The statement will be executed only if any one of the given expressions is true.

For example:

> **If x > 20 Xor y < 10 Then**
> **lblDisplay.Text = "Number is correct"**

End If

In the above example, the string **Number is correct** will be displayed only if the value of the variable **x** is greater than 20 or the value of the variable **y** is less than 10.

The Not Operator

The **Not** operator is used to reverse the logical value of an expression. It means if an expression is true, the **Not** operator will return false and vice-versa. The syntax of the **Not** operator is as follows:

```
If  Not expression Then
statement
End If
```

In this syntax, the given expression is first checked. If it is true, the **Not** operator will return false and if it is false, the **Not** operator will return true.

For example:

```
If Not x > 20 Then
lblDisplay.Text = "Number is correct"
End If
```

In the given example, the expression **x > 20** is checked, whether it is true or false. Next, the **Not** operator is applied. If the value of the variable **x** is not greater than 20, then the message **Number is correct** will be displayed in the **Label** control.

The following application illustrates the use of the logical operators: an application that illustrates the function of the logical operators: **And, Or, Xor**, and **Not**.

Application 11

This application will prompt the user to enter two numbers. It will then display the result according to the operators applied by the user on the entered numbers.

The following steps are required to create this application:

Step 1
Start a new project and save it as **c03_VB_NET_2008_11**.

Step 2
Add three **Label** controls, two **TextBox** controls, and six **Button** controls to the form.

Step 3
Change the values of the **Text** property of the controls as follows:

Label1 to **x**
Label2 to **y**

Button1 to **And**
Button2 to **Or**
Button3 to **Xor**
Button4 to **Not**
Button5 to **Clear**
Button6 to **Exit**

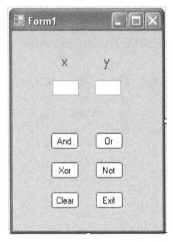

The form will appear as shown in Figure 3-40.

Step 4
Change the values of the **Name** property of the controls as
follows:

Figure 3-40 *Design mode of*
Application 11

Label1 to **lblx**
Label2 to **lbly**
Label3 to **lblDisplay**
TextBox1 to **txtx**
TextBox2 to **txty**
Button1 to **btnAnd**
Button2 to **btnOr**
Button3 to **btnXor**
Button4 to **btnNot**
Button5 to **btnClear**
Button6 to **btnExit**

Step 5
The following is the source code for the **Button** controls:

```
Private Sub btnAnd_Click(ByVal sender As System.Object, _
ByVal e As System.EventArgs) Handles btnAnd.Click          1
Dim x, y As Integer                                        2
x = txtx.Text                                              3
y = txty.Text                                              4
If x > 20 And y < 10 Then                                  5
lblDisplay.Text = "Match Found"                            6
Else                                                       7
lblDisplay.Text = "Try Again"                              8
End If                                                     9
End Sub                                                    10
Private Sub btnOr_Click(ByVal sender As System.Object, _
ByVal e As System.EventArgs) Handles btnOr.Click           11
Dim x, y As Integer                                        12
x = txtx.Text                                              13
y = txty.Text                                              14
If x > 20 Or y < 10 Then                                   15
lblDisplay.Text = "Match Found"                            16
Else                                                       17
```

```
lblDisplay.Text = "Try Again"                                             18
End If                                                                    19
End Sub                                                                   20
Private Sub btnXor_Click(ByVal sender As System.Object, _
ByVal e As System.EventArgs) Handles btnXor.Click                         21
Dim x, y As Integer                                                       22
x = txtx.Text                                                             23
y = txty.Text                                                             24
If x > 20 Xor y < 10 Then                                                 25
lblDisplay.Text = "Match Found"                                           26
Else                                                                      27
lblDisplay.Text = "Try Again"                                             28
End If                                                                    29
End Sub                                                                   30
Private Sub btnNot_Click(ByVal sender As System.Object, _
ByVal e As System.EventArgs) Handles btnNot.Click                         31
Dim x As Integer                                                          32
x = txtx.Text                                                             33
If Not x > 20 Then                                                        34
lblDisplay.Text = "Match Found"                                           35
Else                                                                      36
lblDisplay.Text = "Try Again"                                             37
End If                                                                    38
End Sub                                                                   39
Private Sub btnClear_Click(ByVal sender As System.Object, _
ByVal e As System.EventArgs) Handles btnClear.Click                       40
txtx.Clear()                                                              41
txty.Clear()                                                              42
lblDisplay.Text = ""                                                      43
txtx.Focus()                                                              44
End Sub                                                                   45
Private Sub btnExit_Click(ByVal sender As System.Object, _
ByVal e As System.EventArgs) Handles btnExit.Click                        46
End                                                                       47
End Sub                                                                   48
```

Explanation

The line-by-line explanation of the above given source code is as follows:

Line 5
If x > 20 And y < 10 Then
In this line, the **If-Then** statement is used to check whether **x > 20** and **y < 10**. If both the expressions are evaluated to be true, then the message **Match Found** will be displayed. Otherwise, the message **Try Again** will be displayed, as shown in Figures 3-41 and 3-42, respectively.
Line 15
If x > 20 Or y < 10 Then

Figure 3-41 *Output of Application 11 with valid values for the **And** operator*

Figure 3-42 *Output of Application 11 with invalid values for the **And** operator*

In Line 15, the **If-Then** statement is used to check whether **x > 20** or **y < 10**. Since the **Or** operator is applied to the relational expressions (x > 20 and y < 10), one or both the expressions must be true. If one or both the expressions are true, then the message **Match Found** will be displayed. Otherwise, the message **Try Again** will be displayed, as shown in Figures 3-43 and 3-44, respectively.

Figure 3-43 *Output of Application 11 with valid values for the **Or** operator*

Figure 3-44 *Output of Application 11 with invalid values for the **Or** operator*

Line 25
If x > 20 Xor y < 10 Then
In Line 25, the **If-Then** statement is used to check whether **x > 20** and **y < 10**. If any one of the expressions is evaluated to be true, then the message **Match Found** will be displayed. Otherwise, the message **Try Again** will be displayed, as shown in Figures 3-45 and 3-46, respectively.

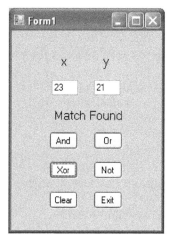

Figure 3-45 *Output of Application 11 with valid values for the **Xor** operator*

Figure 3-46 *Output of Application 11 with invalid values for the **Xor** operator*

Line 34
If Not x > 20 Then
In this line, the expression **x > 20** will be checked first. If it is true, the **Not** operator will return false and if it is false, the **Not** operator will return true. If the variable **x** is assigned a value less than 20 (say 2), then the message **Match Found** will be displayed. Otherwise, the message **Try Again** will be displayed, as shown in Figures 3-47 and 3-48, respectively.

Figure 3-47 *Output of Application 11 with valid values for the **Not** operator*

Figure 3-48 *Output of Application 11 with invalid values for the **Not** operator*

Note
*The **Not** operator is applicable only on one expression at a time, as shown in Figures 3-47 and 3-48.*

Self-Evaluation Test

Answer the following questions and then compare them to those given at the end of this chapter:

1. The _____ loop allows a program to execute a particular statement or a block of statements as long as a specified condition is true.

2. The _____ loop is executed only if the condition is false.

3. The _____ loop is used when the number of iterations in a loop is already known.

4. The **StartValue** is the _____ value assigned to the variable **counter**.

5. The _____ statement indicates the end of the **For** loop.

Review Questions

Answer the following questions:

1. The _____ statement increments the counter variable.

2. A _____ is a loop within the body of another loop.

3. In a nested loop, the outer loop takes control over the _____ loop.

4. The _____ statement is used to perform several operations on the same control.

5. The _____ indicates the end of the **With** block.

Exercises

Exercise 1

Create an application to display odd numbers between 1 to 50 using a loop structure.

Exercise 2

Create an application to check whether a character entered by user is a vowel or not.

Answers to Self-Evaluation Test
1. Do While, 2. Do Until, 3. For Next, 4. initial, **5. Next**

Chapter 4

Arrays and Procedures

Learning Objectives

After completing this chapter, you will be able to understand:

- *Sub procedures.*
- *Functions.*
- *Arrays.*
- *For Each-Next statement.*
- *Parallel arrays.*
- *Multidimensional arrays.*
- *Exception Handling.*

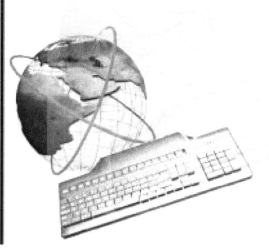

INTRODUCTION

In this chapter, you will learn about arrays, procedures, and functions.

Arrays

An array is a collection of data elements of the same type that are referred together by a common name.

Procedures

A procedure is a group of statements that perform a particular task.

Functions

A function is also a group of statements that perform a particular task. But, it returns a value to the section of the program that executes it.

ARRAYS

An array is a collection of data elements of the same type and these elements are referred by a common name. An individual variable in an array is accessed through a subscript or an index. A subscript is a number which specifies the number of elements within an array. By default, the subscript value starts from 0. The subscript of the first element is 0 and the subscript of the last element is one less than the total number of elements in an array. For example, if an array contains 6 elements, the subscript of the first element will be 0 and the subscript of the last element will be 5. An array has been represented in Figure 4-1.

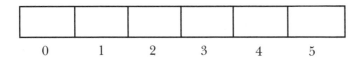

Figure 4-1 *Representation of an array*

Declaring an Array

An array must be declared before it can be used in an application. It must be declared with the keyword **Dim** followed by an array name. Next, the **UpperSubscript** or the maximum size of an array is specified in parentheses. The syntax for declaring an array is as follows:

Dim ArrayName (UpperSubscript) As DataType

In the above syntax, **ArrayName** is the name of the array, **UpperSubscript** is the index of the last element, and the **DataType** specifies the type of data that can be stored in the array.

For example:

Dim pin_code (5) as Integer

In the above example, **pin_code** is declared as an array of the integer type variable and it can store upto six integer values.

Initializing an Array

Initialization means assigning an initial value to an array. Like variables, arrays can also be initialized in the same line where they are declared. The syntax for initializing an array is as follows:

Dim ArrayName (UpperSubscript) As DataType = {value 1, value 2, value 3, ..., value n}

In the above syntax, the values **value 1**, **value 2**, **value 3**, ..., **value n** inside the curly braces are assigned to the elements starting from 0 to n of the given array.

For example:

Dim pin_code () As Integer = {1,5,2,1,0,7}

In this example, the values inside the curly braces are assigned to the array **pin_code** as follows:

pin_code[0] = 1
pin_code[1] = 5
pin_code[2] = 2
pin_code[3] = 1
pin_code[4] = 0
pin_code[5] = 7

Figure 4-2 is the representation of the memory allocation of the array **pin_code**.

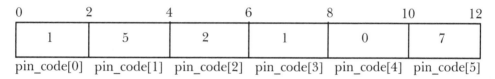

Figure 4-2 *Memory allocation of the array* ***pin_code***

Accessing an Array with a Loop

A number can be stored in a variable and later on, it can be used as a subscript of an array. Moreover, a loop can cycle through the entire array and perform the same operation on each element.

For example:

```
Dim num(7) As Integer
Dim val As Integer
For val = 0 To 6
num(val) = 76
Next val
```

In the above example, the variable **val** is used as a loop counter. When the loop is executed for the first time, the value of the variable **val** is set to 0. So, the statement **num(val) = 76** assigns the value 76 to **num[0]**. When the loop is executed for the second time, the value 76 is assigned to **num[1]** and so on.

Bounds Checking

In VB.NET, the bounds checking is performed on an array during the execution of an application. It means that if a subscript is not within the valid range for subscripts of an array, then VB.NET will not allow the use of this subscript.

For example:

> **Dim num(7) As Integer**

In the above example, due to bounds checking, a subscript which is less than 0 and greater than 7 will not be allowed.

If you write a statement that uses an invalid range of subscript for an array, VB.NET will generate an error message during the execution of the application.

For example:

> **Dim num(7) As Integer**
> **Dim val As Integer**
> **For val = 0 To 8**
> **num(val) = 76**
> **Next val**

In the above example, if you enter a value greater than 7 for **Val**, then an error or an exception: **Index out of range** will be generated. This exception is thrown when an attempt is made to access or insert an element into the array with an index or a subscript greater than the value given in the declaration, or if an index or a subscript is outside the bounds of the array.

FOR EACH-NEXT STATEMENT

This statement is also used to access the values from an array. The syntax for declaring the **For Each-Next** statement is given next.

> For Each ElementVariable In Array
> statement/statements
> Next ElementVariable (optional)

In the above syntax, the **ElementVariable** represents the first element of the given array in the first iteration of the loop during execution. In the second iteration, it represents the second element, and so on. The **Array** represents the array name upon which the loop will iterate. The **statement/statements** are the statements that will be executed during the execution of the loop. The **Next** statement indicates the end of one iteration of the loop and it also increments the value of the **ElementVariable** by one.

The following application illustrates the use of the **For Each-Next** statement:

Application 1

Create an application to display three names in a message box one-by-one, using the **For Each-Next** statement.

This application will display three names: Sam, Tony, and John, one by one, in a message box.

The following steps are required to create this application:

Step 1
Start a new project and save it as **c04_VB_NET_2008_01**.

Step 2
Add a **Button** control to the form.

Step 3
Change the **Text** property of the **Button** control to **Show**.

Step 4
Change the **Name** property of the **Button** control to **btnDisplay**.

Step 5
The source code for the **Show** button is given below. The line numbers given on the right are not a part of the program and are for reference only.

```
Private Sub btnDisplay_Click(ByVal sender As System.Object, _
ByVal e As System.EventArgs) Handles btnDisplay.Click        1
Dim students () As String = {"Sam", "Tony", "John"}          2
Dim identity As String                                       3
For Each identity In students                                4
MessageBox.Show(identity)                                    5
Next identity                                                6
End Sub                                                       7
```

Explanation
The loop will iterate upon the array name **students**. The variable **identity** is the name of the variable that represents an element of the array **students** at the time of execution. The keyword **In** refers to the elements of the array **students**. During execution, in the first iteration of the loop, the variable **identity** represents the first element **Sam**; in the second iteration, it represents the second element **Tony**; and in the third iteration, it represents the third element **John**. The **Next identity** statement indicates the end of one iteration of the loop and also increments the value of the variable **identity** by one.

Step 6
Execute the application; the output form will be displayed, as shown in Figure 4-3. Choose the **Show** button from the output form. A message box with the name **Sam** will be displayed in it, as shown in Figure 4-4. Choose the **OK** button in this message box. Now, the name **Tony** will be displayed, as shown in Figure 4-5. Again, choose the **OK** button; the name **John** will be displayed this time, as shown in Figure 4-6.

Figure 4-3 Output form of Application 1   *Figure 4-4 The first iteration of Application 1*   *Figure 4-5 The second iteration of Application 1*   *Figure 4-6 The third iteration of Application 1*

PARALLEL ARRAYS

Sometimes, you may need to store the related data in more than one array. For example, if you want to store the names and designations of four people, you can use two parallel arrays

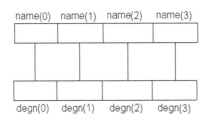

Figure 4-7 Parallel arrays

such as **name** array and **degn** array. Figure 4-7 illustrates the concept of parallel arrays. To access the parallel arrays, you must use the same subscript for both the arrays. For example, to display the names of a group of people and their designations in a list box, you need to use the following source code:

```
For val = 0 To 3
lstDisplay.Items.Add("name" & names(val) & "degn" & degn(val))
Next val
```

In the above source code, the **name** and **degn** are two parallel arrays.

DYNAMICAL ARRAYS

Sometimes you need to store a large volume of data in an array but you may not able to decide the actual size of the array. In VB.NET, you can redimension such an array by declaring it as a dynamic array. This means you can change the number of elements of the upper bound in an array at runtime by using the **ReDim** statement. The syntax for declaring a dynamic array is as follows:

ReDim Preserve ArrayName (UpperSubscript)

In the above syntax, the statement **ReDim** is used to redimension the array. The word **Preserve** following the statement **ReDim** is optional. If you use this word, the existing elements of an array will be preserved, and if it is not used, the existing elements of an array will be destroyed. The word **ArrayName** is the name of the array that is to be resized.

For example:

ReDim Preserve students (11)

In the above example, the dynamic array **students** is resized to the value 11. This means, after execution, the array will have 12 elements because of the **ReDim** statement.

The following application illustrates the use of a dynamic array:

Application 2

Create an application that uses the **ReDim** statement in the source code to redimension an existing array.

This application will use the **ReDim** statement in the source code to redimension the existing array.

The following steps are required to create this application:

Step 1
Start a new project and save it as **c04_VB_NET_2008_02**.

Create the application using the steps given in the previous application.

The following is the source code for the **Show** button:

```
Private Sub btnDisplay_Click(ByVal sender As System.Object, _
ByVal e As System.EventArgs) Handles btnDisplay.Click        1
Dim num As Integer                                           2
Dim arr() As Integer                                         3
num = val(InputBox("Enter a number"))                        4
If num > 5 Then                                              5
ReDim arr(num - 1)                                           6
Else                                                         7
```

MessageBox.Show("Enter a valid number")   8
End If   9
End Sub   10

Explanation

In the above program, Line 4 prompts the user to **Enter a number**. If the user enters a value greater than 5, then the statement **ReDim** in Line 6 will resize the array **arr** to the value **num - 1**.

Execute the application. Next, choose the **Show** button; an input box will be displayed and it will prompt the user to enter a number. If you enter a value greater than 5 (for example, 7), then this will be the **UpperSubscript** of the array **arr** and it will redimension the given array. If you enter a value less than 5 (for example, 3), a message box with the message **Enter a valid number** will be displayed, as shown in Figure 4-8.

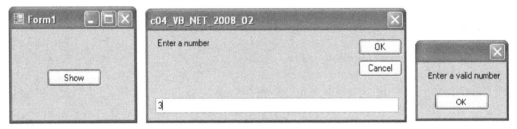

Figure 4-8 Output of Application 2

MULTIDIMENSIONAL ARRAYS

The arrays mentioned in the earlier topics were single-dimensional arrays as they had only one subscript. These arrays can store only a single set of data. Sometimes you need to work with more than one set of data. In such a case, you will not be able to store them in a single-dimensional array. For this purpose, multidimensional arrays have been provided in VB.NET (DOT NET). A multidimensional array has more than one subscript. The .NET framework also supports another type of array, which is known as jagged array.

Two-Dimensional Arrays

A multidimensional array with two upper subscripts is called as a two-dimensional array. A two-dimensional array has two indices. The first index identifies the rows and the second index identifies the columns. The syntax for declaring a two-dimensional array is as follows:

Dim ArrayName(UpperSubscriptRow, UpperSubscriptColumn) As DataType

In the above syntax, **ArrayName** is the name of the array. The **UpperSubscriptRow** specifies the number of rows in an array and the **UpperSubscriptColumn** specifies the number of columns in it. The **DataType** specifies the type of data that can be stored in an array. For example, if you want to declare a two-dimensional array of an integer type that has three rows and three columns, the code will be as follows:

Dim arr (3, 3) As Integer

In the given example, **arr** is the name of the array. The first value (3) in the parentheses specifies the highest subscript of rows and the second value (3) in the parentheses specifies the highest subscript of columns. Figure 4-9 is the diagrammatic representation of this example. The following application illustrates the use of a two-dimensional array:
Create an application to display the elements of a two-dimensional array.

	column 0	column 1	column 2	column 3
row 0	(0, 0)	(0, 1)	(0, 2)	(0, 3)
row 1	(1,0)	(1, 1)	(1, 2)	(1, 3)
row 2	(2, 0)	(2, 1)	(2, 2)	(2, 3)
row 3	(3, 0)	(3, 1)	(3, 2)	(3, 3)

Figure 4-9 A two-dimensional array

Application 3

This application will display the elements of a two-dimensional array.

The following steps are required to create this application:

Step 1
Repeat the steps 1 to 4 of Application 2 to create an application and save it as **c04_VB_NET_2008_03**.

Step 2
The following is the source code for the **Show** button:

```
Private Sub btnShow_Click(ByVal sender As System.Object, _
ByVal e As System.EventArgs) Handles btnOK.Click              1
Dim arr(3, 3) As Single                                       2
Dim rows, columns As Integer                                  3
Dim num As Integer                                            4
For rows = 0 To 3                                             5
For columns = 0 To 3                                          6
num = Val(InputBox("Enter a number"))                         7
arr(rows, columns) = num                                      8
Next columns                                                  9
Next rows                                                     10
For rows = 0 To 3                                             11
For columns = 0 To 3                                          12
lstDisplay.Items.Add(arr(rows, columns))                      13
```

Next columns	14
Next rows	15
End Sub	16

Explanation

Line 2

Dim arr(3, 3) As Single

In the above line, **arr(3, 3)** is declared as a two-dimensional array. This means that there will be four rows and four columns in the given array.

Line 5

For rows = 0 To 3

In this line, the **For** loop is used for the rows only and it is known as the outer loop. The outer loop takes control over the inner loop. In this program, the number of rows is equal to four, therefore, this loop will be executed four times. In each iteration, it will read the values for each row. For example, in the first iteration, it will read for row 0, in the second iteration for row 1, and so on.

Line 6

For columns = 0 To 3

The **For** loop in this line will be executed only if the condition given in Line 5 is true. This loop is used for columns. This loop will also be repeated four times because the number of columns in each row is equal to four. Also, in each iteration, it will load one value in one column.

Line 7

num = Val(InputBox("Enter a number"))

If the condition given in Line 6 is true, then the control will be transferred to Line 7. In this line, the **Val** is a function that is used to convert the string value to a numeric value, and it also returns a numeric value to the calling function. This means that when this line is executed, an input box will be displayed and it will prompt the user to enter a numeric value. This value will be assigned to the variable **num**. Note that in this case, the input box will prompt the user to continue entering values for 16 times because the loop will be repeated 16 times.

Line 13

lstDisplay.Items.Add(arr(rows, columns))

In this line, the values of the variable **num** will be added to the list box vertically in a single row.

Step 3

Execute the application. Next, choose the **Show** button; an input box will be displayed prompting the user 16 times to enter values. Enter the following values in the input box one-by-one:

1	2	3	4	5	6	7	8	9	9	8
7	6	5	4	3						

All these elements will be displayed in the list box. Figure 4-10 shows the memory allocation of the values stored in the array **arr(rows, columns)**.

arr	column 0	column 1	column 2	column 3
row 0	1	2	3	4
row 1	5	6	7	8
row 2	9	9	8	7
row 3	6	5	4	3

*Figure 4-10 Memory allocation of **arr(rows, columns)***

Initializing Two-Dimensional Arrays

You can initialize a two-dimensional array in the same way as a single-dimensional array. The only difference is that while initializing a two-dimensional array, there is no need to provide a subscript. Also, you have to insert a comma between the given values to specify the number of dimensions in a two-dimensional array. For example, if a two-dimensional array has two rows and three columns and you want to initialize it, the syntax for initializing such an array will be as follows:

Dim arr(,) As Integer = {{2, 3, 4}, {7, 4, 1}}

In the above syntax, the values for initializing row 0 are 2, 3, 4 and the initializing values for row 1 are 7, 4, 1.

You can also break the lines of initialization into multiple lines as follows:

Dim arr(,) As Integer = {{2, 3, 4}, _
                                            {7, 4, 1}}

Three-Dimensional Arrays

In VB.NET, you can create arrays upto 32 dimensions. Such arrays are called as three-dimensional arrays. The syntax for declaring a three-dimensional array that consists of 3 sets of 3 rows, and each row containing 3 columns is as follows:

Dim arr(3, 3, 3) As Integer

Figure 4-11 is the diagrammatic representation of the memory allocation of a three-dimensional array **arr(3,3,3)**.

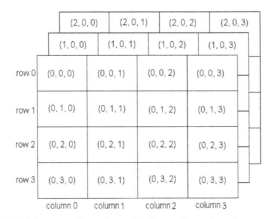

Figure 4-11 *Memory allocation of a three-dimensional array* **arr(3,3,3)**

Jagged Arrays

The array of arrays in which the length of each array differs is called as a jagged array. For example, the following source code will display a jagged array containing the name of months:

```
Dim months(2)() as String                                          1
months(0)=New String(){"January","February","March"}               2
months(1)=New String(){"April","May","June","July"}                3
months(2)=New String(){"August","September",
                "October","November","December"}                    4
```

In the above example, the array **months(2)()** is declared as an array of three arrays in Line 1. In Line 2, the first array is initialized to three members and the values are also assigned to them. Similarly, in Line 3, the second array is initialized to four members and in Line 4, the third array is initialized to five members.

Array Class in VB.NET

The **Array** class is the base class for the implementation of the language that supports arrays. This class provides methods for creating, manipulating, searching, and sorting arrays. There are some functions that can be used to perform some operations on arrays. These functions are as follows:

Sort

The **Sort** is a static method in the class **Array**. The sort method is used to sort the existing array objects. Sorting is usually performed on the primitive data types such as strings and integers. The syntax for using the sort method is as follows:

    Array.Sort(MyArray)

For example:

> **Dim months() As String = {"January", "February", "March", "April", "May",
> "June",   "July"}**
> **Array.Sort(months)**

In the above example, the array **months** is declared as a string type and the values are also assigned to the array objects. **Array.sort (months)** will sort the array objects in an alphabetical order. The output of the example will be as follows:

> April
> February
> January
> July
> June
> March
> May

BinarySearch

This function of the **Array** class is used to search the position of an element in a sorted array. It returns integer type value.

For example:

> **Dim arr() As Integer = {9, 5, 10, 6, 4, 12, 2, 14, 1, 3}**
> **Array.Sort(arr)**
> **MsgBox(Array.BinarySearch(arr, 5))**

In the above example, the array **arr** is declared as an integer type and the values are also assigned to the array objects. The **Sort** method will sort the array and **BinarySearch** method will search the position of the element 5 from the array **arr**. The first element of the sorted array in the above example is shown in Figure 4-12.

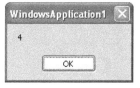

*Figure 4-12 Output of the **BinarySearch** function*

Reverse

The **Reverse** method is used to reverse the sequence of positions of the elements in an array.

For example:

> **Dim arr() As Integer = {9, 5, 10, 6, 4, 12, 2, 14, 1, 3}**
> **Array.Reverse(arr)**

```
For i As Integer = 0 To 9
MsgBox(arr(i))
Next
```

In the above example, the array **arr** is declared as an integer type variable and the values are also assigned to the array objects. The **Reverse** method will reverse the position of the elements of the array **arr**. The output of the example is given below:

3, 1, 14, 2, 12, 4, 6, 10, 5, 9

Clear

The **Clear** method is used to remove certain elements from an array. It will assign a null value to the positions from where it will remove the elements.

For example:

```
Dim arr() As Integer = {9, 5, 10, 6, 4, 12, 2, 14, 1, 3}
Array.Clear(arr, 2, 3)
For i As Integer = 0 To 9
MsgBox(arr(i))
Next
```

In the above example, **Array.Clear** is used to remove three elements from the third position in the array. Therefore, the null value will be assigned to elements **10**, **6**, and **4**. The output of the example is as follows:

9, 5, 0, 0, 0, 12, 2, 14, 1, 3

Copy

The **Copy** method is used to copy an array or a piece of array to another array.

For example:

```
Dim arr() As Integer = {9, 5, 10, 6, 4, 12, 2, 14, 1, 3}
Dim days_s(11) As Integer
Array.Copy(arr, days_s, 5)
For i As Integer = 0 To 11
MsgBox(days_s(i))
Next
```

In the above example, two arrays are declared. The line **Array.Copy(arr, days_s, 5)** will copy the first five elements to the **days_s** array from the **arr** array. And the null value will be assigned to the rest of the elements in the **days_s** array. The output of the above example is as follows:

9, 5, 10, 6, 4, 0, 0, 0, 0, 0, 0

PROCEDURES

In an application, a particular piece of code may be used in multiple parts. In such cases, you have to repeat a particular block of code. However, a particular block of code can create problems in maintaining the code. For example, if you want to make any change in any part of the code at a particular location, then you need to make changes in every section of the application wherever that code has been used. To avoid this repetition of code, the procedures are used. A procedure is a group of statements that perform a particular task. With the help of a procedure, the source code of an application can be divided into small procedures to simplify the program. You can then use those small procedures anywhere in the application. The advantages of using procedures are as follows:

1. With the help of the procedures, you can break the source code of an application into small logical pieces, which can make the application easy and readable.

2. Procedures make debugging of an application easy because it is easier to debug separate units of an application than to debug the whole application.

3. Procedures are reusable throughout the application.

The code that is used to call a procedure is known as a calling code. Whenever a call is made to a procedure, the control is transferred to that procedure and the statements within that procedure are executed. After executing all the statements, the control will be transferred back to the code called as the procedure. There are three types of procedures in VB.NET, which are discussed next.

Sub Procedure

A sub procedure is a block of code that can be used anywhere in an application. This block is enclosed by the **Sub** and **End Sub** statements. Whenever a procedure is called, the statements within the **Sub** and **End Sub** statements are executed. The **Sub** statement indicates the beginning of the sub procedure and the **End Sub** statement indicates the end of the sub procedure. The sub procedure can take arguments such as variables, constants, and expressions, but it cannot return a value.

Declaring a Sub Procedure

A procedure must be declared before being used in the program. A procedure cannot return any value and it cannot be defined within the methods and events. The syntax for declaring a procedure is as follows:

```
AccessSpecifier Sub procedure name(Arguments)
statement/statements
End Sub
```

In the above syntax, the procedure starts with the statement **Sub**, followed by the procedure's name and parentheses. The **AccessSpecifier** and the **Arguments** are optional. The **AccessSpecifier** specifies the visibility of the procedure. The following keywords can be used as access specifiers:

Private

The keyword **Private** is used as an access specifier. It means the procedure can be accessed only by the procedures declared in the same form.

Public

The keyword **Public** is also used as an access specifier. In this case, the sub procedure can be accessed both by the procedures of the same form as well as other forms.

Protected

This access specifier works in a way similar to **Private** except that the derived classes can access the properties and methods of the **Protected** base class.

Consider the following example:

```
Sub Display()
lstShow.Items.Add("Hello")
End Sub
```

In the above example, the statement **Sub** is the beginning of the sub procedure **Display()** and the statement **End Sub** indicates its end. The code **lstShow.Items.Add("Hello")** between the beginning and the end of the sub procedure is its body. Whenever this sub procedure is called, the word **Hello** will be displayed in the list box.

Calling a Sub Procedure

A sub procedure call is made in a program by specifying the name of the procedure followed by a parentheses. The syntax for calling a subprocedure is as follows:

```
procedure name()
```

In the above syntax, the **procedure name** is the name of the procedure that you need to call. During the execution of an application, whenever a sub procedure call is made, the control is transferred to that sub procedure and the statements associated with it are executed.

The following application illustrates the use of a sub procedure:

Application 4

Create an application to display some messages in the **ListBox** control by using a procedure.

This application will display some messages in the **ListBox** control by using a procedure.

The following steps are required to create this application:

Step 1
Start a new project and save it as **c04_VB_NET_2008_04**.

Step 2
Add a **ListBox** control and two **Button** controls to the form.

Step 3
Change the values of the **Text** property of the controls as follows:

Button1 to **OK**
Button2 to **Exit**

The form will appear, as shown in Figure 4-13.

Step 4
Change the values of the **Name** property of the controls as follows:
Button1 to **btnOK**
Button2 to **btnExit**
ListBox1 to **lstDisplay**

Figure 4-13 Design mode of Application 4

Step 5
The source code for the **OK** button is given next.

```
Private Sub btnOK_Click(ByVal sender As System.Object, _
ByVal e As System.EventArgs) Handles btnOK.Click                          1
lstDisplay.Items.Add("John: Where are you going?")                        2
lstDisplay.Items.Add("John: Is it a holiday today?")                      3
DisplayOutput()                                                           4
lstDisplay.Items.Add("John: That is good.")                               5
End Sub                                                                    6
Sub DisplayOutput()                                                       7
lstDisplay.Items.Add("James: I am going to my aunt's place.")             8
End Sub                                                                    9
```

Explanation
Line 2
lstDisplay.Items.Add("John: Where are you going?")
In the above line, the item **John: Where are you going?** will be added to the **ListBox** control.

Line 3
lstDisplay.Items.Add("John: Is it a holiday today?")
In the above line, the item **John: Is it a holiday today?** will be added to the **ListBox** control.

Line 4
DisplayOutput()
In this line, a call is made to the sub procedure **DisplayOutput()** and the control will be transferred to Line 7.

Line 5
lstDisplay.Items.Add("John: That is good.")
Once the sub procedure gets terminated, the control will return to this line and the statement **lstDisplay.Items.Add("John: That is good.")** will be executed. As a result, the item **John: That is good** will be added to the **ListBox** control.

Line 6
End Sub
This line indicates the end of the sub procedure **btnOK_Click**.

Line 7
Sub DisplayOutput()
This line indicates the beginning of the sub procedure **DisplayOutput()**.

Line 8
lstDisplay.Items.Add("James: I am going to my aunt's place")
When the control is transferred to Line 7, the statement, **lstDisplay.Items.Add("James: I am going to my aunt's place")**, associated with it will be executed. As a result, the item **James: I am going to my aunt's place** will be added to the **ListBox** control.

Line 9
End Sub
This line indicates the end of the sub procedure **DisplayOutput()**.

After execution, the form will be displayed, as shown in Figure 4-14.

Figure 4-14 *Output of Application 4*

Passing Arguments to a Procedure

Arguments are the values that are passed to a procedure. An argument or a group of arguments can be passed to a sub procedure through two methods - **ByVal** (passing by value) and **ByRef** (passing by reference). These methods are discussed next.

Passing Arguments By Value

When you pass an argument to a procedure by using the **ByVal** method, a copy of that value will also be passed along with it. In this case, the original argument will not be affected, even if any change is made to the argument within the procedure. This method is used to pass the arguments in all applications illustrated earlier. This is the default method for argument passing in VB.NET. The keyword **ByVal** is used before the argument's name to specify that the arguments are being passed by the value.

For example:

> **Sub ShowValue (ByVal num As Integer)**
> **MessageBox.Show (num)**
> **End Sub**

Here, the variable **num** is preceded by the keyword **ByVal**, which means that the value is passed through the variable **num** by the **ByVal** method.

Passing Arguments By Reference

Passing an argument to a sub procedure using the **ByRef** method means the procedure can access the actual argument and then make changes in it.

For example:
Sub ShowValue (ByRef num As Integer)
MessageBox.Show (num)
End Sub

Here, the variable **num** is preceded by the keyword **ByRef**, which means that the value is passed through the variable **num** by using the **ByRef** method.

The following application illustrates the difference between passing the arguments using the **ByVal** and **ByRef** methods:

Application 5

Create an application to display the values of two variables in a **ListBox** control using the **ByVal** and **ByRef** methods.

This application will display the values of two variables in a **ListBox** control.

The following steps are required to create this application:

Step 1
Start a new project and save it as **c04_VB_NET_2008_05**.

Step 2
Add a **ListBox** control and two **Button** controls to the form.

Step 3
Change the values of the **Text** and **Name** properties of the **ListBox** and **Button** controls as you did in Application 4.

Step 4
Enter the following source code in the code window:

```
Private Sub btnShow_Click(ByVal sender As System.Object, _
ByVal e As System.EventArgs) Handles btnShow.Click        1
Dim num1 As Integer                                       2
num1 = 2                                                  3
ShowVal(num1)                                             4
lstDisplay.Items.Add("The value of num1 is  " & num1)     5
End Sub                                                   6
Sub ShowVal(ByVal num2 As Integer)                        7
num2 = 5                                                  8
lstDisplay.Items.Add("The value of num2 is  " & num2)     9
End Sub                                                   10
```

Line 3
num1 = 2
In this line, the numeric value **2** is assigned to the variable **num 1**.

Line 4
ShowVal(num1)
In this line, a call is made to the sub procedure **ShowVal(num1)** and the variable **num1** is passed as an argument. Whenever this sub procedure is called, the control is transferred to its declaration part and the statements associated with it are executed.

Line 7
Sub ShowVal(ByVal num2 As Integer)
In this line, **num2** is declared as an integer data type variable. The keyword **ByVal** specifies that the value is passed to the variable **num2** by using the **ByVal** method.

Step 5
Execute the application and choose the **Show** button on the form; the following resultant statements will be displayed in the **ListBox** control:

The value of num2 is 5
The value of num1 is 2, as shown in Figure 4-15.

Step 6
Change the keyword **ByVal** to **ByRef** in Line 7. Execute the application again; the following statements will be displayed in the **ListBox** control:

The value of num2 is 5
The value of num1 is 5, as shown in Figure 4-16.

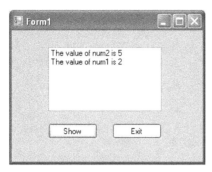

Figure 4-15 Output of Application 5 on using the **ByVal** method

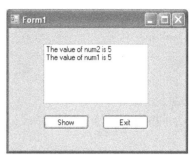

Figure 4-16 Output of Application 5 on using the **ByRef** method

Note that when the argument is passed by using the **ByVal** method, the value of the variable **num1** is not changed. But when the argument is passed by using the **ByRef** method, the value of the variable **num1** is changed to 5.

Passing Multiple Arguments

You can also pass more than one argument to a sub procedure. The following is the example of passing more than one argument to a sub procedure:

> **Private Sub btnShow_Click(ByVal sender As System.Object, _**
> **ByVal e As System.EventArgs) Handles btnShow.Click**

In the above example, the event procedure has two arguments, **sender** and **e**.

The following application illustrates the use of passing multiple arguments to a sub procedure:

Application 6

Create an application to display a message box, which contains the message **The result of multiplication is:-**. It should also display the result of the multiplication.

This application will multiply the numbers 5 and 6, and then display the resultant value 30 in a message box.

The following steps are required to create this application:

Step 1
Start a new project and save it as **c04_VB_NET_2008_06**.

Step 2
Add two **Button** controls to the form.

Step 3
Change the values of the **Text** property of the controls as follows:

Button1 to **Show**
Button2 to **Exit**

Step 4
Change the values of the **Name** property of the controls as follows:

Button1 to **btnshow**
Button2 to **btnExit**

Step 5
Enter the following source code in the code window:

```
Private Sub btnShow_Click(ByVal sender As System.Object,
ByVal e As System.EventArgs) Handles btnShow.Click          1
ShowMul(5, 6)                                               2
End Sub                                                     3
Sub ShowMul(ByVal value1 As Integer, ByVal value2 As Integer) 4
Dim result As Integer                                       5
result = value1 * value2                                    6
MessageBox.Show("The result of multiplication is:- " & result) 7
End Sub                                                     8
```

Explanation

In the given program, when a call is made to the procedure **ShowMul()**, the values 5 and 6 are passed as arguments. These values are then assigned to the variables **value1** and **value2**, respectively. In the body of the procedure **ShowMul()**, the value (5) of the variable **value1** and the value (6) of the variable **value 2** will be multiplied and then the resultant value (30) will be assigned to the variable **result**.

Functions Procedure

Like a sub procedure, a function is also a group of statements that perform a particular task. However, it returns a value to the section of program that executes it. It is a block of code enclosed within the **Function** and **End Function** statements.

Declaring a Function Procedure

The declaration of a function is very much similar to the declaration of a sub procedure. The syntax for declaring a function is as follows:

```
AccessSpecifier Function FunctionName (Arguments) As Data Type
statement/statements
End Function
```

In the above syntax, the working of the **AccessSpecifier** is the same as in the sub procedure. The **AccessSpecifier** is followed by the keyword **Function**, which is in turn followed by the function name and arguments. In this case also, the **AccessSpecifier** and the **Arguments** are optional. The **Data Type** is used as the return type of the function. The last line **End Function**

indicates the end of the function.
For example:

> **Function mul(ByVal num1 As Integer, ByVal num2 As Integer)**
> **Dim result As Integer**
> **result = num1 * num2**
> **Return result**
> **End Function**

In the above example, the keyword **Function** indicates the start of the function declaration, **mul** is the function name, **num1** and **num2** are the arguments passed to it, and the **End Function** indicates the end of the function. When a call is made to the function **mul()**, the statements within **Function** and **End Function** are executed. The **Return result** returns the value of the multiplication to that part of the program, where a call is made to the function **mul()**.

Calling a Function

A function call is made in a program by specifying the function name followed by parentheses and arguments on the right of the assignment statement. The syntax for calling a function is as follows:

> variable = FunctionName (Arguments)

In the above syntax, the **FunctionName** is the name of the function. During the execution of the application, whenever a function call is made, the control is transferred to the function definition, and the statements associated with it are executed.

Application 7

The following application illustrates the concept of function declaration and function call: Create an application to display a message box containing the message **The result of the multiplication is:-** using the concept of the function declaration and the function call. It should also display the result of the multiplication.

This application will multiply the numbers 5 and 6, and then display the resultant value 30 in a message box.

The following steps are required to create this application:

Step 1
Start a new project and save it as **c04_VB_NET_2008_07**.

Step 2
Add two **Button** controls to the form.
Step 3
Change the values of the **Text** property of the controls as follows:

Button1 to **Multiply**

Button2 to **Exit**
Step 4
Change the values of the **Name** property of the controls as follows:

Button1 to **btnMultiply**
Button2 to **btnExit**

Step 5
Enter the following source code in the code window:

```
Private Sub btnMultiply_Click(ByVal sender As System.Object,
ByVal e As System.EventArgs) Handles btnMultiply.Click        1
Dim total As Integer                                          2
total = mul(5, 6)                                             3
MessageBox.Show("The result of the multiplication is:- " & total)   4
End Sub                                                       5
Function mul(ByVal num1 As Integer, ByVal num2 As Integer) As Integer   6
Dim result As Integer                                        7
result = num1 * num2                                         8
Return result                                                9
End Function                                                 10
```

Explanation
Line 2
Dim total As Integer
In the above line, **total** is declared as an integer type variable.

Line 3
total = mul(5, 6)
In the above line, the function **mul()** is called. After executing the statements within the function, the resultant value will be assigned to the variable **total**.

Line 4
MessageBox.Show("The result of the multiplication is:- " & total)
Once the statements of the function are executed, the control will return to Line 4 and the statement **MessageBox.Show("The result of the multiplication is:- " & total)** will be executed. As a result, the message **The result of the multiplication is:-** will be displayed in a message box.

Line 5
End Sub
This line indicates the end of the **btnMultiply_Click** procedure.
Line 6
Function mul(ByVal num1 As Integer, ByVal num2 As Integer) As Integer
The above line is the beginning of the function declaration. In this line, the arguments **num1** and **num2** are passed by the **ByVal** method.

Line 7

Dim result As Integer
In the above line, **result** is declared as an integer data type variable.

Line 8
result = num1 * num2
The arguments **num1** and **num2** have the values 5 and 6, respectively. In this line, these values will be multiplied and the resultant value (30) will be assigned to the variable **result**.

Line 9
Return result
In this line, the resultant value (30) of the multiplication of **num1** (5) and **num2** (6) will be assigned to the variable **total** in Line 3.

Line 10
End Function
This line indicates the end of the function.

Step 6
Execute the application and choose the **Multiply** button on the form; a message box will be displayed with the message **The result of the multiplication is:- 30**.

You can also pass non-numeric arguments such as **Boolean** and **String** to a function, as illustrated in the application given below:

Application 8

Create an application to display a message box containing the message **The name of the student is:- Sam Anthony**, by passing the non-numeric arguments.

This application will display a message box containing the message **The name of the student is:- Sam Anthony**.

The following steps are required to create this application:

Step 1
Start a new project and save it as **c04_VB_NET_2008_08**.

Step 2
Add two **Button** controls to the form.

Step 3
Change the values of the **Text** property of the controls as follows:

Button1 to **Show Name**
Button2 to **Exit**

Step 4

Change the values of the **Name** property of the controls as follows:
Button1 to **btnShow**
Button2 to **btnExit**

Step 5
Enter the following source code in the code window:

```
Private Sub btnShow_Click(ByVal sender As System.Object,
ByVal e As System.EventArgs) Handles btnShow.Click        1
Dim student As String                                     2
student = info("Sam", "Anthony")                          3
MessageBox.Show("The name of the student is:- " & student) 4
End Sub                                                   5
Function info(ByVal first As String, ByVal last As String) As String  6
Dim id As String                                         7
id =  first & " " & last                                  8
Return id                                                9
End Function                                              10
```

Explanation
The working of the above source code is the same as the source code used in the previous application, except that here the value returned by the function **info()** is of the string data type.

Step 6
Execute the application. Choose the **Show Name** button; a message box with the message **The name of the student is:- Sam Anthony** will be displayed.

In the same way, you can also pass the **Boolean** arguments to a function.

Property Procedure
A set of code statements that are used to retrieve or assign the values of the properties declared within a class, a module, or a structure is known as **Property** procedure. Properties are basically the types of variables that store the values for an object in a class. Properties can be accessed as **Public** variables or by **Property** procedures. There are two types of **Property** procedures and they are discussed next.

Get Procedure
These procedures are used to retrieve the values from a property. You can use the **Get** procedure if you need the **Property** procedure to be read-only.

Set Procedure
These procedures are used to assign values to a **Property** procedure. You can use the **Set** procedure, if you need the **Property** procedure to be write-only.

Property procedures can be defined in pairs by using the **Get** and **Set** keywords.

Declaring a Property Procedure

A property is defined by a block of code enclosed within the **Property** statement and the **End Property** statement. Within the **Property** statement and the **End Property** statement, each **Property** procedure is displayed as an internal block enclosed within the **Get** or **Set** statement and the matching **End** statement. The syntax for declaring a property is as follows:

```
AccessSpecifier Property propertyname As Data type
Set (ByVal Value As Data type)
statement1 = newvalue
End Set
Get
Return expression
End Get
End Property
```

In the above syntax, the **Public** keyword can be used as a default **AccessSpecifier**. In the first line, the property is declared. In the second line, the **Set** procedure is used to assign a value to the **Property** procedure and the **End Set** statement indicates the end of the **Set** procedure. The **Get** statement is used to retrieve the value from the property and the **End Get** statement indicates the end of the **Get** statement. In the last line, the **End Property** is the end of the **Property** procedure.

For example:

```
Public Property Name() As String
Set(ByVal value As String)
name = value
End Set
Get
Return name
End Get
End Property
```

In the above example, **Name** is the name of the property and it is declared as the string type. The **Set** procedure is used to the assign the value to the variable that is passed as an argument to its name and the **Get** procedure is used to retrieve the value of the name from the property procedure.

You can invoke the **Property** procedure implicitly using the concept of classes. This topic will be discussed in detail in Chapter 9.

EXCEPTION HANDLING

Exception handling is an in-built mechanism in .NET framework. An exception is basically an error condition that occurs during execution of the application. The exceptions are caused due to user, system, or logic errors. Exception handling is a way to provide an alternate path to the application when it does not execute in the desired way. If the exceptions are not handled, the execution of the application will be terminated abruptly. There are two ways to handle the exceptions caused in VB.NET. These are discussed next.

Structured Exception Handling

Structured exception handling is the standard mechanism of error reporting in VB.NET. In this type of exception handling, the application is divided into blocks. These blocks have the possibility of raising errors, so they are associated with one or more exception handlers. The statements used by the structured exception handling are, **Try**, **Catch**, and **Finally**. The syntax for using the **Try-Catch-Finally** statements is as follows:

```
Try
        statement_1
Catch
        statement_2
Finally
        statement_3
End Try
```

In the above syntax, statement 1 is the code that may cause an error and statement 2 is the code that will execute if the **Try** block throws an error. The **Catch** block will handle the error thrown by the **Try** block. The statement 3 is the code that will perform the final cleaning. Note that the **Finally** block will always execute before the exit of the **Try** block.

For example:

```
Sub job()
Try
Catch e As Exception
MessageBox.Show("An Error Occurred: " & e.ToString())
Finally
End Try
End Sub
```

In the above example, **job** is declared as a sub procedure. The **Try** statement will throw an exception and the **Catch** block will catch the exception and display it in a message box. The **Finally** block will do the final clean up.

Unstructured Exception Handling

In unstructured exception handling, the **On Error GoTo** statement is used within a block of code. The **On Error GoTo** statement is used to enable the exception handling. It also specifies the line number to which the control should pass in case any error occurs in a procedure. If an error occurs in the called procedure that does not have an **On Error GoTo** statement, then the exception will be passed back to the calling procedure. In this case, the error will be handled in the calling procedure. The syntax for using the **On Error GoTo** statement is as follows:

```
On Error {GoTo [Line 0-1] Resume Next}
```

In the above syntax, the **GoTo Line** will enable the exception handling code which starts at the line specified in the given line argument. If an error occurs in the code, the control will pass to this specified line. The **GoTo 0** will disable the enabled exception handling code in the current procedure and reset it to null. The **Resume Next** is used to specify that if an exception occurs, the execution will skip the statement and the control will pass to the next statement.

Self-Evaluation Test

Answer the following questions and then compare them to those given at the end of this chapter:

1. The code of an application can be divided into small procedures with the help of a _____ to simplify the program.

2. An _____ is a collection of data elements of the same type and these elements are referred by a common name.

3. On the termination of a procedure, the _____ variables are destroyed.

4. The _____ indicates the end of the function.

5. _____ is a procedure for assigning initial values to an array.

Review Questions

Answer the following questions:

1. For accessing the parallel arrays, you need to use the same _____ for both the arrays.

2. You can redimension an array at runtime by using the _____ statement.

3. **UpperSubscriptRow** is the value of the last element of the _____.

4. **UpperSubscriptColumn** is the value of the last element of the _____.

5. To initialize a two-dimensional array, you need to insert a comma to specify the number of _____.

Exercise

Exercise 1

Create an application that displays the names of certain cities using the **For Each-Next** statement.

Chapter 5

Common Controls

Learning Objectives

After completing this chapter, you will be able to create:
- *TextBox and MaskedTextBox controls.*
- *Label controls.*
- *LinkLabel controls.*
- *Button and ComboBox controls.*
- *ListBox, CheckedListBox, and PictureBox controls.*
- *NotifyIcon and NumericUpDown controls.*
- *Picker and RadioButton controls.*
- *TreeView and ListView controls.*
- *ProgressBar and Tooltip controls.*

INTRODUCTION

In this chapter, you will learn about various controls such as **TextBox** control, **RichTextBox** control, **ListBox** control, **CheckBox** control, and so on.

TextBox CONTROL

A **TextBox** control is the most commonly used control in the windows user interface. It is a small edit box that can be used to insert, select, and scroll the text if it does not fit into the area of the control. To add a **TextBox** control to the form, double-click on the control in the toolbox. Alternatively, you can drag and drop it directly on the form. When you select the **TextBox** control on the form, a small forward arrow will be displayed on the top-right corner of the control, as shown in Figure 5-1. If you click on the forward arrow, the **Multiline** check box will be displayed, as shown in Figure 5-2. If you select the **Multiline** check box, its **Multiline** property will be set to **True**. Alternatively, this property can be set to **True** in the **Properties** window, where the properties of the **TextBox** control are displayed.

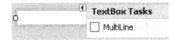

*Figure 5-1 The **TextBox** control*   *Figure 5-2 The **TextBox** control with the **Mutiline** property*

Properties of the TextBox Controls

Some common properties of the **TextBox** control are listed in Table 5-1.

Properties	Functions
BackColor	Sets the background color of the control
BorderStyle	Sets the border style of the control
Cursor	Sets the appearance of the cursor when it is placed over a control
Font	Determines the font and size used to display the text in the control
ForeColor	Sets the foreground color of the display text and graphics in the control
Lines	Sets the lines of text in a multiline edit box
ScrollBars	Indicates the type of scroll bar that should appear in a multiline **TextBox** control
Text	Sets the current text in a **TextBox** control

Properties	Functions
TextAlign	Sets the alignment of the text in a **TextBox** control
MaxLength	Sets the maximum number of characters that can be entered in a **TextBox** control
PasswordChar	Displays the password characters
ReadOnly	Determines whether the text in a **TextBox** control can be changed
WordWrap	Determines whether the lines are automatically wrapped for a multiline **TextBox** control
Name	Sets the name used in the code to identify the control
Anchor	Determines the edge to which a control should be bound
Dock	Determines the borders to be docked to the container

Table 5-1 *Properties of the **TextBox** control*

Adding ScrollBars to the TextBox Controls

There are four ways to add scrollbars to a **TextBox** control, which are given below:

1. None
2. Horizontal
3. Vertical
4. Both

The following steps are required to add scrollbars to a **TextBox** control:

Step 1
Change the value of the **Multiline** property of the **TextBox** control to **True**.

Step 2
Change the default value of the **ScrollBars** property to the desired value.

Aligning the Text in the TextBox Controls

You can align the text in a **TextBox** control with the help of the **TextAlign** property. This property has the following three members:

1. Left
2. Right
3. Center

You can align the text in a **TextBox** control as per your requirement by assigning any one of the given values to the **TextAlign** property of the **TextBox** control.

Read-only Property of the TextBox Controls
Sometimes you do not want the user to change the value of the **Text** property of the **TextBox** control. In such cases, the value **True** should be assigned to the **ReadOnly** property.

Creating a TextBox Control through Source Code
The **TextBox** controls can be created through coding. For example, if you want to create a **TextBox** control of size 100, 30 with the value **TextBox1** assigned to its **Text** property, then enter the following source code for the form load event:

```
Dim TextBox1 As New TextBox                    1
TextBox1.Size = New Size(100, 30)              2
TextBox1.Text = "TextBox1"                     3
Me.Controls.Add(TextBox1)                      4
End Sub                                        5
```

Label CONTROL
A **Label** control is used to display the text on a form. This text cannot be changed by the user at runtime.

Formatting Text in Label Controls
You can format the text in a **Label** control such that the size of the control matches with the size of the text in it. To do so, the value **True** should be assigned to the **AutoSize** property of the **Label** control.

Aligning Text in Label Controls
The **TextAlign** property of the **Label** control has nine members, which are listed below:

1. TopRight
2. TopLeft
3. TopCenter
4. MiddleRight
5. MiddleLeft
6. MiddleCenter
7. BottomRight
8. BottomLeft
9. BottomCenter

You can assign any one of the above mentioned members to the **TextAlign** property of the **Label** control. These values will determine the position of the text in a **Label** control.

LinkLabel CONTROL

These controls are like **Label** controls and they support web-style hyperlinks to other windows forms and internet.

Properties of LinkLabel Controls

Some common properties of the **LinkLabel** control are given in Table 5-2.

Properties	Functions
ActiveLinkColor	Sets the color of the hyperlink when the user clicks on the link
DisabledLinkColor	Sets the color of the disabled link
LinkColor	Determines the color of the default state of the hyperlink
LinkArea	Sets a portion of the text as a hyperlink

*Table 5-2 Properties of the **LinkLabel** control*

Creating a LinkLabel Control

The following steps are required to create a **LinkLabel** control:

Step 1
Double-click on the **LinkLabel** control in the toolbox; it will be added to the form.

Step 2
Enter the following text in the **Text** property of the **LinkLabel** control:

Click here to see the profile.

Step 3
Select the **LinkArea** property of the **LinkLabel** control. Next, choose the button on the right of the **LinkArea** property; the **LinkArea Editor** dialog box will be displayed, as shown in Figure 5-3. Click on the word **here** which is set as a hyperlink and choose the **OK** button in the **LinkArea Editor** dialog box.

*Figure 5-3 The **LinkArea Editor** dialog box*

Step 4
Select the **ActiveLinkColor**, **LinkColor**, and **VisitedLinkColor** properties one-by-one from the **Properties** window. Set their values according to your requirement.

Step 5
Double-click on the **LinkLabel** control; the code window will be displayed. Enter the following source code for the hyperlink:

```
Private Sub LinkLabel1_LinkClicked(ByVal sender As System.Object, _
ByVal e As System.Windows.Forms.LinkLabelLinkClickedEventArgs) Handles
LinkLabel1.LinkVisited = True                                            1
System.Diagnostics.Process.Start("www.cadcim.com")                      2
End Sub                                                                  3
```

Explanation
In the above program, whenever a user chooses the hyperlink portion of the text in the **LinkLabel** control, the **System.Diagnostics.Process.Start** method will to start the navigation.

Step 6
Execute the application; the **controls_demo** form will be displayed, as shown in Figure 5-4.
Step 7

*Figure 5-4 The **controls_demo** form*

Click on the word **here**, which is set as a hyperlink. It will start navigating the site *www.cadcim. com*.

Creating a LinkLabel Control through Source Code
The **LinkLabel** control can also be created through source code. For example, you may need to create a **LinkLabel** control having the value **Click here to see the profile** in its **Text** property.

Also, you need to set the word **here** as a hyperlink and navigate to the site *www.cadcim.com*. To do so, follow the procedure given next.

Enter the following source code for the **Load** event of the form:

```
Dim LinkLabel1 As New LinkLabel                                              1
LinkLabel1.Text = "Click here to see the profile"                            2
LinkLabel1.AutoSize = True                                                   3
LinkLabel1.Links.Add(6, 4)                                                   4
LinkLabel1.LinkVisited = True                                                5
LinkLabel1.Left = 70                                                         6
LinkLabel1.Top = 100                                                         7
AddHandler LinkLabel1.LinkClicked, AddressOf Me.LinkLabel1_Click             8
Me.Controls.Add(LinkLabel1)                                                  9
```

Enter the following source code for the **Click** event of the **LinkLabel** control:

```
System.Diagnostics.Process.Start("www.cadcim.com")                          10
```

Explanation
The line-by-line explanation of the above given source code is as follows:

Line 4
LinkLabel1.Links.Add(6, 4)
In this lines, **Links** is a collection of multiple links where the hyperlink for the **LinkLabel** control is stored. The **Add** method is used to add the new hyperlink.

Line 8
AddHandler LinkLabel1.LinkClicked, AddressOf Me.LinkLabel1_Click
In this line, an event handler **LinkLabel1.LinkClick** is connected to the **Click** event of the **LinkLabel** control using the **AddHandler** method and the **AddressOf** operator.

Line 9
Me.Controls.Add(LinkLabel1)
This line is used to add a **LinkLabel** control to the form.

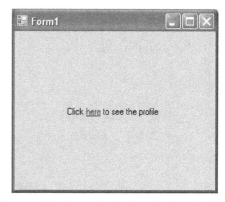

The output of the above source code is shown in Figure 5-5. When you click on the **here** link on the form, the www.cadcim.com website will be displayed, as shown in Figure 5-6.

Figure 5-5 Form displaying the **LinkLabel** control

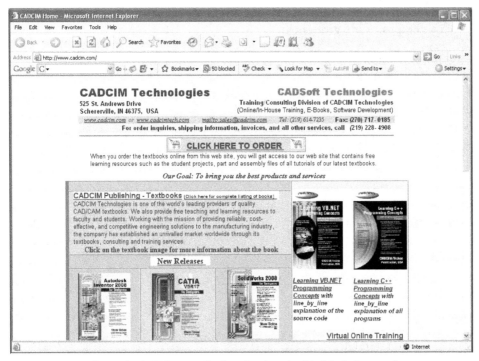

*Figure 5-6 Web page displayed using the **LinkLabel** control*

ListBox CONTROL

A **ListBox** control is used to allow the user to select a single or a set of multiple items from a list of options at runtime.

Creating a ListBox Control

To add a **ListBox** control to a form, double-click on it in the toolbox. Alternatively, drag the **ListBox** control from the toolbox and drop it on the required location of the form. If you select the **ListBox** control on the form, a small forward arrow will be displayed on top right corner of the control, as shown in Figure 5-7. When you click on the forward arrow, two properties, **Use data bound items** and **Edit Items** will be displayed, as shown in Figure 5-8.

*Figure 5-7 The **ListBox** control*   *Figure 5-8 The **ListBox** control with its properties*

If you select the **Use data bound items** check box, the data binding properties will be displayed, as shown in Figure 5-9. These properties will be discussed in detail in the later chapters.

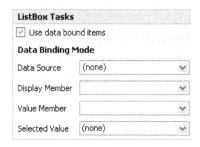

*Figure 5-9 The **Use data bound items** property*

You can use the **Edit Items** link to add the entries in the **ListBox** control. To add the entries, click on the **Edit Items** link; the **String Collection Editor** dialog box will be displayed, as shown in Figure 5-10.

*Figure 5-10 The **String Collection Editor** dialog box*

Properties of the ListBox Controls

Some common properties of a **ListBox** control are listed in Table 5-3.

Properties	Functions
ColumnWidth	Sets the width of each column in a multicolumn **ListBox** control
DrawMode	Sets the drawing mode of a **ListBox** control
HorizontalExtent	Sets the width of the **ListBox** control so that it can scroll horizontally. It can be set only if the **HorizontalScrollbar** property is set to **True**

Properties	Functions
HorizontalScrollbar	Determines whether a horizontal scroll bar will be displayed in a **ListBox** control
MultiColumn	Determines whether more than one column can be selected at a time in a **ListBox** control
ScrollAlwaysVisible	Determines whether the scroll bars are always visible in a **ListBox** control or not
SelectionMode	Sets the mode of selection for the items in a **ListBox** control. It can be multi-selection, single-selection, or none
Sorted	Determines that the items in a **ListBox** control are sorted alphabetically
Items	Stores the list of items in a **ListBox** control

Table 5-3   *Properties of the **ListBox** control*

Creating Multicolumn ListBox Controls

You can create a **ListBox** control with multicolumn using source code. The following source code is required to create a multicolumn **ListBox** control:

```
Private Sub Form1_Load(ByVal sender As System.Object, _
ByVal e As System.EventArgs) Handles MyBase.Load          1
Dim ListBox1 As ListBox                                    2
ListBox1 = New ListBox                                     3
ListBox1.Size = New System.Drawing.Size(600, 95)           4
ListBox1.Location = New System.Drawing.Point(104, 24)      5
Me.Controls.Add(ListBox1)                                  6
ListBox1.MultiColumn = True                                7
Dim list As Integer                                        8
For list= 1 To 40                                          9
ListBox1.Items.Add("Items" & list)                        10
Next list                                                 11
End Sub                                                   12
```

Explanation

The line-by-line explanation of the above mentioned source code is as follows:

Lines 5 and 6
ListBox1.Size = New System.Drawing.Size(600, 95)
ListBox1.Location = New System.Drawing.Point(104, 24)
In these lines, the values 600, 95 are assigned to the **Size** property and the values 104, 24 are assigned to the **Location** property of the **ListBox1** with the help of the namespace **Drawing**.

The output of the above source code is shown in Figure 5-11.

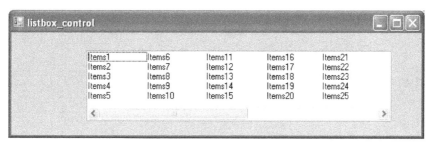

*Figure 5-11 The **listbox_control** form with the output*

 Note
*To view all the items given in Figure 5-11, you need to expand the **listbox_control** form.*

CheckedListBox CONTROL

A **CheckedListBox** control is similar to a **ListBox** control except that it contains a check box for each item. You can create a **CheckedListBox** control in the same way as you did in the **ListBox** control. To add a **CheckedListBox** control to a form, double-click on it or simply drag it from the toolbox and drop it on the form. When the **CheckedListBox** control is selected, a small forward arrow will be displayed on the control, as shown in Figure 5-12. When you click on the arrow, the **Edit Items** property will be displayed, as shown in Figure 5-13.

*Figure 5-12 The **CheckedListBox** control*   *Figure 5-13 The **CheckedListBox** control with the **Edit Items** property*

When you click on the **Edit Items** property, the **String Collection Editor** dialog box will be displayed, as shown in Figure 5-14. You will add the items that can be displayed in the **CheckedListBox** control using the **String Collection Editor** dialog box.

*Figure 5-14 The **String Collection Editor** dialog box*

Adding Items to CheckedListBox Controls

The steps required to add items to a **CheckedListBox** control are given below:

Step 1
Select the **Items** property of the **CheckedListBox** control from the **Properties** window; an ellipses button will be displayed on its right. Choose the button; the **String Collection Editor** dialog box will be displayed.

Step 2
Add the items to the **String Collection Editor** dialog box and choose the **OK** button; the items will be added to the **CheckedListBox** control.

During execution, the items in the **CheckedListBox** control appear as they did in the **ListBox** control, except that in this case, they have a check box in front of them. You can select the check boxes by double-clicking on them. But if the value **True** is assigned to the **CheckOnClick** property of the **CheckedListBox** control, then you can select the check boxes with a single-click.

Creating Multicolumn CheckedListBox Control through Source Code

You can create the **CheckedListBox** control with multicolumn using source code. The following source code is required to create a multicolumn **CheckedListBox** control:

```
Dim CheckedListBox1 As CheckedListBox
CheckedListBox1 = New CheckedListBox
CheckedListBox1.Size = New System.Drawing.Size(100, 95)
CheckedListBox1.Location= New System.Drawing.Point(60, 24)
Me.Controls.Add(CheckedListBox1)
Dim list As Integer
For list = 1 To 40
CheckedListBox1.Items.Add("Items" & list, True)
Next list
```

The output of the above source code is the same as that of the previous source code.

After execution, the **CheckedListBox** control will be displayed, as shown in Figure 5-15.

PictureBox CONTROL

A **PictureBox** control helps you to display the image files such as JPEG, GIF, ico, and so on. To add a **PictureBox** control to a form, double-click on the control or drag and drop it from the toolbox. When you select the **PictureBox** control, a small forward arrow will be displayed on the top right corner of the control. When you click on the arrow, three important properties will be displayed, **Choose Image**, **Size Mode**, and **Dock in parent container**, as shown in Figure 5-16.

Figure 5-15 The listbox_ control form with the new output

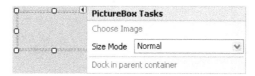

Figure 5-16 The PictureBox control with three properties

These properties are discussed next.

Choose Image

When you choose the **Choose Image** link; the **Select Resource** dialog box will be displayed, as shown in Figure 5-17. Alternatively, you can select the **Image** property from the **Properties** window. In the **Resource context** area of the **Select Resource** dialog box, there are two radio buttons, **Local resource** and **Project resource file**. The **Project resource file** radio button is selected by default. If you select the **Local resource** radio button, the **Import** button associated with the **Local resource** radio button will get enabled. Choose the **Import** button if you want to import an image from any location to your form. To remove the image, choose the **Clear** button. Note that this option is used to add an image only to the form and not to the project.

If you select the **Project resource file** radio button in this dialog box, the **Import** button associated with the **Project resource file** radio button will get enabled. Choose the **Import** button to add an image to the form and also to your project. You can view the entry of the project in the **Resources** folder of the **Solution Explorer** window.

Size Mode

The image can be positioned in a **PictureBox** control with the help of the **Size Mode** property. It has following four members:

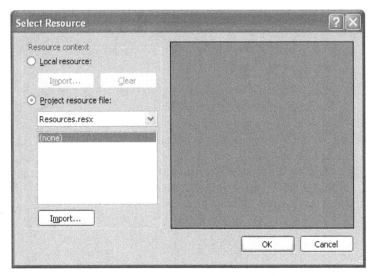

Figure 5-17 *The **Select Resource** dialog box*

Normal
It is the default value of the **Size Mode** property.

StretchImage
This value fits the image to the size of the **Picture Box** control. It means the whole image will be displayed in the **Picture Box** control.

AutoSize
This value displays an image in its original size.

CenterImage
This value of the **Size Mode** property displays the image at the center of the **Picture Box** control. Note that if the size of the **Picture Box** control is small in comparison to the image, then only the center part of the image will be displayed, as shown in Figure 5-18.

Zoom
This value adjusts the size of the image as per the size of the **Picture Box** control.

Adding an Image to the PictureBox Control through Source Code

You can add an image to a **PictureBox** control with the help of the source code. You can also set the **Size Mode** property of the **PictureBox** control through the source code. The following source code is required to add an image and set the **Size Mode** property of the **PictureBox** control:

*Figure 5-18 Image displayed using the **Size Mode** property of the **PictureBox** control*

Private Sub Form1_Load(ByVal sender As System.Object, _
ByVal e As System.EventArgs) Handles MyBase.Load   1
PictureBox1.Image = Image.FromFile("C:\Documents and Settings _
\Cadcim\My Documents\My Pictures\cadcimlogo.jpg")   2
PictureBox1.SizeMode = PictureBoxSizeMode.CenterImage   3
End Sub   4

Explanation
The line-by-line explanation of the above given source code is as follows:

Line 2
**PictureBox1.Image = Image.FromFile("C:\Documents and Settings\Cadcim
\My Documents\My Pictures\cadcimlogo.jpg")**
In this line, the path of the *.jpg* file **cadcimlogo** is assigned to the **Image** property of the
PictureBox1.
Line 3
PictureBox1.SizeMode = PictureBoxSizeMode.CenterImage
In this line, the value **CenterImage** is assigned to the **SizeMode** property of the **PictureBox1**.

PICKERS

VB.NET provides two types of pickers to display a calendar, **DateTimePicker** and **MonthCalendar**.

DateTimePicker Control

This control is used to set the date and time. It has a drop-down list, which displays the date and time. On choosing the down arrow button of this drop-down list, a calendar control will be displayed, as shown in Figure 5-19.

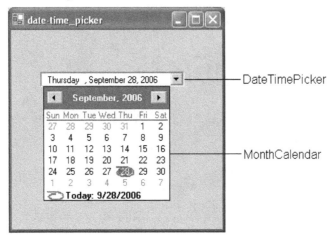

Figure 5-19   The *DateTimePicker* control

The date, month, and year selected by you will become the current value of the drop-down list.

Properties of the DateTimePicker Control

Some important properties of the **DateTimePicker** control are listed as below:

Properties	Functions
CalendarFont	Determines the font used for the calendar
CalendarForeColor	Determines the color of the font used within a month
CalendarMonth Background	Determines the background color within a month

Properties	Functions
CalendarTitle BackColor	Determines the background color of the calendar title
CalendarTitle ForeColor	Determines the foreground color of the calendar title
CalendarTrailing ForeColor	Determines the color of the header and trailing dates
Cursor	Determines the appearance of the cursor when it moves over the control
DropDownAlign	Determines the alignment of the drop-down calendar to the **DateTimePicker** control
Format	Determines the format of the date and time
ShowCheckBox	Determines whether the check box should appear in front of the selected date and time
ShowUpDown	Determines whether the arrows should be used to adjust the date-time values
MaxDate	Determines the maximum selectable date and time
MinDate	Determines the minimum selectable date and time
Value	Determines the current date-time value of the **DateTimePicker** control

Table 5-4 *Properties of the **DateTimePicker** control*

MonthCalendar Control

This control is used to select a date in a month, refer to Figure 5-19.

Properties of the MonthCalendar Control

Some important properties of the **MonthCalendar** control are listed in Table 5-5.

Properties	Functions
CalendarDimensions	Determines the number of rows and columns in months
FirstDayOfWeek	Sets the first day of the week
MaxSelectionCount	Determines the maximum number of days that can be selected for a month
ScrollChange	Determines the scroll rate
SelectionRange	Determines the selected range of dates of a month calendar control
ShowToday	Determines whether today's date should be displayed at the bottom of the **MonthCalendar** control
ShowTodayCircle	Determines whether today's date should be encircled
ShowWeekNumbers	Determines whether the week numbers should be displayed in front of rows of each day
AnnuallyBoldedDates	Determines the day to be made bold
BoldedDates	Determines the date to be made bold
MonthlyBoldedDates	Determines the monthly date to be made bold

*Table 5-5 Properties of the **MonthCalendar** control*

TreeView CONTROL

This control is used to create a tree view for displaying child nodes. Figure 5-20 shows a **TreeView** control.

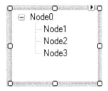

*Figure 5-20 The **TreeView** control*

Properties of TreeView Control

Some important properties of a **TreeView** control are listed Table 5-6.

Properties	Functions
HotTracking	Determines the appearance of the node when the cursor is placed over it
Indent	Sets the distance between the nodes
ItemHeight	Sets the height of the tree node
LabelEdit	Determines whether the user can edit the nodes
Nodes	Used to get the collection of the tree nodes
Scrollable	Determines whether the scroll bars should be displayed, if the **TreeView** control contains more nodes to fit in the visible area of the control
ShowLines	Determines whether the lines should be displayed between the nodes
ShowPlusMinus	Determines whether the plus and minus signs should be displayed in front of the tree nodes
ShowRootLines	Determines whether the root lines should be displayed between the child nodes

*Table 5-6 Properties of the **TreeView** control*

Adding a TreeView Control to a Form

You can add a **TreeView** control to a form in the same way as you added the other controls. Double-click on the **TreeView** control; it will be added to the form. To add nodes, select the **Node** property of the control. Next, choose the button on the right of the **Node** property; the **TreeNode Editor** dialog box will be displayed, as shown in Figure 5-21. Choose the **Add Root** button to add the root node and choose the **Add Child** button to add the child nodes. You can remove the nodes using the **Label** edit box of the **TreeNodeEditor** dialog box.

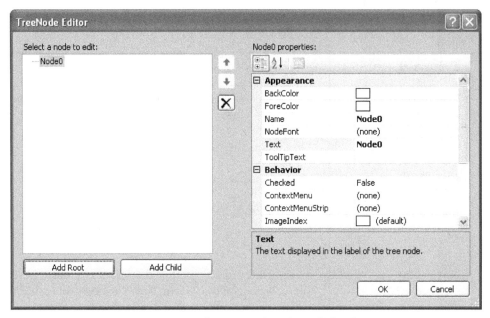

Figure 5-21 The TreeNode Editor dialog box

ListView CONTROL
This control is used to display a list of items on the form.

Adding a ListView Control to a Form
The following steps are required to add the **ListView** control to a form:

Step 1
Double-click on the **ListView** control on the toolbox; it will be added to the form. Adjust it according to your requirement.

Step 2
Change the value of its **View** property to **Details** in the **Properties** window.

Step 3
Select the **Columns** property from the **Properties** window and choose the button on its right; the **ColumnHeader Collection Editor** dialog box will be displayed, as shown in Figure 5-22.

Step 4
To add the columns, choose the **Add** button. If you want to edit the **Text** property of these buttons, you can do so by entering the value in the **Text** property of the **ColumnHeader Collection Editor** dialog box and then choosing the **OK** button.

Step 5
To add the items to these columns, select the **Items** property of the **ListView** control.

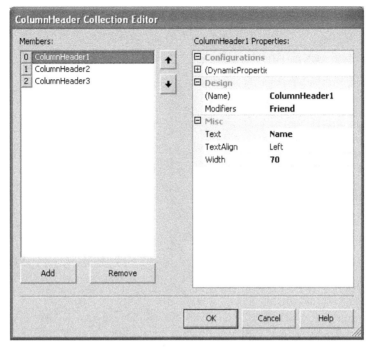

*Figure 5-22 The **ColumnHeader Collection Editor** dialog box*

Step 6
Choose the button on its right side; the **ListViewItem Collection Editor** dialog box will be displayed, as shown in Figure 5-23.

Step 7
Choose the **Add** button. Enter the value **John** in its **Text** property and then choose the **OK** button; the value **John** will be added to the **ListView** control.

Step 8
To add the sub items, select the **SubItems** property of the **ListViewItem** in the **ListViewItem Collection Editor** dialog box. Choose the button on its right; the **ListViewSubItem Collection Editor** dialog box will be displayed, as shown in Figure 5-24.

Step 9
Choose the **Add** button to add subitems to the **Name** field. Enter the value **Doctor** (for Designation) in the **Text** property. Again, choose the **Add** button and enter the value **876567** (for Contact Number) in the **Text** property; a list will be created, refer to Figure 5-24.

Step 10
To add more items and subitems, repeat the steps from 5 to 9.

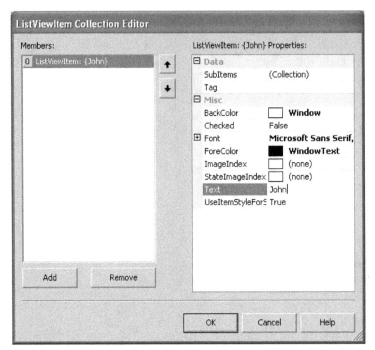

Figure 5-23　The **ListViewItem Collection Editor** *dialog box*

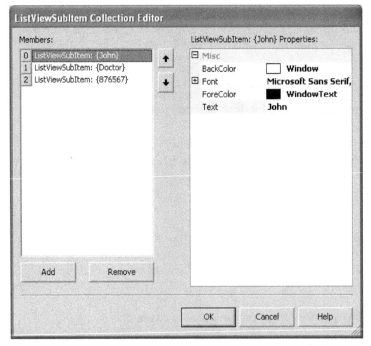

Figure 5-24　The **ListViewSubItem Collection Editor** *dialog box*

RichTextBox CONTROL

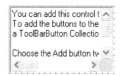

A **RichTextBox** control is similar to a **TextBox** control, except that the scroll bars can be added to it. It can also display fonts, colors, and links. Figure 5-25 shows the **RichTextBox** control.

Figure 5-25 *The* *RichTextBox* *control*

Adding a RichTextBox Control to a Form

The following steps are required to add a **RichTextBox** control to a form:

Step 1
Double-click on the **RichTextBox** control in the toolbox; it will be added to the form. Alternatively, you can drag it from the toolbox and then drop it on the form.

Step 2
To add multiple lines of text to the **RichTextBox** control, select the **Lines** property from the **Properties** window. Choose the button on the right of the **Lines** property; the **String Collection Editor** dialog box will be displayed, as shown in Figure 5-26. Enter some lines of text in the **String Collection Editor** dialog box and choose the **OK** button; the lines of the text will be added to the **RichTextBox** control. Make sure the value of the **Multiline** property of the **RichTextBox** control is **True**.

Figure 5-26 *The* *String Collection Editor* *dialog box*

Adding Scroll Bars to the RichTextBox Control

If the lines of the text exceed the visible area of the **RichTextBox** control, a vertical scroll bar will be added automatically to it. If you want to add a horizontal scroll bar, then change the value of the **WordWrap** property of the **RichTextBox** control to **False**. To add both scroll bars simultaneously, change the value of the **ScrollBars** property to **Both**.

Creating RichTextBox Control through Source Code

You can create a **RichTextBox** control with the help of source code. Add a **Button** control to the form and double-click on it; the code window will be displayed. Enter the following source code for the **Load** event of the form:

```
Private Sub Form1_Load(ByVal sender As System.Object,
ByVal e As System.EventArgs) Handles MyBase.Load                           1
Dim RichTextBox1 As New RichTextBox                                        2
RichTextBox1.Size = New Size(144, 88)                                      3
RichTextBox1.Text = "If the lines of the text exceed the visible area of
the TextBox control, a vertical scroll bar will be added automatically to it"   4
RichTextBox1.Location = New Point(28, 32)                                  5
Me.Controls.Add(RichTextBox1)                                             6
End Sub                                                                     7
```

Execute the application; the output of the form will be the same as shown in Figure 5-25.

Button CONTROL

A **Button** control is a small rectangular shaped box that is used to handle events in coding. The default text of the **Button** control is **Button1** and the default event is the **Click** event. It means if you click on the **Button** control, some action will be performed.

To add a **Button** control to a form, double-click on it from the toolbox. Alternatively, you can drag the **Button** control and drop it on the form.

Properties of Button Controls

Some of the important properties of the **Button** control are as follows:

Properties	Functions
BackColor	Sets the background color of the control
Forecolor	Sets the color of the display text in the control
Font	Determines the font used to display the text in the control
FlatStyle	Determines the appearance of the control
Text	Sets the current text in the control
TextAlign	Sets the alignment of the text in the control
Dock	Determines the location of border to be docked to the form

*Table 5-7 Properties of the **Button** control*

Creating a Button Control through Source Code

The **Button** control can be created through coding. For example, if you want to create a **Button** control of size 100, 30 with the value **Button1** assigned to its **Text** property, then enter the following source code in the code window:

```
Private Sub Form2_Load(ByVal sender As System.Object, _
ByVal e As System.EventArgs) Handles MyBase.Load                1
Dim Button1 As New Button                                       2
Button1.Size = New Size(100, 30)                                3
Button1.Text = "Button1"                                        4
Me.Controls.Add(Button1)                                        5
End Sub                                                          6
```

Explanation

The line-by-line explanation of the above source code is as follows:

Line 2
Dim Button1 As New Button
In the above line, the variable **Button1** is declared as a new instance of the **Button** class.

Line 3
Button1.Size = New Size(100, 30)
In the above line, values 100 and 30 are passed as an argument to the **Size** property of the **Button** control. It means the values for the length and width of the **Button** control are 100 and 30, respectively.

Line 4
Button1.Text = "Button1"
In the above line, the value **Button1** is assigned to the **Text** property of the **Button** control.

Line 5
Me.Controls.Add(Button1)
In the above line, the value **Button1** is passed as an argument to the **Controls.Add** property of the form. Here, **Me** defines the current form. So, it means that a new **Button** control named as **Button1** will be added to the current form.

The **Button** control created through this method is shown in Figure 5-27.

*Figure 5-27 The **Button** control created through source code*

CheckBox CONTROL

The **CheckBox** control looks similar to a **Label** control with a small square box associated with it. This control is used to select or clear the options from a list of given options. When an option is selected, a tick mark appears in the corresponding small square box, as shown in Figure 5-28.

To add this control to a form, double-click on it in the toolbox. Alternatively, you can drag it from the toolbox and drop it on the form.

Figure 5-28 The CheckBox control

Properties of the CheckBox Controls

Some of the important properties of the **CheckBox** control are listed in Table 5-8.

Properties	Functions
Appearance	Determines the appearance of the control
CheckAlign	Determines the position of the box inside the control
CheckState	Determines the display of check mark in the box
FlatStyle	Determines the style of appearance of the control

Table 5-8 Properties of the CheckBox control

Creating a CheckBox Control through Source Code

The **CheckBox** control can be created using the following source code is as follows:

```
Dim CheckBox1 As New CheckBox                                    1
CheckBox1.Size = New Size(100, 30)                              2
CheckBox1.Text = "CheckBox1"                                    3
CheckBox1.CheckAlign = ContentAlignment.MiddleLeft             4
CheckBox1.FlatStyle = FlatStyle.Standard                       5
CheckBox1.Appearance = Appearance.Normal                       6
CheckBox1.CheckState = CheckState.Unchecked                    7
Me.Controls.Add(CheckBox1)                                     8
```

Explanation

The line-by-line explanation of the above source code is as follows:

Line 1
Dim CheckBox1 As New CheckBox
In the above line, the variable **CheckBox1** is declared as **CheckBox**.

Line 2
CheckBox1.Size = New Size(100, 30)
In this line, values 100 and 30 are assigned to the **Size** property of the **CheckBox** control.

Line 3
CheckBox1.Text = "CheckBox1"
In the above line, the value **CheckBox1** is assigned to the **Text** property of the **CheckBox** control.

Line 4
CheckBox1.CheckAlign = ContentAlignment.MiddleLeft
In the above line, the value **ContentAlignment.MiddleLeft** is assigned to the **CheckAlign** property of the **CheckBox** control, which means the box will appear in the middle-left of the control.

Line 5
CheckBox1.FlatStyle = FlatStyle.Standard
In the above line, the value **Standard** is assigned to the **FlatStyle** property of the **CheckBox** control.

Line 6
CheckBox1.Appearance = Appearance.Normal
In the above line, the value **Normal** is assigned to the **Appearance** property of the **CheckBox** control.

Line 7
CheckBox1.CheckState = CheckState.Unchecked
In the above line, the value **Unchecked** is assigned to the **CheckState** property of the **CheckBox** control. It means the **CheckBox** control will appear unchecked.

Line 8
Me.Controls.Add(CheckBox1)
In the above line, the value **CheckBox1** is passed as an argument to the **Controls.Add** property of the form. Here, **Me** defines the current form. It indicates that a new **CheckBox** control named as **CheckBox1** will be added to the current form.

ComboBox CONTROL

A **ComboBox** control comprises a **TextBox** control associated with a drop-down **ListBox** control. From the drop-down **ListBox** control, you can select any option, and it will be displayed in the edit box. There is a small forward arrow located at the upper right corner of the **ComboBox** control, as shown in Figure 5-29.

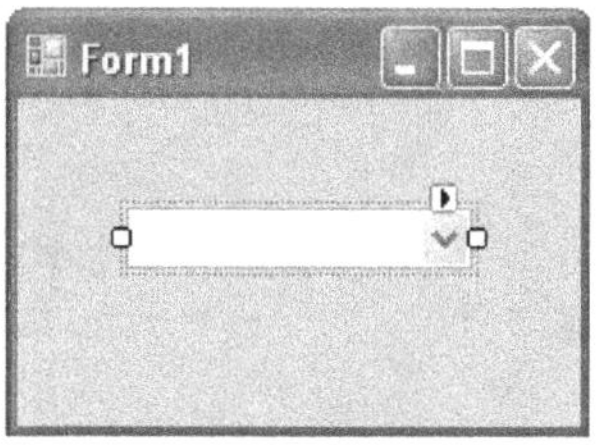

Figure 5-29 The *ComboBox* control

When you click on the arrow, two properties will be displayed, **Use data bound items** and **Edit Items**. When you choose the **Edit Items** property; the **String Collection Editor** dialog box will be displayed. In the **Enter the strings in collection (one per line)** area, you can add the required values for the **ComboBox** control. The **Use data bound items** property will be discussed in later the chapters.

Creating a ComboBox Control through Source Code

You can create a **ComboBox** control through coding. Enter the following source code for the **Load** event of the form:

Dim ComboBox1 As New ComboBox
ComboBox1.Size = New Size(100, 30)
ComboBox1.Text = ""
Me.Controls.Add(ComboBox1)

The explanation of this coding is same as that of the previous source code.

MaskedTextBox CONTROL

This control is just like a simple **TextBox** control with a specific property. With the help of this property, you can set any format such as **Numeric**, **Phone Number**, **Zip Code**, and so on. You can also add this control to your form as you added the other controls. When you click on the small forward arrow on the upper right corner of the **Masked TextBox** control, the **Set Mask** property will be displayed. If you choose this property; the **Input Mask** dialog box will be displayed, as shown in Figure 5-30.

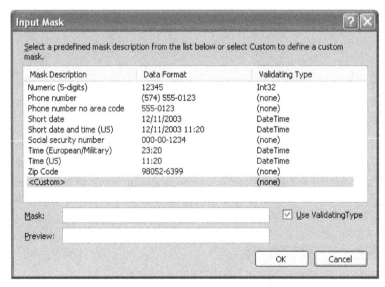

*Figure 5-30 The **Input Mask** dialog box*

You can set any format for the **Masked TextBox** control using this dialog box according to your requirement. For example, if you want to display phone number in your **MaskedTextBox** control, select the **Phone number** option from the dialog box; it will get added to the **Mask** edit box. Also, you can preview its format in the **Preview** edit box, as shown in Figure 5-31. Similarly, you can set other formats also.

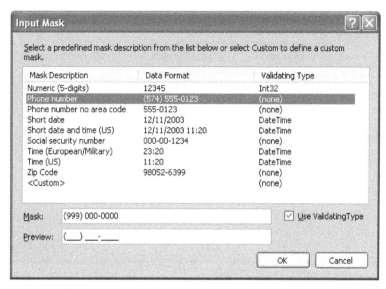

Figure 5-31 *The **Input Mask** dialog box with the **Phone number** option selected*

NotifyIcon CONTROL

The **NotifyIcon** control is located on the left of the taskbar of your system, as shown in Figure 5-32. This control is used to activate any application to a visible state from its hidden state.

Figure 5-32 *Taskbar with notify icons*

A **NotifyIcon** control can handle both the **Click** and the **Double-click** events. It means, the icon will be activated either by a single-click or by double-click. For example, if you double-click on the **Windows Live Messenger** icon in the taskbar, the **Windows Live Messenger** window will be activated.

To add the **NotifyIcon** control to the form, double-click on it in the toolbar; the **NotifyIcon** control will be added to the component tray.

You can add an icon of your choice in the **Icon** property of the **NotifyIcon** control. To add an icon, select the **Icon** property of the **NotifyIcon** control; an ellipse button will be displayed in front of the property. Choose the button; the **Open** dialog box will be displayed, as shown in Figure 5-33. Choose any of the icons and then choose the **Open** button; the icon will be added to the **Icon** property. When you execute this application, you will notice the icon is added to the taskbar.

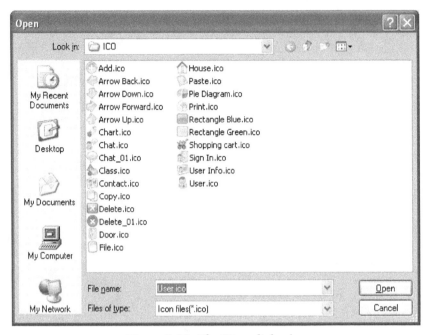

Figure 5-33 *The* **Open** *dialog box*

Creating a NotifyIcon

You can create your own **NotifyIcon** with the help of the icon designer. The following steps are required to create a **NotifyIcon**:

1. Choose **Project > Add New Item** from the menu bar; the **Add New Item** dialog box will be displayed. Select the **General** subnode under the **Common Items** node in the **Categories** area.

2. Select the **Icon File** option from the **Templates** area. Next, choose the **Add** button; the icon designer window will be displayed, as shown in Figure 5-34.

3. Now, you can design the icon using the tools displayed in the toolbar that is just above the icon. These tools can be used to draw different shapes, color them, edit them, and so on.

NumericUpDown CONTROL

A **NumericUpDown** control is formed by the combination of the **TextBox** control and two arrows, as shown in Figure 5-35. The **TextBox** control is used to display a numeric value and the arrows are used to increase or decrease the value. You can use the **UP** arrow to increase the value and the **DOWN** arrow to decrease the value.

The **NumericUpDowm** control has two important properties, **Maximum** and **Minimum**. The default value for the **Minimum** property is 0 and for the **Maximum** property is 100. It means you can specify the values from 0 to 100. You can change the default values if needed.

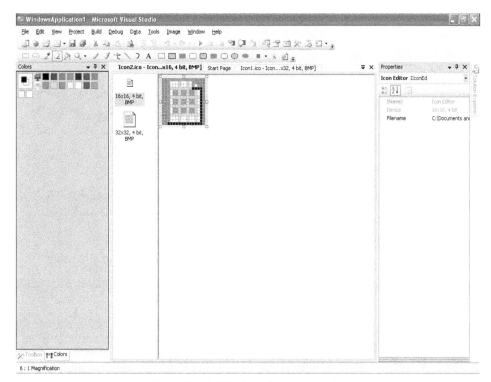

Figure 5-34 *The icon designer window*

ProgressBar CONTROL

A **ProgressBar** control is a horizontal bar that is used to indicate the completion of an action by displaying small rectangles in the bar. When the horizontal bar is completely filled with rectangles, it means the action is complete. These small rectangles provide an idea to the user about the progress of the current action. To add a **ProgressBar** control to the form, you need to double-click on it.

Figure 5-35 *The **NumericUpDown** control*

Properties of ProgressBar Controls

The important properties of the **ProgressBar** control are listed in Table 5-9.

Properties	Functions
Maximum	Determines the upper range of the **ProgressBar** control within the application
Minimum	Determines the lower range of the **ProgressBar** control within the application
Style	Sets the style of the **ProgressBar** control
Value	Determines the current value of the **ProgressBar** control in the range specified in the **Maximum** and **Minimum** properties
Step	It is an integer value used to increment the value of the **ProgressBar** control

*Table 5-9　Properties of the **ProgressBar** control*

RadioButton CONTROL

A **RadioButton** control is used to select only one option from the possible multiple options. It is similar to the **CheckBox** control. The only difference is that the **CheckBox** control can be used to select multiple options at a time, whereas the **RadioButton** control can be used to select only one option from the possible multiple options. The **RadioButton** control is shown in Figure 5-36.

*Figure 5-36　The **RadioButton** control*

Some of the important properties of the **RadioButton** control are given in Table 5-10.

Properties	Functions
Appearance	Sets the appearance of the **RadioButton** control
Checked	Determines whether the **RadioButton** control is selected or not
CheckAlign	Determines the position of the check box within the control
TextAlign	Determines the alignment of the text
AutoClick	Determines the state of the **RadioButton** control on a click

*Table 5-10　Properties of the **RadioButton** control*

ToolTip CONTROL

Whenever you place the mouse cursor over a control, a **ToolTip** control is displayed. A tooltip is a small rectangular box that gives a short description about the working of the control. Tooltips are used to provide quick help to the user. Whenever you double-click on this control, it is added to the component tray of the form but is not visible at runtime.

Some of the important properties of the **ToolTip** component are given in Table 5-11.

Properties	Functions
AutoPopDelay	Determines the duration for which a tool tip will be displayed on the screen
InitialDelay	Determines the time taken to display the tooltip when you place the cursor over a control
ReshowDelay	Determines the duration of time between the display of different tooltip windows as you move the mouse pointer from one control to another
AutomaticDelay	Sets the values of all the above mentioned properties of the **ToolTip** control to some appropriate values

Table 5-11 *Properties of the **ToolTip** control*

WebBrowser CONTROL

The **WebBrowser** control provides a wrapper that allows you to display web pages in your windows forms application.

Some important properties of the **WebBrowser** control are listed in Table 5-12.

Properties	Functions
Url	Specifies the **Url** that the **WebBrowser** control has to navigate
AllowNavigation	Specifies whether the **WebBrowser** control can browse to another web page once it is initially loaded

Table 5-12 *Properties of the **WebBrowser** control*

The following application illustrates the use of the **Label** control, **LinkLabel** control, **TextBox** control, and **ListBox** control:

Application 1

Create an application that will prompt the user to enter his name and the book name that he wants to order.

In this application, the user will be prompted to enter his name and the book name that he wants to order. The application will then display the entire details in a message box.

The following steps are required to create this application:

Step 1
Start a new project and save it as **c05_VB_NET_2008_01**.

Step 2
Add three **Label** controls, two **TextBox** controls, a **LinkLabel** control, and a **ListBox** control to the form. The form will be displayed, as shown in Figure 5-37.

Step 3
Change the **Text** property of the controls as follows:

Label1 to **Name**
Label2 to **Address**
Label3 to **Book Name**
LinkLabel to **Order Now**

Step 4
Select the **Items** property of the **ListBox** control from the **Properties** window. Choose the ellipse button; the **String Collection Editor** dialog box will be displayed, as shown in Figure 5-38. Add the following items to the editor:

Figure 5-37 *The form after adding the controls*

VB.NET   Java
Oracle   Dreamweaver
C++   Excel

Figure 5-38 *The **String Collection Editor** dialog box*

Step 5

Double-click on the **LinkLabel** control; the code window will be displayed. Enter the following source code for the **Click** event of the **LinkLabel** control in the code window:

MsgBox(" Mr. " & TextBox1.Text & " has place the " & Chr(13) & "order for the " & ListBox1. SelectedItem & " book. " & Chr(13) & "His mailing address is:" & Chr(13) & TextBox2.Text, MsgBoxStyle.YesNo)

Note that the entire above mentioned code will be entered in a single line.

Explanation

In the above source code, the concatenation operator **&** is used to concatenate the text values of the **TextBox** control and the **ListBox** control. **(13)** is the ASCII value of the ENTER key. The result of this application will be displayed in a message box.

Step 6

Execute the application. To do so, press the F5 key. Alternatively, choose **Debug > Start Debugging** from the menu bar. The final form will be displayed, as shown in Figure 5-39.

Step 7

Enter the required values in the **Name** and **Address** textboxes and then select any one option from the **Book Name** listbox.

Step 8

Next, choose the **Order Now** link; a message box with the complete details of the order will be displayed, as shown in Figure 5-40.

Figure 5-39 *The final form*

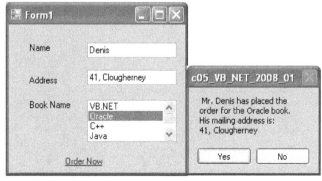

Figure 5-40 *Message box displaying the details of an order*

The following application illustrates the use of the **PictureBox** control, **Button** control, and **CheckedListBox** control:

Application 2

Create an application that will prompt the user to select an option from the existing three options to display a picture.

In the following application, the user will be prompted to select any one option from the multiple options to display a picture.

Step 1
Start a new project and save it as **c05_VB_NET_2008_02**.

Step 2
Add a **Label** control, a **CheckedListBox** control, a **PictureBox** control, and a **Button** control to the form.
Step 3
Change the **Text** property of the controls as follows:
Label1 to **Select the picture to display**
Button1 to **Show Picture**

The resultant form will be shown in Figure 5-41.

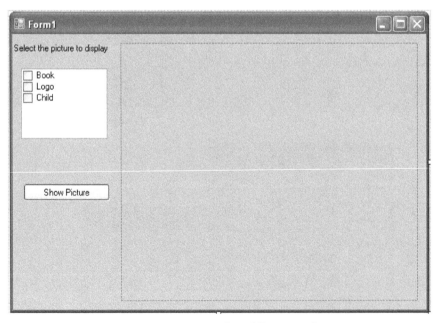

Figure 5-41 *Form after adding controls*

Step 4
Double-click on the **Show Picture** button; the code window will be displayed. Enter the following code for the **Click** event of the **Button** control:

```
Dim FileName As String                                                        1
Dim I_Ctr As Integer                                                          2
PictureBox1.ImageLocation = FileName                                          3
PictureBox1.Show()                                                            4
```

Step 5
Double-click on the **CheckedListBox** control and enter the following source code:

```
If CheckedListBox1.SelectedIndex = 0 Then                                     5
FileName = "C:\cadcim\small_front_cover_page_vb_net.gif"                       6
ElseIf CheckedListBox1.SelectedIndex = 1 Then                                 7
FileName = "C:\logo-cadcim\logo-5.bmp"                                        8
Else                                                                          9
FileName = "C:\Documents and Settings\CADCIM\My Documents\
            My Pictures\untitled3.bmp"                                       10
End If                                                                       11
```

 Note
You need to specify the paths for the images in the above source code according to location of the files on your system.

Explanation
The line-by-line explanation of the above source code is as follows:

Line 1
Dim FileName As String
In the above line, the variable **FileName** is declared as **String**.

Line 2
Dim I_Ctr As Integer
In the above line, **I_Ctr** is declared as an **Integer**.

Line 3
PictureBox1.ImageLocation = FileName
In the above line, the value of the variable **FileName** is assigned to the **ImageLocation** property of the **PictureBox** control.

Line 4
PictureBox1.Show()
In the above line, **Show()** is the method of the **PictureBox** control. The **Show()** method is used to call the image files to be displayed in the **PictureBox** control.

Line 5
If CheckedListBox1.SelectedIndex = 0 Then
In the above line, if the value of the **SelectedIndex** property of the **CheckedListBox** control is 0, then the control will be transferred to the next line (line 6) and the image mentioned in that line will be displayed.

Line 6
FileName = "C:\cadcim\small_front_cover_page_vb_net.gif"
In the above line, the path **C:\cadcim\small_front_cover_page_vb_net.gif** is assigned to the variable **FileName**.

Line 7
ElseIf CheckedListBox1.SelectedIndex = 1 Then
If the statement in the line 5 is not evaluated to **True**, then the control will be transferred to this line. In this line, if the value of the **SelectedIndex** of the **CheckedListBox** control is 1, then the control will be transferred to the next line (line 8) and the image mentioned in the line will be displayed.

Line 8
FileName = "C:\logo-cadcim\logo-5.bmp"
In the above line, the path **C:\logo-cadcim\logo-5.bmp** is assigned to the variable **FileName**.

Line 9
Else
The **Else** statement in this line is used for the **If** statement in line 5. If both the conditions within the body of the **If** and the **ElseIf** statement are evaluated to false, then the control will be transferred to this line. It means the statement within the **Else** block will be executed.

Line 10
FileName = "C:\Documents and Settings\CADCIM\My Documents
                My Pictures\untitled3.bmp"
In the above line, the path **C:\Documents and Settings\CADCIM\My Documents\My Pictures\untitled3.bmp** of the image is assigned to the variable **FileName**.

Line 11
End If
The above line indicates the end of the **If** statement.

Step 6
Execute the application. To do so, press the F5 key. Alternatively, choose **Start > Start Debugging** from the menu bar. If you select the **Child** check box and then choose the **Show Picture** button, the image of the child will be displayed, as shown in Figure 5-42.

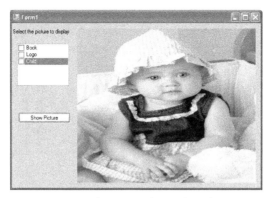

Figure 5-42 *The output form of Application 2*

The following application illustrates the use of the **DateTimePicker** control, **RadioButton** control, **ComboBox** control, and **RichTextBox** control:

Application 3

Create an application that will prompt the user to enter his personal details.

In this application, the user will be prompted to enter his/her personal details using different controls.

The following steps are required to create this application:

Step 1
Start a new project and save it as **c05_VB_NET_2008_03**.

Step 2
Add seven **Label** controls, two **TextBox** controls, a **RichTextBox** control, two **RadioButton** controls, two **CheckBox** controls, and a **DateTimePicker** control to the form. Arrange the controls, as shown in Figure 5-43.
Step 3
Change the **Text** property of the controls as follows:

Label1 to **Name**
Label2 to **Date of Birth**
Label3 to **Designation**
Label4 to **Gender**
Label5 to **Phone No**
Label6 to **Tell about yourself**
Label7 to **About 500 characters**
Button1 to **Submit**
RadioButton1 to **Male**
RadioButton2 to **Female**
CheckBox1 to **Residential**
CheckBox2 to **Office**

Step 4
Change the **Name** property of the controls
as follows:

TextBox1 to **TxtName**
TextBox2 to **TxtPhone**
ComboBox1 to **CmbRole**
RadioButton1 to **RbMale**
RadioButton2 to **Rbfemale**
Button1 to **Brn_Submit**

Step 5
Double-click on the **DateTimePicker** control;
the code window will be displayed. Enter the
following source code:

TextBox1.Text = DateTimePicker1.Value
In the above source code, the value of the
DateTime Picker control is assigned to the
Text property of the associated **TextBox**
control.

Step 6
Double-click on the **Submit** button and enter
the following source code in the code window:

Figure 5-43 Design mode of Application 3

MsgBox("Thanks for submitting details to
CADCIM Technologies, USA", , "CADCIM Technologies")
In the above source code, a message box with the message **"Thanks for submitting details
to CADCIM Technologies, USA", , "CADCIM Technologies** will be displayed whenever the
user chooses the button.

Step 7
Execute the application; the output form will be displayed, as shown in Figure 5-44. Enter
the details as follows:
Name: John
Date of Birth: 05/12/81
Designation: Team Leader
Gender: Male
Phone No: 614-7532

Next, choose the **Submit** button; a message box will be displayed, as shown in Figure 5-45.

Figure 5-44 *The output form of Application 3*

Figure 5-45 *Message box displayed*

Self-Evaluation Test

Answer the following questions and then compare them to those given at the end of this chapter:

1. Sometimes you do not want the user to change the value of the **Text** property of the **TextBox** control. To do so, the value of the _____ property should be set to **True**.

2. You can align the text in the **TextBox** control using the _____ property.

3. The _____ property is used to set a portion of the text as hyperlink.

4. The _____ property is used to set the color of the hyperlink when the user clicks on it.

5. The _____ property is used to set the drawing mode of a **ListBox** control.

Review Questions

Answer the following questions:

1. The image can be positioned in the **PictureBox** control with the help of the _____ property.

2. _____ is the default value of the **Size Mode** property of a **PictureBox** control.

3. A _____ is displayed in a small rectangular box that gives a short description about the working of the control.

4. The _____ control is used to set the date and time.

5. The _____ property determines whether today's date should be displayed at the bottom of the **MonthCalendar** control.

Exercise

Exercise 1

Create an application that will prompt the user to enter his username and password in a form. When the user chooses the **OK** button on the form, the application should verify the username and password as **Sam** and **computer**, respectively. If the username and password entered by the user are correct, a registration form, similar to Figure 5-46, will be displayed. After entering the details, when the user chooses the **OK** button on the registration form, the application will display a message box with the message **Form submitted**.

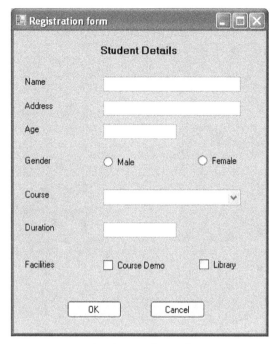

Figure 5-46 *Output form of Exercise 1*

Answers to Self-Evaluation Test
1. ReadOnly, 2. TextAlign, 3. LinkArea, 4. ActiveLinkColor, 5. DrawMode

Chapter 6

Containers, Menus, and Toolbars

Learning Objectives

After completing this chapter, you will be able to*:*
- *Work with the GroupBox control.*
- *Work with the Panel control.*
- *Work with the SplitContainer control.*
- *Work with the TabControl control.*
- *Work with the TableLayout control.*
- *Work with the FlowLayout control.*
- *Work with the MenuStrip control.*
- *Work with the StatusStrip control.*
- *Work with the ContextMenuStrip control.*
- *Work with the ToolStrip control.*
- *Work with the ToolStripContainer control.*

INTRODUCTION

There are a number of controls in VB.NET and they are categorized based upon their functionality. In the previous chapter, you learned about the common controls or the controls that are most commonly used. In this chapter, you will learn about the containers, menus, toolbars, and data.

CONTAINERS

The controls that can hold other controls are known as containers. In this section, you will learn about different containers used in VB.NET.

FlowLayoutPanel Control

The **FlowLayoutPanel** control is a container that arranges the controls in a horizontal or vertical direction. You can use this control to wrap the controls into a single row or single column.

Some of the important properties of the **FlowLayoutPanel** control are listed below:

FlowDirection

This property is used to determine the direction in which the controls will be placed in the **FlowLayoutPanel** control. This property has the following four members:

LeftToRight

This value is used to place the controls in the left-to-right direction.

TopDown

This value is used to place the controls in the top-to-down direction.

RightToLeft

This value is used to place the controls in the right-to-left direction.

BottomUp

This value is used to place the controls in the bottom-to-up direction.

Using the FlowDirection Property

The default direction for placing controls in the **FlowLayoutPanel** control is **LeftToRight**. To change the direction, you need to select the **FlowDirection** of the **FlowLayoutPanel** control from the **Properties** window and then select any one of the values from the drop-down list. For example, if you change the default value to the **TopDown** option, the controls will be arranged one after the other depending upon the size of the **FlowLayoutPanel** control, as shown in Figure 6-1.

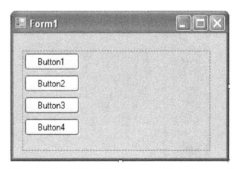

Figure 6-1 *The **FlowLayoutPanel** control*

Padding

The **Padding** property is used to determine the interior spacing of the controls. Its default value is 0. You can arrange the controls using this property. For example, if there are four controls placed within the **FlowLayoutPanel** control with the value 3 as its **Padding** property, the form will appear, as shown in Figure 6-2. Next, if you change the value of the **Padding** property to 10, the form will appear, as shown in Figure 6-3.

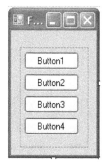

Figure 6-2 The *FlowLayoutPanel* controls with the default **Padding** property

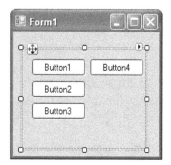

Figure 6-3 The *FlowLayoutPanel* controls with value 10 as its **Padding** property

GroupBox Control

A box with a rectangular border and an optional title, which appears in the upper left corner, is called as the group box. It is a container type control in which you can place other controls. If you move the **GroupBox** control, all controls within it will also move. The **GroupBox** control is used to subdivide a form into different categories depending upon the function. For example, to fill an admission form, you need various details such as personal details, official details, and so on. Therefore, the **GroupBox** control can be used to subdivide the form under different headings.

Creating GroupBox Control through Source Code

You can create the **GroupBox** control through source code. The following is the source code that will create a **GroupBox** control in the center of the form:

```
Dim GroupBox1 As New GroupBox                                    1
GroupBox1.Text = "Personal details"                             2
GroupBox1.Location = New Size(50, 50)                           3
Me.Controls.Add(GroupBox1)                                      4
```

Explanation

The following is the line-by-line explanation of the above source code:

Line 1
Dim GroupBox1 As New GroupBox
In the above line, the variable **GroupBox1** is declared as **New GroupBox**.

Line 2
GroupBox1.Text = "Personal details"
In the above line, the string **Personal details** is assigned to the **Text** property of the variable **GroupBox1**.

Line 3
GroupBox1.Location = New Size(50, 50)
In the above line, the value **50, 50** is assigned to the **Location** property of the variable **GroupBox1**.

Line 4
Me.Controls.Add(GroupBox1)
In the above line, **Me** refers to the current form and the statement **Controls.Add(GroupBox1)** will add the **GroupBox** control to the form.

When you execute the application, the output form will be displayed, as shown in Figure 6-4.

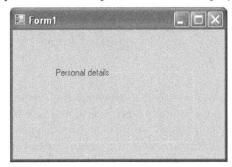

*Figure 6-4 The **GroupBox** control created through source code*

Panel Control

The **Panel** control is also a container similar to the **GroupBox** control. The only difference is that the **Panel** control has scroll bars whereas they are missing in the **GroupBox** control. When you move the **Panel** control, all the controls inside it will also move.

Important Properties of the Panel Control
Some of the important properties of the **Panel** control are as follows:

AutoScroll
In case the contents inside the control exceed its visible area, the **AutoScroll** property determines whether the scroll bars will be added to the **Panel** control or not.

BorderStyle
The **BorderStyle** property determines the appearance of the border of the **Panel** control. For example, if the **BorderStyle** property is set to the value **None**, which is the default value, no border will be visible.

Creating Panel Control through the Source Code

You can create the **Panel** control through source code. The following source code will create a **Panel** control in the center of the form:

```
Dim Panel1 As New Panel                                          1
Panel1.BorderStyle = BorderStyle.Fixed3D                         2
Panel1.Location = New Size(50, 50)                               3
Me.Controls.Add(Panel1)                                          4
```

Explanation

The line-by-line explanation of the above source code is given below:

Line 1
Dim Panel1 As New Panel
In the above line, the variable **Panel1** is declared as **New Panel**.

Line 2
Panel1.BorderStyle = BorderStyle.Fixed3D
In the above line, the value **Fixed3D** is assigned to the **BorderStyle** property of the **Panel** control. It means that the appearance of the border of the **Panel** control will be like a shadowed line.

Line 3
Panel1.Location = New Size(50, 50)
In the above line, the value **50, 50** is assigned to the **Location** property of the variable **Panel1**.

Line 4
Me.Controls.Add(Panel1)
In the above line, **Me** refers to the current form and the statement **Controls.Add(Panel1)** will add the **Panel** control to the form.

When you execute the application, the output form will be displayed, as shown in Figure 6-5.

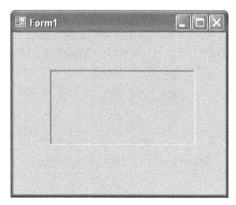

Figure 6-5 The **Panel** control created through code

SplitContainer Control

The **SplitContainer** control is the combination of two **Panel** controls that are separated by a movable bar. If you move the cursor over the separating bar, the cursor will change its shape that will enable you to resize your **Panel** control, as shown in Figure 6-6. The advantage of using this control is that you can select a topic in one **Panel** control and the contents of that particular topic will be displayed in another Panel. For

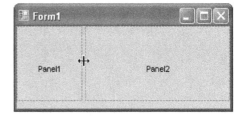

Figure 6-6 The SplitContainer control

example, in the Microsoft Visual Studio window, there is a toolbar on the left side and the window on the right side. Both toolbar and window are separated by a bar. Similarly, you can create another set up using the **SplitContainer** control, as shown in Figure 6-7.

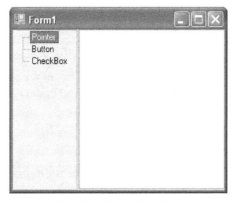

Figure 6-7 Example of the SplitContainer control

TabControl Control

The **TabControl** control displays multiple tabs on the form, as shown in Figure 6-8. The **TabControl** control can be used to create multiple page dialog box, in which similar type of properties will be grouped under one tab. If you click on the forward arrow located on the upper right corner of the control, two properties, **Add Tab** and **Remove Tab** will be displayed. If you choose the **Add Tab** property; a tab will be added to the form. If you choose the **Remove Tab** property; a tab will be removed from the form.

Figure 6-8 The TabControl control

Other Important Properties of the TabControl Control

The other important properties of the **TabControl** control are given next.

TabPages

The **TabPages** property contains details of the individual tabs. Select the **TabPages** property of the **TabControl** control from the **Properties** window. Choose the **Collection** ellipses button; the **TabPage Collection Editor** dialog box will be displayed, as shown in Figure 6-9. In this dialog box, you can change the properties of the individual tabs. To change the properties of the tabs, select them one-by-one; different properties will be displayed on the right side of the dialog box. You can also add or delete the tabs with the help of this dialog box. To add a tab, choose the **Add** button and to delete a tab, choose the **Remove** button.

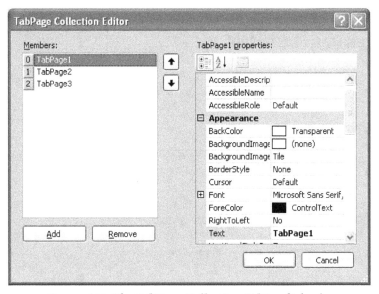

*Figure 6-9 The **TabPage Collection Editor** dialog box*

BackgroundImage

The **BackgroundImage** property is used to set the background image of the control.

Multiline

The **Multiline** property of the **TabControl** control determines whether the multiline tabs are allowed or not. The default value of the **Multiline** property is false. You can change it to true, if you want to add multiline tabs.

Appearance

The **Appearance** property determines the layout of the tabs. The tabs can be set either as simple buttons or flat buttons.

Adding Controls to the TabControl Control

You can add controls to the individual pages of the **TabControl** control. To add the controls to different pages of the **TabControl** control, choose the tabs one-by-one and add the controls as you have done with the forms. For example, if there are three tabs in the **TabControl** control, choose the first tab and double-click on the **Button** control in the toolbox; the **Button** control will be added to the first page. Similarly, add a **Button** control to the second page.

You can add the controls to the **TabControl** control through the source code also. If you want to add a **Button** control to the first page of the **TabControl** control, use the following source code:

```
TabPage1.Controls.Add(New Button())
```

A **Button** control, without any display text, will be added to the first page.

TableLayoutPanel Control

The **TabelLayoutPanel** control allows the controls to be arranged in grids.

The following application illustrates the use of the containers:

Application 1

Create an application that will display the description about some controls using the **SplitContainer** control.

This application will display the description of the **PictureBox**, **ProgressBar**, and **NumericUpDown** controls using the **SplitContainer** control.

The following steps are required to create this application:

Step 1
Create a new project and save it as **c06_VB_NET_2008_01**.

Step 2
Add a **SplitContainer**, two **PictureBox** controls, two **ProgressBar** controls, two **NumericUpDown** controls, three **LinkLabel** controls, and three **FlowLayoutPanel** controls to the form.

Step 3
Arrange the controls, as shown in Figure 6-10.

Step 4
Double-click on the form and enter the following source code:

```
Label1.Text = "The Button control is a small rectangular shaped box that is used for " & _
              "handling events in coding. The default text of the Button control is " & _
              "Button1. The default event of Button control is Click. That means if " & _
              "you click on the Button control, some action will be performed."
```

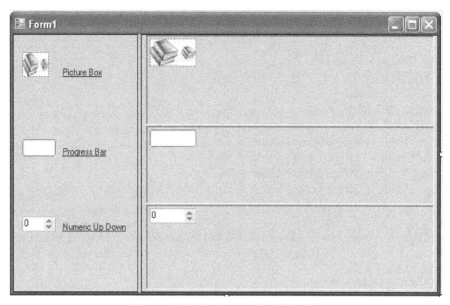

Figure 6-10 *Design mode of the form*

Label2.Text = "The ProgressBar control is a horizontal bar used to indicate the " & _
            "completion of an action by displaying small rectangles in the bar. " & _
            "When the horizontal bar is completely filled with rectangles that " & _
            "means the action is complete. These small rectangles are just to give " & _
            "the user an idea about the progress of the action."

Label3.Text = "The NumericUpDown control appears like a combination of " & _
            "TextBox control and two arrows. The TextBox control is used " & _
            "to display a numeric value and with the help of these arrows " & _
            "the user can increase or decrease the value. That means you can use " & _
            "UP arrow to increase the value and DOWN arrow to decrease the value."
FlowLayoutPanel1.Visible = False
FlowLayoutPanel2.Visible = False
FlowLayoutPanel3.Visible = False
ProgressBar1.Value = 0
ProgressBar2.Value = 0

Step 5
Double-click on the **Picture Box** link label and enter the following source code:

ProgressBar1.Value = 0
ProgressBar2.Value = 0
FlowLayoutPanel1.Visible = True
FlowLayoutPanel2.Visible = False
FlowLayoutPanel3.Visible = False

Step 6
Double-click on the **Progress Bar** link label and enter the following source code:

```
ProgressBar1.Value = 0
ProgressBar2.Value = 0
FlowLayoutPanel1.Visible = False
FlowLayoutPanel2.Visible = True
FlowLayoutPanel3.Visible = False
ProgressBar1.Value = ProgressBar1.Value + 10
ProgressBar2.Value = ProgressBar2.Value + 20
ProgressBar1.Value = ProgressBar1.Value + 10
ProgressBar2.Value = ProgressBar2.Value + 20
```

Step 7
Double-click on the **Numeric Up Down** link label and enter the following source code:

```
ProgressBar1.Value = 0
ProgressBar2.Value = 0
FlowLayoutPanel1.Visible = False
FlowLayoutPanel2.Visible = False
FlowLayoutPanel3.Visible = True
NumericUpDown1.Value = 0
NumericUpDown2.Value = 0
```

The following is the explanation of the above mentioned source code:

In the above mentioned source code, Step 4 is used to assign values to the **LinkLabel** controls, make the **Visible** property of the **FlowLayoutPanel** control as false. And, also it is used to assign the value 0 to the **Value** property of **ProgressBar1** and **ProgressBar2**. In Step 5, the **Visible** property of the **FlowLayoutPanel1** is set to true. Therefore, whenever you click on the **LinkLabel1**, only the contents in the **FlowLayoutPanel1** will be displayed. In Step 6, the **Visible** property of the **FlowLayoutPanel2** is set to true. Also, the values of the **Value** property of the **ProgressBar** controls are increased. In Step 7, the **Visible** property of only the **FlowLayoutPanel3** is set to true.

Step 8
Execute the application, the output of the form will be displayed, as shown in Figure 6-11.

Step 9
Click on the **ProgressBar** link label; the description of the control will be displayed on the right side of the separator bar of the **SplitContainer** control, as shown in Figure 6-12.

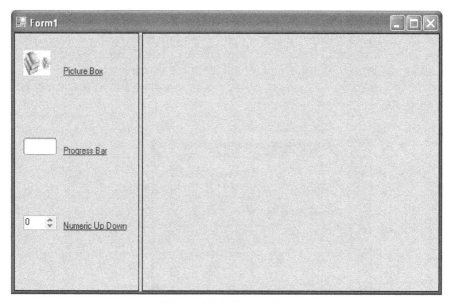

Figure 6-11 *Output form*

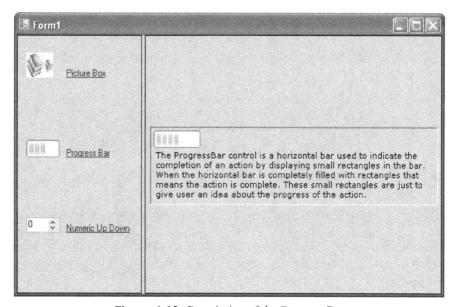

Figure 6-12 *Description of the **ProgressBar***

MENUS & TOOLBARS

Menus and toolbars are the structures that provide commands in an organized manner. The menus and toolbars are commonly used when an application has several operations and the user has to choose any one of them. The menus and toolbars are discussed next.

ContextMenuStrip

The context menus, also called as shortcut menus, are the menus that are displayed when you right-click on a control or in the area of form window. The **ContextMenuStrip** component is used to add the items to the shortcut menu. To add a **ContextMenuStrip** component to a form, double-click on it in the toolbox; the component will be added to the component tray, as shown in Figure 6-13.

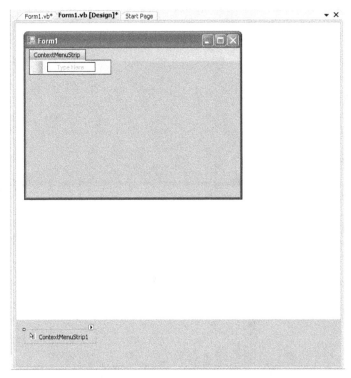

*Figure 6-13 The **ContextMenuStrip** component*

If you click on the forward arrow on the upper right corner of the **ContextMenuStrip** component in the component tray, three properties will be displayed, **RenderMode**, **ShowImageMargin**, and **ShowCheckMargin**. These properties are discussed next.

RenderMode
This property is used to apply the pant styles to the control. It has three options, **System**, **Professional**, **ManageRenderMode**.

ShowImageMargin
This property is used to determine whether the space will be shown on the left of the image in the **ToolStripMenu** or not. Its default value is true.

ShowCheckMargin
This property determines whether the space for a check mark will be shown on the left of the **ToolStripMenu** or not. Its default value is false.

Adding ContextMenuStrip to a Control

You can add the **ContextMenuSrtip** to a control. The following steps are required to add a **ContextMenuStrip** to a control, such as **Button** control:

1. Add a **ContextMenuStrip** component to the form.

2. When the **ContextMenuStrip** is added, it will prompt you to enter the item that you want to add as a context menu.

3. Next, add a **Button** control to the form.

4. Set the **ContextMenuStrip** property of the **Button** control to the value **ContextMenuStrip1**.

5. When you execute the application and right-click on the **Button** control, the added items will be displayed, as shown in Figure 6-14.

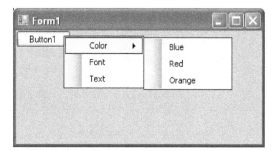

*Figure 6-14 The **ContextMenuStrip** associated to the **Button** control*

MenuStrip

The **MenuStrip** component will help you to add a menu bar to your application. To add the **MenuStrip** component to your form, double-click on the **MenuStrip** control in the toolbar; it will be added to the component tray and you can notice a bar on the form, as shown in Figure 6-15. When you add items to this bar, it will work as the menu bar, as shown in Figure 6-16. If you click on the **Type Here** area of the bar, refer to Figure 6-15, a down arrow will be displayed. Click on the arrow, three options will be displayed. You can add any option to the menu bar. For example, if you want to add a combo box to the menu bar, select that option from the list; the combo box will be added to the menu bar, as shown in Figure 6-17. You can also add items to the combo box from the **Properties** window. To add the items to the combo box, select the **ComboBox** control located on the form. Next, from the **Properties** window, select the **Items** property; an ellipses button will be displayed. Choose the button; the **String Collection Editor** dialog box will be displayed, as shown in Figure 6-18. Enter the items you need to add to the **ComboBox** control and then choose the **OK** button; the selected items will be added to the **ComboBox** control.

Figure 6-15 *The MenuStrip component*

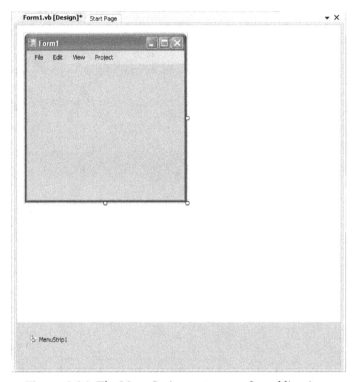

Figure 6-16 *The MenuStrip component after adding items*

Some Important Properties of the MenuStrip Control

When you click on the forward arrow located on the upper right corner of the **MenuStrip** control, some important properties of the **MenuStrip** control will be displayed in a SmartTags window, as shown in Figure 6-19. These properties are discussed next.

Embed in ToolStripContainer

When you choose the **Embed in ToolStripContainer** property, a **ToolStripContainer** will be added to the form and it will embed the **MenuStrip** control.

Insert Standard Items

This property is used to add the in-built menu items to the menu bar. To add an in-built menu item to the menu bar, select the **Insert Standard Items** property from the SmartTags window; the menu items will be added to the menu bar, as shown in Figure 6-20.

Figure 6-17 *Combo box added to the menu bar*

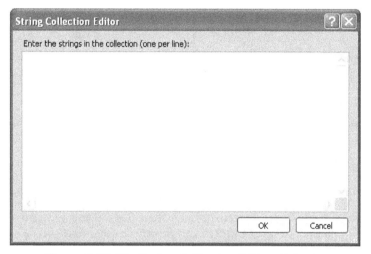

Figure 6-18 *The* **String Collection Editor** *dialog box*

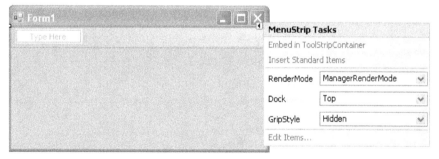

Figure 6-19 *Properties of the* **MenuStrip** *control*

RenderMode
This property is used to apply the paint styles to the control. It has three options, **System**, **Professional**, **ManageRenderMode**.

Dock
This property is used to determine which of the borders of the control are bound to the container. It has six options, as shown in Figure 6-21.

Figure 6-20 *Form with an in-built menu bar*

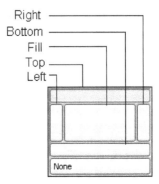

Figure 6-21 *Options of the* **Dock** *property*

GripStyle

This property is used to determine the visibility of the grip on the **ToolStrip**. It has two options, **Hidden** and **Visibility**. When you select the **Visibility** option, a grip will be displayed on the left of the **ToolStrip**.

Edit Items

This property is used to edit the items. For example, you can add new items to the **MenuStrip** or edit the existing items of the **MenuStrip** using this property. To edit the items, choose the **Edit Items** property from the SmartTags window; the **Items Collection Editor** dialog box will be displayed, as shown in Figure 6-22. In this dialog box, you can select an item from the **Select item and add to list below** drop-down list and then choose the **Add** button; the item will be added to the **Members** area. Now, you can set the properties of the added items on the right of the **Items Collection Editor** dialog box.

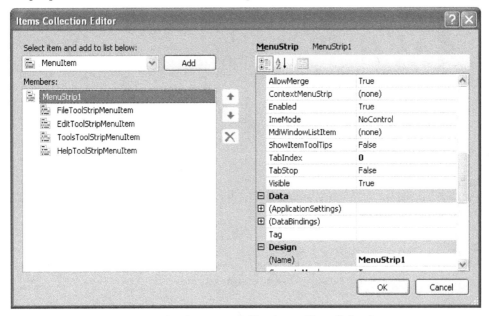

Figure 6-22 *The* **Items Collection Editor** *dialog box*

StatusStrip

The **StatusStrip** area is mostly located at the bottom of a window to show the status of the current operating program. The status is displayed in the form of text or icons. To add the **StatusStrip** control to the form, double-click on the control in the toolbox; the control will be added to the bottom of the form, as shown in Figure 6-23.

Figure 6-23 The StatusStrip control

If you want to add items to the **StatusStrip** control, click on the down arrow located in the **StatusStrip** control; a list of items will be displayed, as shown in Figure 6-24. These items are discussed next.

StatusLabel

This item is used to add text to the **StatusStrip** control. To add this item, select it from the list and then change its text as required from the **Properties** window. For example, if you want to change its **Text** property to Status Bar, select its **Text** property from the **Properties** window and enter the string **Status Bar** in the edit-box. Once you enter the text and press ENTER; the text will be displayed, as shown in Figure 6-25.

Figure 6-24 Items associated with the StatusStrip control

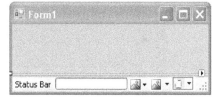

Figure 6-25 The StatusStrip control with all its options

ProgressBar

This item is used to add a progress bar to the **StatusStrip** control. It will help in displaying the current status of the application. To add this item, select it from the list; it will be added to the **StatusStrip** control, refer to Figure 6-25.

DropDownButton

This property is similar to the **ToolStripMenuItem** of the **MenuStrip**. It is a small icon image with a drop-down arrow, as shown in Figure 6-25. You can add any item to the **StatusStrip** by clicking on the arrow.

SplitButton

The function of the **SplitButton** is similar to that of the **DropDownButton**.

ToolStrip

The **ToolStrip** control is similar to **StatusStrip**, but it has some additional options, as shown in Figure 6-26. The **ToolStrip** control is used as a shortcut for the menu options. For example, if you need to start a new project, then choose **File > New Project** from the menu bar, but with the help of **ToolStrip** control, you can create shortcut for the **New Project** option.

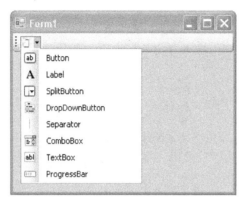

Figure 6-26 The **ToolStrip** control with all its options

Some Important Properties of the ToolStrip Control

When you click on the forward arrow at the upper right corner of the control, some important properties of the **ToolStrip** control will be displayed, as shown in Figure 6-27. The description of the properties is given next.

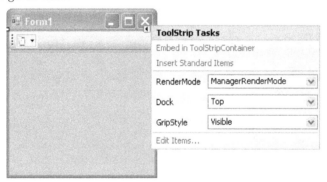

Figure 6-27 The **ToolStrip** control with its properties

Embed in ToolStripContainer

When you choose the **Embed in ToolStripContainer**, a **ToolStripContainer** will be added to the form and it will embed the **ToolStrip** control, as shown in Figure 6-28.

Insert Standard Items

The **Insert Standard Items** property will add the in-built **ToolStrip** items to the **ToolStrip** control, as shown in Figure 6-29.

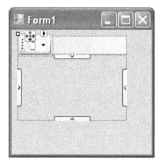

Figure 6-28 The **Embed in ToolStripContainer** *property of the* **ToolStripContainer** *control*

Figure 6-29 The **Insert Standard Items** *property of the* **ToolStrip** *control*

ToolStripContainer

It is similar to the **SplitContainer** having four side panels and a central panel, as shown in Figure 6-30. If you put multiple **ToolStrip** controls in the left or right panel, the items will be displayed vertically. And, if you put multiple **ToolStrip** controls in the top or bottom panel, the items will be displayed horizontally. The central panel is used to accommodate the common controls such as **Label** control, **TextBox** control, and so on. You cannot delete these panels. However, you can hide them by changing the value of the **BottomToolStripPanelVisible**, **TopToolStripPanelVisible**, **LeftToolStripPanelVisible**, and **RightToolStripPanelVisible** properties to false.

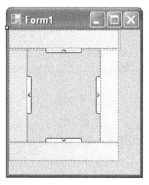

Figure 6-30 The **ToolStripContainer** *control*

The following application illustrates the use of the toolbars:

Application 2

Create an application that will display a web page using the controls, **WebBrowser**, **ToolStrip**, and **StatusStrip**.

The following application will browse any web site or URL:

Step 1
Create a new project and save it as **c06_VB_NET_2008_02**.

Step 2
Add a **ToolStrip** control, **StatusStrip** control, and **WebBrowser** control to the form.

Step 3
Select the **ToolStrip** control and add four **Buttons** and a **DropDownButton** from the drop-down list of the **Toolstrip** control, as shown in Figure 6-31.

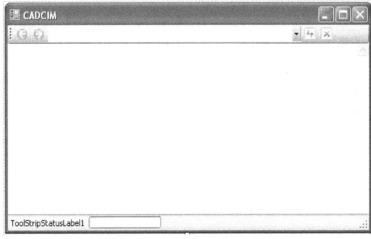

Figure 6-31 *Design mode of the Application 2*

Step 4
Select the **StatusStrip** control and add a **StatusLabel** and **ProgressBar** from the drop-down list of the **StatusStrip** control, as shown in Figure 6-31.

Step 5
Double-click on the form and enter the following code:

```
Private Sub ToolStripComboBox1_KeyPress(ByVal sender As Object, _
ByVal e As System.Windows.Forms.KeyPressEventArgs) _
Handles ToolStripComboBox1.KeyPress                                    1
Dim KeyCode As Integer = Asc(e.KeyChar)                                2
```

```
If Not KeyCode = 13 Then Exit Sub                                        3
If ToolStripComboBox1.Text = "" Then                                     4
Exit Sub                                                                 5
Else                                                                     6
WebBrowser1.Navigate(ToolStripComboBox1.Text)                            7
ToolStripStatusLabel1.Text = WebBrowser1.DocumentTitle                   8
Me.Text = WebBrowser1.DocumentTitle                                      9
End If                                                                  10
End Sub                                                                 11

Private Sub WebBrowser1_Navigated(ByVal sender As Object, _
ByVal e As System.Windows.Forms.WebBrowserNavigatedEventArgs) _
Handles WebBrowser1.Navigated                                          12
ToolStripProgressBar1.Value = ToolStripProgressBar1.Value + 15         13
ToolStripComboBox1.Text = e.Url.ToString                               14
ToolStripProgressBar1.Value = ToolStripProgressBar1.Value + 15         15
Me.Text = WebBrowser1.DocumentTitle                                    16
ToolStripProgressBar1.Value = ToolStripProgressBar1.Value + 15         17
ToolStripStatusLabel1.Text = WebBrowser1.DocumentTitle                 18
ToolStripProgressBar1.Value = ToolStripProgressBar1.Value + 1          19
End Sub                                                                20

Private Sub Form1_Load(ByVal sender As Object, _
ByVal e As System.EventArgs) Handles Me.Load                           21
Me.Width = 1190                                                        22
Me.Height = 725                                                        23
End Sub                                                                24
Private Sub ToolStripButton1_Click(ByVal sender As System.Object, _
ByVal e As System.EventArgs) Handles ToolStripButton1.Click            25
If WebBrowser1.CanGoForward Then                                       26
WebBrowser1.GoForward()                                                27
ToolStripStatusLabel1.Text = WebBrowser1.DocumentTitle                 28
Me.Text = WebBrowser1.DocumentTitle                                    29
End If                                                                 30
End Sub                                                                31
Private Sub ToolStripButton2_Click(ByVal sender As System.Object, _
ByVal e As System.EventArgs) Handles ToolStripButton2.Click            32
If WebBrowser1.CanGoBack Then                                          33
WebBrowser1.GoBack()                                                   34
ToolStripStatusLabel1.Text = WebBrowser1.DocumentTitle                 35
Me.Text = WebBrowser1.DocumentTitle                                    36
End If                                                                 37
End Sub                                                                38
Private Sub ToolStripButton4_Click(ByVal sender As System.Object, _
ByVal e As System.EventArgs) Handles ToolStripButton4.Click            39
WebBrowser1.Stop()                                                     40
End Sub                                                                41
```

Explanation
The line-by-line explanation of the above source code is given next.

Line 1
Private Sub ToolStripComboBox1_KeyPress(ByVal sender As Object, _
ByVal e As System.Windows.Forms.KeyPressEventArgs) _
Handles ToolStripComboBox1.KeyPress
In the above line, you need to code the **KeyPress** event of the **ToolStripComboBox1** control.

Line 2
Dim KeyCode As Integer = Asc(e.KeyChar)
In the above line, the variable **KeyCode** is declared as an integer value. The **Asc** function is used to find the ASCII value of the character key. The ASCII value of the **e.KeyChar** is assigned to the variable **KeyCode**.

Line 3
If Not KeyCode = 13 Then Exit Sub
In the above line, the **If** statement is used to evaluate the value of the **KeyCode**. If the value is not 13, which is the ASCII value of the ENTER key, the application will exit from the sub procedure.

Line 4-7
If ToolStripComboBox1.Text = "" Then
Exit Sub
Else
WebBrowser1.Navigate(ToolStripComboBox1.Text)
In the above line, the **If** statement is used to check the value of the **Text** property of the **ToolStripComboBox**. If the value is null, the control will be transferred to Line 5 and the code will exit from the sub procedure. Otherwise, the control will be transferred to the **Else** block and the application will start navigating the URL entered for the **Text** value of the **ToolStripComboBox1**.

Line 8
ToolStripStatusLabel1.Text = WebBrowser1.DocumentTitle
In Line 8, the title of the navigating URL page will be assigned to the **Text** property of the **ToolStripStatusLabel1**. Each time the user enters a new URL, the value of the **Text** property of the **ToolStripStatusLabel1** will change accordingly.

Line 9
Me.Text = WebBrowser1.DocumentTitle
In the above line, the title of the navigating URL page will be assigned to the **Text** property of the form.

Line 10
End If
The above line indicates the end of the **If** statement.

Line 11
End Sub
The above line indicates the end of the sub procedure.

Line 12
Private Sub WebBrowser1_Navigated(ByVal sender As Object, _
ByVal e As System.Windows.Forms.WebBrowserNavigatedEventArgs) _
Handles WebBrowser1.Navigated

In the above line, the **Navigated** event of the **WebBrowser1** is coded.

Line 13
ToolStripProgressBar1.Value = ToolStripProgressBar1.Value + 15
In the above line, the value of the **Value** property of the **ProgressBar** is incremented by 15.

Line 14
ToolStripComboBox1.Text = e.Url.ToString
In the above line, the **e.Url** represents the navigated URL. The string value **e.Url.ToString** is assigned to the **Text** property of the **ToolStripComboBox1**.

Line 16
Me.Text = WebBrowser1.DocumentTitle
In the above line, the title of the navigated URL will be assigned to the **Text** property of the form.

Line 17
ToolStripProgressBar1.Value = ToolStripProgressBar1.Value + 15
In the above line, the counter value of the **Value** property of the **ToolStripProgressBar1** is incremented by 15.

Line 21
Private Sub Form1_Load(ByVal sender As Object, _
ByVal e As System.EventArgs) Handles Me.Load
In the above line, the **Load** event of the form is coded.

Line 22-23
Me.Width = 1190
Me.Height = 725
In these lines, **Me** indicates the active window form. Here the values 1190 and 725 are assigned to the **Width** and **Height** properties of the form, respectively.

Line 26-27
If WebBrowser1.CanGoForward Then
WebBrowser1.GoForward()
In these lines, if the **CanGoForward** property evaluates to true, then the web browser will navigate to the existing next page.

Line 33-34
If WebBrowser1.CanGoBack Then
WebBrowser1.GoBack()
In the above lines, if the **CanGoBack** property evaluates to true, then the web browser will navigate to the existing previous page.

Line 40
WebBrowser1.Stop()
In the above line, the navigation of the URL will be stopped.

Step 6
Execute the application; the form will be displayed, as shown in Figure 6-32. You can enter any URL address in the **ComboBox** control and then press ENTER; it will navigate to the URL address entered. For example, if you enter **www.cadcim.com**, the application will navigate to the cadcim website, as shown in Figure 6-33.

Figure 6-32 Output mode of Application 2

The following application illustrates the use of the toolbars:

Application 3

Create an application that will display a notepad window using the controls, **ContextMenuStrip**, **MenuStrip**, **StatusStrip**, **OpenFileDialog**, **RichTextBox**, and **SaveFileDialog**. The **OpenFileDialog** and **SaveFileDialog** controls will be discussed in the next chapter.

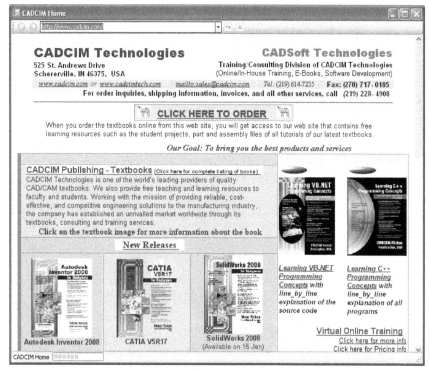

Figure 6-33 *Output of Application 2 after entering a URL address*

The following steps will display a notepad window:

Step 1
Create a new project and save it as **c06_VB_NET_2008_03**.

Step 2
Add **MenuStrip**, **StatusStrip**, **RichTextBox**, **ContextMenuStrip**, **OpenFileDialog**, and **Save-FileDialog** controls to the form.

Step 3
Select the **MenuStrip** control in the component tray and add the following options to it:

File > New, Open, Save, Save As, and Exit
Edit > Undo, Delete,   and Select All
View > Status Bar

The resultant form will appear as shown in Figure 6-34.

Step 4
Select the **ContextMenuStrip** control in the component tray and add the following options to it: **Undo**, **Delete**, and **Select All**.

Step 5
Double-click on the form and enter the following source code:

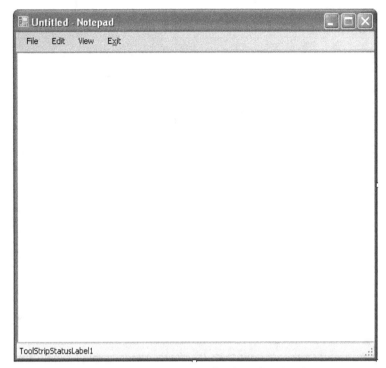

Figure 6-34 *Design mode of Application 3*

Public Class Form1	1
Dim Copy_string As String	2
Dim Bol_True As Boolean	3
Dim Del_text As String	4
Private Sub Form1_Load(ByVal sender As System.Object, _	
ByVal e As System.EventArgs) Handles MyBase.Load	5
ContextMenuStrip1.Visible = True	6
ContextMenuStrip1.Enabled = False	7
StatusStrip1.Visible = False	8
Bol_True = True	9
End Sub	10

Step 6
Double-click on the **StatusBar** option of the **View** menu and enter the following source code:

Private Sub StatusBarToolStripMenuItem_Click(ByVal sender As System.Object, _	
ByVal e As System.EventArgs) Handles StatusBarToolStripMenuItem.Click	11
If Bol_True Then	12
StatusStrip1.Visible = True	13
Bol_True = False	14
Rftbox.Width = Me.Width - 10	15

Rftbox.Height = Me.Height - 75	16
Else	17
StatusStrip1.Visible = False	18
Bol_True = True	19
Rftbox.Width = Me.Width - 10	20
Rftbox.Height = Me.Height - 10	21
End If	22
End Sub	23

Step 7
Enter the following source code for the **Resize** event of the form:

Private Sub Form1_Resize(ByVal sender As Object, _	
ByVal e As System.EventArgs) Handles Me.Resize	24
Rftbox.Width = Me.Width - 10	25
Rftbox.Height = Me.Height - 10	26
End Sub	27

Step 8
Double-click on the **New** option of the **File** menu and enter the following source code:

Private Sub NewToolStripMenuItem_Click(ByVal sender As System.Object, _	
ByVal e As System.EventArgs) Handles NewToolStripMenuItem.Click	28
Rftbox.Clear()	29
Me.Text = "Untitled_Notepad"	30
End Sub	31

Step 9
Double-click on the **Open** option of the **File** menu and enter the following source code:

Private Sub OpenToolStripMenuItem_Click(ByVal sender As System.Object, _	
ByVal e As System.EventArgs) Handles EditToolStripMenuItem.Click	
Dim Str_File As String	32
Dim Str_cont As String	33
Dim oRead As System.IO.StreamReader	34
OpenFileDialog1.ShowDialog()	35
Str_File = OpenFileDialog1.FileName	36
If Str_File = "" Or Str_File = "OpenFileDialog" Then Exit Sub	37
oRead = OpenText(Str_File)	38
Str_cont = ""	39
Do While oRead.Peek <> -1	40
Str_cont = Str_cont & oRead.ReadLine & Chr(13)	41
Loop	42
Rftbox.Text = Str_cont	43
Me.Text = Str_File & "- Notepad"	44
oRead.Close()	45
End Sub	46

Step 10
Enter the following source code for the **TextChanged** event of the extended **RichTextBox**:

```
Private Sub Rftbox_TextChanged(ByVal sender As System.Object, _
ByVal e As System.EventArgs)                                          47
If Not Rftbox.Text = "" Then                                         48
ContextMenuStrip1.Enabled = True                                     49
End If                                                               50
End Sub                                                              51
```

Step 11
Double-click on the **Save** option of the **File** menu and enter the following source code:

```
Private Sub SaveToolStripMenuItem1_Click(ByVal sender As System.Object, _
ByVal e As System.EventArgs) Handles SaveToolStripMenuItem1.Click    52
Dim oWrite As IO.StreamWriter                                        53
SaveFileDialog1.ShowDialog()                                         54
If SaveFileDialog1.FileName = " " Then Exit Sub                      55
oWrite = CreateText(SaveFileDialog1.FileName & ".txt")               56
oWrite.Write(Rftbox.Text)                                            57
oWrite.Close()                                                       58
Me.Text = SaveFileDialog1.FileName & " - Notepad"                    59
End Sub                                                              60
```

Step 12
Double-click on the **Exit** option of the **File** menu and enter the following source code:

```
Private Sub ExitToolStripMenuItem_Click(ByVal sender As System.Object,
ByVal e As System.EventArgs) Handles ExitToolStripMenuItem.Click     61
End                                                                 62
End Sub                                                              63
```

Step 13
Double-click on the **Delete** option of the **Edit** menu and enter the following source code:

```
Private Sub DeleteToolStripMenuItem_Click(ByVal sender As System.Object, _
ByVal e As System.EventArgs) Handles DeleteToolStripMenuItem.Click   64
Dim Bol_M As Boolean                                                 65
ContextMenuStrip1.Enabled = False                                    66
If Rftbox.SelectedText = "" Then                                     67
Bol_M = MsgBox("No text to delete", MsgBoxStyle.Critical, "CADCIM")68
ElseIf Not Len(Trim(Rftbox.SelectedText)) = Rftbox.TextLength Then   69
Bol_M = MsgBox("Please select all the text", MsgBoxStyle.Critical, "CADCIM")  70
End If                                                               71
If Bol_M = True Then Exit Sub                                        72
Del_text = Trim(Rftbox.Text)                                         73
Rftbox.Clear()                                                      74
End Sub                                                              75
```

Step 14
Double-click on the **Select All** option of the **Edit** menu and enter the following source code:

```
Private Sub SelectAllToolStripMenuItem1_Click
(ByVal sender As System.Object, ByVal e As System.EventArgs)
Handles SelectAllToolStripMenuItem1.Click                         76
Rftbox.SelectAll()                                                77
End Sub                                                           78
```

Step 15
Double-click on the **Undo** option of the **Edit** menu and enter the following source code:

```
Private Sub UndoToolStripMenuItem1_Click(ByVal sender As System.Object,
ByVal e As System.EventArgs) Handles UndoToolStripMenuItem1.Click  79
Rftbox.Text = Del_text                                            80
End Sub                                                           81


Private Sub UndoContextToolStripMenuItem_Click
(ByVal sender As System.Object, ByVal e As System.EventArgs)
Handles UndoContextToolStripMenuItem.Click                        82
If Not Rftbox.Text = "" Then                                      83
Exit Sub                                                          84
End If                                                            85
Rftbox.Text = Del_text                                            86
End Sub                                                           87


Private Sub DeletecontextToolStripMenuItem2_Click
(ByVal sender As System.Object, ByVal e As System.EventArgs)
Handles DeletecontextToolStripMenuItem2.Click                     88
Dim Bol_M As Boolean                                              89
ContextMenuStrip1.Enabled = True                                  90
If Rftbox.Text = "" Then                                          91
Exit Sub                                                          92
End If                                                            93
If Rftbox.SelectedText = "" Then                                  94
Bol_M = MsgBox("Please select all the text", MsgBoxStyle.Critical, "CADCIM")  95
ElseIf Not Len(Trim(Rftbox.SelectedText)) = Rftbox.TextLength Then  96
Bol_M = MsgBox("Please select all the text", MsgBoxStyle.Critical, "CADCIM")  97
End If                                                            98
If Bol_M = True Then Exit Sub                                     99
Del_text = Trim(Rftbox.Text)                                     100
Rftbox.Clear()                                                   101
End Sub                                                          102


Private Sub SelectAllContextToolStripMenuItem_Click
(ByVal sender As System.Object, ByVal e As System.EventArgs)
Handles SelectAllContextToolStripMenuItem.Click                  103
```

```
Rftbox.SelectAll()                                              104
End Sub                                                         105


Private Sub Rftbox_TextChanged_1(ByVal sender As System.Object,
ByVal e As System.EventArgs) Handles Rftbox.TextChanged         106
If Rftbox.Text <> "" Then                                       107
ContextMenuStrip1.Enabled = True                                108
Else                                                            109
ContextMenuStrip1.Enabled = True                                110
End If                                                          111
ToolStripStatusLabel1.Text = "Number of words " & Rftbox.TextLength   112
End Sub                                                         113


Private Sub SaveAsToolStripMenuItem_Click(ByVal sender As System.Object,
ByVal e As System.EventArgs) Handles SaveAsToolStripMenuItem.Click   114
Dim oWrite As IO.StreamWriter                                   115
SaveFileDialog1.ShowDialog()                                    116
oWrite = CreateText(SaveFileDialog1.FileName & ".txt")          117
oWrite.Write(Rftbox.Text)                                       118
oWrite.Close()                                                  119
Me.Text = SaveFileDialog1.FileName & " - Notepad"               120
End Sub                                                         121


Private Sub ExitToolStripMenuItem1_Click(ByVal sender As System.Object,
ByVal e As System.EventArgs) Handles ExitToolStripMenuItem1.Click    122
End                                                             123
End Sub                                                         124
End Class                                                       125
```

Explanation
The following is the line-by-line explanation of the above source code:

Lines 1-4
Public Class Form1
Dim Copy_string As String
Dim Bol_True As Boolean
Dim Del_text As String
In the above mentioned lines, the variable **Copy_string** is declared as a string data type, the variable **Bol_True** is declared as a boolean data type, and the variable **Del_text** is declared as a string data type. These are declared under the **Public** class of the form.

Lines 5-10
Private Sub Form1_Load(ByVal sender As System.Object, _
ByVal e As System.EventArgs) Handles MyBase.Load
ContextMenuStrip1.Visible = True
ContextMenuStrip1.Enabled = False
StatusStrip1.Visible = False

Bol_True = True
End Sub

In the above mentioned lines, the value **True** is assigned to the **Visible** property of the **ContextMenuStrip** control, which means the options of the **ContextMenuStrip** control will be visible to the user. The value **False** is assigned to the **Enabled** property of the **Context-MenuStrip** control, which means the options of the **ContextMenuStrip** control will not be highlighted when displayed. Moreover, the value **False** is assigned to the **Visible** property of the **StatusStrip** control, which means that the **StatusStrip** control will not be displayed on the form at the runtime.

The value **True** is assigned to the variable **Bol_True**.

Lines 11-23
Private Sub StatusBarToolStripMenuItem_Click(ByVal sender As System.Object, _
ByVal e As System.EventArgs) Handles StatusBarToolStripMenuItem.Click
If Bol_True Then
StatusStrip1.Visible = True
Bol_True = False
Rftbox.Width = Me.Width - 10
Rftbox.Height = Me.Height - 75
Else
StatusStrip1.Visible = False
Bol_True = True
Rftbox.Width = Me.Width - 10
Rftbox.Height = Me.Height - 10
End If
End Sub

In the above mentioned lines, if the value of the boolean variable **Bol_True** is true, then the **StatusStrip** control will be visible in the form window. And, when the **StatusStrip** is visible, the size of the **RichTextBox** is adjusted according to the size of **StatusStrip**. If the **StatusStrip** control is not visible, the size of the **RichTextBox** is readjusted to its original size.

Lines 28-30
Private Sub NewToolStripMenuItem_Click(ByVal sender As System.Object, _
ByVal e As System.EventArgs) Handles NewToolStripMenuItem.Click
Rftbox.Clear()
Me.Text = "Untitled-Notepad"
End Sub

The above given source code is for the **Click** event of the **New** option of the **File** menu. The **Clear** method of the **RichTextBox** control is used to clear or remove the text from the **RichTextBox** control. The string value **Untitled-Notepad** is assigned to the **Text** property of the form.

Lines 31-45
Private Sub OpenToolStripMenuItem_Click(ByVal sender As System.Object, _
ByVal e As System.EventArgs) Handles OpenToolStripMenuItem.Click

```
Dim Str_File As String
Dim Str_cont As String
Dim oRead As System.IO.StreamReader
OpenFileDialog1.ShowDialog()
Str_File = OpenFileDialog1.FileName
If Str_File = " " Or Str_File = "OpenEditDialog" Then Exit Sub
oRead = OpenText(Str_File)
Str_cont = ""
Do While oRead.Peek <> -1
Str_cont = Str_cont & oRead.ReadLine & Chr(13)
Loop
Rftbox.Text = Str_cont
Me.Text = Str_File & "- Notepad"
oRead.Close()
End Sub
```

In these lines, the source code is for the **Open** option of the **File** menu is mentioned. Whenever you select the **Open** option from the **File** menu; the **Open** dialog box will be displayed with the help of the **OpenFileDialog1.ShowDialog()** line of source code. In the **Open** dialog box, you will be prompted to enter a file name that you want to open. Once the file name is entered, it will be assigned to the variable **Str_File** with the help of **Str_File = OpenFileDialog1.FileName oRead = OpenText(OpenFileDialog1.FileName**. The code **oRead.ReadLine** reads the lines of the text from the file. The **Do While** loop continues to execute till **oRead. ReadLine** reads the last line.

Lines 49-53

```
Private Sub Rftbox_TextChanged(ByVal sender As System.Object, _
ByVal e As System.EventArgs)
If Not Rftbox.Text = "" Then
ContextMenuStrip1.Enabled = True
End If
End Sub
```

In the above given source code, the value of the **Text** property of the **RichTextBox** control is checked. If the **Rftbox** is not blank, then the value true will be assigned to the **Enabled** property of the **ContextMenuStrip**.

Lines 54-61

```
Private Sub SaveToolStripMenuItem1_Click(ByVal sender As System.Object, _
ByVal e As System.EventArgs) Handles SaveToolStripMenuItem1.Click
Dim oWrite As IO.StreamWriter
SaveFileDialog1.ShowDialog()
If SaveFileDialog1.FileName = " " Then Exit Sub
oWrite = CreateText(SaveFileDialog1.FileName & ".txt")
oWrite.Write(Rftbox.Text)
oWrite.Close()
Me.Text = SaveFileDialog1.FileName & " - Notepad"
End Sub
```

The above mentioned lines are for the **Save As** option of the **File** menu. Whenever you select the **Save** option from the **File** menu, the **Save As** dialog box will be displayed with the help of **SaveFileDialog1.ShowDialog()** line of the source code and it will prompt you to enter the file name. The line **oWrite = CreateText(SaveFileDialog1.FileName & ".txt")** will create the file with the extension *.txt*. Once you choose the **Save** button in the **Save As** dialog box, the file name will be added to the **Text** property of the form concatenated with **- Notepad**. The line **owrite.Close()** will close **StreamWriter**.

Lines 62-64
Private Sub ExitToolStripMenuItem_Click(ByVal sender As System.Object, _
ByVal e As System.EventArgs) Handles ExitToolStripMenuItem.Click
End
End Sub
The above lines of the source code are used for the **Exit** option of the **File** menu. With the help of these lines, you can exit from the application.
Lines 65-76
Private Sub DeleteToolStripMenuItem_Click(ByVal sender As System.Object,
ByVal e As System.EventArgs) Handles DeleteToolStripMenuItem.Click
Dim Bol_M As Boolean
ContextMenuStrip1.Enabled = False
If Rftbox.SelectedText = "" Then
Bol_M = MsgBox("No text to delete", MsgBoxStyle.Critical, "CADCIM")
ElseIf Not Len(Trim(Rftbox.SelectedText)) = Rftbox.TextLength Then
Bol_M = MsgBox("Please select all the text", MsgBoxStyle.Critical, "CADCIM")
End If
If Bol_M = True Then Exit Sub
Del_text = Trim(Rftbox.Text)
Rftbox.Clear()
End Sub
In the above mentioned lines, the **Delete** option of the **Edit** menu has been coded. If you do not select the whole text in the notepad file, the message **Please select all the text** will be displayed in the message box. And if you try to delete an empty file, it will give the message **No text to delete**.

Lines 77-79
Private Sub SelectAllToolStripMenuItem1_Click
(ByVal sender As System.Object, ByVal e As System.EventArgs)
Handles SelectAllToolStripMenuItem1.Click
Rftbox.SelectAll()
End Sub
The above mentioned lines are the source code for the **Select All** option. Whenever you choose the **Select All** option from the **Edit** menu, **Rftbox.SelectAll()** will select the entire text in the current file.

All the remaining options are coded using the same method as mentioned above.

Step 15
Execute the application; the output of the application will be displayed, as shown in Figure 6-35.

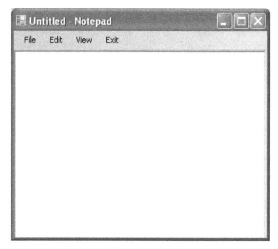

Figure 6-35   *Output of Application 3*

Step 16

If you choose **View > Status Bar** from the menu in this application, the status bar will be displayed, as shown in Figure 6-36. And if you want to hide the status bar, again choose **View > Status Bar**.

Step 17

If you right-click on the form, the context menu will be displayed, as shown in Figure 6-37.

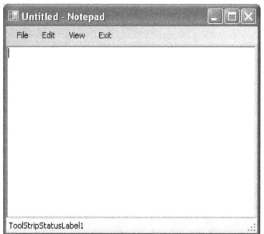

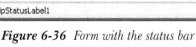

Figure 6-36   *Form with the status bar*

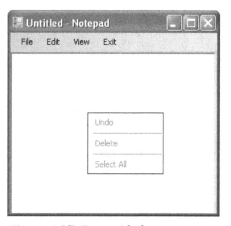

Figure 6-37   *Form with the context menu*

The following application illustrates the use of the **TabControl**:

Application 4

Create an application that will display an employee's and his department's details with the help of the **TabControl** controls.

This application will display a **TabControl** control with two tab pages, one having the entries for the employees's details and the other having entries for the department's details.

The following steps are required to create this application:

Step 1
Create a new project and save it as **c06_VB_NET_2008_04**.

Step 2
Add a **TabControl** control with two tab pages on the form.

Step 3
Change the **Text** property of the first tab page to **Employee Details**. Under this **TabControl**, add six **Label** controls, six **TextBox** controls, and three **Button** controls to the form.

Step 4
Change the **Text** property of the controls as follows:

Label1 to **Emp Id**
Label2 to **Emp Name**
Label3 to **Emp Address**
Label4 to **City**
Label5 to **State**
Label6 to **Country**

The form will appear as shown in Figure 6-38.

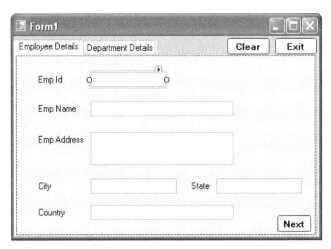

Figure 6-38 *Design mode of Application 4 with the* ***Employee Details*** *tab*

Step 5
Change the name property of the controls as follows:

TextBox1 to **Txt_Empno**
TextBox2 to **Txt_Ename**
TextBox3 to **Txt_Eadd**
TextBox4 to **Txt_City**
TextBox5 to **Txt_State**
TextBox6 to **Txt_Country**

Step 6
Change the **Text** property of the second tab page to **Department Details**. Under this tab page, add five **Label** controls, five **TextBox** controls, and three **Button** controls to the form.

Step 7
Change the **Text** property of the controls, as shown in Figure 6-39.

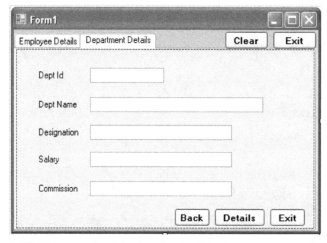

Figure 6-39 *Design mode of Application 4 with the* **Department Details** *tab*

Step 8
Change the **Name** property of the controls as follows:

TextBox1 to **Txt_Deptno**
TextBox2 to **Txt_Dname**
TextBox3 to **Txt_Desg**
TextBox4 to **Txt_Salary**
TextBox5 to **Txt_Comm**
Step 9
Double-click on the **Next** button and enter the following source code in the code window:

```
If Txt_Empno.Text = "" Or Txt_Ename.Text = "" Or _
Txt_Eadd.Text = "" Or Txt_City.Text = "" Or _
Txt_State.Text = "" Or Txt_Country.Text = "" Then          1
MsgBox("Please Fill All The Details", , "CADCIM, Employee Details")   2
Exit Sub                                                   3
End If                                                     4
```

```
If TabControl1.TabCount > 1 And TabControl1.SelectedIndex _
< TabControl1.TabCount - 1 Then                                              5
TabControl1.SelectedIndex = TabControl1.SelectedIndex + 1                    6
End If                                                                        7
```

Step 10
Doulble-click on the **Clear** button and enter the following source code:

```
Dim Ctrl As System.Windows.Forms.Control                                     8
If TabControl1.SelectedIndex = 0 Then                                        9
For Each Ctrl In TabPage2.Controls                                          10
If TypeOf Ctrl Is TextBox Then Ctrl.Text = ""                              11
Next                                                                        12
Else                                                                        13
For Each Ctrl In TabPage1.Controls                                         14
If TypeOf Ctrl Is TextBox Then Ctrl.Text = ""                             15
Next                                                                        16
End If                                                                      17
```

Step 11
Double-click on the **Back** button and enter the following source code:
```
If TabControl1.TabCount > 1 And _                                          18
TabControl1.SelectedIndex < TabControl1.TabCount + 1 Then                  19
TabControl1.SelectedIndex = TabControl1.SelectedIndex - 1                  20
End If                                                                      21
```

Step 12
Double-click on the **Details** button and enter the following source code:

```
If Txt_Deptno.Text = "" Or Txt_Dname.Text = "" Or _
Txt_Desg.Text = "" Or Txt_Salary.Text = "" Or Txt_Comm.Text = "" Then      22
MsgBox("Please Fill All The Details", , "CADCIM, Department Details")       23
Exit Sub                                                                    24
End If                                                                      25
MsgBox("Employee Name:" & Space(3) & _
Txt_Ename.Text & Chr(10) & Chr(13) & "Employee Address: " & _
Txt_Eadd.Text & Chr(10) & Chr(13) _& Space(18) & _
Txt_City.Text & ", " & Txt_State.Text & Chr(10) & _
Chr(13) & Space(Len("Employee Address: ")) _& _
Txt_Country.Text, , "CADCIM, Employee Details")                            26
MsgBox("Department Name: " & Txt_Dname.Text &
Chr(10) & Chr(13) & "Designation:    " & Txt_Desg.Text &
Chr(10) & Chr(13) & "Salary:        " _ & Txt_Salary.Text &
Chr(10) & Chr(13) & "Commission:     " &
Txt_Comm.Text, , "CADCIM Department Details")                              27
```

Explanation
The following is the line-by-line explanation of the above given source code:

Lines 1-7
If Txt_Empno.Text = "" Or Txt_Ename.Text = "" Or
Txt_Eadd.Text = "" Or Txt_City.Text = "" Or
Txt_State.Text = "" Or Txt_Country.Text = "" Then
MsgBox("Please Fill All The Details", , "CADCIM, Employee Details")
Exit Sub
End If
If TabControl1.TabCount > 1 And TabControl1.SelectedIndex
< TabControl1.TabCount - 1 Then
TabControl1.SelectedIndex = TabControl1.SelectedIndex + 1
End If

In the above source code, the **If** statement is used. The application will first check if the values for all the fields have been entered. If this is the case, then the control will be transferred to the next **If** statement. Here, it will check if there are more than one tabs in the application. Also, it will check if the current tab is not the last tab. If all these conditions are true, then the application will move to another tab control, once the values for all the fields have been entered. If you leave any of the fields blank or do not enter any value in any field at all, then the message **Please Fill All The Details** will be displayed.

Lines 8-17
Dim Ctrl As System.Windows.Forms.Control
If TabControl1.SelectedIndex = 0 Then
For Each Ctrl In TabPage2.Controls
If TypeOf Ctrl Is TextBox Then Ctrl.Text = ""
Next
Else
For Each Ctrl In TabPage1.Controls
If TypeOf Ctrl Is TextBox Then Ctrl.Text = ""
Next
End If

In the above lines, all the controls in the current form are declared as variable **Ctrl**. First, the application will check the values in all the fields. Next, it will check if the these controls are **TextBox** controls. If this condition is true, then the null string will be assigned to the controls. This condition will be checked for both the first and the second tab.

Lines 22-27
If Txt_Deptno.Text = "" Or Txt_Dname.Text = "" Or
Txt_Desg.Text = "" Or Txt_Salary.Text = "" Or Txt_Comm.Text = "" Then
MsgBox("Please Fill All The Details", , "CADCIM, Department Details")
Exit Sub
End If
MsgBox("Employee Name:" & Space(3) &
Txt_Ename.Text & Chr(10) & Chr(13) & "Employee Address: " &

Txt_Eadd.Text & Chr(10) & Chr(13) _& Space(18) &
Txt_City.Text & ", " & Txt_State.Text & Chr(10) &
Chr(13) & Space(Len("Employee Address: ")) _&
Txt_Country.Text, , "CADCIM, Employee Details")
MsgBox("Department Name: " & Txt_Dname.Text &
Chr(10) & Chr(13) & "Designation: " & Txt_Desg.Text &
Chr(10) & Chr(13) & "Salary: " _ & Txt_Salary.Text &
Chr(10) & Chr(13) & "Commission: " &
Txt_Comm.Text, , "CADCIM Department Details")

In the above lines, the source code will first check if the values for all the fields in the **Department Details** tab have been entered. If this is the case, then a message box with all the details entered for both the tabs will be displayed one-by-one. Otherwise, it will give the message **Please Fill All The Details** in a message box.

Step 13
Execute the application; the output of the form will be displayed, as shown in Figure 6-40. Enter the values in the fields and choose the **Next** button; the form will be displayed, as shown in Figure 6-41. Enter the values in the next tab and choose the **Details** button; a message box with entire information of the employee will be displayed, as shown in Figure 6-42. If you choose **OK** button from the message box; the **CADCIM, Department Details** message box will be displayed, as shown Figure 6-43.

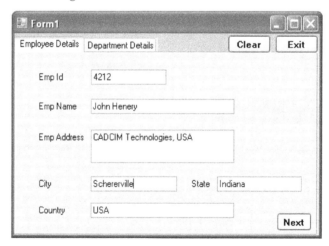

Figure 6-40 Output with the *Employee Details* tab chosen

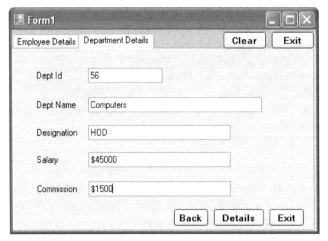

*Figure 6-41 Output with the **Department Details** tab chosen*

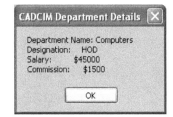

*Figure 6-42 The **CADCIM, Employee** Details message box*

*Figure 6-43 The **CADCIM Department** Details message box*

Self-Evaluation Test

Answer the following questions and then compare them to those given at the end of this chapter:

1. The controls that can hold other controls are known as _____.

2. The _____ property is used to determine the interior spacing between the controls.

3. The _____ property will determine the appearance of the border of the **Panel** control.

4. The _____ is a control that displays multiple tabs.

5. The _____ property is used to add the in-built menus to the form.

Review Questions

Answer the following questions:

1. The _____ property is used to determine the visibility of the grip on the **ToolStrip**.

2. The _____ is the area that is mostly located at the bottom of a window to show the status of the current operating program.

3. The _____ item is used to add text to the **StatusStrip** control.

4. The _____ property is used to determine the borders of the control that are bound to the container.

5. The _____ is also known as the shortcut menu.

Exercises

Exercise 1

Create an application to display a menu system with the menu names: **File**, **Format**, and **Help**, as shown in Figure 6-44. The following is the list of menu commands with the respective menu names:

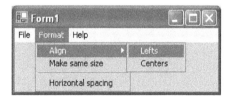

Figure 6-44 Form for Exercise 1

File: **New** and **Open**
Format: **Align**, **Make same size**, and **Horizontal spacing**
Help: **About**

Also, insert a separator bar between the **Make same size** and **Horizontal spacing** options.

The following are the submenus of the menu commands:

New: **New** and **Open**
Align: **Lefts** and **Centers**

Exercise 2

Create an application to display a context menu for the **Show** button with the menu commands: **Build**, **Debug**, and **Design**, as shown in Figure 6-45.

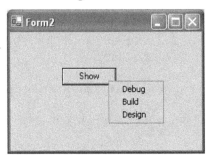

Figure 6-45 *Form for Exercise 2*

Answers to Self-Evaluation Test
1. containers, **2. Padding**, **3. BorderStyle**, **4. TabControl**, **5. Insert Standard Items**

Chapter 7

Components

Learning Objectives

After completing this chapter, you will be able to:
- *Work with BackgroundWorker component.*
- *Work with ErrorProvider component.*
- *Work with EventLog component.*
- *Work with FileSystemWatcher component.*
- *Work with HelpProvider component.*
- *Work with ImageList component.*
- *Work with MessageQueue component.*
- *Work with PerformanceCounter component.*
- *Work with ServiceController.*
- *Work with Process component.*
- *Work with Timer component.*

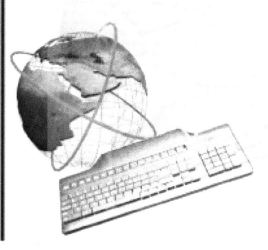

INTRODUCTION

In this chapter, you will learn about various components used in VB.NET and their implementation. These components are discussed next.

BackgroundWorker Component

The **BackgroundWorker** component is used to execute the time-consuming operations of the applications asynchronously in the background. To add the **BackgroundWorker** component to a form; double-click on it in the toolbar. Alternatively, drag and drop it on the form, it will be added to the component tray. You can view its properties in the **Properties** window. The **BackgroundWorker** component has four events, **Disposed**, **DoWork**, **ProgressChanged**, and **RunWorkerCompleted**. These events are discussed later in this chapter with the help of an application.

ErrorProvider Component

The **ErrorProvider** component is used to validate the user's input on a control. It is an indication of an error associated with a control on a form. The **ErrorProvider** component displays an error icon next to the target control. The default error icon is indicated by an exclamatory mark, which is red in color. When a user moves the cursor over the icon, a tooltip with the error message strip gets displayed. To add the **ErrorProvider** component to the form; double-click on it in the toolbar. Alternatively, drag and drop it on the form; it will be added to the component tray. You can view its properties in the **Properties** window. An example of the implementation of the **ErrorProvider** component is given below:

Step 1
Start a new project. Add an **ErrorProvider** component, a **TextBox** control, and a **Button** control to the form.

Step 2
Double-click on the **Button** control and enter the following source code to the code window:

```
If Not IsDate(TextBox1.Text) Then
ErrorProvider1.SetError(TextBox1, "Not a valid date.")
Else
ErrorProvider1.SetError(TextBox1, "")
End If
```

In the above given source code, if you enter an invalid date in the **TextBox** control and choose the **Button1** control; an error icon will be displayed next to the **TextBox** control, as shown in Figure 7-1. If you move the cursor over the icon; the error message **Not a valid date.** will be displayed.

Figure 7-1 *The form with the error icon*

EventLog Component

Event logging is a standard method with which an application in your system keeps a record of some software and hardware related events. With the help of this record, the system administrator can determine the cause of any hardware or software error in the system. Also, it tries to recover any lost data and prevent the errors from occurring again and again. The **EventLog** component is used to determine the conditions due to which an error has occurred. With the help of this component, you can connect the event logs both to local and remote computers. You can write the entries for these logs and also read the entries from the existing logs. To add the **EventLog** component to your form, double-click on it in the toolbar. Alternatively, you can drag and drop it on the form; it will be added to the component tray. You can view its properties in the **Properties** window.

You can also view the list of event logs of the servers that you have accessed. You can also add the event logs from the list to your form. To view the list, choose **Server Explorer > Servers > Event Logs**. Next, drag an event log from the list and drop it on the form; an instance of the added event log will be created. There are three event logs that are available on every system, **System**, **Security**, and **Application**. The **System** event log tracks the events that occur on the system component such as drivers and services. The **Security** event log tracks the security changes, user log-in, and so on. The **Application** event log tracks the events that occur in the registered application.

Writing an Event Source

The concept of event source is used in the event log system. The event source is used to determine whether an application can write an event log entry and the events with which those entries should associate. Before writing an event log, your application must register itself to the existing event source or create a new event source, which is given below:

Creating an Event Log

You can use the **EventLog.CreateEventSource()** method to create a new event source that will be associated with an event log. The following source code is used to check if an event source "**App**" exists in the application. If the event source does not exist in the application, then this code will create a new event source.

```
If Not EventLog.Exists("App") Then
EventLog.CreateEventSource("App", "Application")
```

FileSystemWatcher Component

The **FileSystemWatcher** component is connected to the directories and it monitors the changes in the directories or the files contained in it. The changes in the directories include creation of new files, addition of subdirectories, and renaming of subdirectories or files. The **FileSystemWatcher** component basically conveys the information about the changes made in the file system by raising relevant events. The **FileSystemWatcher** component can view the files on a local system, a network, or a remote computer. Note that it can view the changes within a directory, but not the changes made in the attributes of the root directory. For example, if you are working in a directory called **C:\My Pictures**, the component will view the changes within the **My Pictures** directory and not in the root directory, **C:**.

Some Important Properties of FileSystemWatcher Component

Some important properties of the **FileSystemWatcher** component are as follows:

EnableRaisingEvents

The **EnableRaisingEvents** property determines whether the component is active or not.

Filter

The **Filter** property is a string value, which is used to determine the files that are being viewed or monitored in a directory. Its default value is ***.***. If you want to view the changes in all the files, then set the value of the **Filter** property to "" (empty string).

IncludeSubdirectories

The **IncludeSubdirectories** property determines whether the subdirectories within the specified directory should be viewed or not.

NotifyFilter

The **NotifyFilter** property determines the type of changes to be viewed.

Path

The **Path** property determines the path of the directory to be viewed.

HelpProvider Component

The **HelpProvider** component provides the pop-up help or the online help for various controls, when the F1 key is pressed. With the help of the **HelpProvider** component, an HTML file is displayed with the linked topics. Help is associated with the **HelpProvider** component using the **HelpNamespace** property. You can use the **SetHelpString** method of the **HelpProvider** component to associate a specific help string with other controls, such as **Button** control. The string is associated with a control with the help of the **SetHelpString** method. It is displayed when you press the F1 key while the control is in focus. Similarly, you can use the **SetHelpKeyword** method to determine the help keyword associated with a control and the **SetHelpNavigator** method to determine the help in the form of table of contents, index, and so on. Also, the **HelpProvider** component provides additional properties to a control on the form. These properties are discussed next.

HelpKeyWord

It determines whether the **Help** keyword will be associated with the control or not.

HelpNavigator

It determines the constant that indicates the element of the help file to be displayed. It provides seven values to navigate **Topic**, **TopicOfContents**, **Index**, **Find**, **AssociatedIndex**, **Keywordindex**, and **TopicId**.

HelpString

It determines the **Help** string associated with the control.

ImageList Component

The **ImageList** component is used to store the collection of images. These images can be displayed with the help of different controls. To add the **ImageList** component to the form, drag and drop it on the form; it will be added to the component tray. To view some of the important properties of the **ImageList** component, choose the forward arrow on the top right corner of the **ImageList** component, as shown in Figure 7-2.

Figure 7-2 *Some important properties of the **ImageList** component*

Some important properties of the **ImageList** component are discussed next.

Image Size

The **Image Size** property is used to set the size of the image to be displayed.

Image Bit Depth

The **Image Bit Depth** property is used to change the bit depth of images that are imported to the form.

Choose Images

The **Choose Images** property is used to add images to the image collection list of the **ImageList** component. To add an image to the **ImageList** control, choose the **Choose images** property from the Smart Tags or choose **Images** from the **Properties** window; the **Images Collection Editor** dialog box will be displayed, as shown in Figure 7-3. Choose the **Add** button; the **Open** dialog box will be displayed. Select the image that you want to add to the **ImageList** component; the image will be added in the **Images Collection Editor** dialog box. Choose the **OK** button from the **Images Collection Editor** dialog box. You can use the **ImageList** component with all the controls that have the **ImageList** property.

MessageQueue Component

The **MessageQueue** component is used to introduce a message-based communication within an application. With the help of this component, an application can send and receive messages in a queue on the **Message Queuing** servers, create and delete queues, explore the existing queues, and so on. The **MessageQueue** component basically provides a central place to store and remove the data. To add the **MessageQueue** component, double-click on it in the toolbox. Alternatively, you can drag and drop it on the form. Note that this component will be added in the component tray only if you have message queue configured on your system. If an error message is displayed while adding this component to the form, it means that the message queue is not configured on your system. To configure the message queue, follow the steps given next.

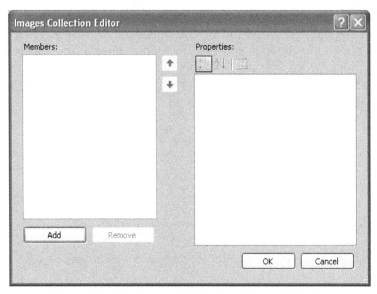

Figure 7-3 *The **Images Collection Editor** dialog box*

1.   Choose **Start > Settings > Control Panel**; the **Control Panel** window will be displayed, as shown in Figure 7-4.

Figure 7-4 *The **Control Panel** window*

2. Double-click on the **Add or Remove Programs** icon; the **Add or Remove Programs** window will be displayed, as shown in Figure 7-5. Choose the **Add/Remove Windows Components** button on the left of the window; the **Windows Components Wizard** dialog box will be displayed, as shown in Figure 7-6.

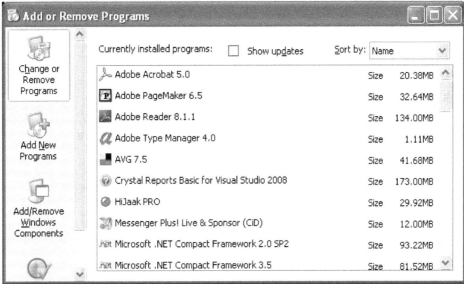

Figure 7-5 The Add or Remove Programs window

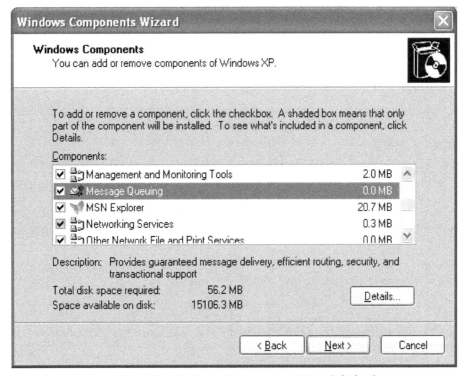

Figure 7-6 The Windows Components Wizard dialog box

3.   Select the **Message Queuing** check box from the **Components** area.

4.   Choose the **Details** button in the dialog box; the **Message Queuing** dialog box will be displayed, as shown in Figure 7-7. Select all the check boxes in the **Subcomponents of Message Queuing** area. Choose the **OK** button; it will return to the **Windows Components Wizard** dialog box.

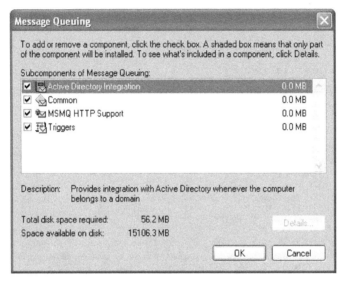

*Figure 7-7 The **Message Queuing** dialog box*

5.   Choose the **Next** button in the **Windows Components Wizard** dialog box; it will prompt you to insert the CD of the operating system, which is already installed on your system. Insert the CD. After the configuration is completed, choose the **Finish** button.

There are four types of queue in the **MessageQueue** component, which are as follows:

Outgoing
The **Outgoing** queue is used to store the messages temporarily before they are sent to their destinations.

Public
The **Public** queue can be used by different application on different servers within a network.

Private
These type of queues can be used only by the local server.

System
It contains the messages sent from the system and the dead messages. These dead messages are not meant for delivery.

PerformanceCounter Component

The **PerformanceCounter** component is used to view the behavior of the performance objects such as processors, memory, disks, and so on. There is a specific category for all the performance counters. For example, the **Available Bytes** and **Cache Bytes** counters fall under the **Memory** category. You can create your own category and then specify the counters. There are two ways of creating the category, using the **Server Explorer** and through coding. In this section, you will learn to create it using the **Server Explorer** only.

Creating New Category of Performance Counter Using Server Explorer

To create a new category of performance counters, choose **Server Explorer > Servers > Computer name > Performance Counters** from the design window of the current application. Right-click on **Performance Counter** and then choose **Create New Category**; the **Performance Counter Builder** dialog box will be displayed, as shown in Figure 7-8. You can enter the values for all the parameters according to your requirement and then, choose the **OK** button; the new category will be added to the **Performance Counter** list.

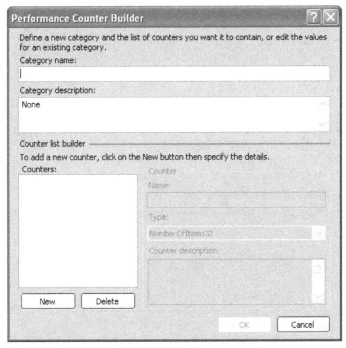

*Figure 7-8 The **Performance Counter Builder** dialog box*

ServiceController Component

The **ServiceController** component is used to connect to windows services and it also allows you to control the behavior of the existing services. Additionally, you can run or stop a service, manipulate a service or get information about a specific service. To add the **ServiceController** component to your form, double-click on it in the toolbar. Alternatively, drag and drop it on the form; it will be added to the component tray. You can view its properties in the **Properties** window.

Process Component

The **Process** component is used to provide access to the processes that are running on computer. The **Process** component can be used to access the processes on both the remote and the local computers. On local computers, you can control most of the functions such as starting and terminating a process, querying it for any specific information, and so on. But on the remote computers, you cannot start and stop a process. You can only query it for any specific information. For starting a process on a local computer, you can use the following source code:

```
Private Sub Button1_Click(ByVal sender As System.Object,
ByVal e As System.EventArgs) Handles Button1.Click
Dim Process As New Process()
Process.StartInfo.FileName = "D:\process.txt"
Process.StartInfo.WindowStyle = ProcessWindowStyle.Maximized
Process.Start()
End Sub
```

In this source code, you are coding a **Button** control to start a process. Here, the process name is **info_text**. For starting any process, you need to specify its full path. The **Start()** method starts the process. In this case, when you choose **Button1** on the form, the text file **info_text** will be displayed.

Timer Component

The **Timer** component sets the time interval for executing an event. This control helps you in executing the event regularly after a given time interval.

Properties of the Timer Component

There are two important properties of the **Timer** control, which are as follows:

Enabled

The **Enabled** property of the **Timer** control can be used to turn the timer on and off.

Interval

It sets the time interval between the events. The time is set in milliseconds.

The following application illustrates the use of the **BackgroundWorker** Component:

Application 1

Create an application that will start a process and show its progress with the help of the **BackgroundWorker** component.

The following steps are required to create this application:

Step 1
Start a new project and save it as **c07_VB_NET_2008_01**.

Step 2
Add two **Button** controls, a **Label** control, a **ProgressBar** control, a **ListView** control, and a **BackgroundWorker** component to the form.

Step 3
Change the **Text** property of the controls as follows:

Form1 to **BackgroundWorker**
Button1 to **Start**
Button2 to **Cancel**
Label1 to **Progress......**

The design mode of the form will be similar to Figure 7-9.

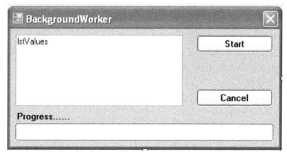

Figure 7-9 *The design mode of Application 1*

Step 4
Change the **Name** property of the controls as follows:

ListView to **lstValues**
Button1 to **btnStart**
Button2 to **btnCancel**
ProgressBar1 to **prgThread**
BackgroundWorker1 to **TestWorker**

Step 5
Double-click on the form and enter the following source code in the code window. The line numbers on the right are not a part of the program and are for reference only.

```
Option Strict Off                                                    1
Public Class Form1                                                   2
Public Glb_Var As Integer                                           3
Public Glb_Str As String                                            4
Private Sub btnStart_Click(ByVal sender As System.Object, _
```

```
ByVal e As System.EventArgs) Handles btnStart.Click                    5
btnStart.Enabled = False                                               6
btnCancel.Enabled = True                                               7
lstValues.Items.Clear()                                                8
prgThread.Value = 0                                                    9
TestWorker = New System.ComponentModel.BackgroundWorker                10
TestWorker.WorkerReportsProgress = True                                11
TestWorker.WorkerSupportsCancellation = True                           12
TestWorker.RunWorkerAsync()                                            13
End Sub                                                                14

Private Sub TestWorker_DoWork(ByVal sender As Object, _
ByVal e As System.ComponentModel.DoWorkEventArgs) _
Handles TestWorker.DoWork                                              15
Dim ListText As String                                                 16
For Value As Integer = 0 To 100                                        17
If TestWorker.CancellationPending Then                                 18
Exit For                                                               19
End If                                                                 20
ListText = String.Concat("CADCIM ", Value)                             21
TestWorker.ReportProgress(Value, ListText)                             22
Threading.Thread.Sleep(100)                                            23
Next                                                                   24
End Sub                                                                25

Private Sub TestWorker_ProgressChanged(ByVal sender As Object, _
ByVal e As System.ComponentModel.ProgressChangedEventArgs) _
Handles TestWorker.ProgressChanged                                     26
prgThread.Value = e.ProgressPercentage                                 27
lstValues.Items.Add(e.UserState)                                       28
End Sub                                                                29

Private Sub TestWorker_RunWorkerCompleted(ByVal sender As Object, _
ByVal e As System.ComponentModel.RunWorkerCompletedEventArgs) _
Handles TestWorker.RunWorkerCompleted                                  30
btnStart.Enabled = True                                                31
btnCancel.Enabled = False                                              32
End Sub                                                                33

Private Sub btnCancel_Click(ByVal sender As Object, _
ByVal e As System.EventArgs) Handles btnCancel.Click                   34
TestWorker.CancelAsync()                                               35
End Sub                                                                36
End Class                                                              37
```

Explanation
The line-by-line explanation of the above given source code is as follows:

Line 1
Option Strict Off
In this line, the **Option Strict** is set to **Off**. So, all the variables should be declared before using them.

Line 2
Public Class Form1
This is the declaration of the form.

Line 3
Public Glb_Var As Integer
In this line, the **Integer** variable **Glb_Var** is declared as a global variable.

Line 4
Public Glb_Str As String
In this line, the **String** variable **Glb_Str** is declared as a global variable.

Line 5
Private Sub btnStart_Click(ByVal sender As System.Object, _
ByVal e As System.EventArgs) Handles btnStart.Click
In this line, the coding for the **Click** event of the **Start** button is done.

Lines 6-14
btnStart.Enabled = False
btnCancel.Enabled = True
lstValues.Items.Clear()
prgThread.Value = 0
TestWorker = New System.ComponentModel.BackgroundWorker
TestWorker.WorkerReportsProgress = True
TestWorker.WorkerSupportsCancellation = True
TestWorker.RunWorkerAsync()
End Sub
In these lines, when the user chooses the **Start** button, the process will start and the **Start** button will be disabled, while the **Cancel** button will be enabled. At the starting point, the **ListView** control will be blank and the value of the **ProgressBar** control will also be set to zero. The **WorkerReportProgress** property and the **WorkerSupportsCancellation** property of the **BackgroundWorker** component are set to **True**. The **RunWorkerAsync** property will start the execution of the background operation. The **End Sub** indicates the end of the procedure.

Line 15
Private Sub TestWorker_DoWork(ByVal sender As Object, _
ByVal e As System.ComponentModel.DoWorkEventArgs) _
Handles TestWorker.DoWork
This line refers to the **DoWork** event of the **BackgroundWorker** component.

Lines 16-25

```
Dim ListText As String
For Value As Integer = 0 To 100
If TestWorker.CancellationPending Then
Exit For
End If
ListText = String.Concat("CADCIM ", Value)
TestWorker.ReportProgress(Value, ListText)
Threading.Thread.Sleep(100)
Next
End Sub
```

In these lines, the variable **ListText** is declared as a string data type. Another variable **Value** is declared as an integer data type and the value 0 to 100 is assigned to it. This code will basically concatenate the values of the **ListText** and **Value** variables and display them in the **ListView** control. The **ReportProgress** method of the **BackgroundWorker** component raises the **ProgressChanged** event of the **BackgroundWorker** component. The **Threading** namespace contains the **Thread** class and the **Sleep** is the method of the **Thread** class. The **Sleep** method is used to suspend the current thread for a specific period of time.

Lines 26-29

```
Private Sub TestWorker_ProgressChanged(ByVal sender As Object, _
ByVal e As System.ComponentModel.ProgressChangedEventArgs) _
Handles TestWorker.ProgressChanged
prgThread.Value = e.ProgressPercentage
lstValues.Items.Add(e.UserState)
End Sub
```

These lines refer to the **ProgressChanged** event of the **BackgroundWorker** component. The **e.ProgressPercentage** will return the integer value, which is assigned to the **Value** property of the progress bar **PrgThread**. This value will be added to the listview **lstValues**.

Line 30

```
Private Sub TestWorker_RunWorkerCompleted(ByVal sender As Object, _
ByVal e As System.ComponentModel.RunWorkerCompletedEventArgs) _
Handles TestWorker.RunWorkerCompleted
```

This line refers to the **RunWorkerCompleted** event of the **BackgroundWorker** component.

Lines 31-33

```
btnStart.Enabled = True
btnCancel.Enabled = False
End Sub
```

In these lines, the **Start** button is enabled and the **Cancel** button is disabled.

Lines 34-35

```
Private Sub btnCancel_Click(ByVal sender As Object, _
ByVal e As System.EventArgs) Handles btnCancel.Click
TestWorker.CancelAsync()
```

These lines refer to the **Click** event of the **Cancel** button. The **CancelAsync** method of the **BackgroundWorker** component is used to cancel the pending background operations.

Line 35
End Sub
This line indicates the end of the procedure.

Line 36
End Class
This line indicates the end of the class **Form1**.

Step 6
Execute the application; the output form will be displayed. Choose the **Start** button on the form; the output will be displayed, as shown in Figure 7-10.

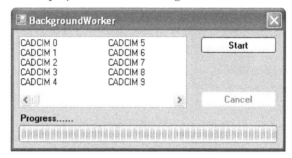

Figure 7-10 The output of Application 1

The following application illustrates use of the **ErrorProvider** and **ImageList** components:

Application 2

Create an application that will prompt the user to enter his personal details in a form and then submit them.

In this application, the user will be prompted to enter his personal details in a form. In case, the user leaves any of the fields blank, an error icon will be displayed.

The following steps are required to create this application:

Step 1
Start a new project and save it as **c07_VB_NET_2008_02**.

Step 2
Add six **Label** controls, six **TextBox** controls, three **Button** controls, a **ListView** control, and a **GroupBox** control to the form. Also, add an **ErrorProvider** component and an **ImageList** component that will be added to the component tray.

The design mode of the application will be similar to Figure 7-11.

Figure 7-11 *The design mode of Application 2*

Step 3
Change the **Name** property of the controls as follows:

TextBox1 to **Txt_Name**
TextBox2 to **Txt_Address**
TextBox3 to **Txt_Phone**
TextBox4 to **Txt_Designation**
TextBox5 to **Txt_JDate**
TextBox6 to **Txt_image**
Button1 to **Btn_upload**
Button2 to **Btn_Submit**
Button3 to **Btn_Exit**
GroupBox1 to **Grp_image**
ListView1 to **LstView_Image**

Step 4
Double-click on the form and enter the following source code in the code window:

```
Dim Bol As Boolean                                                      1
Private Sub Form1_Load(ByVal sender As System.Object, _
ByVal e As System.EventArgs) Handles MyBase.Load                        2
Grp_Image.Visible = False                                               3
Bol = False                                                             4
End Sub                                                                 5
Private Function ValidateTextBox(ByVal Txt As TextBox) As Boolean       6
```

```
If Txt.Text = "" Then                                                    7
Me.ErrorProvider1.SetError(Txt, "Please enter the text")                 8
Txt.Focus()                                                              9
End If                                                                   10
End Function                                                             11

Private Sub Btn_upload_Click(ByVal sender As System.Object, _
ByVal e As System.EventArgs) Handles Btn_upload.Click                    12
Grp_Image.Visible = True                                                 13
End Sub                                                                  14

Private Sub Btn_Exit_Click(ByVal sender As System.Object, _
ByVal e As System.EventArgs) Handles Btn_Exit.Click                      15
End                                                                      16
End Sub                                                                  17

Private Sub LstView_Image_DoubleClick(ByVal sender As Object, _
ByVal e As System.EventArgs) Handles LstView_Image.DoubleClick           18
Dim str As String                                                        19
Dim indexs As Integer = (LstView_Image.SelectedItems(0).Index)           20
str = LstView_Image.Items(indexs).Text                                   21
Txt_image.Text = str                                                     22
If Txt_image.Text = "" Then                                              23
Me.ErrorProvider1.SetError(Txt_image, _
"Please select the image from the Listview")                             24
Exit Sub                                                                 25
End If                                                                    26
Grp_Image.Visible = False                                                27
End Sub                                                                  28

Private Sub Txt_Address_GotFocus(ByVal sender As Object, _
ByVal e As System.EventArgs) Handles Txt_Address.GotFocus                29
ValidateTextBox(Txt_Name)                                                30
Text_Checked(Txt_Name)                                                   31
End Sub                                                                  32

Private Sub Txt_JDate_GotFocus(ByVal sender As Object, _
ByVal e As System.EventArgs) Handles Txt_JDate.GotFocus                  33
ValidateTextBox(Txt_Desgination)                                         34
Text_Checked(Txt_Desgination)                                            35
End Sub                                                                  36

Private Sub Txt_Phone_GotFocus(ByVal sender As Object, _
ByVal e As System.EventArgs) Handles Txt_Phone.GotFocus                  37
ValidateTextBox(Txt_Address)                                             38
Text_Checked(Txt_Address)                                                39
End Sub                                                                  40
```

```
Private Sub Txt_image_GotFocus(ByVal sender As Object, _
ByVal e As System.EventArgs) Handles Txt_image.GotFocus          41
ValidateTextBox(Txt_JDate)                                        42
Text_Checked(Txt_JDate)                                           43
End Sub                                                           44

Private Sub Txt_image_KeyPress(ByVal sender As Object, _
ByVal e As System.Windows.Forms.KeyPressEventArgs) _
Handles Txt_image.KeyPress                                        45
Me.Btn_upload.Focus()                                             46
End Sub                                                           47

Private Sub Btn_Submit_Click(ByVal sender As System.Object, _
ByVal e As System.EventArgs) Handles Btn_Submit.Click             48
If Txt_image.Text = "" Then                                       49
Me.ErrorProvider1.SetError(Txt_image, _
"Please select the image from the Listview")                      50
Exit Sub                                                          51
End If                                                            52
MsgBox("Thanks For The Registration")                             53
End Sub                                                           54
Private Sub Text_Checked(ByVal txt As TextBox)                    55
If Not txt.Text = "" Then                                         56
Me.ErrorProvider1.Clear()                                         57
End If                                                            58
End Sub                                                           59
```

Explanation
The line-by-line explanation of the above given source code is as follows:

Lines 6-11
Private Function ValidateTextBox(ByVal Txt As TextBox) As Boolean
If Txt.Text = "" Then
Me.ErrorProvider1.SetError(Txt, "Please enter the text")
Txt.Focus()
End If
End Function
In these lines, the function **ValidateTextBox** is declared as **Boolean** type. If an empty string is assigned to the **Text** property of the **TextBox** control, an error icon will be displayed because of the **ErrorProvider** component. If you move the cursor over the icon, the message **Please enter the text** will be displayed.

Lines 18-28
Private Sub LstView_Image_DoubleClick(ByVal sender As Object, _
ByVal e As System.EventArgs) Handles LstView_Image.DoubleClick
Dim str As String
Dim indexs As Integer = (LstView_Image.SelectedItems(0).Index)

str = LstView_Image.Items(indexs).Text
Txt_image.Text = str
If Txt_image.Text = "" Then
Me.ErrorProvider1.SetError(Txt_image,
"Please select the image from the Listview")
Exit Sub
End If
Grp_Image.Visible = False
End Sub

In these lines, the **Double-Click** event of the **ListView** control is coded. It means whenever you double-click on an image from the **ListView** control, the image name will be added to the **TextBox** control associated with it. If you do not select any image, then the **ErrorProvider** component will give an error message **Please select the image from the Listview**.

Lines 29-32
Private Sub Txt_Address_GotFocus(ByVal sender As Object, _
ByVal e As System.EventArgs) Handles Txt_Address.GotFocus
ValidateTextBox(Txt_Name)
Text_Checked(Txt_Name)
End Sub

These lines refer to the **GotFocus** event of the **Txt_Address** textbox. Here, the **Txt_Name** textbox will be validated and checked.

Step 5
Execute the application; the output form will be displayed, as shown in Figure 7-12. Enter the values in all the textboxes and then choose the **Submit** button; a message box with the message **Thanks For The Registration** will be displayed, as shown in Figure 7-13.

Figure 7-12 *The output form of Application 2*

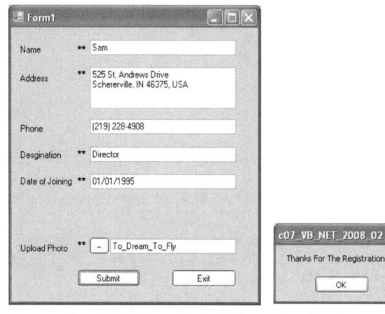

Figure 7-13 *Message displayed after entering the values*

The following application illustrates the use of the **FileSystemWatcher** component:

Application 3

Create an application that will use the **FileSystemWatcher** component to keep a watch on a particular directory.

The following steps are required to create this application:

Step 1
Start a new project and save it as **c07_VB_NET_2008_03**.

Step 2
Add a **FileSystemWatcher** component to the form.

Step 3
Double-click on the form and enter the following source code in the code window:

```
Private Sub Form1_Load(ByVal sender As Object, _
ByVal e As System.EventArgs) Handles Me.Load                          1
With FileSystemWatcher1                                               2
.Path = My.Computer.FileSystem.CurrentDirectory & "\FilesystemWatcher" 3
.EnableRaisingEvents = True                                           4
.IncludeSubdirectories = False                                       5
.Filter = "TxtFilesystem.txt"                                        6
```

```
End With                                                          7
End Sub                                                           8

Private Sub FileSystemWatcher1_Created(ByVal sender As Object, _
ByVal e As System.IO.FileSystemEventArgs) _
Handles FileSystemWatcher1.Created                               9
MsgBox("New Text file" & e.Name & " has been created")          10
End Sub                                                          11

Private Sub FileSystemWatcher1_Deleted(ByVal sender As Object, _
ByVal e As System.IO.FileSystemEventArgs) _
Handles FileSystemWatcher1.Deleted                              12
MsgBox("Text file" & e.Name & " has been deleted")             13
End Sub                                                         14
```

Explanation

In the above source code, the **Load** event of the form is coded first. Then, the **With-End With** statements are used for assigning the values to different properties of the **FileSystemWatcher** component. The **FileSystemWatcher** component will keep a watch on the current directory of the file system. Therefore, whenever a new file is created in the particular directory, the application will give the message **Text file has been created** and whenever an existing file has been deleted, the message **Text file has been deleted** will be displayed.

The following application illustrates the use of the **Process** component:

Application 4

Create an application that will search and display the current processes and applications. It should also display the list of visible applications, processes, and ids.

This application will prompt the user to enter the name of a process or an application to check whether the process or the application exists or not. The application will also enable the user to view the list of visible applications, processes, and ids.

The following steps are required to create this application:

Step 1
Start a new project and save it as **c07_VB_NET_2008_04**.

Step 2
Add three **GroupBox** controls, five **Button** controls, and three **TextBox** controls. The resultant form will appear similar to Figure 7-14.

Step 3
Go to **Solution Explorer** and double-click on the **My Project** option; a window with different options will be displayed, as shown in Figure 7-15.

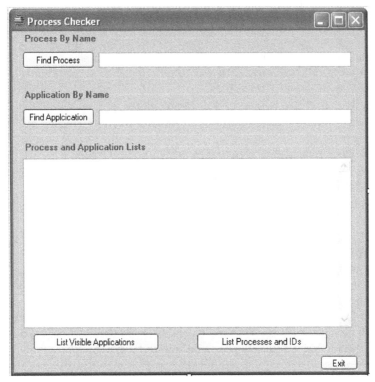

Figure 7-14 *The design mode of Application 4*

Step 4
Select the **References** option from the window and then choose the **Add** button; the **Add Reference** dialog box will be displayed, as shown in Figure 7-16. Now, go back to the design window.

Step 5
Change the **Name** property of the controls as follows:

Form1 to **Frm_ProcessChk**
Button1 to **Btn_Proc**
Button2 to **Btn_App**
Button3 to **Btn_Application**
Button4 to **Btn_Process**
Button5 to **Btn_Exit**
TextBox1 to **Txt_Process**
TextBox2 to **Txt_Application**
TextBox3 to **Txt_ListProcess**

Step 6
Double-click on the form and enter the following source code in the code window:

```
Imports System.Text                                                     1
Imports System.Management                                               2
```

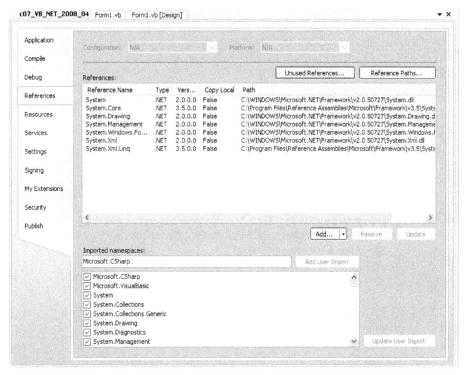

Figure 7-15 *The window displayed on double-clicking on the* **MyProject** *option*

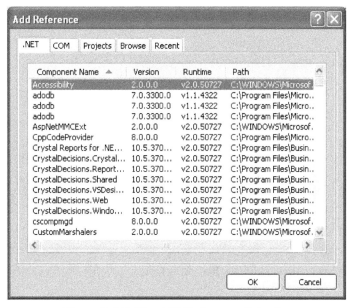

Figure 7-16 *The* **Add Reference** *dialog box*

```vbnet
Public Class Frm_ProcessChk                                          3

Private Sub Btn_Application_Click(ByVal sender As System.Object, _
ByVal e As System.EventArgs) Handles Btn_Application.Click           4
Dim StrBlder As New StringBuilder()                                  5
Dim pProc As New Process()                                           6

For Each pProc In Process.GetProcesses(".")                          7
If pProc.MainWindowTitle.Length > 0 Then
StrBlder.Append("Window Title: "+ _
pProc.MainWindowTitle.ToString() + Environment.NewLine)             8
StrBlder.Append("Process Name: " + _
pProc.ProcessName.ToString() + Environment.NewLine)                 9
StrBlder.Append("Window Handle: " + _
pProc.MainWindowHandle.ToString() + Environment.NewLine)            10
StrBlder.Append("Memory Allocation:  " + _
pProc.PrivateMemorySize64.ToString() + Environment.NewLine)         11
StrBlder.Append(Environment.NewLine)                                12
End If                                                              13
Next                                                               14
Txt_ListProcess.Text = StrBlder.ToString                           15
End Sub                                                             16

Private Sub Btn_Exit_Click(ByVal sender As System.Object, _
ByVal e As System.EventArgs) Handles Btn_Exit.Click                17
End                                                                18
End Sub                                                            19

Private Sub Btn_Process_Click(ByVal sender As System.Object, _
ByVal e As System.EventArgs) Handles Btn_Process.Click             20
Dim Str_Bld As New StringBuilder()                                 21
Dim MgtClass As New ManagementClass("Win32_Process")               22
Dim MgtObj As New ManagementObject()                               23
For Each MgtObj In MgtClass.GetInstances                           24
Str_Bld.Append("Name:  " & MgtObj("Name") & Environment.NewLine)   25
Str_Bld.Append("ID:  " & MgtObj("ProcessId") & Environment.NewLine) 26
Str_Bld.Append(Environment.NewLine)                                27
Next                                                               28
Txt_ListProcess.Text = Str_Bld.ToString                            29
End Sub                                                            30

Private Sub Btn_App_Click(ByVal sender As System.Object,
ByVal e As System.EventArgs) Handles Btn_App.Click                 31
Dim Bol_Proc As Boolean = False                                    32
Dim Proc As New Process()                                          33
Dim AppName As String = Trim(Txt_Application.Text)                 34
For Each Proc In Process.GetProcesses(".")                         35
If Proc.ProcessName.ToLower() = AppName.ToLower() Then             36
```

```
Bol_Proc = True                                                          37
End If                                                                   38
Next                                                                     39
If Bol_Proc = True Then                                                  40
MessageBox.Show(Txt_Application.Text + " process name found.", _
"CADCIM Technologies")                                                   41
Else                                                                     42
MessageBox.Show(Txt_Application.Text + " process name not found.", _
"CADCIM Technologies")                                                   43
End If                                                                   44
End Sub                                                                  45

Private Sub Btn_Proc_Click(ByVal sender As System.Object, _
ByVal e As System.EventArgs) Handles Btn_Proc.Click                      46
Dim MgtClass As New ManagementClass("Win32_Process")                     47
Dim MgtObj As New ManagementObject()                                     48
Dim Bol_Proc As Boolean = False                                          49
Dim Str_Proc As String = Trim(Txt_Process.Text)                          50
For Each MgtObj In MgtClass.GetInstances()                               51
If MgtObj("Name").ToString().ToLower() = Str_Proc.ToLower() Then         52
Bol_Proc = True                                                          53
End If                                                                   54
Next                                                                     55
If Bol_Proc = True Then                                                  56
MessageBox.Show(Txt_Process.Text & " process name found.", _
"CADCIM Technologies")                                                   57
Else                                                                     58
MessageBox.Show(Txt_Process.Text & " process name not found.", _
"CADCIM Technologies")                                                   59
End If                                                                   60
End Sub                                                                  61
End Class                                                                62
```

Explanation

The line-by-line explanation of the above given source code is given as follows:

Lines 1-2
Imports System.Text
Imports System.Management
In these lines, the **Text** and **Management** namespaces are imported.

Line 3
Public Class Frm_ProcessChk
In this line, the class **Frm_ProcessChk** is declared.

Lines 7-15
For Each pProc In Process.GetProcesses(".")
If pProc.MainWindowTitle.Length > 0 Then

```
StrBlder.Append("Window Title: " + pProc.MainWindowTitle.ToString() + _ Environment.
NewLine)
StrBlder.Append("Process Name: " + pProc.ProcessName.ToString() + _ Environment.
NewLine)
StrBlder.Append("Window Handle: " + pProc.MainWindowHandle.ToString() + _ Envi-
ronment.NewLine)
StrBlder.Append("Memory Allocation:  " + pProc.PrivateMemorySize64.ToString() + _
Environment.NewLine)
StrBlder.Append(Environment.NewLine)
End If
Next
Txt_ListProcess.Text = StrBlder.ToString
```

In these lines, the **For** loop is used to check all the processes in the system. Whenever a user chooses the **ListAvailableApplications** button, all the applications running on the system will be listed in the multiline **TextBox** control and the information about **Window Title**, **Process Name**, **Window Handle**, and **Memory Allocation** will be displayed.

Lines 20-29

```
Private Sub Btn_Process_Click(ByVal sender As System.Object, _
ByVal e As System.EventArgs) Handles Btn_Process.Click
Dim Str_Bld As New StringBuilder()
Dim MgtClass As New ManagementClass("Win32_Process")
Dim MgtObj As New ManagementObject()
For Each MgtObj In MgtClass.GetInstances
Str_Bld.Append("Name:  " & MgtObj("Name") & Environment.NewLine)
Str_Bld.Append("ID:  " & MgtObj("ProcessId") & Environment.NewLine)
Str_Bld.Append(Environment.NewLine)
Next
Txt_ListProcess.Text = Str_Bld.ToString
```

In these lines, the variable **MgtClass** is declared as the **ManagementClass** type. The variable **MgtObj** is declared as an instance of the **ManagementObject** class. The **For Each** loop is used to check the processes of the system. Whenever a user chooses the **ListProcesses and IDs** button, the **For** loop starts searching for all the executable processes on the system and all of them will be displayed in the multiline **TextBox** control.

Step 7

Execute the application; the output of the application will be displayed. Enter any process that you want to search, for example, **smss.exe**, in the **Find Process** textbox. Next, choose the **Find Process** button; a message box with the message **smss.exe process name found.** will be displayed, as shown in Figure 7-17. Similarly, if you want to search any application, then enter the name of the application in the textbox on the right of the **Find Application** button, and then choose the **Find Application** button. Next, if you want to view all the currently visible applications, the choose **List Visible Applications** button; all the visible applications will be listed in the textbox, as shown in Figure 7-18. Similarly, to view all the processes, choose the **List Processes and IDs** button, all the processes will be listed in the textbox, as shown in Figure 7-19.

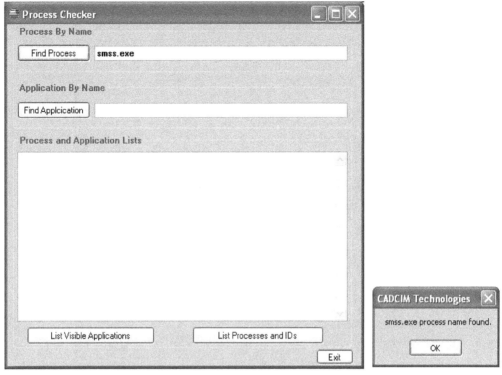

Figure 7-17 *The output of the Application 4 in case of finding a process*

The following application illustrates the use of the **ServiceController** component:

Application 5

Create an application that will start and stop a process.

The following application will start and stop a process. If you enter the process that does not exist in the system, the application will give an error message.

The following steps are required to create this application:

Step 1
Start an application and save it as **c07_VB_NET_2008_05**.

Step 2
Add a **Label** control, a **TextBox** control, a **ServiceController** component, and two **Button** controls to the form.

The resultant form will appear as shown in Figure 7-20.

Step 3
Change the **Name** property of the controls as follows:

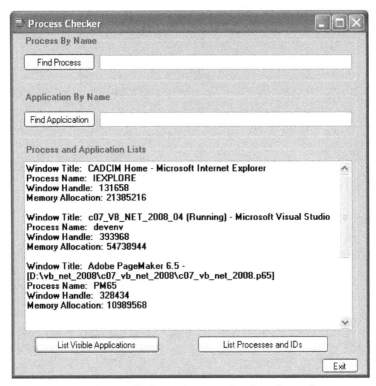

Figure 7-18 *All the applications listed in the textbox*

TextBox1 to **Txt_SerName**
ServiceController1 to **ServiceContr**

Step 4
Double-click on the form and enter the following source code:

Imports System.Collections.Generic	1
Imports System.ComponentModel	2
Imports System.ServiceProcess	3
Public Class Form1	4
Private Sub Form1_Load(ByVal sender As Object, _	
ByVal e As System.EventArgs) Handles Me.Load	5
Button2.Enabled = False	6
Txt_SerName.Focus()	7
End Sub	8
Private Sub Button1_Click(ByVal sender As System.Object, _	
ByVal e As System.EventArgs) Handles Button1.Click	9
Try	10
If Trim(Txt_SerName.Text) = "" Then	
MessageBox.Show("Enter the Service Name", "CADCIM Technologies")	11
Exit Sub	12

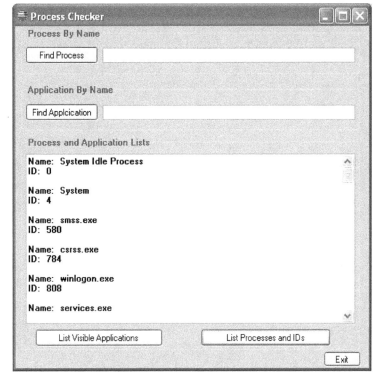

Figure 7-19 *All the applications listed in textbox*

Figure 7-20 *The design mode of Application 5*

ServiceContr = New ServiceController(Trim(Txt_SerName.Text))	13
If ServiceContr.Status = ServiceControllerStatus.Running Then	14
MessageBox.Show("Service already running...........", "CADCIM Technologies", _	
MessageBoxButtons.OK, MessageBoxIcon.Information)	15
Button2.Enabled = True	16
Button1.Enabled = False	17
Exit Sub	18
End If	19
If Not Trim(Txt_SerName.Text) = "" Then	20
ServiceContr.Start()	21

```
Button2.Enabled = True                                                    22
Button1.Enabled = False                                                   23
Label1.Text = Txt_SerName.Text & " " & "Service started........"          24
Else                                                                      25
End If                                                                    26
Catch ex As Exception                                                     27
MsgBox(ex.Message)                                                        28
End Try                                                                   29
End Sub                                                                   30

Private Sub Button2_Click(ByVal sender As System.Object, _
ByVal e As System.EventArgs) Handles Button2.Click                        31
ServiceContr = New ServiceController(Trim(Txt_SerName.Text))              32
If ServiceContr.Status = ServiceControllerStatus.Stopped Then             33
Button2.Enabled = False                                                   34
Button1.Enabled = True                                                    35
MessageBox.Show("Service already stopped...........", "CADCIM Technologies", _
MessageBoxButtons.OK, MessageBoxIcon.Information)                         36
Exit Sub                                                                  37
End If                                                                    38
If ServiceContr.CanStop Then                                             39
ServiceContr.Stop()                                                       40
Label1.Text = Txt_SerName.Text & " " & "Service stopped........"          41
Button2.Enabled = False                                                   42
Button1.Enabled = True                                                    43
End If                                                                    44
End Sub                                                                   45
End Class                                                                 46
```

Explanation
The line-by-line explanation of the above given source code is as follows:

Lines 1-3
Imports System.Collections.Generic
Imports System.ComponentModel
Imports System.ServiceProcess
In these lines, the namespaces **System.Collections.Generic**, **System.ComponentModel**, **System.ServiceProcess** are imported.

Lines 9-30
Private Sub Button1_Click(ByVal sender As System.Object, _
ByVal e As System.EventArgs) Handles Button1.Click
Try
If Trim(Txt_SerName.Text) = "" Then
MessageBox.Show("Enter the Service Name", "CADCIM Technologies")
Exit Sub
ServiceContr = New ServiceController(Trim(Txt_SerName.Text))

If ServiceContr.Status = ServiceControllerStatus.Running Then
MessageBox.Show("Service already running............", "CADCIM Technologies", _
MessageBoxButtons.OK, MessageBoxIcon.Information)
Button2.Enabled = True
Button1.Enabled = False
Exit Sub
Label1.Text = Txt_SerName.Text & " " & "Service started........"
Else
End If
Catch ex As Exception
MsgBox(ex.Message)
End Try
End Sub

In these lines, the **Try-End Try** statement is used to handle exceptions, if there are any exceptions. If a null value is assigned to the **TextBox** control, a message box with the message **Enter the Service Name** will be displayed. In the line **ServiceContr = New ServiceController(Trim(Txt_SerName.Text))**, any value that the user enters in the **TextBox** control will be assigned to the **ServerController** component. If the service name that you have entered is already running, the message box with the message **Service already running...........** will be displayed. In this case, **Button2** will be enabled and **Button1** will be disabled. The service name with the message **Service started.........** will be displayed in the **Label** control. The **Catch** statement will catch the system exception and display a message. Similarly, the service control will stop when the user chooses the **Button2** control.

Step 5
Execute the application; the output form will be displayed. Enter any service in the **Server Name** textbox such as **FTP Publishing** and choose the **Start Service** button; the service will started. Check the service in the **Computer Management** window. To check the service, double-click on **My Computer**; the **Computer Management** window will be displayed. Next, expand the **Services and Applications** nodes and then double-click on the **Services** node; all the services will be displayed. In this case, status of the service is **Started**, as shown in Figure 7-21.

Step 6
Choose the **Stop Service** button; the service will be stopped. Check the status of the service again, the value of the status will be null, as shown in Figure 7-22.

The following application illustrates the use of the **PerformaneCounter** and **Timer** components:

Application 6

Create an application to check whether the name of the performance counter entered by the user exists or not.

In this application, the user will be prompted to enter the **ObjectName**, **CounterName**, and **InstanceName**. The application will check whether the data entered by the user exists or not and then it will display a message.

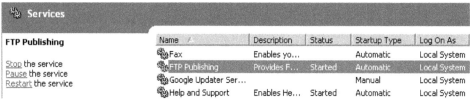

Figure 7-21 *The output of Application 5 in case of starting the service*

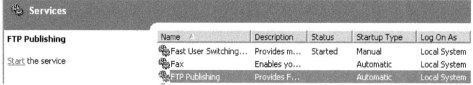

Figure 7-22 *The output of Application 5 in case of stopping the service*

The following steps are required to create this application:

Step 1
Start a new project and save it as **c07_VB_NET_2008_06**.
Step 2
Add three **Label** controls, three **TextBox** controls, a **PerformanceCounter** component, and two **Button** controls to the form.

The resultant form will appear as shown in Figure 7-23.
Step 3
Change the **Name** property of the controls as follows:

Figure 7-23 *The design mode of Application 6*

TextBox1 to **Txt_objectName**
TextBox2 to **Txt_CounterName**
TextBox3 to **Txt_InstanceName**

Step 4
Double-click on the **CheckPerformance** button. Now, declare the global variables and then enter the source code for the **Click** event of the button as follows:

Public Class Form1	1
Public objectName As String	2
Public counterName As String	3
Public instanceName As String	4
Public Counter As PerformanceCounter	5
Public Sub Button1_Click(ByVal sender As Object, _	
ByVal e As System.EventArgs) Handles Button1.Click	6
If Txt_CounterName.Text = "" Or Txt_objectName.Text = "" Or _	
Txt_InstanceName.Text = "" Then Exit Sub	7
objectName = Txt_objectName.Text	8
counterName = Txt_CounterName.Text	9
instanceName = Txt_InstanceName.Text	10
objectName = objectName.Trim()	11
counterName = counterName.Trim()	12
instanceName = instanceName.Trim()	13
If (Not PerformanceCounterCategory.Exists(objectName)) Then	14
MessageBox.Show("Object" & objectName & " does not exists! ", _	
"CADCIM Technologies.....")	15
Exit Sub	16
End If	17
If (Not PerformanceCounterCategory.CounterExists(counterName, _	
objectName)) Then	18
MessageBox.Show("Counter " & counterName & " does not exist! ", _	
"CADCIM Technologies.....")	19
Exit Sub	20
End If	21

```
MessageBox.Show("Object Name :" & objectName & Chr(13) & _
"Counter Name: " & counterName & Chr(13) & "& Instance Name: " _
& instanceName & Chr(13) & " exists", "CADCIM Technologies")          22
End Sub                                                                23

Private Sub Button2_Click(ByVal sender As System.Object, _
ByVal e As System.EventArgs) Handles Button2.Click                     24
End                                                                    25
End Sub                                                                26
End Class                                                              27
```

Explanation
The line-by-line explanation of the above mentioned source code is as follows:

Lines 1-5
Public Class Form1
Public objectName As String
Public counterName As String
Public instanceName As String
Public theCounter As PerformanceCounter
In these lines, the class **Form1** is declared. Also, the variables are declared globally.

Lines 6-13
Public Sub Button1_Click(ByVal sender As Object, _
ByVal e As System.EventArgs) Handles Button1.Click
If Txt_CounterName.Text = "" Or Txt_objectName.Text = "" Or _
Txt_InstanceName.Text = "" Then Exit Sub
objectName = Txt_objectName.Text
counterName = Txt_CounterName.Text
instanceName = Txt_InstanceName.Text
objectName = objectName.Trim()
counterName = counterName.Trim()
instanceName = instanceName.Trim()
In these lines, the **Click** event of **Button1** is coded. If the null value is assigned to all the
TextBox controls or any one of them, the control will exit the sub procedure. The value of
the **Txt_objectName** textbox will be assigned to the variable **objectName**. The value of the
Txt_CounterName textbox will be assigned to the variable **counterName**. The value of the
Txt_InstanceName textbox will be assigned to the variable **instanceName**. The **objectName.**
Trim() is used to trim the extra spaces, if any.

Lines 14-23
If (Not PerformanceCounterCategory.Exists(objectName)) Then
MessageBox.Show("Object " & objectName & " does not exist! ", _
 "CADCIM Technologies.....")
Exit Sub
End If
MessageBox.Show("Object Name :" & objectName & Chr(13) & _

"Counter Name: " & counterName & Chr(13) & "& Instance Name: " _
& instanceName & Chr(13) & " exists", "CADCIM Technologies")
End Sub

In the above lines, if the object name entered by the user does not exist, then a message box with the message **does not exist** concatenated with the object name will be displayed. And, if the object name entered by the user exists, then a message box with the **Object Name**, **Counter Name**, and **Instance Name** will be displayed. In these lines, 13 is the ASCII value of the ENTER key.

Step 5
Execute the application; the output of the form will be displayed. Enter the values **FTP Service**, **Bytes Received/sec**, and **_Total** for the **ObjectName**, **CounterName**, and **InstanceName** parameters, respectively. Next, choose the **Check Performance** button; the output will be displayed, as shown in Figure 7-24. If you enter the invalid entries, the output will be displayed, as shown in Figure 7-25.

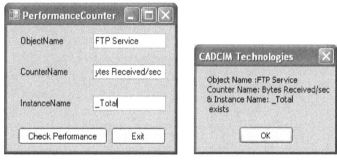

Figure 7-24 *The output of Application 6 in case of valid entries*

Figure 7-25 *The output of Application 6 in case of invalid entries*

The following application illustrates the use of the **MessageQueue** component.

Application 7

Create an application to send the messages to the local server and also to retrieve those messages.

In this application, the user will be prompted to enter a subject and message on a form. This message will then be displayed in the **Read the Message** area.

The following steps are required to create this application:

Step 1
Start a new project and save it as **c07_VB_NET_2008_07**.

Step 2
Add two **GroupBox** controls, three **TextBox** controls, one **ComboBox** control, and a **Button** control to the form.

The resultant form will appear as shown in Figure 7-26.

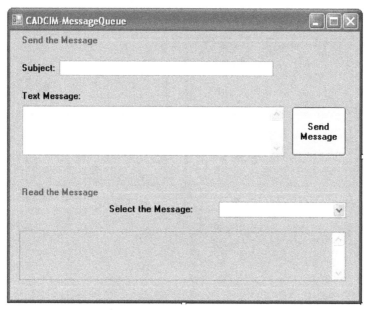

Figure 7-26 The design mode of Application 7

Step 3
Change the value of the **Name** property of controls as follows:

TextBox1 to **Txt_Label**
TextBox2 to **Txt_Send**
TextBox3 to **Txt_Read**
ComboBox1 to **CmbQueue**
Button1 to **Btn_Send**

Step 4
Enter the following source code in the code window:

```vbnet
Imports System.Messaging                                          1
Public Class Form1                                               2
Dim MsgQ As MessageQueue                                         3
Private Sub Form1_Load(ByVal sender As Object, _
ByVal e As System.EventArgs) Handles Me.Load                     4
If Not (MessageQueue.Exists(".\Private$\CADCIM")) Then           5
MsgQ = MessageQueue.Create(".\Private$\CADCIM")                  6
Else                                                             7
MsgQ = New MessageQueue(".\Private$\CADCIM")                     8
End If                                                           9
End Sub                                                          10


Private Sub Btn_Send_Click(ByVal sender As System.Object, _
ByVal e As System.EventArgs) Handles Btn_Send.Click              11
Dim msg As Message                                               12
Try                                                              13
If Txt_Label.Text = "" Then                                      14
MessageBox.Show("Enter the subject", "CADCIM")                   15
Exit Sub                                                         16
End If                                                           17
If Txt_Send.Text = "" Then                                       18
MessageBox.Show("Enter the text for the message", "CADCIM")   19
Exit Sub                                                         20
End If                                                           21


msg = New Message                                                22
msg.Priority = MessagePriority.Normal                            23
msg.Label = Txt_Label.Text                                       24
msg.Body = Txt_Send.Text                                         25
MsgQ.Send(msg)                                                   26
MessageBox.Show("Message sent.")                                 27
For Each msg In MsgQ                                             28
CmbQueue.Items.Add(msg.Label)                                    29
Next                                                             30
Catch ex As Exception                                            31
MessageBox.Show("Error: " + ex.ToString())                       32
End Try                                                       33
End Sub                                                          34


Private Sub Btn_Read_Click(ByVal sender As System.Object, _
ByVal e As System.EventArgs)                                     35
End Sub                                                          36


Private Sub CmbQueue_SelectedIndexChanged(ByVal sender As System.Object, _
ByVal e As System.EventArgs) Handles CmbQueue.SelectedIndexChanged  37
Dim str() As String = {"System.String,mscorlib"}                 38
MsgQ.Formatter = New XmlMessageFormatter(str)                    39
```

```
Dim Mymessage As Message = MsgQ.Receive()                              40
Txt_Read.Text = Mymessage.Body                                         41
End Sub                                                                42
End Class                                                              43
```

Explanation

The line-by-line explanation of the above given source code is as follows:

Line 1
Imports System.Messaging
In this line, the namespace **System.Messaging** is imported.

Line 2
Public Class Form1
In this line, the class **Form1** is declared.

Line 3
Dim MsgQ As MessageQueue
In this line, the variable **MsgQ** is declared as **MessageQueue** that will provide the access to queue on the message queuing server.

Line 4
Private Sub Form1_Load(ByVal sender As Object,
ByVal e As System.EventArgs) Handles Me.Load
In this line, the form load event is declared.

Line 5
If Not (MessageQueue.Exists(".\Private$\CADCIM")) Then
This line will determine whether the message queuing exists on the specified path or not. If it exists, then the control will be transferred to the next line.

Line 6
MsgQ = MessageQueue.Create(".\Private$\CADCIM")
This line will create a non-transactional message queuing queue at the specified path.

Lines 7-9
Else
MsgQ = New MessageQueue(".\Private$\CADCIM")
End If
If the condition in the previous line does not satisfy, the control will be transferred to line 7. In this line, the keyword **New** is used to create a new object instance of **MessageQueue**. **EndIf** indicates the end of the **If** statement.

Line 11
Private Sub Btn_Send_Click(ByVal sender As System.Object, _
ByVal e As System.EventArgs) Handles Btn_Send.Click
In this line, the **Click** event of the **Button** control is declared.

Lines 13-17
Try
If Txt_Label.Text = "" Then
MessageBox.Show("Enter the Subject", "CADCIM")
Exit Sub
End If
In these lines, the **Try-Catch** block is used to catch the exceptions, if any. If the null string is assigned to the **Txt_Label** textbox, then a message box with the message **Enter the subject** will be displayed.

Lines 18-21
If Txt_Send.Text = "" Then
MessageBox.Show("Enter the Text for the Message", "CADCIM")
Exit Sub
End If
In these lines, if the null string is assigned to the **Txt_Send** textbox, then the message **Enter the text for the message** will be displayed.

Line 23
msg.Priority = MessagePriority.Normal
In this line, the priority of the messages will be set. This indicates that the messages will be placed in the queue according to the priority.

Line 24
msg.Label = Txt_Label.Text
In this line, the text entered in the **Txt_Label** textbox will be assigned to the **Label** property of **msg**.

Line 25
msg.Body = Txt_Send.Text
In this line, the text entered in the **Txt_Send** textbox will be assigned to the **Body** property of **msg**.
Line 26
MsgQ.Send(msg)
In this line, the message will be sent within the local server.

Lines 28-30
For Each msg In MsgQ
CmbQueue.Items.Add(msg.Label)
Next
In these lines, each message entered by the user will be added to the **ComboBox** control.

Lines 31-34
Catch ex As Exception
MessageBox.Show("Error: " + ex.ToString())
End Try
End Sub

In these lines, **Catch** will catch the exception, if any. A message box with a specified text will be displayed. The **EndTry** statement indicates the end of the **Try** statement.

Line 37
Private Sub CmbQueue_SelectedIndexChanged(ByVal sender As System.Object, _
ByVal e As System.EventArgs) Handles CmbQueue.SelectedIndexChanged
In this line, the **SelectedIndexChanged** event of the **ComboBox** control is declared.

Line 38
Dim str() As String = {"System.String,mscorlib"}
In this line, the variable **str()** is declared as a string data type.

Line 39
MsgQ.Formatter = New XmlMessageFormatter(str)
XmlMessageFormatter is the default formatter that is used by an instance of **MessageQueue** to serialize the messages written for the queue. The message is then assigned to the formatter of **MessageQueue**.

Line 40
Dim Mymessage As Message = MsgQ.Receive()
In this line, **MsgQ.Receive()** will receive the message first and then assign it to the variable **Message**.

Step 5
Execute the application; the output form will be displayed. Enter message such as **Hello** in the **Subject** textbox and **How are you?** in the **Text Message** textbox. Choose the **Send Message** button; a message box with the message **Message Sent.** will be displayed, as shown in Figure 7-27. To view the message , select the subject from the **Select the Message** combo box; the message you have sent will be displayed in the textbox, as shown in Figure 7-28.

Figure 7-27 *The output of Application 7 in case a message is sent*

Figure 7-28 *The output of Application 7 in case a message is retrieved*

Self-Evaluation Test

Answer the following questions and then compare them to those given at the end of this chapter:

1. The _____ component is used to execute the time-consuming operations asynchronously in the background of an application.

2. The _____ component is used to validate the user's input on a control.

3. The _____ property determines whether the component is active or not.

4. The _____ component is used to store the collection of images.

5. The _____ component is used to access the processes on both the remote and local computers.

Review Questions

Answer the following questions:

1. The _____ is a standard method used by an application in your system to store a record of some software and hardware related events.

2. The _____ component is used to determine the conditions due to which an error has occurred.

3. The _____ property is used to import an image to the form.

4. With the help of the _____ component, an application can create and delete queues, explore the existing queues, send and receive messages to a queue on the **Message Queuing** servers, and so on.

5. You can use the _____ method to create a new event source that will be associated with an event log.

Exercise

Exercise 1

Create an application to display any process on your system using the **Process** component. The output of your application will be similar to Figure 7-29. The process should start when you choose the **Start** button and stop when you choose the **Stop** button.

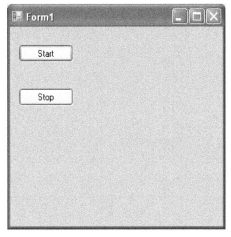

Figure 7-29 *The output of Exercise 1*

Answers to Self-Evaluation Test
1. BackgroundWorker, 2. ErrorProvider, 3. EnableRaisingEvents, 4. ImageList, 5. Process

Chapter 8

Working with MDI, In-built Dialogs, and Printing Controls

Learning Objectives

After completing this chapter, you will be able to:
- *Create multi document interface.*
- *Work with in-built dialogs.*
- *Work with printing controls.*

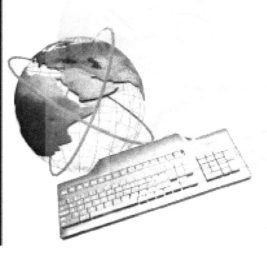

INTRODUCTION

In this chapter, you will be able to work with the in-built dialog boxes and the printing controls. You will also learn to create menus and work with multiple document interface forms.

Creating Multiple Document Interface (MDI) Applications

The MDI applications allow you to display multiple documents simultaneously, wherein each document has its own document window. To create your own MDI, follow the steps given below:

1. Start a new project. Set the **IsMdiContainer** property of the Form 1 to **True**; the color of the form will be changed to dark grey. Also, change the **WindowState** property of the form to **Maximize**.

2. Add two more windows forms, **Form2** and **Form3** to **Form1**.

3. Add a **MenuStrip** control and three main menus, **Form2**, **Form3**, and **Exit** to **Form 1**.

4. Double-click on the **Form2** main menu and enter the following source code:

```
Dim child1 As New Form2
    child1.MdiParent = Me
child1.Show()
```

5. Double-click on the **Form3** main menu and enter the following source code:

```
Dim child2 As New Form3
child2.MdiParent = Me
child2.Show()
```

6. Double-click on the **Exit** main menu and enter the following source code:

```
Me.Close()
```

7. Execute the application; **Form1** will be displayed to its maximized state. Click on the **Form2** and **Form3** main menus; two forms will be displayed, as shown in Figure 8-1.

Alternatively, choose the **Solution Explorer** tab and right-click on the project name in the **Solution Explorer** window. Now, choose **Add > New Items** from the context menu; the **Add New Item** dialog box will be displayed, as shown in Figure 8-2. Select **Windows Forms** from the **Categories** list and **MDI Parent Form** from the **Templates** area.

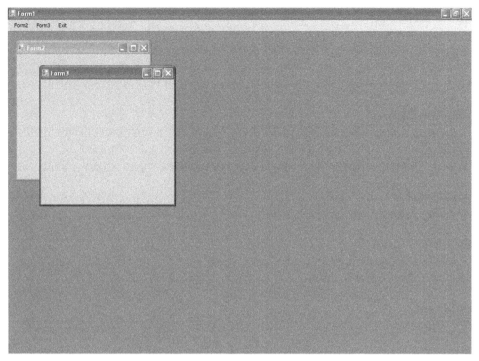

Figure 8-1 *The MDI application*

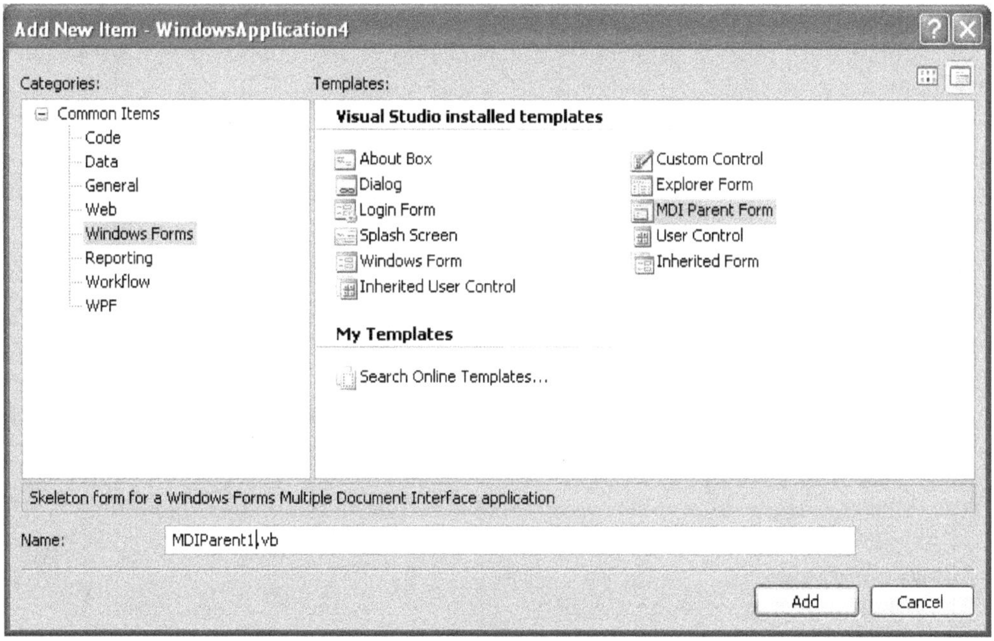

Figure 8-2 *The **Add New Item** dialog box*

In-built Dialogs

VB.NET framework provides with some in-built dialogs. These dialogs require less coding in comparison to other dialogs. You can call these dialogs through simple source code. For example, if you want to print any document, you can call the in-built printing dialogs in your application. There are several in-built dialogs provided by VB.NET, and they are discussed next.

PageSetupDialog

The **PageSetupDialog** component can be used to specify the page details for printing. For adding this dialog to the form, double-click on it; the dialog will be added to the component tray. Some of the important properties of the **PageSetupDialog** are discussed next.

AllowMargins

The **AllowMargins** property is used to enable or disable the editing of the margins.

AllowOrientation

The **AllowOrientation** property is used to enable or disable the orientation of the radio buttons at the time of printing.

AllowPaper

The **AllowPaper** property allows you to change the settings of the paper size.

AllowPrinter

The **AllowPrinter** property is used to enable or disable the printer buttons.

Document

The **Document** property determines the print document for which you need to set the print options.

PrintDialog

The **PrintDialog** component allows the user to select the printer and choose the document to print. Some of the important properties of the **PrintDialog** component are as follows:

AllowCurrentPage

The **AllowCurrentPage** property is used to enable or disable the **Current Page** option.

AllowPrintToFile

The **AllowPrintToFile** property is used to enable or disable the **Print to File** check box.

AllowSelection

The **AllowSelection** property is used to enable or disable the **Selection** button.

AllowSomePages

The **AllowSomePages** property is used to enable or disable the **Pages** button.

PrintDocument

The **PrintDocument** component is used to define a reusable object, which sends the output to the printer, in case the printing is done through the windows application. Some of the important properties of the **PrintDocument** component are as follows:

DocumentName

The **DocumentName** property is used to determine the name of the document that is to be shown to the user.

GenerateMember

The **GenerateMember** property is used to indicate whether a member variable of this component will be generated.

PrintPreviewControl

The **PrintPreviewControl** component lets the user preview the document before it gets printed. You can use this control to create your own customized print preview window. To add it to the form, double-click on it; the **PrintPreviewControl** component will be displayed, as shown in Figure 8-3. To use this control, you need to set its **Document** property to print the document.

Figure 8-3 The *PrintPreviewControl* component

Some of the important properties of the **PrintPreviewControl** are as follows:

AutoZoom

When the **AutoZoom** property is set to true, all the contents are resized and they become visible.

Columns

The **Columns** property is used to set the number of pages that are displayed horizontally in the **PrintPreviewControl** component.

Rows

The **Rows** property is used to set the number of pages that are displayed vertically in the **PrintPreviewControl** component.

StartPage

The **StartPage** property is used to set the page number from which you can preview the document.

Zoom

The **Zoom** property is used to set a value that will specify the length of the pages displayed.

PrintPreviewDialog

The **PrintPreviewDialog** component is used to preview the document before printing. It is supported by the **PrintPreviewDialog** class. For previewing any document, you need to set its **Document** property to **PrintDocument**.

ColorDialog

The **ColorDialog** component allows the user to select a color of his choice for the printing document. It is supported by the **ColorDialog** class.

Some of the important properties of the **ColorDialog** component are as follows:

AllowFullOpen

The **AllowFullOpen** property is used to determine whether the user can use the entire **ColorDialog** dialog box to define the custom color.

AnyColor

The **AnyColor** property is used to determine whether the dialog box displays all the available colors in the set of basic colors.

Color

The **Color** property is used to set the color selected by the user.

FullOpen

The **FullOpen** property is used to determine whether the **Custom** color section will get displayed when the **ColorDialog** dialog box opens.

SolidColorOnly

The **SolidColorOnly** property is used to determine whether the dialog box will restrict the user to a set of selected colors only.

FolderBrowserDialog

The **FolderBrowserDialog** component is used to browse and select the folders. You can also create new folders with the help of the **FolderBrowserDialog** component. The **RootFolder** property of the **FolderBrowserDialog** component is used to set the location of the root folder from where you want to start browsing the subfolders. The selected root folder and the subfolders will be displayed in a dialog box. The default value of the **FolderBrowserDialog** component is **Desktop**. You can locate the path of the selected folder with the help of the **SelectedPath** property. You can also create a new folder with the help of this property. To create a new folder or to select a path, choose the ellipses button associated with the **SelectedPath** property; the **Browse For Folder** dialog box will be displayed, as shown in Figure 8-4. To create a new folder, choose the **Make New Folder** button. To browse a folder, select the folder and then choose the **OK** button.

FontDialog

The **FontDialog** component is used to select the font size, color, style, and so on of the text in a document with the help of the Font dialog box, as shown in Figure 8-5. Some of the important properties of the **FontDialog** component are as follows:

AllowVectorFont

The **AllowVectorFont** property determines whether the vector fonts can be selected.

Figure 8-4 The **Browse For Folder** *dialog box*

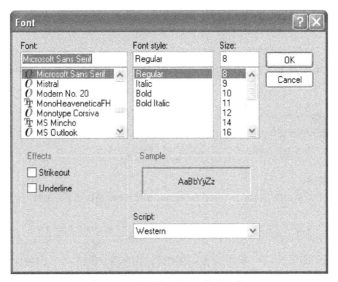

Figure 8-5 The **Font** *dialog box*

AllowVerticalFonts
The **AllowVerticalFonts** property is used to determine whether the vertical fonts can be displayed.

Color
The **Color** property is used to set the color selected by the user.

Font
The **Font** property is used to set the font selected by the user.

FontMustExist

The **FontMustExist** property is used to determine whether a message will be displayed, if the user selects a font that does not exist.

ShowApply

The **ShowApply** property is used to determine whether the **Apply** button will exist or not.

ShowColor

The **ShowColor** property is used to determine whether the choice of color option will be displayed or not.

ShowEffects

The **ShowEffects** property is used to determine whether the effects such as underline, strike, subscript, and so on will be displayed or not.

OpenFileDialog

The **OpenFileDialog** component is used to determine the name and path of files that you want to use. This component is supported by the **OpenFileDialog** class. Some of the important properties of the **OpenFileDialog** control are as follows:

AddExtension

The **AddExtension** property is used to determine whether the extensions are automatically added to the files or not.

CheckFileExists

The **CheckFileExists** property is used to determine whether an error message will be displayed, if the user tries to open a file that does not exist.

CheckPathExists

The **CheckPathExist** property is used to determine whether the path selected by the user exists or not.

DefaultExt

The **DefaultExt** property is used to add a default extension to a file, if the user does not specify it.

FileName

The **FileName** property is used to set the file name of the file opened by the user.

Multiselect

The **Multiselect** property is used to determine whether multiple files can be selected at a time.

ReadOnlyChecked

The **ReadOnlyChecked** property is used to determine whether the **Read-Only** check box is selected or not.

SupportMultiDottedExtensions

The **SupportMultiDottedExtensions** property is used to determine whether the multi-dotted extensions can be selected.

Title

The **Title** property is used to set the title of a dialog box.

SaveFileDialog

The **SaveFileDialog** component is used to browse the files and select a location for saving the file. The path of the file selected by the user will be displayed in a dialog box. Some of the important properties of the **SaveFileDialog** component are as follows:

CheckFileExists

The **CheckFileExists** property is used to check whether the file specified by the user exists or not.

CheckPathExists

The **CheckPathExists** property is used to check whether the path specified by the user exists or not.

CreatePrompt

The **CreatePrompt** property is used to check whether the user should be prompted, in case a new file is created. The value of the **CreatePrompt** property can be true only if the value of the **ValidateNames** property is set to true.

FileName

The **FileName** property is used to set the file name selected by the user in the **File** dialog box.

OverwritePrompt

The **OverwritePrompt** property is used to prompt a message in case the user specifies the name of file that already exists.

SupportMultiDottedExtensions

The **SupportMultiDottedExtensions** property is used to determine whether the multidotted extensions can be saved or selected.

The following application illustrates the use of all the Printing and Dialog components: Create an application to form an editor using the printing and dialog components.

In this application, you will create a text editor.

Application 1

The following steps are required to create this application:

Step 1

Start a new project and save it as **c08_VB_NET_2008_01**. Right-click on any control in the toolbox and choose the **Choose Items** option from the context menu; the **Choose Toolbox Items** dialog box will be displayed. In this dialog box, choose the **Browse** button; the **Open** dialog box will be displayed. Browse to the **ExtendedRichTextBox** file; it will be added to the form.

Step 2

Add a **RichTextBox** control, a **MenuStrip** component, a **ContextMenu** component, a **ToolStrip** component, a **OpenFileDialog** component, a **SaveFileDialog** component, a **PageSetUpDialog** component, a **PrintDocument** component, a **PrintDialog** component, a **FontDialog** component, a **ColorDialog** component, two **Panel** controls, and a **PrintPreviewDialog** component to the form.

Step 3

Add the following menu items to the **MenuStrip**:

1. **File > New, Open, Save, Save As, PageSetUp, Print Preview, Print,** and **Exit**
2. **Edit > Undo, Redo, Find, Find and Replace, Select All, Cut, Copy, Paste, Insert image**
3. **Font > Select Font, Font Color, Bold, Italic, Underline, Normal,** and **Page Color**
4. **Paragraph > Indent > None, 5 pts, 10 pts, 15 pts, 20 pts** and **Align > Left, Center, Right**
5. **Bullets > Add Bullets** and **Remove Bullets**

You can also assign shortcut keys to these commands. To use an alphabet as a shortcut key, enter '**&**' before the specified alphabet in the **Text** property. You will notice a small line under the alphabet that you want to use as a shortcut key. Now, to use the shortcut key, you need to press ALT and the specified alphabet simultaneously.

Step 4

Add the following items to the **ContextMenuStrip**:

1. Undo
2. Cut
3. Copy
4. Paste
5. Select All

Step 5

Add two **Label** controls, two **TextBox** controls, five **Button** controls, and a **CheckBox** control to **Panel1**.

Step 6

Add a **Label** control, a **TextBox** control, three **Button** controls, and a **CheckBox** control to **Panel2**.

Step 7

Add icons to the **ToolStrip**.

Step 8
Select **Panel1** and right-click on it; the context menu will be displayed. Choose **Bring to Front** option. Next, pull **Panel1** over **Panel2**. The form, in this case will appear similar to Figure 8-6. Next, pull **Panel2** over **Panel1**, as shown in Figure 8-7.

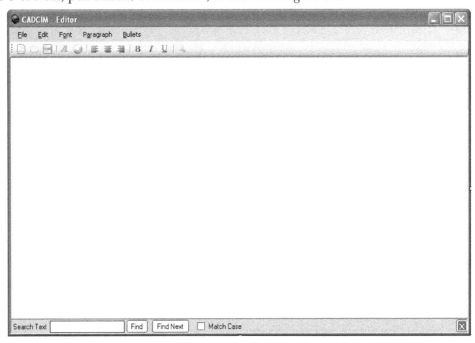

*Figure 8-6 The design mode of Application1 with **Panel1***

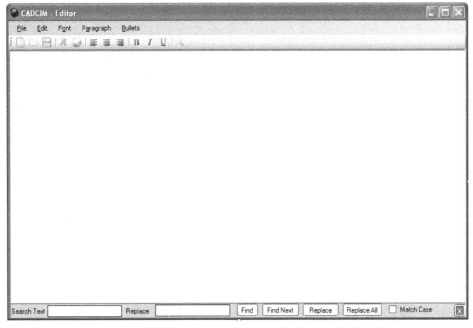

*Figure 8-7 The design mode of Application1 with **Panel2***

Step 9
Enter the following source code in the code window:

```
Imports System.Drawing                                              1
Imports System.IO                                                   2
Imports System.IO.File                                              3
Imports System                                                      4
Imports System.Collections.Generic                                  5
Imports System.ComponentModel                                       6
Imports System.Drawing.Imaging                                      7
Imports System.Text                                                 8
Imports System.Windows.Forms                                        9
Imports ExtendedRichTextBox                                        10

Public Class FrmMain                                               11
Dim Bol_True As Boolean                                            12
Dim Bol_WordWarp As Boolean                                        13
Private currentFile As String                                      14
Private checkPrint As Integer                                      15

Private Sub FrmMain_FormClosing(ByVal sender As Object, ByVal e As _
System.Windows.Forms.FormClosingEventArgs) Handles Me.FormClosing  16
If Rftbox.Modified = True Then                                     17
Dim Ans As DialogResult                                           18
Ans = MessageBox.Show("Save current document before exit?", _
"Unsaved Document", MessageBoxButtons.YesNo, MessageBoxIcon.Question)  19

If Ans = System.Windows.Forms.DialogResult.No Then                 20
Rftbox.Modified = False                                           21
Rftbox.Clear()                                                    22
Return                                                            23
Else                                                              24
SaveMenuItem_Click(Me, New EventArgs())                           25
End If                                                            26
Else                                                              27
Rftbox.Clear()                                                    28
currentFile = ""                                                  29
Me.Text = "CADCIM: New Document"                                  30
End If                                                             31
End Sub                                                           32

Private Sub FrmMain_Load(ByVal sender As System.Object, _
ByVal e As System.EventArgs) Handles MyBase.Load                   33
Dim RichTextbox As New ExtendedRichTextBox.RichTextBoxPrintCtrl    34

RichTextbox.Name = "Rftbox"                                       35
RichTextbox.Dock = DockStyle.Fill                                 36
RichTextbox.Location = New Size(0, 50)                            37
```

```
Me.Controls.Add(RichTextbox)                                              38

ContextMenuStrip1.Visible = True                                          39
ContextMenuStrip1.Enabled = False                                         40
FindPanel.Visible = False                                                 41
Me.ReplacePanel.Visible = False                                           42
Bol_True = True                                                           43
Bol_WordWarp = False                                                      44
Btn_FindNext.Enabled = False                                              45
Btn_RF_Next.Enabled = False                                               46
End Sub                                                                   47

Private Sub Form1_Resize(ByVal sender As Object,
ByVal e As System.EventArgs) Handles Me.Resize                            48
Rftbox.Width = Me.Width - 10                                              49
Rftbox.Height = Me.Height - 80                                            50
End Sub                                                                   51

Private Sub Rftbox_TextChanged(ByVal sender As System.Object,
ByVal e As System.EventArgs)                                              52
If Not Rftbox.Text = "" Then                                              53
ContextMenuStrip1.Enabled = True                                          54
End If                                                                    55
End Sub                                                                   56

Private Sub UndoContextToolStripMenuItem_Click(ByVal sender _
As System.Object, ByVal e As _
System.EventArgs) Handles UndoContextToolStripMenuItem.Click              57
Rftbox.Undo()                                                             58
End Sub                                                                   59

Private Sub SelectAllContextToolStripMenuItem_Click(ByVal sender _
As System.Object, ByVal e As System.EventArgs) _
Handles SelectAllContextToolStripMenuItem.Click                           60
Rftbox.SelectAll()                                                        61
End Sub                                                                   62

Private Sub Rftbox_TextChanged_1(ByVal sender As System.Object, _
ByVal e As System.EventArgs) Handles Rftbox.TextChanged                   63
If Rftbox.Text <> "" Then                                                 64
ContextMenuStrip1.Enabled = True                                          65
Else                                                                      66
ContextMenuStrip1.Enabled = False                                         67
End If                                                                    68
End Sub                                                                   69

Private Sub NewMenuItem_Click(ByVal sender As System.Object, _
ByVal e As System.EventArgs) Handles NewMenuItem.Click                    70
```

```
If Rftbox.Modified = True Then                                          71
Dim Ans As DialogResult                                                 72
Ans = MessageBox.Show("Save current document before
creating new document?", "Unsaved Document", _
MessageBoxButtons.YesNo, MessageBoxIcon.Question)                       73
If Ans = Windows.Forms.DialogResult.No Then                             74
currentFile = ""                                                        75
Me.Text = "CADCIM - New Document"                                       76
Rftbox.Modified = False                                                 77
Rftbox.Clear()                                                          78
Else                                                                    79
SaveMenuItem_Click(Me, New EventArgs)                                   80
Me.Text = "CADCIM - New Document"                                       81
Rftbox.Modified = False                                                 82
Rftbox.Clear()                                                          83
Return                                                                  84
End If                                                                  85
Else                                                                    86
currentFile = ""                                                        87
Me.Text = "CADCIM - New Document"                                       88
Rftbox.Modified = False                                                 89
Rftbox.Clear()                                                          90
Return                                                                  91
End If                                                                  92
End Sub                                                                 93

Public Sub OpenFile()                                                   94
OpenFileDialog1.Title = "CADCIM - Open File"                            95
OpenFileDialog1.DefaultExt = "rtf"                                      96
OpenFileDialog1.Filter = "Rich Text Files|*.rtf|Text Files|*
.txt|HTML Files|*.htm|All Files|*.*"                                    97
OpenFileDialog1.FilterIndex = 1                                         98
OpenFileDialog1.FileName = String.Empty                                 99

If OpenFileDialog1.ShowDialog = Windows.Forms.DialogResult.OK Then      100
If OpenFileDialog1.FileName = "" Then                                   101
Exit Sub                                                                102
End If                                                                  103
Dim StrExt As String                                                    104
StrExt = Path.GetExtension(OpenFileDialog1.FileName)                    105
StrExt = StrExt.ToUpper                                                 106
If StrExt = ".RTF" Then                                                 107
Rftbox.LoadFile(OpenFileDialog1.FileName, _
RichTextBoxStreamType.RichText)                                         108
Else                                                                    109
Dim Str_cont As String                                                  110
Dim oRead As System.IO.StreamReader                                     111
```

```
oRead = OpenText(OpenFileDialog1.FileName)                              112
Str_cont = ""                                                          113

Do While oRead.Peek <> -1                                              114
Str_cont = Str_cont & oRead.ReadLine                                   115
Str_cont = Str_cont & Chr(13)                                          116
Loop                                                                   117
Rftbox.Text = Str_cont                                                 118
currentFile = OpenFileDialog1.FileName                                 119

Me.Text = "CADCIM - " & currentFile                                    120
oRead.Close()                                                          121
End If                                                                 122
Else
MessageBox.Show("Open File request cancelled by user.", "Cancelled")   123
End If                                                                 124
End Sub                                                                125

Private Sub OpenMenuItem_Click(ByVal sender As System.Object, _
ByVal e As System.EventArgs) Handles OpenMenuItem.Click                126
If Rftbox.Modified = True Then                                         127
Dim Ans As DialogResult                                                128
Ans = MessageBox.Show("Save current document before creating
new document?", "Unsaved Document",
MessageBoxButtons.YesNo, MessageBoxIcon.Question)                      129

If Ans = Windows.Forms.DialogResult.No Then                            130
Rftbox.Modified = False                                                131
OpenFile()                                                             132
Else                                                                  133
SaveMenuItem_Click(Me, New EventArgs)                                  134
End If                                                                 135
Else                                                                  136
OpenFile()                                                             137
End If                                                                 138
End Sub                                                                139

Private Sub SaveMenuItem_Click(ByVal sender As System.Object, _
ByVal e As System.EventArgs) Handles SaveMenuItem.Click                140
Try                                                                   141
If currentFile = String.Empty Then                                    142
SaveAsMenuItem_Click(Me, New EventArgs)                                143
Exit Sub                                                              144
End If                                                                145

Dim StrExt As String                                                  146
StrExt = Path.GetExtension(currentFile)                                147
```

```
If StrExt = ".RFT" Then                                             148
Rftbox.SaveFile(currentFile)                                        149
Else                                                                150
Dim oWrite As IO.StreamWriter                                       151
oWrite = CreateText(currentFile)                                    152
oWrite.Write(Rftbox.Text)                                           153
oWrite.Close()                                                      154
oWrite = Nothing                                                    155
Rftbox.SelectionStart = 0                                           156
Rftbox.SelectionLength = 0                                          157
End If                                                              158

Me.Text = "CADCIM - " & currentFile                                 159
Rftbox.Modified = False                                             160

Catch ex As Exception                                               161
MessageBox.Show(ex.Message.ToString(), "Error-CADCIM")              162
End Try                                                             163
End Sub                                                             164
Private Sub SaveAsMenuItem_Click(ByVal sender As System.Object, _
ByVal e As System.EventArgs) Handles SaveAsMenuItem.Click           165
Try                                                                 166
SaveFileDialog1.Title = "CADCIM - Save File"                        167
SaveFileDialog1.DefaultExt = "rtf"                                  168
SaveFileDialog1.Filter = "Rich Text Files|*.rtf|Text Files|*
.txt|HTML Files|*.htm|All Files|*.*"                                169
SaveFileDialog1.FilterIndex = 1                                     170

If SaveFileDialog1.ShowDialog() = Windows.Forms.DialogResult.OK Then  171
If SaveFileDialog1.FileName = "" Then                               172
Exit Sub                                                            173
End If                                                              174

Dim StrExt As String                                                175
StrExt = Path.GetExtension(SaveFileDialog1.FileName)                176
StrExt = StrExt.ToUpper                                             177

If StrExt = ".RTF" Then                                             178
Rftbox.SaveFile(SaveFileDialog1.FileName, RichTextBoxStreamType.RichText)  179
Else                                                                180
Dim oWrite As IO.StreamWriter                                       181

oWrite = New IO.StreamWriter(SaveFileDialog1.FileName)              182
oWrite.Write(Rftbox.Text)                                           183
oWrite.Close()                                                      184
oWrite = Nothing                                                    185
```

```
Rftbox.SelectionStart = 0                                                    186
Rftbox.SelectionLength = 0                                                   187
End If                                                                       188
currentFile = SaveFileDialog1.FileName                                       189
Rftbox.Modified = False                                                      190
Me.Text = "CADCIM - " + currentFile.ToString()                               191
MessageBox.Show(currentFile.ToString() + " saved.", "File Save")             192
Else                                                                         193
MessageBox.Show("Save File request cancelled by user...", "Cancelled")       194
End If                                                                       195

Catch ex As Exception                                                        196

MessageBox.Show(ex.Message.ToString(), "Error-CADCIM")                       197
End Try                                                                      198
End Sub                                                                      199

Private Sub BoldMenuItem_Click(ByVal sender As System.Object, _
ByVal e As System.EventArgs) Handles BoldMenuItem.Click                      200
If Not Rftbox.SelectedText = "" Then                                         201
Dim CurrentFont As Font = Rftbox.SelectionFont                               202
Dim newFontStyle As FontStyle                                                203

If Rftbox.SelectionFont.Style = FontStyle.Bold Then                          204
newFontStyle = FontStyle.Regular                                             205
Else                                                                         206
newFontStyle = FontStyle.Bold Or Rftbox.SelectionFont.Style                  207
End If                                                                        208

Rftbox.SelectionFont = New Font(CurrentFont.FontFamily,
CurrentFont.Size, newFontStyle)                                              209
End If                                                                        210
End Sub                                                                       211

Private Sub ItalicMenuItem_Click(ByVal sender As System.Object, _
ByVal e As System.EventArgs) Handles ItalicMenuItem.Click                    212
If Not Rftbox.SelectedText = "" Then                                         213
Dim CurrentFont As Font = Rftbox.SelectionFont                               214
Dim newFontStyle As FontStyle                                                215

If Rftbox.SelectionFont.Style = FontStyle.Italic Then                        216
newFontStyle = FontStyle.Regular                                             217
Else                                                                         218
newFontStyle = FontStyle.Italic Or Rftbox.SelectionFont.Style                219
End If                                                                        220
Rftbox.SelectionFont = New Font(CurrentFont.FontFamily, CurrentFont.Size,
newFontStyle)                                                                221
```

```
End If                                                                      222
End Sub                                                                     223

Private Sub UnderlineMenuItem_Click(ByVal sender As System.Object, _
ByVal e As System.EventArgs) Handles UnderlineMenuItem.Click               224
If Not Rftbox.SelectedText = "" Then                                       225
Dim CurrentFont As Font = Rftbox.SelectionFont                            226
Dim newFontStyle As FontStyle                                             227

If Rftbox.SelectionFont.Style = FontStyle.Underline Then                  228
newFontStyle = FontStyle.Regular                                          229
Else                                                                       230
newFontStyle = FontStyle.Underline Or Rftbox.SelectionFont.Style         231
End If                                                                      232

Rftbox.SelectionFont = New Font(CurrentFont.FontFamily,
CurrentFont.Size, newFontStyle)                                           233
End If                                                                      234
End Sub                                                                     235

Private Sub NormalMenuItem_Click(ByVal sender As System.Object, _
ByVal e As System.EventArgs) Handles NormalMenuItem.Click                 236
If Not Rftbox.SelectedText = "" Then                                       237
Dim CurrentFont As Font = Rftbox.SelectionFont                            238
Dim newFontStyle As FontStyle                                             239

newFontStyle = FontStyle.Regular                                         240
Rftbox.SelectionFont = New Font(CurrentFont.FontFamily,
CurrentFont.Size, newFontStyle)                                           241
End If                                                                      242
End Sub                                                                     243

Private Sub PageColorMenuItem_Click(ByVal sender As System.Object, _
ByVal e As System.EventArgs) Handles PageColorMenuItem.Click              244
ColorDialog1.Color = Rftbox.BackColor                                     245

If ColorDialog1.ShowDialog = Windows.Forms.DialogResult.OK Then           246
Rftbox.BackColor = ColorDialog1.Color                                     247
End If                                                                      248
End Sub                                                                     249

Private Sub FontColorMenuItem_Click(ByVal sender As System.Object, _
ByVal e As System.EventArgs) Handles FontColorMenuItem.Click              250
If ColorDialog1.ShowDialog = Windows.Forms.DialogResult.OK Then           251
If ColorDialog1.Color = Rftbox.SelectionColor Then Exit Sub               252
Rftbox.SelectionColor = ColorDialog1.Color                               253
```

```
End If                                                                    254
End Sub                                                                   255

Private Sub tbrBold_Click(ByVal sender As System.Object, _
ByVal e As System.EventArgs) Handles tbrBold.Click                        256
BoldMenuItem_Click(Me, New EventArgs)                                     257
End Sub                                                                   258

Private Sub tbrItalic_Click(ByVal sender As System.Object, _
ByVal e As System.EventArgs) Handles tbrItalic.Click                      259
ItalicMenuItem_Click(Me, New EventArgs)                                   260
End Sub                                                                   261

Private Sub tbrUnderline_Click(ByVal sender As System.Object, _
ByVal e As System.EventArgs) Handles tbrUnderline.Click                   262
UnderlineMenuItem_Click(Me, New EventArgs)                                263
End Sub                                                                   264

Private Sub LeftToolStripMenuItem_Click(ByVal sender As System.Object, _
ByVal e As System.EventArgs) Handles LeftToolStripMenuItem.Click          265
Rftbox.SelectionAlignment = HorizontalAlignment.Left                      266
End Sub                                                                   267

Private Sub CenterToolStripMenuItem_Click(ByVal sender As System.Object, _
ByVal e As System.EventArgs) Handles CenterToolStripMenuItem.Click        268
Rftbox.SelectionAlignment = HorizontalAlignment.Center                    269
End Sub                                                                   270

Private Sub RightToolStripMenuItem_Click(ByVal sender As System.Object, _
ByVal e As System.EventArgs) Handles RightToolStripMenuItem.Click         271
Rftbox.SelectionAlignment = HorizontalAlignment.Right                     272
End Sub                                                                   273

Private Sub tbrLeft_Click(ByVal sender As System.Object, _
ByVal e As System.EventArgs) Handles tbrLeft.Click                        274
LeftToolStripMenuItem_Click(Me, New EventArgs)                            275
End Sub                                                                   276

Private Sub tbrCenter_Click(ByVal sender As System.Object, _
ByVal e As System.EventArgs) Handles tbrCenter.Click                      277
CenterToolStripMenuItem_Click(Me, New EventArgs)                          278
End Sub                                                                   279

Private Sub tbrRight_Click(ByVal sender As System.Object, _
ByVal e As System.EventArgs) Handles tbrRight.Click                       280
RightToolStripMenuItem_Click(Me, New EventArgs)                           281
End Sub                                                                   282
```

```
Private Sub PageSetupMenuItem_Click(ByVal sender As System.Object, _
ByVal e As System.EventArgs) Handles PageSetupMenuItem.Click          283
PageSetupDialog1.Document = PrintDocument1                            284
PageSetupDialog1.ShowDialog()                                        285
End Sub                                                              286


Private Sub ExitMenuItem_Click(ByVal sender As System.Object, _
ByVal e As System.EventArgs) Handles ExitMenuItem.Click              287
End                                                                 288
End Sub                                                             289


Private Sub PrintDocument1_BeginPrint(ByVal sender As Object, _
ByVal e As System.Drawing.Printing.PrintEventArgs) Handles _
PrintDocument1.BeginPrint                                           290
checkPrint = 0                                                      291
End Sub                                                             292


Private Sub PrintDocument1_PrintPage(ByVal sender As Object, _
ByVal e As System.Drawing.Printing.PrintPageEventArgs) Handles _
PrintDocument1.PrintPage                                            293
checkPrint = Rftbox.Print(checkPrint, Rftbox.TextLength, e)         294

If checkPrint < Rftbox.TextLength Then                              295
e.HasMorePages = True                                              296
Else                                                               297
e.HasMorePages = False                                             298
End If                                                             299
End Sub                                                            300


Private Sub UndoMenuItem_Click(ByVal sender As System.Object, _
ByVal e As System.EventArgs) Handles UndoMenuItem.Click             301
If Rftbox.CanUndo Then                                             302
Rftbox.Undo()                                                      303
End If                                                             304
End Sub                                                            305


Private Sub RedoMenuItem_Click(ByVal sender As System.Object, _
ByVal e As System.EventArgs) Handles RedoMenuItem.Click             306
If Rftbox.CanRedo Then                                             307
Rftbox.Redo()                                                      308
End If                                                             309
End Sub                                                            310


Private Sub tspColor_Click(ByVal sender As System.Object, _
ByVal e As System.EventArgs) Handles tspColor.Click                311
FontColorMenuItem_Click(Me, New EventArgs)                         312
End Sub                                                            313
```

```
Private Sub FindAndReplaceMenuItem_Click(ByVal sender As System.Object, _
ByVal e As System.EventArgs) Handles FindAndReplaceMenuItem.Click          314

If FindPanel.Visible = True Then                                           315
FindPanel.Visible = False                                                  316
Me.ReplacePanel.Visible = True                                             317
Txt_search.Text = TxtFind.Text                                             318
Txt_Replace.Focus()                                                        319
Else                                                                       320
Me.ReplacePanel.Visible = True                                             321
Txt_search.Focus()                                                         322
End If                                                                      323
End Sub                                                                     324

Private Sub tbrFind_Click(ByVal sender As System.Object, _
ByVal e As System.EventArgs) Handles tbrFind.Click                         325
FindAndReplaceMenuItem_Click(Me, New EventArgs)                            326
End Sub                                                                     327
Private Sub FindMenuItem_Click(ByVal sender As System.Object, _
ByVal e As System.EventArgs) Handles FindMenuItem.Click                    328
FindPanel.Visible = True                                                   329
TxtFind.Focus()                                                            330
End Sub                                                                     331

Private Sub PreviewMenuItem_Click(ByVal sender As System.Object, _
ByVal e As System.EventArgs) Handles PreviewMenuItem.Click                 332
PrintPreviewDialog1.Document = PrintDocument1                              333
PrintPreviewDialog1.ShowDialog()                                           334
End Sub                                                                     335

Private Sub PrintMenuItem_Click(ByVal sender As System.Object, _
ByVal e As System.EventArgs) Handles PrintMenuItem.Click                   336
PrintDialog1.Document = PrintDocument1                                     337
If PrintDialog1.ShowDialog() = System.Windows.Forms.DialogResult.OK Then   338
PrintDocument1.Print()                                                     339
End If                                                                      340
End Sub                                                                     341

Private Sub InsertImageMenuItem_Click(ByVal sender As System.Object, _
ByVal e As System.EventArgs) Handles InsertImageMenuItem.Click             342
Try                                                                         343
OpenFileDialog1.Title = "CADCIM - Insert Image File"                       344
OpenFileDialog1.DefaultExt = "rtf"                                         345
OpenFileDialog1.Filter = "Bitmap Files|*.bmp|JPEG Files|*.jpg|GIF Files|   346
*.gif"
OpenFileDialog1.FilterIndex = 1                                            347
OpenFileDialog1.ShowDialog()                                              348
```

```
If OpenFileDialog1.FileName = "" Then                                    349
Exit Sub                                                                 350
End If                                                                   351

Dim StrImagePath As String = OpenFileDialog1.FileName                    352
Dim Img As Image                                                         353
Dim Df As DataFormats.Format                                             354

Img = Image.FromFile(StrImagePath)                                       355
Clipboard.SetDataObject(Img)                                             356
Df = DataFormats.GetFormat(DataFormats.Bitmap)                           357

If Me.Rftbox.CanPaste(Df) Then                                           358
Me.Rftbox.Paste(Df)                                                      359
Else                                                                     360
MessageBox.Show("Cannot insert the image", "CADCIM")                     361
End If                                                                   362
Catch ex As Exception                                                    363
MessageBox.Show(ex.Message.ToString(), "Error-CADCIM")                   364
End Try                                                                  365
End Sub                                                                  366

Private Sub SelectAllMenuItem_Click(ByVal sender As System.Object, _
ByVal e As System.EventArgs) Handles SelectAllMenuItem.Click             367
Rftbox.SelectAll()                                                       368
End Sub                                                                  369

Private Sub CopyMenuItem_Click(ByVal sender As Object, _
ByVal e As System.EventArgs) Handles CopyMenuItem.Click                  370
Rftbox.Copy()                                                            371
End Sub                                                                  372

Private Sub CutMenuItem_Click(ByVal sender As Object, _
ByVal e As System.EventArgs) Handles CutMenuItem.Click                   373
Rftbox.Cut()                                                             374
End Sub                                                                  375

Private Sub PasteMenuItem_Click(ByVal sender As System.Object, _
ByVal e As System.EventArgs) Handles PasteMenuItem.Click                 376
Rftbox.Paste()                                                           377
End Sub                                                                  378

Private Sub NoneIndentMenuItem_Click(ByVal sender As System.Object, _
ByVal e As System.EventArgs) Handles NoneIndentMenuItem.Click
Rftbox.SelectionIndent = 0                                               379
End Sub                                                                  380
```

```
Private Sub Indent5MenuItem_Click(ByVal sender As System.Object, _
ByVal e As System.EventArgs) Handles Indent5MenuItem.Click          381
Rftbox.SelectionIndent = 5                                          382
End Sub                                                             383

Private Sub Indent10MenuItem_Click(ByVal sender As System.Object, _
ByVal e As System.EventArgs) Handles Indent10MenuItem.Click         384
Rftbox.SelectionIndent = 10                                         385
End Sub                                                             386

Private Sub Indent15MenuItem_Click(ByVal sender As System.Object, _
ByVal e As System.EventArgs) Handles Indent15MenuItem.Click         387
Rftbox.SelectionIndent = 15                                         388
End Sub                                                             389

Private Sub Indent20MenuItem_Click(ByVal sender As System.Object, _
ByVal e As System.EventArgs) Handles Indent20MenuItem.Click         390
Rftbox.SelectionIndent = 20                                         391
End Sub                                                             392
Private Sub AddBulletsMenuItem_Click(ByVal sender As System.Object, _
ByVal e As System.EventArgs) Handles AddBulletsMenuItem.Click       393
Rftbox.SelectionIndent = 10                                         394
Rftbox.SelectionBullet = True                                       395
End Sub                                                             396

Private Sub RemoveBulletsMenuItem_Click(ByVal sender As System.Object, _
ByVal e As System.EventArgs) Handles RemoveBulletsMenuItem.Click    397
Rftbox.SelectionIndent = 0                                          398
Rftbox.SelectionBullet = False                                      399
End Sub                                                             400

Private Sub ToolStripMenuItem3_Click(ByVal sender As System.Object, _
ByVal e As System.EventArgs) Handles ToolStripMenuItem3.Click       401
Rftbox.Cut()                                                        402
End Sub                                                             403

Private Sub ToolStripMenuItem2_Click(ByVal sender As System.Object, _
ByVal e As System.EventArgs) Handles ToolStripMenuItem2.Click       404
Rftbox.Paste()                                                      405
End Sub                                                             406

Private Sub tbrSave_Click(ByVal sender As System.Object, _
ByVal e As System.EventArgs) Handles tbrSave.Click                  407
SaveMenuItem_Click(Me, New EventArgs)                               408
End Sub                                                             409

Private Sub tbrNew_Click(ByVal sender As System.Object, _
```

```
ByVal e As System.EventArgs) Handles tbrNew.Click                         410
NewMenuItem_Click(Me, New EventArgs)                                      411
End Sub                                                                   412


Private Sub SelectFontMenuItem_Click(ByVal sender As System.Object, _
ByVal e As System.EventArgs) Handles SelectFontMenuItem.Click            413
Try                                                                       414
If Rftbox.SelectionFont.Name = "" Then                                   415
FontDialog1.Font = Rftbox.SelectionFont                                  416
Else                                                                      417
FontDialog1.Font = Nothing                                               418
End If                                                                    419


FontDialog1.ShowApply = True                                             420
If FontDialog1.ShowDialog = System.Windows.Forms.DialogResult.OK Then    421
Rftbox.SelectionFont = FontDialog1.Font                                  422
End If                                                                    423
Catch ex As Exception                                                    424
MessageBox.Show(ex.Message.ToString(), "Error-CADCIM")                   425
End Try                                                                   426
End Sub                                                                   427


Private Sub tbrFont_Click(ByVal sender As System.Object, _
ByVal e As System.EventArgs) Handles tbrFont.Click                       428
SelectFontMenuItem_Click(Me, New EventArgs)                              429
End Sub                                                                   430


Private Sub Btn_Find_Click_1(ByVal sender As System.Object, _
ByVal e As System.EventArgs) Handles Btn_Find.Click                      431
Try                                                                       432
If Trim(Rftbox.Text) = "" Then Exit Sub                                  433
Dim StartPosition As Integer                                             434
Dim SearchType As StringComparison                                       435


If ChkMatchCase.Checked = True Then                                      436
SearchType = StringComparison.Ordinal                                    437
Else                                                                      438
SearchType = StringComparison.OrdinalIgnoreCase                          439
End If                                                                    440


StartPosition = Rftbox.Text.IndexOf(TxtFind.Text, SearchType)           441


If StartPosition = 0 Then                                                442
MessageBox.Show("String: " + TxtFind.Text.ToString() + " not found", _
"No Matches", MessageBoxButtons.OK, MessageBoxIcon.Asterisk)            443
Exit Sub                                                                 444
End If                                                                   445
```

```
Rftbox.Select(StartPosition, TxtFind.TextLength)                         446
Rftbox.ScrollToCaret()                                                    447
Rftbox.Focus()                                                            448
Btn_FindNext.Enabled = True                                               449

Catch ex As Exception                                                     450
MessageBox.Show(ex.Message.ToString(), "Error-CADCIM")                    451
End Try                                                                   452
End Sub                                                                   453

Private Sub Btn_FindNext_Click_1(ByVal sender As System.Object, _
ByVal e As System.EventArgs) Handles Btn_FindNext.Click                   454
Try                                                                       455
If Trim(Rftbox.Text) = "" Then Exit Sub                                   456
Dim StartPosition As Integer = Rftbox.SelectionStart + 2                  457
Dim SearchType As StringComparison                                        458
If ChkMatchCase.Checked = True Then                                       459
SearchType = StringComparison.Ordinal                                     460
Else                                                                      461
SearchType = StringComparison.OrdinalIgnoreCase                           462
End If                                                                    463

StartPosition = Rftbox.Text.IndexOf(TxtFind.Text, StartPosition, SearchType)   464

If StartPosition = 0 Or StartPosition < 0 Then                            465
MessageBox.Show("String: " + TxtFind.Text.ToString() + " not found", _
"No Matches", MessageBoxButtons.OK, MessageBoxIcon.Asterisk)              466
Exit Sub                                                                  467
End If                                                                    468

Rftbox.Select(StartPosition, TxtFind.Text.Length)                         469
Rftbox.ScrollToCaret()                                                    470
Rftbox.Focus()                                                            471
Btn_FindNext.Enabled = True                                               472

Catch ex As Exception                                                     473
MessageBox.Show(ex.Message.ToString(), "Error-CADCIM")                    474
End Try                                                                   475
End Sub                                                                   476

Private Sub Btn_FClose_Click(ByVal sender As System.Object, _
ByVal e As System.EventArgs) Handles Btn_FClose.Click                     477
FindPanel.Visible = False                                                 478
End Sub                                                                   479

Private Sub Btn_Replace_Click(ByVal sender As System.Object, _
ByVal e As System.EventArgs) Handles Btn_Replace.Click                    480
```

```
Try                                                                   481
If Trim(Rftbox.Text) = "" Then Exit Sub                               482
If Rftbox.SelectedText.Length <> 0 Then                               483
Rftbox.SelectedText = Txt_Replace.Text                                484
End If                                                                485

Dim StartPosition As Integer                                         486
Dim SearchType As StringComparison                                    487

If Chk_Matchcase.Checked = True Then                                  488

SearchType = StringComparison.Ordinal                                489
Else                                                                  490
SearchType = StringComparison.OrdinalIgnoreCase                       491
End If                                                                492

StartPosition = Rftbox.Text.IndexOf(Txt_search.Text, SearchType)      493

If StartPosition = 0 Or StartPosition < 0 Then                        494
MessageBox.Show("String: " + Txt_search.Text.ToString() + " not found", _
"No Matches", MessageBoxButtons.OK, MessageBoxIcon.Asterisk)          495
Exit Sub                                                              496
End If                                                                497
Rftbox.Select(StartPosition, Txt_search.Text.Length)                  498
Rftbox.ScrollToCaret()                                                499

Catch ex As Exception                                                 500
MessageBox.Show(ex.Message.ToString(), "Error-CADCIM")                501
End Try                                                               502
End Sub                                                               503

Private Sub Btn_RFind_Click(ByVal sender As System.Object, _
ByVal e As System.EventArgs) Handles Btn_RFind.Click                  504
Try                                                                   505
If Trim(Rftbox.Text) = "" Then Exit Sub                               506
Dim StartPosition As Integer = Rftbox.SelectionStart + 2              507
Dim SearchType As StringComparison                                    508

If Chk_Matchcase.Checked = True Then                                  509
SearchType = StringComparison.Ordinal                                510
Else                                                                  511
SearchType = StringComparison.OrdinalIgnoreCase                       512
End If                                                                513

StartPosition = Rftbox.Text.IndexOf(Txt_search.Text, _
StartPosition, SearchType)                                            514
```

```
If StartPosition = 0 Or StartPosition < 0 Then                                    515
MessageBox.Show("String: " + Txt_search.Text.ToString() + " not found", _
"No Matches", MessageBoxButtons.OK, MessageBoxIcon.Asterisk)                      516
Exit Sub                                                                          517
End If                                                                            518

Rftbox.Select(StartPosition, Txt_search.Text.Length)                              519
Rftbox.ScrollToCaret()                                                            520
Rftbox.Focus()                                                                    521
Btn_RF_Next.Enabled = True                                                        522
Catch ex As Exception                                                             523
MessageBox.Show(ex.Message.ToString(), "Error-CADCIM")                            524
End Try                                                                           525
End Sub                                                                           526

Private Sub Btn_RF_Next_Click(ByVal sender As System.Object, _
ByVal e As System.EventArgs) Handles Btn_RF_Next.Click                            527
Try                                                                               528
If Trim(Rftbox.Text) = "" Then Exit Sub                                           529
Dim StartPosition As Integer = Rftbox.SelectionStart + 2                          530
Dim SearchType As StringComparison                                                531

If Chk_Matchcase.Checked = True Then                                              532
SearchType = StringComparison.Ordinal                                             533
Else                                                                              534
SearchType = StringComparison.OrdinalIgnoreCase                                   535
End If                                                                            536

StartPosition = Rftbox.Text.IndexOf(Txt_search.Text, StartPosition, _
SearchType)                                                                       537

If StartPosition = 0 Or StartPosition < 0 Then                                    538
MessageBox.Show("String: " + Txt_search.Text.ToString() + " not found", _
"No Matches", MessageBoxButtons.OK, MessageBoxIcon.Asterisk)                      539
Exit Sub                                                                          540
End If                                                                            541

Rftbox.Select(StartPosition, Txt_search.Text.Length)                              542
Rftbox.ScrollToCaret()                                                            543
Rftbox.Focus()                                                                    544
Btn_RFind.Enabled = True                                                          545

Catch ex As Exception                                                             546
MessageBox.Show(ex.Message.ToString(), "Error-CADCIM")                            547
End Try                                                                           548
End Sub                                                                           549
```

```
Private Sub Btn_AReplace_Click(ByVal sender As System.Object, _
ByVal e As System.EventArgs) Handles Btn_AReplace.Click                550
Try                                                                     551
If Trim(Rftbox.Text) = "" Then Exit Sub                                552
Rftbox.Rtf = Rftbox.Rtf.Replace(Txt_search.Text.Trim(), _
Txt_Replace.Text.Trim())                                               553

Dim StartPosition As Integer                                           554
Dim SearchType As StringComparison                                     555

If Chk_Matchcase.Checked = True Then                                   556
SearchType = StringComparison.Ordinal                                  557
Else                                                                    558
SearchType = StringComparison.OrdinalIgnoreCase                        559
End If                                                                   560

StartPosition = Rftbox.Text.IndexOf(Txt_Replace.Text, SearchType)      561

Rftbox.Select(StartPosition, Txt_Replace.Text.Length)                  562
Rftbox.ScrollToCaret()                                                  563

Catch ex As Exception                                                   564
MessageBox.Show(ex.Message.ToString(), "Error-CADCIM")                 565
End Try                                                                  566
End Sub                                                                  567

Private Sub Btn_RClose_Click(ByVal sender As System.Object, _
ByVal e As System.EventArgs) Handles Btn_RClose.Click                  568
ReplacePanel.Visible = False                                           569
End Sub                                                                  570

Private Sub tbrOpen_Click(ByVal sender As System.Object, _
ByVal e As System.EventArgs) Handles tbrOpen.Click                     571
OpenMenuItem_Click(Me, New EventArgs)                                  572
End Sub                                                                  573

Private Sub FileToolStripMenuItem_Click(ByVal sender As System.Object, _
ByVal e As System.EventArgs) Handles FileToolStripMenuItem.Click        574
End Sub                                                                  575
Private Sub ToolStripMenuItem1_Click(ByVal sender As System.Object, _
ByVal e As System.EventArgs)                                            576
End Sub                                                                  577
End Class                                                                578
```

Explanation

The line-by-line explanation of the above given source code is as follows:

Lines 16-32

The lines from 16-32 include the source code for the **FormClosing** event of the form. In these lines, if the user tries to close the text file without saving it, then the **Unsaved Document** message box with the message **Save current document before exit?** will be displayed, as shown in Figure 8-8. If the user chooses the **No** button, the contents of the **RichTextBox** will be cleared and the user will get a new file to use. If the user chooses the **Yes** button, then the **Save File** dialog box will be displayed, as shown in Figure 8-9. You can save the file with any name by entering the name in the **File name** edit box and using the following formats:

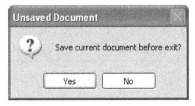

*Figure 8-8 The **Unsaved Document** message box*

*Figure 8-9 The **Save File** dialog box*

1. Rich Text Files
2. Text Files
3. HTML Files
4. All Files

Lines 33-47

The lines from 33-47 include the source code for the **Load** event of the form. In these lines, the values are assigned to different properties. The values assigned to the properties are as follows:

Control	Property	Value
RichTextbox	Name	Rftbox
RichTextbox	Dock	Fill
RichTextbox	Size	0, 5
ContextMenuStrip1	Visible	True
ContextMenuStrip1	Enabled	False
FindPanel	Visible	False
Btn_FindNext	Enabled	False
Btn_RF_Next	Enabled	False

Lines 63-69
The lines from 63-69 include the source code for the **TextChanged** event of the **ExtendedRichTextbox**. In these lines, the **If-End If** statement is used. If null value is assigned to the **Text** property of the **ExtendedRichTextbox**, then the **ContextMenu1** will be disabled. Otherwise, it will be enabled.

Lines 70-93
The lines from 70-93 include the source code for the **Click** event of the **NewMenuItem**. If the user tries to create a new text file without saving the previous file, a message box titled **Unsaved Document** with the message **Save current document before creating New Document?** will be displayed. If the user chooses the **No** button, then the content of the **RichTextBox** will be cleared and the user will get a new file to use. If the user chooses the **Yes** button, then the **Save File** dialog box will be displayed. You can save the file with any name by entering the name in the **File name** edit box.

Lines 94-99
In these lines, the sub procedure **OpenFile()** is declared. The value **CADCIM - Open File** is assigned to the **Title** value of the **OpenFile**. Similarly, the value **rtf** is assigned to the **DefaultExt** property of the **OpenFile**, the value **Rich Text Files|*.rtf|Text Files|*.txt|HTML Files|*.htm|All Files|*.*** is assigned to the **Filter** property, the value **1** is assigned to the **FilterIndex** property, and the value **String.empty** is assigned to the **FileName** of the **OpenFile**.

Lines 100-125
If the sub procedure **OpenFile** is called and the null value has been assigned to the **File name**, the sub procedure will exit. The variable **StrExt** is declared as string. The statement **Path. GetExtension** will get the file extension in the **Open** dialog box. This path will then be assigned to the variable **StrExt**. If the value *.RTF* is assigned to the variable **StrExt**, then the file will be loaded directly. Otherwise, the **StreamReader** will read the text of the file line-by-line and then load it. If the user cancels the **Open** dialog box, a message **Open File request cancelled by user** will be displayed in the **Cancelled** message box.

Lines 126-139
When the user chooses the **OpenMenu** option from the menu bar, the message **Save current document before creating new document** will be displayed in the **Unsaved Document** message box. If the user chooses the **No** button, the **OpenFile** sub procedure will be called. Otherwise, the sub procedure **SaveMenuItem_Click** will be called.

Lines 140-164
The lines from 140-164 include the source code for the **Click** event of the **SaveMenuItem**. If the value *.RTF* is assigned to the variable **StrExt**, then the file will be saved directly. Otherwise, the **StreamWriter** will open a file for writing and then write the string to the stream. Then, the **Close()** method will close the **StreamWriter** and the file name will be displayed on the title bar of the form.

Lines 200-211
The lines from 208-219 include the source code for the **Click** event of the **BoldMenuItem**. In these lines, whenever the user chooses the **Bold** option, the application will first check if the text is already bold. If it is already bold, then the **Bold** option will make it unbold. But, if the text is unbold, then choosing the **Bold** option will make it bold.

Lines 290-292
These lines will start the printing procedure. It will first check the number of pages before printing and then print the required document.

Lines 293-300
These lines include the source code for the **PrintPage** event of the **PrintDocument1** component. Before the printing process starts, it will check if the additional pages should also be printed or not.

Step 10
Execute the application; the output will be displayed, as shown in Figure 8-10.

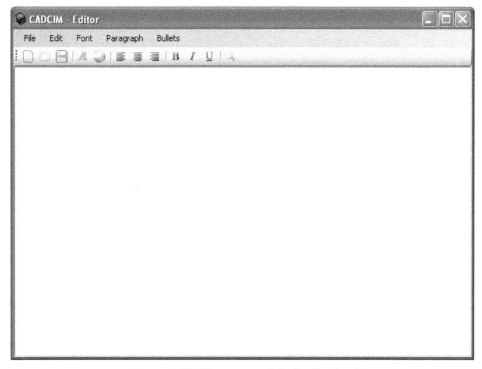

Figure 8-10 *The output of the Application 1*

Step 11
Enter the required text on the editor. Choose **File > Save** from the menu bar and save the file as the text document. You will notice the name of the file on the title bar, as shown in Figure 8-11.

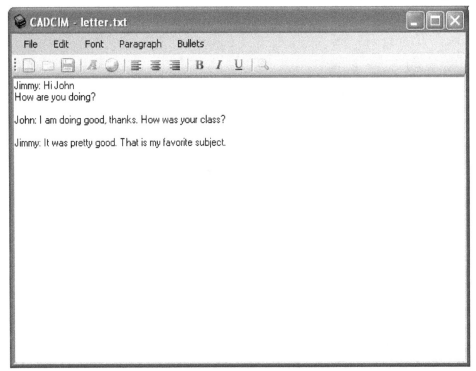

Figure 8-11 The name of the file displayed on the title bar

Step 12
Choose **Edit > Insert image** from the menu bar; the **Insert Image File** dialog box will be displayed, as shown in Figure 8-12. Select any image and choose the **OK** button; the image will be added at the position of cursor, as shown in Figure 8-13.

Step 13
Choose **File > Page Setup**; the **Page Setup** dialog box will be displayed, as shown in Figure 8-14. You can set the margin, size, orientation, and so on of the document with the help of this dialog box. After setting the values, choose the **OK** button on the **Page Setup** dialog box.

Step 14
Choose **File > Preview** from the menu bar; the **Print preview** screen will be displayed, as shown in Figure 8-15.

Step 15
Choose **File > Print** from the menu bar; the **Print** dialog box will be displayed, as shown in Figure 8-16. Select a printer and then choose the **Printer** button; the document will start printing.

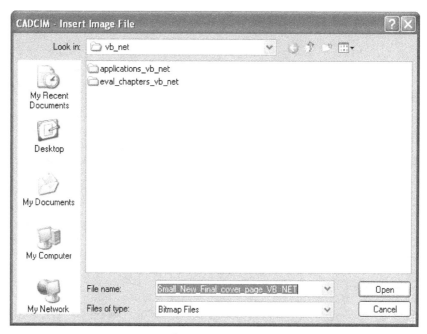

*Figure 8-12 The **Insert Image File** dialog box*

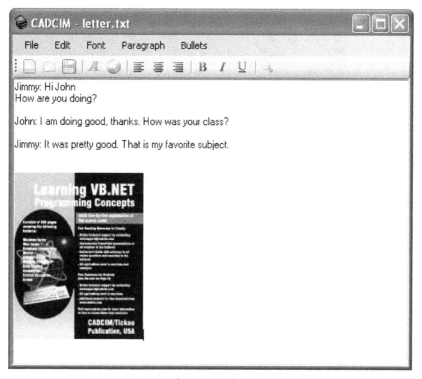

Figure 8-13 The output form with an image

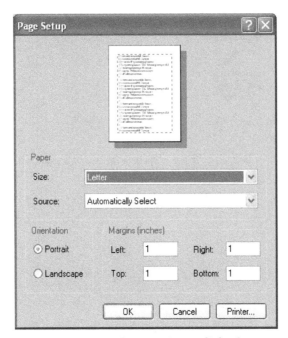

Figure 8-14 *The* **Page Setup** *dialog box*

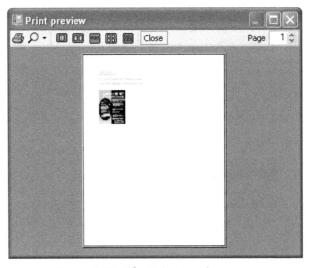

Figure 8-15 *The* **Print preview** *screen*

Step 16

To find and replace any string, choose **Edit > Find and Replace** from the menu bar; the toolstrip will be displayed, as shown in Figure 8-17. You can hide the toolstrip by choosing the (X) cross button located on the right side of the toolstrip.

Figure 8-16 The **Print** dialog box

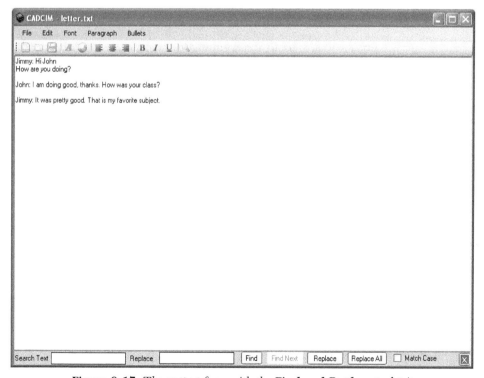

Figure 8-17 The output form with the **Find and Replace** toolstrip

Self-Evaluation Test

Answer the following questions and then compare them to those given at the end of this chapter:

1. The _____ can be used to specify the page details for printing.

2. The _____ property is used to enable or disable the editing of the margins.

3. The _____ component is used to let the user preview a document before it gets printed.

4. The _____ control is used to browse and select the folders.

5. The _____ property is used to check whether the file specified by the user exists or not.

Review Questions

Answer the following questions:

1. The _____ property is used to prompt a message in case the user specifies a file name that already exists.

2. The _____ property is used to determine whether the **Read-Only** check box is selected or not.

3. The _____ property of the **FolderBrowserDialog** component is used to set the location of the root folder from where you want to start browsing any subfolder.

4. The _____ property is used to set the font selected by the user.

5. The _____ applications allow you to display multiple documents simultaneously, wherein each document has its own document window.

Answers to Self-Evaluation Test
1. PageSetupDialog, 2. AllowMargin, 3. PrintPreviewControl, 4. FolderBrowserDialog, 5. CheckFileExists

Chapter 9

Concepts of Object-oriented Programming

Learning Objectives

After completing this chapter, you will be able to understand:
- *Structures.*
- *Classes.*
- *Use of the Is keyword.*
- *Constructors.*
- *Destructors.*
- *Inheritance.*
- *Overriding.*
- *Polymorphism.*
- *Overloading.*

INTRODUCTION

In this chapter, you will learn about the objects, structures, and classes. You will also understand the concepts of object-oriented programming in detail with its features such as Abstraction, Polymorphism, Encapsulation, and Inheritance. Also, you will learn about Overloading, Overriding, Shadowing, Constructors and Destructors.

STRUCTURES

In the earlier applications, you used arrays to group certain items. But while grouping with arrays, all the items were of the same data type. In case, you need to group items of different data types, then the concept of structures is used. Structures are used to handle a group of logically related data items. Structures are basically similar to classes. The only difference is that the structures are of the reference type whereas, the classes are of the value type. Moreover, the structures are used for smaller objects that do not persist in the memory for a long period whereas, the classes are used for larger objects that are expected to retain in the memory for a longer period. In VB.NET, the structures are declared using the keyword **Structure**.

The syntax for declaring a structure is as follows:

        AccessSpecifier Structure StructName
        FieldDeclaration
        End Structure

In the above syntax, **AccessSpecifier** is optional, **StructName** is the name of the structure, and **FieldDeclaration** is the declaration of field/fields. The **End Structure** marks the end of the structure.

For example:

        Structure Student
        Dim name As String
        Dim age As Integer
        Dim section As String
        End Structure

In the above example, the keyword **Structure** is used to direct the compiler that a structure is being declared. Here, **Student** is the name of the structure and the **End Structure** indicates the end of the structure. The statements between the declaration and the end of the structure represent the field declaration.

Note that you cannot create variables using the keyword **Structure**. It can only direct the compiler about the type of variables that you need to use within the body of the structure. To declare variables of the structure type, you have to use the keyword **Dim**.

For example:

```
Dim std As Student
std.name = "Mary"
std.age = 21
std.section = "A"
```

In this example, **std** is declared as a variable of the **Student** type. The **name, age**, and **section**, which are declared in the structure body are the fields of the structure **Student**. The dot (.) operator associated with the variable **std** is used to access the fields declared within the structure. You can also use the **With** statement to access the fields of a structure, as shown in the example given below:

```
Dim std As Student
With std
.name = "Mary"
.age = 21
.section = "A"
End With
```

The following application illustrates the use of the structures:

Application 1

Create an application to display the name of a student in the **ListBox** control using the concept of structures.

This application will display the name of a student in the **ListBox** control on a form.

The following steps are required to create this application:

Step 1
Start a new project and save it as **c09_VB_NET_2008_01**.

Step 2
Add a **Button** control and a **ListBox** control to the form.

Step 3
Double-click on the **Button** control; the code window will be displayed. Enter the source code given below in the code window. The line numbers on the right are not a part of the application and are for reference only.

```
Structure Student                                                1
Dim name As String                                               2
Dim age As Integer                                               3
Dim section As String                                            4
```

```
End Structure                                                           5
Private Sub Button1_Click(ByVal sender As System.Object, _
ByVal e As System.EventArgs) Handles Button1.Click                      6
Dim std As Student                                                      7
std.name = "Mary"                                                       8
std.age = 21                                                            9
std.section = "A"                                                       10
lstDisplay.Items.Add(std.name)                                          11
```

Explanation
The line-by-line explanation of the above given source code is as follows:

Line 1
Structure Student
In this line, the string **Student** is declared as a structure.

Line 5
End Structure
This line indicates the end of the structure **Student**.

Line 7
Dim std As Student
In this line, **std** is declared as a variable of the **Student** type.

Line 8
std.name = "Mary"
In this line, the value **Mary** is assigned to the **name** field of the variable **std** with the dot (.) operator.

Line 11
lstDisplay.Items.Add(std.name)
In the above line, the value **Mary** of the **name** field of the variable **std** will be added to the **ListBox** control.

Step 4
Execute the application. Choose the **Button** control on the form; the name **Mary** will be added to the **ListBox** control, as shown in Figure 9-1.

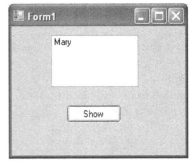

Figure 9-1 *Output of Application 1*

CLASSES

A class is a collection of data members and functions. These members and functions are used to manipulate the data. If needed, the class hides the data members and member functions from external use. In other words, it works like a protection cover for the data and functions. With the help of classes, you can write the code that can be used in multiple applications. All the controls that are used in VB.NET are examples of classes.

Defining a Class

The syntax for defining a class is as follows:

```
AccessSpecifier Class class_name
statement/statements
End Class
```

In the above syntax, the **AccessSpecifier** represents the visibility of the class to the outer code. Here, **Class** is a keyword and **class_name** represents the name of the class. **End Class** represents the end of the class. The various types of **AccessSpecifier** are discussed next.

Public

The **Public** members of a class can be accessed by the members of the same class and also the members of the other classes.

Private

By default, the members of a class are **Private**. These members can only be accessed by the other members of the same class.

Protected

The scope of the **Protected** members is between the **Public** and the **Private** access specifiers. Therefore, these members can be accessed either by the members of their own class or by the members of a class derived from their own class.

Friend

The **Friend** members can be accessed within the source code containing their declaration, as well as anywhere else in the same assembly.

Objects

An object is an instance of a class. The mode of communication among various objects of a program is determined by the methods and properties defined in the class of an object. For example, the **TextBox** class has the properties such as **BorderStyle**, **Text**, and **Name**. But different objects of this class contain their own values for these properties. For example, if there are two **TextBox** objects (controls) added to a form, you can set different values for the properties of both the **TextBox** controls according to your requirement.

Creating a Class

The steps required to create a class are given next.

Step1
Start a new project and save it as **class_demo**.

Step 2
Right-click on the name of the project in the **Solution Explorer** window. Choose **Add > Class** from the context menu to invoke the **Add New Item** dialog box, as shown in Figure 9-2.

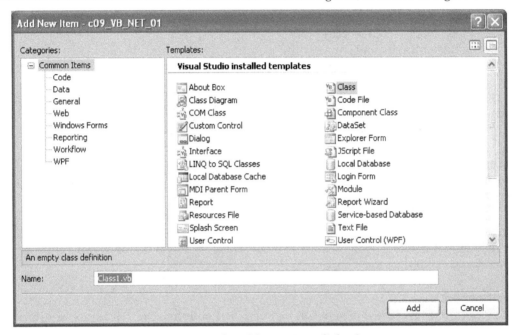

*Figure 9-2 The **Add New Item** dialog box*

Step 3
Select the **Class** option from the **Templates** area. Change the name of the class as **Employee** in the **Name** edit-box.

Step 4
Choose the **Add** button on the **Add New Item** dialog box; the code window will be displayed with the following source code:

```
Public Class Employee
End Class
```

You can add your code between the above lines.

For example:

        Public Class Employee
        Public Name As String
        Public Age As Integer
        Public Designation As String
        End Class

In the above example, **Employee** is declared as a class, and **Name** (String type), **Age** (Integer type), and **Designation** (String type) are declared as the data members of the class **Employee**.

Creating an Object of a Class

After creating a class, you can create instances of that class. These instances are known as the objects of a class. The objects of a class inherit the properties of their base class. You can identify each class on the basis of some of their specific properties. The syntax for creating an object of a class is as follows:

        Dim obj_name As New class_name

In the above syntax, the object **obj_name** is created from the class **class_name** with the help of the keyword **New**.

For example:

        Dim emp As New Employee

In the above example, **emp** is an object and the keyword **New** creates a new object instance of the class **Employee**.

You can also write the above example using another method, which is as follows:

        Dim emp As Employee
        emp = New Employee

In the above source code, the keyword **Dim** in the first line creates an object **emp** of the class **Employee**. The keyword **New** in the second line creates a new instance of the class **Employee**.

Accessing the Members of a Class

Like structures, you can also access the members of a class with the help of the dot (**.**) operator. For example, if **emp** is the object of the class **Employee**, then the following source code will help you store the values in the **Public** data members of the class **Employee**:

        emp.Name = "Joe"
        emp.Age = 25
        emp.Designation = "Doctor"

In the this code, **Name** is the data member of the class **Employee** and **Joe** is the value assigned to the data member **Name**. Similarly, the values **25** and **Doctor** are assigned to the **Age** and **Designation** data members, respectively.

Using the 'Is' Keyword to Compare Objects

Sometimes multiple variables may refer to the same object in the memory. In such cases, you cannot use the assignment operator to compare the two variables that are referring to the same object. For this purpose, the **Is** keyword is used. For example, you may have a class **Employee** in your application having two objects, **cmp1Employee** and **cmp2Employee**. As both the objects in this case are referring to the same instance of the class **Employee**, therefore the keyword **Is** is used. The source code for using the **Is** keyword is given next.

```
Dim cmp1Employee As Employee
Dim cmp2Employee As Employee
Private Sub Button1_Click(ByVal sender As System.Object, _
ByVal e As System.EventArgs) Handles Button1.Click
cmp1Employee = New Employee
cmp1Employee = cmp2Employee
If cmp1Employee Is cmp2Employee Then
TextBox1.Text = "This is the use of the Is keyword"
End If
End Sub
```

CONSTRUCTORS

A constructor is a special member function that is used to initialize the objects of a class. For creating a constructor, you need to create a sub procedure called **New** in the class. The **New** sub procedure will be executed each time an instance of the class is created.

The following application illustrates the use of a constructor:

Application 2

Create an application to display the message **This is use of the constructor**, using the concept of constructors.

This application will display the message **This is use of the constructor** on a windows form.

The following steps are required to create this application:

Step 1
Start a new project and save it as **c09_VB_NET_2008_02**.

Step 2
Add a **Button** control and a **TextBox** control to the form.

Step 3
Enter the following source code in the code window:

```
Public Class Employee                                              1
Private name As String                                             2
Private designation As String                                      3
Private id As Integer                                              4
Public Sub New()                                                   5
name = ""                                                          6
designation = ""                                                   7
id = 0.0                                                           8
End Sub                                                            9
End Class                                                         10

Public Class Form1                                                11
Dim cmp1Employee As Employee                                      12
Dim cmp2Employee As Employee                                      13
Private Sub Button1_Click(ByVal sender As System.Object, _
ByVal e As System.EventArgs) Handles Button1.Click                14
cmp1Employee = New Employee                                       15
cmp1Employee = cmp2Employee                                       16
If cmp1Employee Is cmp2Employee Then                              17
TextBox1.Text = "This is use of the constructor"                  18
End If                                                            19
End Sub                                                           20
End Class                                                         21
```

Explanation
The line-by-line explanation of the above given source code is as follows:

Line 1
Public Class Employee
In this line, the class named **Employee** is declared as **Public**.

Line 2
Private name As String
In this line, the string type variable **name** is declared as a **Private** data member of the class **Employee**.

Line 3
Private designation As String
In this line, the string type variable **designation** is declared as **Private**.

Line 4
Private id As Integer
In this line, the integer type variable **id** is declared as **Private**.

Line 5
Public Sub New()
In this line, the constructor is created using the sub procedure **New**.

Line 12
Dim cmp1Employee As Employee
In this line, **cmp1Employee** is declared as an object of the class **Employee**.

Line 13
Dim cmp2Employee As Employee
In this line, the variable **cmp2Employee** is declared as an object of the class **Employee**.

Line 17
If cmp1Employee Is cmp2Employee Then
In this line, the **Is** keyword is used to determine whether the two objects **cmp1Employee** and **cmp2Employee** of the class **Employee** refer to the same memory locations.

Step 4
Execute the application. Choose the **Button** control; the message **This is use of the constructor** will be displayed in a **TextBox** control, as shown in Figure 9-3.

Figure 9-3 *Output of Application 2*

DESTRUCTORS

When an object is no longer required in a program, it is destroyed from the memory using the destructors. Therefore, the destructors or finalizers are run by a class at the end of a program. You can place code within a destructor to clean up the object, after it is no longer in use. The clean up of objects might include releasing the resources or decrementing the counters. To do so, the **Finalize** method is used. This method is automatically called when the .NET runtime determines that the object is no longer required. While working with destructors, you need to use the **Overrides** keyword. Usually, the **Finalize** method is used to deallocate the resources and inform the other objects that the current object is going to be destroyed. The syntax for using the destructors is as follows:

```
Public Class ClassA
Protected Overrides Sub Finalize()
MyBase.Finalize()
End Sub
End Class
```

INHERITANCE

In this section, you will learn about some more features of VB.NET such as reusability and inheritance. Reusability is a mechanism with which you can reuse a class that is already available. This mechanism saves a lot of time because you do not need to create the same code repeatedly. Once a class has been created and debugged, it can be used in several ways. In VB.NET, reusability is also used for creating a new class from an existing one by reusing its properties. The technique of creating a new class from an old one is known as inheritance. The new class is known as the derived class and the old one is known as the base class. A derived class can inherit some or all the properties of a base class and can also add some other properties of its own. The following is the syntax for inheriting properties of a base class:

```
Public Class DerivedClassName
Inherits BaseClassName
Member variables
End Class
```

In the above syntax, the derived class is specified by the **DerivedClassName**. The keyword **Inherits** associated with the **BaseClassName** is used to inherit some or all the properties of the base class. In the third line, you can declare the data member of the derived class. In the last line, the **End Class** indicates the end of the derived class.

The following application illustrates the use of inheritance in the programs:

Application 3

Create an application to display the details of a book in a **ListBox** control.

This application will display the details of a book in the **ListBox** control, using a class named **Book**.

The following steps are required to create this application:

Step 1
Start a new project and save it as **c09_VB_NET_2008_03**.

Step 2
Add a **Button** control and a **ListBox** control to the form.

Step 3
Enter the following source code in the code window:

```
Public Class Books                                          1
Private numPage As Integer                                  2
Private Title As String                                     3
Public Property Pages() As Integer                          4
Get                                                         5
```

```
Return numPage                                              6
End Get                                                     7
Set(ByVal Value As Integer)                                8
numPage = Value                                            9
End Set                                                    10
End Property                                               11
Public Property BookTitle() As String                     12
Get                                                        13
Return Title                                              14
End Get                                                    15
Set(ByVal Value As String)                                16
Title = Value                                             17
End Set                                                    18
End Property                                               19
End Class                                                  20
```

Step 4

Double-click on the **Button** control and enter the following source code:

```
Public Class VB                                           21
Inherits Books                                            22
Private Weight As Single                                  23
Public Property MaxWeight() As Single                     24
Get                                                        25
Return Weight                                             26
End Get                                                    27
Set(ByVal Value As Single)                                28
Weight = Value                                            29
End Set                                                    30
End Property                                               31
End Class                                                  32
Private Sub Button1_Click(ByVal sender As System.Object,
ByVal e As System.EventArgs) Handles Button1.Click        33
Dim edition As VB                                         34
edition = New VB                                          35
edition.Pages = 390                                       36
edition.BookTitle = "Programming"                         37
edition.MaxWeight = 500                                   38
ListBox1.Items.Add(edition.MaxWeight)                     39
ListBox1.Items.Add(edition.Pages)                         40
ListBox1.Items.Add(edition.BookTitle)                     41
End Sub                                                    42
```

Explanation

The line-by-line explanation of the above given source code is given next.

Line 1
Public Class Books
In this line, the class **Books** is declared as **Public**. It is the base class.

Line 2
Private numPage As Integer
In this line, the **Integer** data member **numPage** is declared as **Private**. It is used to specify the number of pages in the book.

Line 3
Private Title As String
In this line, the **String** data member, **Title** is declared as **Private**. It is used to specify the title of the book.

Line 4
Public Property Pages() As Integer
In this line, **Property Pages** is declared as **Public** and its return type is integer.

Line 5
Get
The **Get** procedure is used to retrieve the value from a property.

Line 6
Return numPage
In this line, the value of the variable **numPage** will be returned to the **Get** procedure.

Line 7
End Get
This line indicates the end of the **Get** procedure.

Line 8
Set(ByVal Value As Integer)
In this line, the **Set** procedure is used to hold the code that is executed when the value is stored in the property.

Line 9
numPage = Value
In this line, the value of the variable **Value** is assigned to the **numPage**.

Line 10
End Set
This line indicates the end of the **Set** procedure.

Line 11
End Property
This line indicates the end of the **Property Pages** procedure.

Line 21
Public Class VB
In this line, the class **VB** is declared as **Public**. It is the derived class.

Line 22
Inherits Books
In this line, the keyword **Inherits** associated with the base class **Books** is used to inherit some or all the properties of the base class **Books** to the derived class **VB**.

Step 5
Execute the application and choose the **Button** control on the form; the details of the book will be displayed in the **ListBox** control, as shown in Figure 9-4.

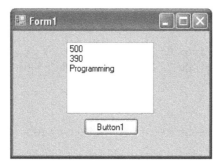

Figure 9-4 *Output of Application 3*

Public Inheritance

Declaring the member of a class as **Public** indicates that it can be used anywhere in the program. If the members of a base class are declared as **Public**, then they will be declared as **Public** in the derived class by default. This is known as **Public** inheritance. To declare the members of a class as **Public**, you need to add the keyword **Public** with them.

Application 4

The following application illustrates the use of **Public** inheritance:
Create an application to illustrate the use of **Public** inheritance.

This application will create a base class **Animal** and a derived class **Horse** using the **Public** inheritance.

The following steps are required to create this application:

Step 1
Start a new project and save it as **c09_VB_NET_2008_04**.

Step 2

Add a **Button** control and a **TextBox** control to the window form.

Step 3
Set the **Text** property of the **TextBox** control to the string **Null**.

Step 4
Enter the following source code in the code window:

```
Public Class Form1                                              1
Dim anml As Horse                                               2
Private Sub Button1_Click(ByVal sender As System.Object, _
ByVal e As System.EventArgs) Handles Button1.Click              3
anml = New Horse(Me)                                            4
anml.Running()                                                  5
End Sub                                                         6
End Class                                                       7
Public Class Animal                                             8
Protected frm As Form1                                          9
Public Sub New(ByVal form1 As Form1)                            10
frm = form1                                                     11
End Sub                                                         12
Public Sub Running()                                            13
frm.TextBox1.Text = "Running"                                   14
End Sub                                                         15
End Class                                                       16

Public Class Horse                                              17
Inherits Animal                                                 18
Public Sub New(ByVal form1 As Form1)                            19
MyBase.New(form1)                                               20
End Sub                                                         21
Public Sub Drinking()                                           22
frm.TextBox1.Text = "Drinking"                                  23
End Sub                                                         24
End Class                                                       25
```

Explanation
The line-by-line explanation of the above given source code is as follows:

Line 4
anml = New Horse(Me)
In this line, the keyword **New** is associated with the class **Animal** from which the new instance can be created. In this application, the new instance of the class **Horse** is created. The keyword **Me** refers to the current form.

Line 5
anml.Running()

This line is used to call the method **Running** of the class **Animal** through the object **anml**.

Line 10
Public Sub New(ByVal form1 As Form1)
In this line, the procedure **New** is declared as **Public**.

Step 5
Execute the application and choose the **Button** control; the word **Running** will be displayed in the **TextBox** control.

Protected Inheritance
Declaring the data member of a class as **Protected** indicates that it can be accessed both by the class in which it is declared as well as the members of the derived class.

Private Inheritance
Declaring the member of a class as **Private** indicates that it can be accessed only by the given class and not by any other class. The members which are declared as **Private** cannot be accessed even by the derived classes. All the applications given in the earlier chapters used the **Private** inheritance.

Friend Inheritance
The members that are declared as **Friend** are accessible both within the source code where they are declared as well as anywhere else in the given assembly. The keyword **Friend** can be used with the following statements:

1. Class Statement_
2. Const Statement_
3. Declare Statement_
4. Delegate Statement
5. Dim Statement_
6. Enum Statement_
7. Event Statement_
8. Function Statement_
9. Interface Statement_
10. Module Statement
11. Property Statement_
12. Structure Statement_
13. Sub Statement

Application 5

The following application illustrates the use of the **Friend** inheritance:
Create an application to illustrate the use of the **Friend** inheritance.

This application will display the message **Programming world** using the **Friend** inheritance.

The following steps are required to create this application:

Step 1
Start a new project and save it as **c09_VB_NET_2008_05**.

Step 2
Add a **Button** control to the window form.

Step 3
Change the **Text** property of the **Button** control to **Display**.

Step 4
Enter the following source code in the code window:

```
Public Class Choose                                                    1
Friend Sub Display(ByVal Text As String)                               2
MsgBox(Text)                                                           3
End Sub                                                                4
End Class                                                              5

Public Class Form1                                                     6
Private Sub Button1_Click(ByVal sender As System.Object, _
ByVal e As System.EventArgs) Handles Button1.Click                     7
Dim show As New Choose                                                 8
show.Display("Programming world")                                      9
End Sub                                                                10
End Class                                                              11
```

Explanation
The line-by-line explanation of the above mentioned source code is as follows:

Line 1
Public Class Choose
In the above line, the class **Choose** is declared as **Public**.

Line 2
Friend Sub Display(ByVal Text As String)
In the above line, the keyword **Friend** is used so that the procedure **Display(ByVal Text As String)** can be accessed within the source code containing its declaration and by any other component of the same source code.

Line 3
MsgBox(Text)
When this line is executed, a message box will be displayed containing the string declared in Line 8.
Line 9

show.Display("Programming world")
In the above line, the control will be transferred to the sub procedure declared in Line 6.

Step 5
Execute the application and choose the **Display** button on the form; a message box containing the message **Programming world** will be displayed, as shown in Figure 9-5.

Figure 9-5   *Output of Application 5*

OVERRIDING

In VB.NET, the base class procedure or method can be overridden by writing it with the same name and the same number of parameters and data types in the derived class. This can be done by using the keyword **Overridable**. In such cases, when a property is accessed or a method is called by an object, then instead of the base class version, the overridden version gets executed. For example, the property procedure for the class **Books** in **c09_VB_NET_2008_03** is as follows:

```
Public Property Pages() As Integer
Get
Return numPage
End Get
Set(ByVal Value As Integer)
numPage = Value
End Set
End Property
```

In the above example, any value that is passed to the variable **numPage** is stored in the **Set** section. If you want to restrict the number of pages in the class **Books**, you can override the **Pages** property procedure by writing another version of it in the class **Books**.

For writing another version of the **Pages** property procedure, you have to add the keyword **Overridable** to the property procedure of the class **Books**, as given next.

```
Public Overridable Property Pages() As Integer
Get
Return numPage
End Get
Set(ByVal Value As Integer)
numPage = Value
End Set
End Property
```

In the above example, the keyword **Overridable** indicates that the procedure is overridden in the derived class. You can also restrict the number of pages by adding the source code within the property procedure. The source code to be added is as given next.

Public Overrides Property Pages() As Integer

Get
Return MyBase.Pages
End Get
Set(ByVal Value As Integer)
If Value >= 1 And Value <= 390 Then
MyBase.Pages = Value
Else
MsgBox("The value should be within the range", "Confirm")
End If
End Set
End Property
End Class

In the above source code, the keyword **MyBase** is the reference to the base class. So, the expression **MyBase.Pages** refers to the **Pages** property of the class **Books**. The **If** statement is used within the **Set** procedure to restrict the value of the **numPage** between 1 and 390. If the statement associated with the **If** statement is evaluated to true, the following source code will be executed:

MyBase.Pages = Value

If the value of the variable is not within the specified range, an error message will be displayed.

MustInherit Keyword

The keyword **MustInherit** is used to specify that a particular class can be used only as a base class. It means no instance can be created of that particular class.

The following example illustrates the use of the keyword **MustInherit**:

```
Public MustInherit Class Animal
Protected frm As Form1
Public Sub New(ByVal form3 As Form1)
frm = form3
End Sub
Public Overridable Sub Running()
frm.TextBox1.Text = "Running"
End Sub
End Class

Public Class Horse
Inherits Animal
Public Sub New(ByVal form3 As Form1)
MyBase.New(Form1)
End Sub
End Class

Public Class Cat
```

```
Inherits Animal
Public Sub New(ByVal form3 As Form1)
MyBase.New(Form1)
End Sub
End Class


Public Class Form1
Dim anml As Animal
Private Sub Button1_Click(ByVal sender As System.Object, _
ByVal e As System.EventArgs) Handles Button1.Click
anml = New Horse(Me)
anml.Running()
End Sub
End Class
```

OVERLOADING

VB.NET allows you to define different versions of a method in a class, and the compiler automatically selects the most appropriate method based on the parameters given. Generally, overloading is considered as a method that takes different parameters, but conceptually performs the same function. For example, the method **Draw** can be used to draw both rectangles as well as triangles. For drawing triangles, it will need six arguments corresponding to the x and y coordinates of three vertices. However, for drawing rectangles, it will need only four arguments. You can use the keyword **Overloads** with the overloading method.

Procedure Overloading

Procedure overloading defines multiple procedures using the same name but with different argument lists. The procedures can be overloaded to define similar procedures without differentiating them by name.

For example:

```
Private Overloads Sub ShowDateTime(ByVal dDate As Date, _
ByVal iOffset As Integer, ByVal sText As String)
MessageBox.Show(dDate.AddDays(iOffset).ToString() & " " & sText)
End Sub

Private Overloads Sub ShowDateTime(ByVal dDate As Date)
MessageBox.Show(dDate.ToString())
End Sub

Private Sub Form1_Load(ByVal sender As System.Object, _
ByVal e As System.EventArgs) Handles MyBase.Load
Call ShowDateTime(Now)
Call ShowDateTime(Now, 2, "info")
End Sub
```

POLYMORPHISM

Polymorphism is a greek term that consists of two words, **poly** and **morph**. **Poly** means many and **morph** means forms. So, polymorphism means 'one name, many forms'. There are two types of polymorphism used in VB.NET, which are as follows:

1. Inheritance-based Polymorphism
2. Interface-based Polymorphism

Inheritance-based Polymorphism

This is a type of polymorphism in which the methods are defined in the base class and you can override these methods with new implementations in the derived classes. For example, suppose a class **Animal** and a derived class **Horse** has been created. Also, a method **Shown** is created, so that you can pass an object of the class **Animal** to it. In such cases, inheritance-based polymorphism can be used to pass the objects of the class **Animal** or the objects of the class **Horse** to the method **Shown**. The following is the source code of this example:

```
Public Class Animal                                                 1
Overridable Sub Running()                                           2
MsgBox("Running")                                                   3
End Sub                                                             4
End Class                                                           5

Public Class Form1                                                  6
Public Class Horse                                                  7
Inherits Animal                                                     8
Overrides Sub Running()                                             9
MsgBox("Drinking")                                                 10
End Sub                                                            11
End Class                                                          12
Private Sub Button1_Click(ByVal sender As System.Object, _
ByVal e As System.EventArgs) Handles Button1.Click                 13
Dim dog As New Animal                                              14
Dim horse As New Horse                                             15
Shown(dog)                                                         16
Shown(horse)                                                       17
End Sub                                                            18
Public Sub Shown(ByVal Obj As Animal)                              19
Obj.Running()                                                      20
End Sub                                                            21
End Class                                                          22
```

Explanation

The line-by-line explanation of the above source code is given next.

Line 1
Public Class Animal
In the above line, the class **Animal** is declared as **Public**.

Line 2
Overridable Sub Running()
In the above line, the keyword **Overridable** is used to specify that the procedure **Running()** can be overridden in the derived class **Horse**.

Line 3
MsgBox("Running")
In the above line, the **MsgBox** function is used to display the message **Running** in the message box.

Line 4
End Sub
This line indicates the end of the method **Running**.

Line 5
End Class
This line indicates the end of the class **Animal**.

Line 7
Public Class Horse
In the above line, the class **Horse** is declared as **Public**.

Line 8
Inherits Animal
In the above line, the keyword **Inherits** is used to help the derived class **Horse** inherit the attributes, fields, properties, methods, and events of the class **Animal**.

Line 9
Overrides Sub Running()
In the above line, the keyword **Overrides** is used to specify that the procedure **Running** overrides the inherited member of the base class.

Line 10
MsgBox("Drinking")
In the above line, the **MsgBox** function is used to display the message **Drinking** in the message box.

Line 11
End Sub
This line indicates the end of the sub procedure **Running**.

Line 12
End Class
This line indicates the end of the class **Horse**.

Line 14
Dim dog As New Animal
In this line, the variable **dog** is declared as a new object member of the class **Animal**.

Line 15
Dim horse As New Horse
In this line, the variable **horse** is declared as a new object member of the class **Horse**.

Line 16
Shown(dog)
In this line, the method **Shown** is used to call the **Shown** method. The object **dog** of the class **Animal** is passed as an argument to the **Shown** method.

Line 17
Shown(horse)
In this line, the method **Shown** is used to call the **Shown** method. The object **horse** of the class **Animal** is passed as an argument to the **Shown** method.

Line 19
Public Sub Shown(ByVal Obj As Animal)
In this line, the parameters variable **Obj** is declared using the keyword **ByVal**. It means that the given argument is passed by the value to the parameter.

Line 20
Obj.Running()
This line is used to call the sub procedure **Running** of the object **Obj** of the class **Animal**.

On executing the application, the message **Running** (associated with the **Running** method of the class **Animal**) will be displayed in the message box, and then the message **Drinking** (associated with the **Drinking** method of the derived class **Horse**) will override the **Running** method.

Interface-based Polymorphism

In this type of polymorphism, you can create an interface and then implement it in different ways in different classes. For example, you can create an interface **AnimalIntr** and declare a method or a sub procedure **Run** for it. In this case, the interface-based polymorphism can be used to implement the **Run** method in different classes such as the **Dog** and **Horse** classes. An example of the interface-based polymorphism is illustrated in the following source code:

```
Public Interface AnimalIntr                                      1
Sub Run()                                                        2
End Interface                                                    3
Public Class Dog                                                 4
Implements AnimalIntr                                           5
Sub Run() Implements AnimalIntr.Run                             6
MsgBox("Running")                                               7
End Sub                                                          8
End Class                                                        9

Public Class Horse                                              10
Implements AnimalIntr                                          11
```

```
Sub Run() Implements AnimalIntr.Run                              12
MsgBox("Drinking")                                               13
End Sub                                                          14
End Class                                                        15
Public Class Form1                                               16
Private Sub Button1_Click(ByVal sender As System.Object, _
ByVal e As System.EventArgs) Handles Button1.Click               17
Dim dog As New Dog                                               18
Dim horse As New Horse                                           19
Shown(dog)                                                       20
Shown(horse)                                                     21
End Sub                                                          22
Public Sub Shown(ByVal Obj As AnimalIntr)                        23
Obj.Run()                                                        24
End Sub                                                          25
End Class                                                        26
```

Explanation
The line-by-line explanation of the above given source code is as follows:

Line 1
Public Interface AnimalIntr
In this line, **AnimalIntr** is declared as **Public Interface**.

Line 2
Sub Run()
In this line, the sub procedure **Run** is declared.

Line 3
End Interface
This line indicates the end of the interface **AnimalIntr**.

Lines 4 and 5
Public Class Dog
Implements AnimalIntr
The statement **Implements** is used to implement the methods, properties, and events of an interface. In the above lines, the class **Dog** is used to implement the members of the **AnimalIntr** interface.

Line 6
Sub Run() Implements AnimalIntr.Run
In this line, the sub procedure **Run**, declared in the **AnimalIntr** interface, is implemented on the class **Dog**.

The output of this source code is similar to the previous code.

The following application illustrates the use of the procedure overloading:

Application 6

Create an application to understand the concept of class and procedure overloading.

This application will display a form that will prompt the user to enter his personal details, and then it will display the details on the form.

The following steps are required to create this application:

Step 1
Start a new project and save it as **c09_VB_NET_2008_06**.

Step 2
Add six **TextBox** controls, five **Button** controls, and twelve **Label** controls to the window form. The resultant form will appear, as shown in Figure 9-6.
Step 3
Change the **Name** property of the control as follows:

TextBox1 to **TxtC_ID**
TextBox2 to **TxtFName**
TextBox3 to **TxtLName**
TextBox4 to **TxtAdd**

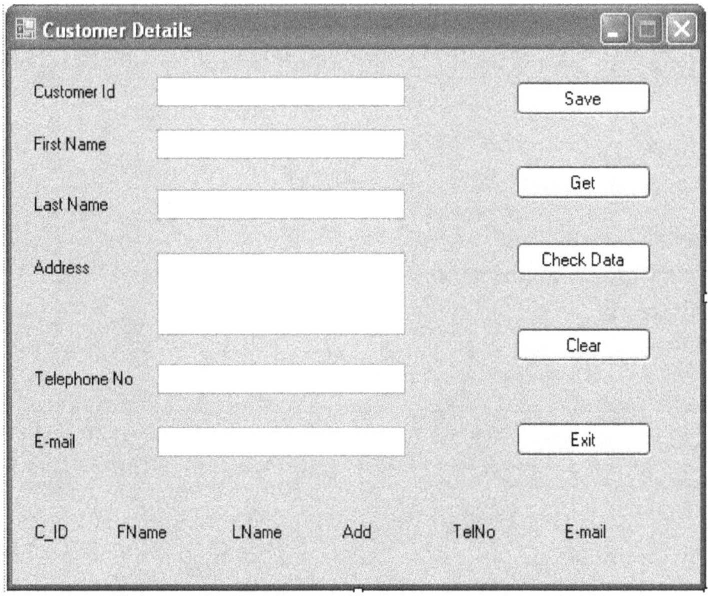

Figure 9-6 *The design mode of Application 6*

TextBox5 to **TxtTelNo**
TextBox6 to **TxtEmail**
Button1 to **BtnSave**
Button2 to **BtnGet**
Button3 to **BtnChkData**
Button4 to **BtnClear**
Button5 to **BtnExit**
Label7 to **LblC_ID**
Label8 to **LblFname**
Label9 to **LblLname**
Label10 to **LblAdd**
Label11 to **LblTelNo**
Label12 to **LblEmail**
Also, set the **MaximizeBox** property of the form to **False**.

Step 4
To add a class, choose the **Solution Explorer** tab. Right-click on the project name and choose **Add > Class** from the context menu; the **Add New Item** dialog box will be displayed. Change the name of the class to **Customer.vb** in the **Name** edit box and choose the **Add** button; the class name will be added to the **Solution Explorer** window and the class window will be displayed, as shown in Figure 9-7. Enter the following source code in the class **Customer** source code window:

Public Cid as String
Public Fname as String
Public Lname as String
Public Add as String
Public Telno as Long
Public Email as String
Step 5
Enter the following source code in the code window:

```
Public Class FrmCustomerDetails                            1
Dim ObjCust As New Customer                                2
Dim Bol_Txt As Boolean                                     3
Dim Bol_Int As Boolean                                     4
```

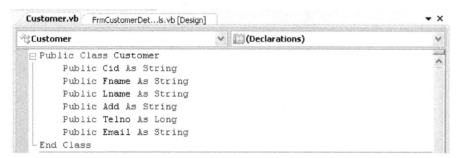

Figure 9-7 *The* **Customer** *class code window*

```
Private Sub FrmCustomerDetails_Load(ByVal sender As Object, _
ByVal e As System.EventArgs) Handles Me.Load                          5
Bol_Txt = False                                                        6
Bol_Int = False                                                        7
End Sub                                                                8


Private Sub BtnSave_Click(ByVal sender As Object, _
ByVal e As System.EventArgs) Handles BtnSave.Click                     9
With ObjCust                                                          10
.Cid = TxtC_ID.Text                                                  11
.Fname = TxtLName.Text                                               12
.Lname = TxtLName.Text                                               13
.Add = TxtAdd.Text                                                   14
.Telno = Val(TxtTelNo.Text)                                          15
.Email = TxtEmail.Text                                               16
End With                                                             17
End Sub                                                              18


Public Sub Validate_Data(ByVal Cid As String)                        19
Dim Chk_I As Integer                                                 20
Dim Chk_II As String                                                 21
Dim Chk_III As Boolean                                               22
Chk_I = Len(Cid)                                                     23
Chk_II = Mid(Cid, 1, 1)                                              24
Chk_III = Val(Mid(Cid, 2, 4))                                        25
If Chk_I <> 4 Or Chk_II <> "C" Or Chk_III <> True Then               26
MessageBox.Show("Please enter the valid data. The Customer id _
should start with letter 'C' " & Chr(13) & "and followed _
by three digits.", "Error-CADCIM", MessageBoxButtons.OK, _
MessageBoxIcon.Error)                                                27
Bol_Txt = True                                                       28
End If                                                               29
End Sub                                                              30


Public Sub Validate_Data(ByVal Telno As Long)                        31
If Len(Trim(Telno)) < 10 Or Len(Trim(Telno)) > 10 Then               32
MessageBox.Show("Please enter the valid data. The Telephone _
number should be of 10 digits", "Error-CADCIM", MessageBoxButtons.OK, _
MessageBoxIcon.Error)                                                33
Bol_Int = True                                                       34
End If                                                               35
End Sub                                                              36


Private Sub BtnGet_Click(ByVal sender As System.Object, _
ByVal e As System.EventArgs) Handles BtnGet.Click                    37
With ObjCust                                                         38
LblC_ID.Text = .Cid                                                  39
```

```vbnet
LblFName.Text = .Fname                                            40
LblLName.Text = .Lname                                            41
LblAdd.Text = .Add                                                42
LblTelNo.Text = .Telno                                            43
LblEmail.Text = .Email                                            44
End With                                                          45
End Sub                                                           46


Private Sub BtnChkData_Click(ByVal sender As System.Object, _
ByVal e As System.EventArgs) Handles BtnChkData.Click             47
Try                                                               48
Validate_Data(TxtC_ID.Text)                                       49
If Bol_Txt = True Then                                            50
Bol_Txt = False                                                   51
TxtC_ID.Clear()                                                   52
TxtC_ID.Focus()                                                   53
Exit Sub                                                          54
End If                                                            55
Dim Ctr_I As Long                                                 56
If Len(TxtTelNo.Text) = 0 Then                                    57
MessageBox.Show("Please enter the Telephone number")              58
Exit Sub                                                          59
ElseIf Val(TxtTelNo.Text) <> 0 Then                               60
Ctr_I = CType(TxtTelNo.Text, Long)                                61
Validate_Data(Ctr_I)                                              62
End If                                                            63
If Bol_Int = True Then                                            64
End If                                                            65
Catch ex As Exception                                             66
MessageBox.Show(ex.Message.ToString(), "Error-CADCIM", _
MessageBoxButtons.OK, MessageBoxIcon.Error)                       67
End Try                                                           68
End Sub                                                           69


Private Sub TxtTelNo_KeyPress(ByVal sender As Object, _
ByVal e As System.Windows.Forms.KeyPressEventArgs) _
Handles TxtTelNo.KeyPress                                         70
If Asc(e.KeyChar) = 8 Then Exit Sub                               71
If Asc(e.KeyChar) < 48 Or Asc(e.KeyChar) > 57 Then                72
e.KeyChar = ""                                                    73
Exit Sub                                                          74
End If                                                            75
End Sub                                                           76


Private Sub BtnClear_Click(ByVal sender As System.Object, _
ByVal e As System.EventArgs) Handles BtnClear.Click               77
Dim Ctrl As Control                                               78
```

```
For Each Ctrl In Me.Controls                                    79
If TypeOf Ctrl Is TextBox Then                                  80
Ctrl.Text = ""                                                  81
End If                                                          82
Next                                                            83
LblC_ID.Text = "C_ID"                                           84
LblFName.Text = "Fname"                                         85
LblLName.Text = "Lname"                                         86
LblAdd.Text = "Add"                                             87
LblTelNo.Text = "TelNo"                                         88
LblEmail.Text = "E-mail"                                        89
End Sub                                                         90

Private Sub BtnExit_Click(ByVal sender As System.Object, _
ByVal e As System.EventArgs) Handles BtnExit.Click              91
End                                                             92
End Sub                                                         93
End Class                                                       94
```

Explanation

The line-by-line explanation of the above given source code is as follows:

Lines 1-2
In these lines, the class **FrmCustomerDetails** is declared as **Public** and **ObjCust** is created as an object of the class **Customer**.

Lines 9-18
In these lines, the customer information is stored in the member variable of the **Customer** class through the object **ObjCust**.

Lines 19-30
In these lines, the procedure **Validate_Data** is declared as **Public** with the string variable passed as an argument. This source code checks the customer id entered by the user. If the user enters an invalid customer id, then an error message will be displayed.

Lines 31-36
In these lines, the procedure **Validate_Data** is declared as **Public** with the long variable passed as an argument. This source code checks the telephone number entered by the user. If the user enters an invalid telephone number, then an error message will be displayed on the form.

Lines 37-46
In these lines, the values are retrieved from the member variables of the **Customer** class and then they are assigned to the **Label** controls.

Lines 47-69
In these lines, if the customer id entered by the user is not valid, then the code will prompt the user to enter the customer id again and also the telephone number will be validated.

Lines 70-76
In these lines, the ASCII value of the keys pressed by the user are checked. If the keys pressed by the user are not the numeric keys, then it will exit the procedure.

Lines 76-90
In these lines, the values in the **TextBox** controls are cleared and the values in the **Label** controls are set to default.

Step 6
Execute the application; the resultant form will be displayed, as shown in Figure 9-8.

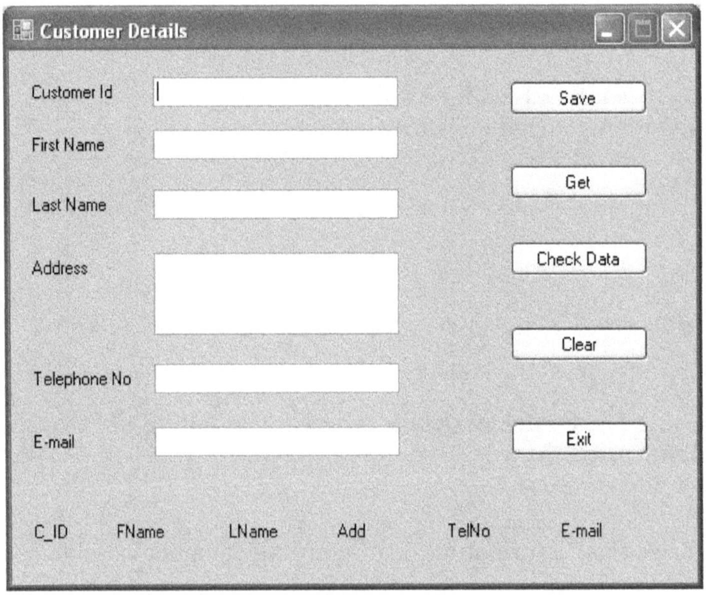

Figure 9-8 *The resultant form of Application 6*

Step 7
Enter the following values in the **Textbox** controls:
Customer Id: **C001**
First Name: **David**
Last Name: **Robert**
Address: **525, Indiana**
Telephone No: **2196147325**
E-mail: **david@yahoo.com**

Next, choose the **Get** button from the form; the information that you entered will be displayed on the form, as shown in Figure 9-9.
Step 8
In the **Customer Id** textbox, if you enter an id that does not start with the character C, then an error message will be displayed on choosing the **Check Data** button, as shown in Figure 9-10.

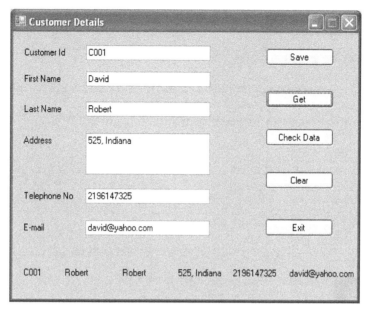

Figure 9-9 *The output of Application 6*

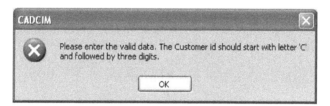

Figure 9-10 *The error message*

Self-Evaluation Test

Answer the following questions and then compare them to those given at the end of this chapter:

1. A _____ is a data type, in which you can group different fields.

2. The _____ members of a class can be accessed by the members of the same class and also by the members of the other class.

3. The _____ members can only be accessed by the other members of the same class.

4. The _____ members have the scope between the **Public** and **Private** access specifiers.

5. The _____ members can be accessed within the program containing their declaration and by any other components of the same application.

Review Questions

Answer the following questions:

1. A_____ is a special member function that is used to initialize the objects of a class.

2. For creating a constructor, you need to create a sub procedure named _____ in a class.

3. _____ provides a mechanism with which you can reuse something that is already available.

4. Reusability is used in case of _____.

5. The technique of creating a new class from an old one is known as _____.

Exercise

Exercise 1

Create an application to display the personal details of a person. The application should contain a class named **Details**. The class **Details** should include the following details of the person:

His name, address, e-mail address, and contact number

Answers to Self-Evaluation Test
1. structure, 2. **Public**, 3. **Private**, 4. **Protected**, 5. **Friend**

Chapter 10

Working with Database

INTRODUCTION

In this chapter, you will learn about the basic databases used in VB.NET and the procedure of their creation. Additionally, you will about learn the concept of data binding using various controls such as **TextBox** control, **ComboBox** control, **ListBox** control, and so on.

DATABASES

Database is a collection of tables that contain related data. Data in the tables are arranged in the form of rows and columns. Each column in a table is known as field. A field contains a piece of information related to a particular item. Each row is known as a record. A record is a set of data related to an item. A record can consist of one or more fields. Tables in a database also have a primary key. A primary key is a particular field or a combination of fields that can identify each row in a table uniquely. For example, you may have an employee table containing the following three fields:

Id

Name

Address

And, the following three records:

6778, 'Sam', '204-A, Holland'

6779, 'Mary', '709-B, Washington'

7000, 'John', '899-C, Florida'

In such a case, all the employees cannot have the same Id, so you can set the field **Id** as the primary key. Table 10-1 shows a database table.

Id	Name	Address
6778	Sam	204-A, Holland
6779	Mary	709-B, Washington
7000	John	899-C, Florida

Table 10-1 Representation of a database table

Data Providers, Data Adapters, and Datasets

To work with databases, you need to follow the steps given below one-by-one:

1. Get connection to a data source
2. Work with the data
3. Use the data from the databases through source code

Get Connection to a Data Source

While working with databases, first of all, you need to get a connection to the data source. To do so, you need to use a data provider that can access the data. Microsoft SQL Server is the default data provider for VB.NET. But VB.NET can also work with the other data providers such as Oracle, Access, and so on. You have to use ADO.NET **SQLConnection** objects for working with SQL Server. If you need to work with the other data providers, then use ADO. NET **OleDbConnection** objects. ADO.NET (ADO means ActiveX Data Objects) is used as a primary data access and manipulation protocol in VB.NET.

Work with the Data

After getting the data connection to a data source, you need to work with the data in the database. The data adapters are used to work with the data. Basically, there are some datasets containing the data that is required from a database. But these datasets are not connected to the database. Therefore, the data adapters are used to apply the commands to the database.

Use the Data from the Databases through Source Code

After getting a data adapter, you can generate datasets. For example, if you need to access a table from a database, first create a connection to that database and then get an adapter using the SQL Server, so that you can retrieve the required table from the database. Next, you need work on the data in the dataset. Figure 10-1 represents the sequence of the database connection.

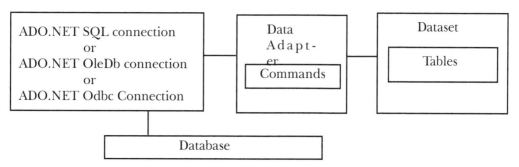

Figure 10-1 *A database connection*

One dataset can store multiple tables at a time, but only one query can be handled by the data adapter at a time. For multiple tables, you need to use multiple data adapters.

SERVER EXPLORER

In VB.NET, the **Server Explorer** helps you create connections to the databases. The following steps are required to create a connection to a database:

1. To display the **Server Explorer** window, choose **View > Server Explorer** from the menu bar or press the **Ctrl+Alt+S** keys; the **Server Explorer** window will be displayed, as shown in Figure 10-2.

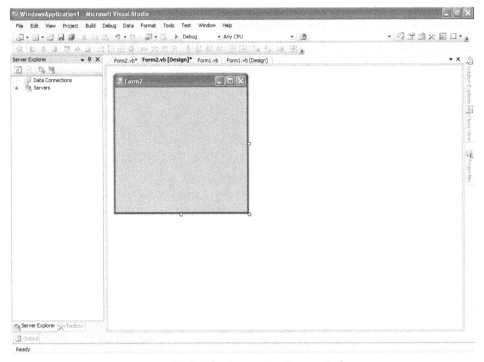

*Figure 10-2 The **Server Explorer** window*

2. Right-click on the **Data Connections** node and then choose **Add Connection** from the context menu in the **Server Explorer** window; the **Change Data Source** dialog box will be displayed, as shown in Figure 10-3. Select the **Microsoft SQL Server** option from the **Data source** list box and the **.NET Framework Data Provider for SQL Server** option from the **Data provider** drop-down list. Also, select the **Always use this selection** check box, and then choose the **OK** button; the **Add Connection** dialog box will be displayed, as shown in Figure 10-4.

3. Select the server that you need to use from the **Server name** drop-down list. If you do not have any server, then enter dot (**.**) in the drop-down list, which is the default server. Next, select the **Use Windows Authentication** radio button from the **Log on to the server** area. Then, select the **pubs** option from the **Select or enter a database name** drop-down list in the **Connect to a database** area. Next, choose the **Test Connection** button; the message **Test connection succeeded** will be displayed in a message box. Choose the **OK** button from the message box.

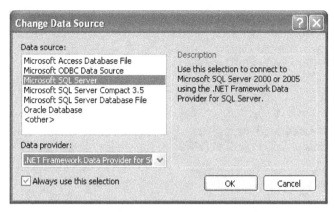

*Figure 10-3 The **Change Data Source** dialog box*

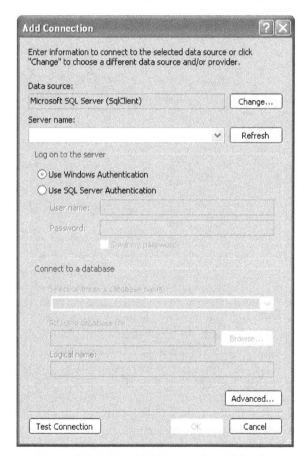

*Figure 10-4 The **Add Connection** dialog box*

4. Next, choose the **OK** button in the **Add Connection** dialog box; the **pubs** database will be added to the **Server Explorer** window.

5. Expand the **pubs** node in the **Server Explorer** window; a list of items will be displayed. Next, expand the **Tables** node; a list of existing tables will be displayed.

6. Add a **DataGridView** control to the form. Choose the forward arrow at the upper right corner of the **DataGridView** control; a list of properties will be displayed. Select the **Add Project Data Source** option from the **Choose Data Source** drop-down list; the **Data Source Configuration Wizard** will be displayed, as shown in Figure 10-5.

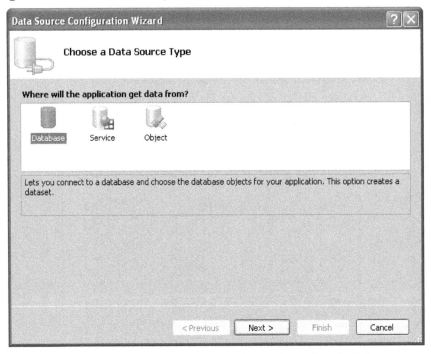

*Figure 10-5 The **Data Source Configuration Wizard** window*

7. Choose the **Next** button on the **Data Source Configuration Wizard** to go to the next step. Select the data connection that you want to use in the application from the drop-down list and again choose the **Next** button; the **Save the Connection String to the Application Configuration File** page of the **Data Source Configuration Wizard** window will be displayed, as shown in Figure 10-6. Choose the **Next** button; the **Choose Your Database Objects** window will be displayed, as shown in Figure 10-7.

8. Expand the **Tables** node; all the tables of the **pubs** database will be displayed in the form of check boxes. Select the **employee** check box. Next, choose the **Finish** button; the **employee** table will be added to the **DataGridView** control and three components, **PubsDataSet**, **EmployeeBindingSource**, and **EmployeeTableAdapter** will be added to the component tray of the form, as shown in Figure 10-8.

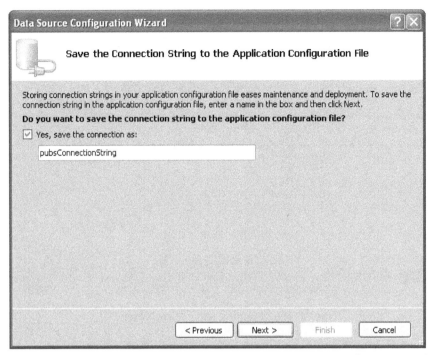

*Figure 10-6 The **Save the Connection String to the Application Configuration File** page*

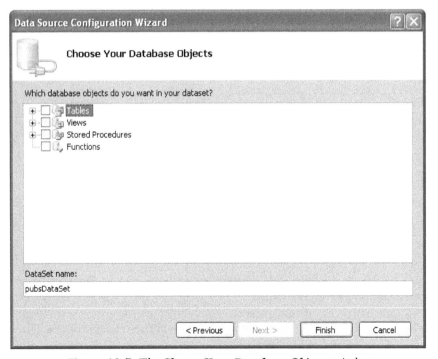

*Figure 10-7 The **Choose Your Database Objects** window*

9. Execute the application; the data of the **employee** table will be displayed on the form, as shown in Figure 10-9. You can resize the form to view the entire data, if it is not visible.

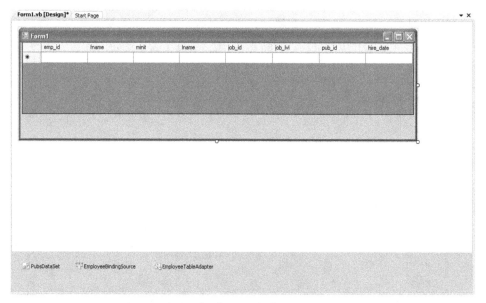

Figure 10-8 *The form with the* **employee** *table*

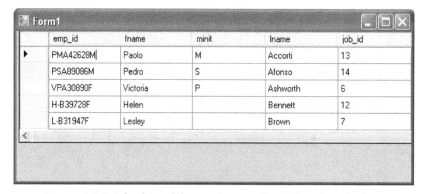

Figure 10-9 *The data of the* **employee** *table displayed on the form*

Editing the Columns of the DataGridView Control

To edit the columns of the **DataGridView** control, follow the steps given below:

1. Right-click on the **DataGridView** control and choose the **Edit Columns** option from the context menu; the **Edit Columns** dialog box will be displayed, as shown in Figure 10-10.

2. Select any field from the **Selected Columns** area and change its **Header Text** value from the **Bound Column Properties** area.

3. Next, choose the **OK** button; the header text value of the selected field will be changed.

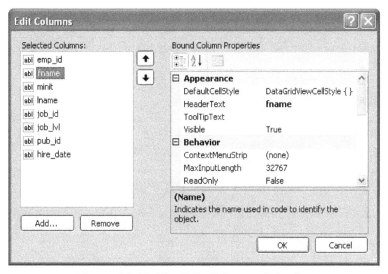

*Figure 10-10 The **Edit Columns** dialog box*

BASIC SQL COMMANDS

In this section, you will learn about the basic SQL (Structured Query Language) commands. Some of the important SQL commands are listed below:

1. SELECT
2. WHERE
3. BETWEEN
4. LIKE
5. ORDER BY
6. DISTINCT
7. IN
8. AS
9. NOT IN

To understand the above given commands, consider that you are working with the **employee** table of the **pubs** database.

SELECT Command

The **SELECT** command is used to retrieve some or all the fields from the table. If you need to get all the records from a table, in this case, the **employee** table, use the following statement:

SELECT * FROM employee

In the above statement, the * character is used to retrieve all the records from the **employee** table.

If you need to select the specific fields, use the following statement:

SELECT emp_id, fname, minit, lname FROM employee

In the above statement, **emp_id**, **fname**, **minit**, and **lname** fields will be retrieved from the **employee** table.

WHERE Command

The **WHERE** command is used to specify some criteria. The records required by the user should meet this specified criteria. To get the details of the employees having the value **A** in the **minit** field, use the following statement with the **WHERE** command:

SELECT * FROM employee WHERE (minit = 'A')

The above statement returns only those records that have the value **A** in the **minit** field.

BETWEEN Command

The **BETWEEN** command is used to specify a range of values according to your requirement. For example, if you want to display details of employees having the values between **A** and **C** for the **minit** field, then use the **BETWEEN** command, as given below:

SELECT * FROM employee WHERE (minit BETWEEN 'A' AND 'C')

The above statement returns only those records that have the value ranging between **A** and **C** in the **minit** field.

LIKE Command

The **LIKE** command uses partial string matching. For example, if you need to display the names of employees starting with the alphabets **Pa** from the **employee** table, then use the following statement:

SELECT * FROM employee WHERE fname LIKE 'Pa%'

The **LIKE** command recognizes various pattern-matching characters. The following is the list of some of the pattern-matching characters that can be used with the **LIKE** command:

% Character

This character matches any number of characters. For example, if you type **Pa%**, all the names starting with **Pa** such as, **Paolo**, **Paul**, and so on will be displayed.

_ Character

This _ (underscore) character matches a single alphabetic character. For example, if you enter **P_o%**, only those names will be displayed which contain the alphabets **P** and **O**, such as **Paolo**.

ORDER BY Command

This command is used to view the data of a table in a sorted order. By default, this command sorts a record in the ascending order. The statement for using the **ORDER BY** command is given below:

SELECT * FROM employee ORDER BY fname

In the above statement, the **ORDER BY** command will sort records of the **employee** table in an ascending order.

DISTINCT Command

Consider a situation when you have a database with duplicate values in the fields of the record. For example, there is a field **City** in the **Customers** table. You may need to know the total number of cities in a table. If the name of a city is mentioned multiple times, its value will also be counted accordingly. So, if you want to display the name of a particular city only once at a time, you can use the **DISTINCT** command. This will ensure that a particular city is listed only once. The following statement will display the names of the cities without duplication:

SELECT DISTINCT City FROM Customers

IN Command

This command can be used with the **WHERE** command to select the data that matches with the list of constant values in a table. For example, if you want to display the records of two cities, such as **Berlin** and **London** in the **Customers** table, use the following statement:

SELECT * FROM Customers WHERE City IN ('Berlin', 'London')

AS Command

You can use the **AS** command when you need to change the name of any field in a table. For example, to change the name of the field **ContactTitle** to **Title**, use the following statement:

SELECT ContactTitle AS Title FROM Customers

In the above statement, the **AS** command is used to change the name **ContactTitle** to **Title**.

NOT IN Command

This command is used to select the data that does not match with the list of the constant values in a table. For example, if you want to delete the rows containing the values **Berlin** and **London** in the **City** field of the **Customers** table, use the following statement:

SELECT * FROM Customers WHERE City NOT IN ('Berlin', 'London')

RELATIONAL DATABASE

When the data in two tables can be related to each other through a common entity (primary key), it is known as relational database. The concept of relational database can be illustrated through the following example:

Employee	
emp_name	emp_id
Mary	A433
Robert	A434
Maria	A435

Department	
emp_id	dept
A433	Physics
A434	Chemistry
A435	Biology

The above example represents a relational database, which contains two tables: **Employee** and **Department**. These tables are related to each other through a common entity, **emp_id**. This common entity is also known as the primary key.

Joins

You have already learnt that the tables in a relational database can be related to each other with the help of keys or common entities. In this type of database, you can retrieve the data from more than one table using joins. There are various types of joins. In this section, you will learn about the **INNER JOIN**.

INNER JOIN

The **INNER JOIN** is considered as the default join and it displays the intersection of two tables. The **INNER JOIN** returns only those rows from both the tables where a match is found. If there are some rows in one table that do not have any match in the other, then those rows will not be displayed.

The following example illustrates the working of the **INNER JOIN**:

employee			pub_info	
fname	lname	Id	Id	pub_id
Bruce	Wills	1042	1042	25
Will	Smith	1043	1045	25
Sara	Feder	1044	1012	150
John	Taravolta	1045	1041	120

In the above example, there are two tables: **employee** and **pub_info**. You can join these two tables with the help of the **INNER JOIN**. The following query will illustrate the working of the **INNER JOIN**:

SELECT employee.id, employee.lname, employee.fname,
    pub_info.id
        pub_info.pub_id AS Expr1
FROM   employee INNER JOIN
        pub_info ON employee.pub_id = pub_info.pub_id

In the above query, the **INNER JOIN** command is used to join the **employee** table to the **pub_info** table. The joining will be displayed with the help of the **Query Builder** dialog box, as shown in Figure 10-11.

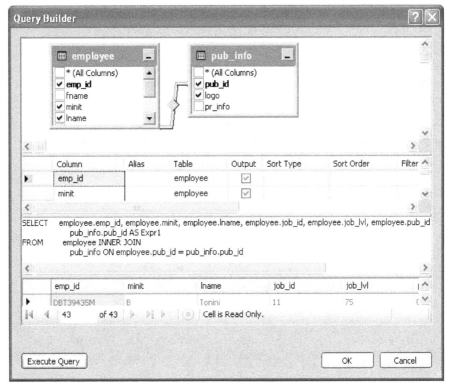

Figure 10-11 The **Query Builder** *dialog box*

DATA BINDING

The binding of controls with the data source is called as data binding. Visual Studio 2008 provides the **Data Source Configuration Wizard** which helps in connecting the application to the data in a database.

Architecture of Data Binding

The architecture of data binding consists of three steps, which are as follows:

Creating Data Connection

In this step, the user creates a connection string and also a connection object that provides connection to the database.

Creating DataAdapter and Dataset

After creating data connection, the next step is to create **DataAdapter** and **Dataset**. These are used to set the data connection.

Calling the Fill method

The next step is to call the **Fill** method of the **DataAdapter**. This method is used to fill the data in the **Dataset** using the **DataAdapter** and the connection object.

There are two types of data bindings, simple binding and complex binding. These are discussed next.

Simple Binding

The process of binding the controls to a single value data in the database is known as the simple data binding. For example, if you want to bind a **TextBox** control to the field **fname** in the **employee** table, then follow the steps given below:

Step 1
Start a new project.

Step 2
Create connection to the **pubs** database.

Step 3
Next, add a **TextBox** control to the form.

Step 4
Select the **DataBindings** property of the **TextBox** control and expand it.

Step 5
Select the **Advance** option from the **DataBindings** property of the **TextBox** control and choose the button on its right; the **Formatting and Advanced Binding** dialog box will be displayed, as shown in Figure 10-12.

Step 6
Select the **Text** option from the **Common** node in the **Property** area of the **Formatting and Advanced Binding** dialog box.
Step 7
Next, select the field of the **employee** table from the **Binding** drop-down list and choose the **OK** button.

Step 8
Execute the application; the value of the **minit** field of the **employee** table will be displayed in the **TextBox** control, as shown in Figure 10-13. Note that in the case of simple binding, only one value of the **fname** field is displayed in the specified control. To display more values, you need to add a **BindingNavigator** control to the form.

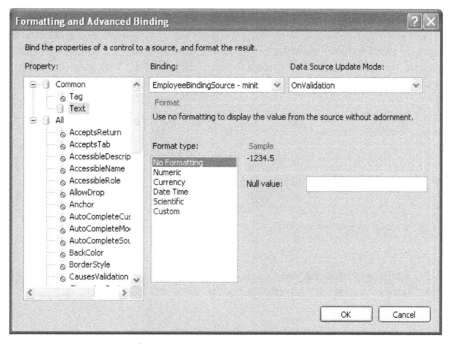

Figure 10-12 The **Formatting and Advanced Binding** dialog box

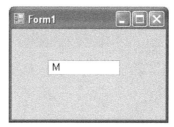

Figure 10-13 The simple binding of the **TextBox** control

Step 9
Set the value **EmployeeBindingSource** to the **BindingSource** property of the **BindingNavigator** control. Also, change the value of the **Dock** property to **Bottom**.

Step 10
Execute the application again; the output form with the **BindingNavigator** will be displayed, as shown in Figure 10-14.

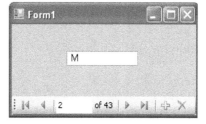

Figure 10-14 The output form with the **BindingNavigator** displayed

Complex Binding

In the previous section, you learnt to bind a single value of a field to the **TextBox** control. Sometimes you need to bind multiple or all values of a field to a control. To do so, you need to use the complex binding. For example, if you want to bind a **ListBox** control to the field **lname** in the **employee** table, then follow the steps given below:

Step 1
Start a new project.

Step 2
Create an SQL database connection as mentioned earlier.

Step 3
Add a **ListBox** control to the form.

Step 4
Set the value **EmployeeBindingSource1** in the **DataSource** property and the value **lname** in the **DisplayMember** property from the respective drop-down lists.

Step 5
Execute the application; the values of the **lname** field of the **employee** table will be displayed in the **ListBox** control, as shown in Figure 10-15.

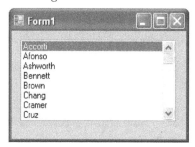

Figure 10-15 *The complex binding with the* ***ListBox*** *control*

DATA BINDING WITH CONTROLS

In this section, you will learn about binding different controls to the database.

Data Binding with the ComboBox Control

The following steps are required to bind the data with the **ComboBox** control:

1. Create a database connection for your application.

2. Add a **ComboBox** control to the form.

3. Set the value **EmployeeBindingSource** to the **DataSource** property of the **ComboBox** control.

4. Set the value **pub_id** to the **DisplayMember** property.

5. Expand the **DataBindings** property of the **ComboBox** control and select the **Advance** property; the **Formatting and Advanced Binding** dialog box will be displayed. Select the **Text** node from the **Property** area. Next, select the **Binding** combo box and expand the **EmployeeBindingSource** node; the list of fields in the **employee** table will be displayed, as shown in Figure 10-16. Next, select the **pub_id** from the list and then choose the **OK** button from the **Formatting and Advanced Binding** dialog box.

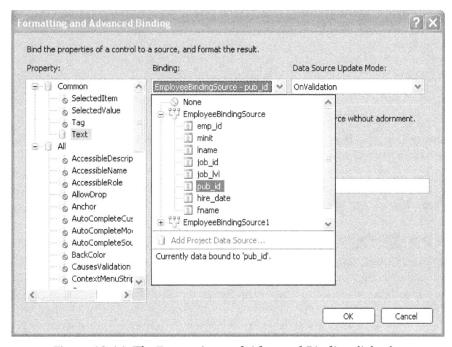

Figure 10-16 The Formatting and Advanced Binding dialog box

6. Execute the application; the output form will be displayed, as shown in Figure 10-17. Select the **ComboBox** control, all the values of the **pub_id** field will be displayed, as shown in Figure 10-18.

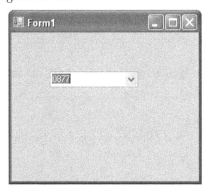

Figure 10-17 The output form

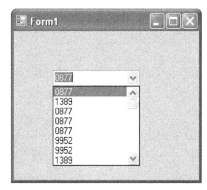

Figure 10-18 The values of the pub_id field

Data Binding with the CheckBox Control

The following steps are required to bind the data with the **CheckBox** control:

1. Create a database connection for your application.

2. Add a **CheckBox** control to the form.

3. Expand the **DataBindings** property and select the **Advance** property; the **Formatting and Advanced Binding** dialog box will be displayed. You can bind any of the following properties of the **CheckBox** control:
   a. CheckAlign
   b. Checked
   c. CheckState
   d. Tag
   e. Text

   In this section, the **Text** property of the **CheckBox** control will be bound to the **lname** field of the **employee** table.

4. Execute the application; the output of the form will be displayed, as shown in Figure 10-19.

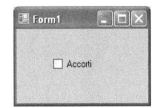

Figure 10-19 *The output of the form*

DATABASE CONNECTION FOR WEB APPLICATIONS

The database connection in web forms is almost the same as in the windows forms. However, the process of data binding is different in the case of web forms. In windows forms, whenever a page is uploaded, the data binding in the forms also updates automatically, but in the web forms, there is no direct connection between the dataset and the controls. Whenever the page is uploaded in the web forms, you have to refresh the data binding connection. Also, you can display the in-built tables on the form in web applications. For example, if you want to display the **employee** table on the web form, then follow the steps given below:

Step 1
Start a new project.

Step 2
Create database connection of the **pubs** database as you did in the case of windows forms.

Step 3
Next, expand the **database** node and then expand the **Tables** node; all the tables in the **pubs** database will be displayed.

Step 4
Drag the **employee** table from the list of tables and drop it on the web form; the table will be added to the web form, as shown in Figure 10-20.

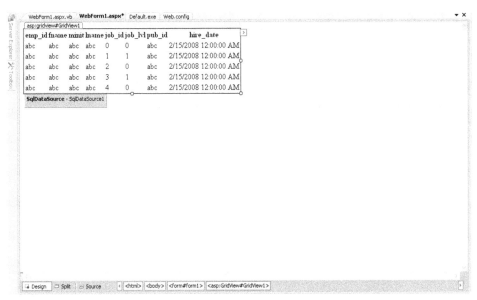

*Figure 10-20 The **employee** table added to the web form*

Step 5
Next, execute the application; the **employee** table will be displayed on the output form, as shown in Figure 10-21.

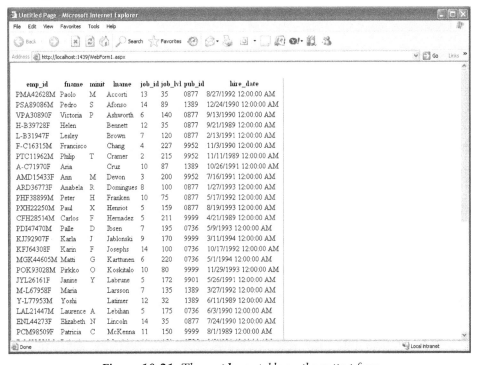

*Figure 10-21 The **employee** table on the output form*

CREATING TABLES

In the earlier sections, you worked on the in-built tables. However, you can also create all your own customized tables.

The following steps are required to create a table:

Step 1
Start a new project.

Step 2
In the **Server Explorer** window, select any data connection. Next, right-click on the **Table** node and choose **Add New Table** from the context menu; the **dbo** window will be displayed. Save the table as **university_details**, as shown in Figure 10-22.

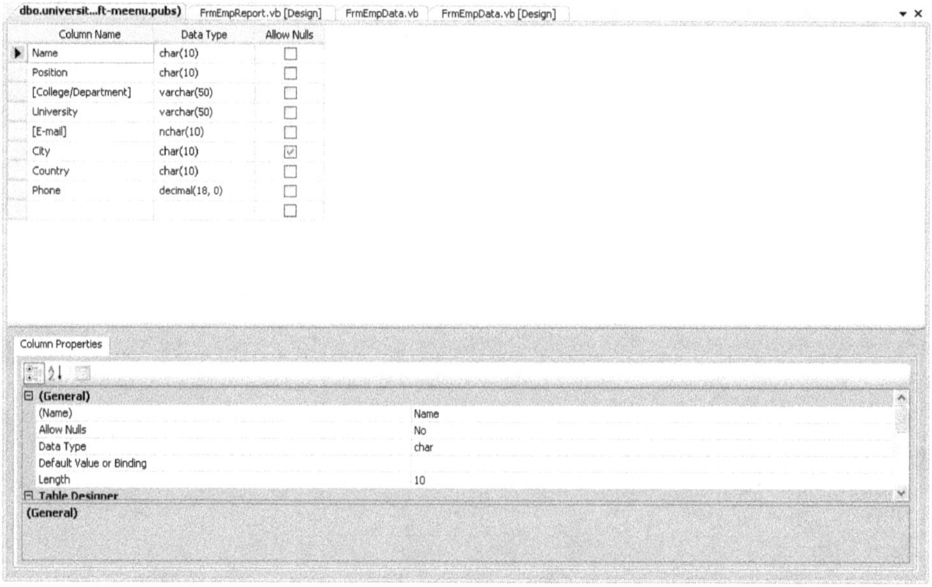

*Figure 10-22 The design mode of the **university_details** table*

Step 3
Next, to add the entries to the table, open the **SQL Server Enterprise Manager** window, as shown in Figure 10-23. Expand the **pubs** node in the **Server Explorer** window and then double-click on the **Tables** node; all the tables will be listed.

Step 4
Right-click on the **university_details** table and choose **Open Table > Return all rows** from the context menu; the **Data in Table** window will be displayed, as shown in Figure 10-24. You can add the required entries in this window.

Step 5
Next, create the database connection. Add the **university_details** table to the form.

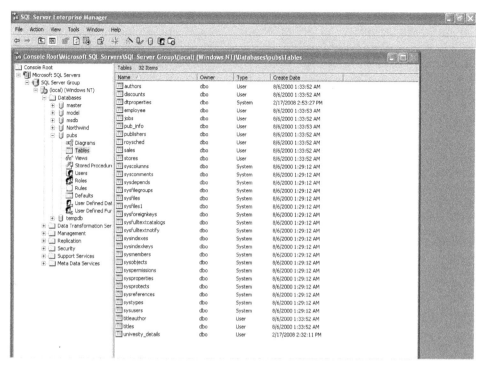

*Figure 10-23 The **SQL Server Enterprise Manager** window*

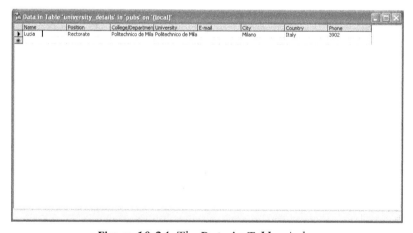

*Figure 10-24 The **Data in Table** window*

Step 6

Execute the application; the **university_details** table will be displayed, as shown in Figure 10-25. The following application illustrates the use of database connection:

Create an application that will display the details of an employee on a form.

This application will prompt the user to enter his personal details and then save them. It will also update and search the data.

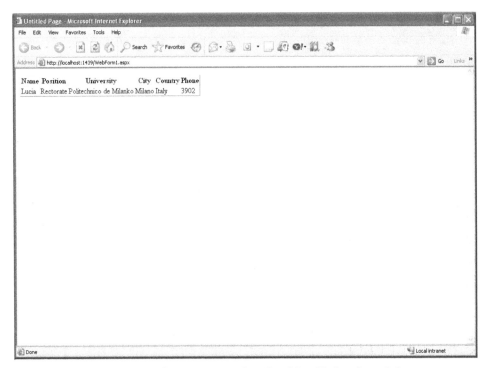

*Figure 10-25 The **university_details** table added to the web form*

Before starting the application, you need to create a database named **employee_data** in SQL Server. Also, you need to create a table **EmpData,** as shown in Table 10-2. In the Table 10-2, the value 0 of the column **Allow Nulls** represents that the Null value is not allowed in that particular column and the value 1 represents that the Null value is allowed.

The following steps are required to create this application:

Step 1
Start a new project and save it as **c10_VB_NET_2008_01**.

Step 2
Add the controls to the **Form1** and arrange them, as shown in Figure 10-26.

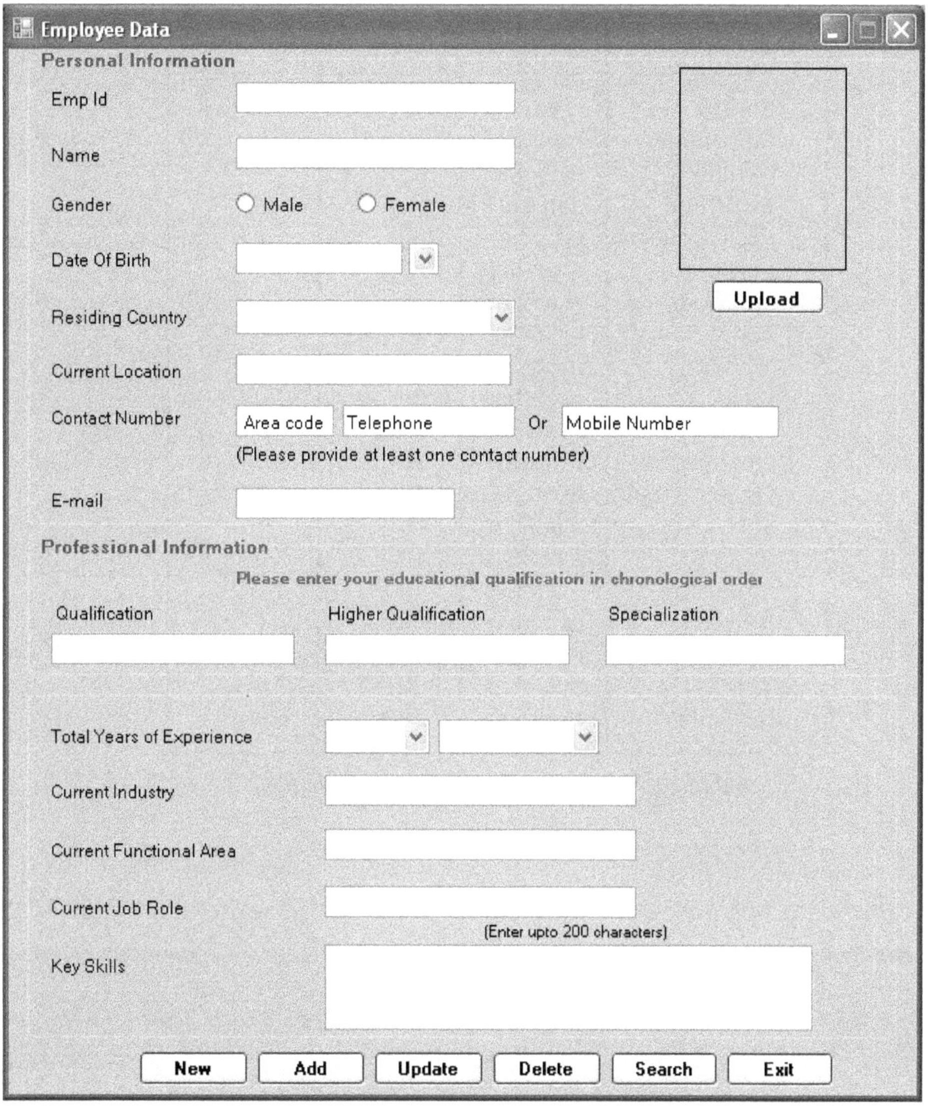

Figure 10-26 *The* ***Form1*** *of Application 1*

Column Name	Data Type	Length	Allow Nulls
EmpId	varchar	4	0
EmpName	nvarchar	50	0
Gender	nvarchar	6	0
BirthDate	datetime	8	0
Resd_Country	nvarchar	80	1
Location	nvarchar	80	0
Std_Code	nvarchar	5	1
Phone	nvarchar	10	1
Mobile	nvarchar	10	1
Email	nvarchar	80	0
Photo	nvarchar	200	0
Qualification	nvarchar	80	0
Higher_Qual	nvarchar	50	0
Specialization	nvarchar	50	1
Yr_Exp	nvarchar	10	0
Mon_Exp	nvarchar	10	1
Industry	nvarchar	80	1
Func_Area	nvarchar	80	1
Role	nvarchar	80	0
KeySkills	nvarchar	200	0

*Table 10-2 The structure of the **EmpData** table*

Step 3
Add **Form2** to the application and then add the controls to it, as shown in Figure 10-27.

*Figure 10-27 The **Form 2** of Application 1*

Step 4

Add a module to the application. To do so, right-click on the name of the application in the **Solution Explorer** window and then choose **Add > Module** from the context menu; the **Add New Item** dialog box will be displayed. Change the name of the module to **Library.vb** in the **Name** edit box. Choose the **Add** button from the **Add New Item** dialog box; the code window for the module will be displayed. Enter the source code for the database connection in the code window, as shown in Figure 10-28.

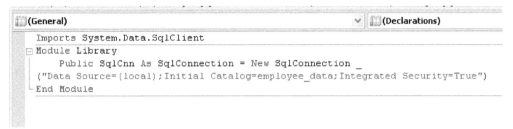

```
(General)                                                          (Declarations)
    Imports System.Data.SqlClient
Module Library
    Public SqlCnn As SqlConnection = New SqlConnection _
  ("Data Source=(local);Initial Catalog=employee_data;Integrated Security=True")
End Module
```

Figure 10-28 *The module code window*

Step 5

The source code for this application is given below. The line numbers on the right are not a part of the application and are for reference only.

```
Imports System.Data.SqlClient                                               1
Public Class FrmEmpData                                                     2
Dim Dr As SqlDataReader                                                     3
Dim Da As SqlDataAdapter                                                    4
Dim Dc As SqlCommand                                                        5
Dim Ds As New DataSet                                                       6
Dim Upload_file As String                                                   7

Private Sub Form1_FormClosing(ByVal sender As Object, _
ByVal e As System.Windows.Forms.FormClosingEventArgs) _
Handles Me.FormClosing                                                      8
If SqlCnn.State = ConnectionState.Open Then SqlCnn.Close()                  9
End Sub                                                                     10

Private Sub Form1_Load(ByVal sender As Object, _
ByVal e As System.EventArgs) Handles Me.Load                                11
If SqlCnn.State = ConnectionState.Closed Then SqlCnn.Open()                 12
Btn_Add.Enabled = False                                                     13
TxtEmpId.ReadOnly = True                                                    14
TxtName.Focus()                                                             15
LoadData()                                                                  16
End Sub                                                                     17

Public Sub LoadData()                                                       18
```

```
Dim Dt As DataTable                                                      19
Da = New SqlDataAdapter("Select * from country order by country", SqlCnn)  20
Dt = New DataTable                                                       21
Da.Fill(Dt)                                                              22
CmbCountry.DataSource = Dt                                               23
CmbCountry.DisplayMember = "Country"                                     24
CmbCountry.ValueMember = "Country"                                       25
Dt = Nothing                                                             26
CmbCountry.SelectedIndex = 0                                             27
TxtName.Focus()                                                          28
CmbYrs.Items.Add("—Year—")                                              29
CmbMonth.Items.Add("—Month—")                                           30
For I_Ctr As Integer = 0 To 40                                          31
CmbYrs.Items.Add(I_Ctr)                                                  32
Next                                                                     33
For i_ctr As Integer = 0 To 11                                          34
CmbMonth.Items.Add(i_ctr)                                                35
Next                                                                     36
CmbMonth.SelectedIndex = 0                                              37
CmbYrs.SelectedIndex = 0                                                38
End Sub                                                                  39

Private Sub DateTimePicker1_ValueChanged(ByVal sender As Object, _
ByVal e As System.EventArgs) Handles DateTimePicker1.ValueChanged        40
TxtDateB.Text = DateValue(DateTimePicker1.Value)                         41
End Sub                                                                  42

Private Sub Btn_Update_Click(ByVal sender As System.Object, _
ByVal e As System.EventArgs) Handles Btn_Update.Click                    43
FrmEmpReport.Show(Me)                                                    44
End Sub                                                                  45

Private Sub Btn_Exit_Click(ByVal sender As System.Object, _
ByVal e As System.EventArgs) Handles Btn_Exit.Click                      46
End                                                                      47
End Sub                                                                  48

Private Sub Btn_Delete_Click(ByVal sender As System.Object, _
ByVal e As System.EventArgs) Handles Btn_Delete.Click                    49
Dim Str_emp As String                                                    50
Str_emp = InputBox("Enter the EmpId")                                    51
If Str_emp = "" Then Exit Sub
Dc = New SqlCommand("delete from EmpData where Empid='" & _
Str_emp & "'", SqlCnn)                                                   52
Dc.ExecuteNonQuery()                                                     53
MessageBox.Show("Record Deleted", "Employee Data")                       54
End Sub                                                                  55
```

```
Private Sub Btn_Add_Click(ByVal sender As System.Object, _
ByVal e As System.EventArgs) Handles Btn_Add.Click                      56
Dim Str_sql As String                                                   57
If Upload_file = "" Then                                                58
MessageBox.Show("Please upload the photo", "CADCIM - ERROR", _
MessageBoxButtons.OK)                                                   59
Exit Sub                                                                60
End If                                                                  61
Dim EmpId, EmpName, Gender, BirthDate, Resd_Country, Location, _
Std_Code, Phone, Mobile, Email, Photo, _Qualification, Higher_Qual, _
Specialization, Yr_Exp, Mon_Exp, Industry, Func_Area, Role, _KeySkills _
As SqlParameter                                                         62
Str_sql = "INSERT INTO EmpData (EmpId, EmpName, Gender, _
BirthDate, Resd_Country, Location, Std_Code, Phone, " & _"Mobile, _
Email, Photo, Qualification, Higher_Qual, Specialization,  Yr_Exp, _
Mon_Exp, Industry, " & _"Func_Area, Role, KeySkills) VALUES _
(@EmpId, @EmpName, @Gender, @BirthDate, @Resd_Country, " & _
"@Location, @Std_Code, @Phone, @Mobile, @Email, @Photo, _
@Qualification, @Higher_Qual, @Specialization, " & _
"@Yr_Exp, @Mon_Exp, @Industry, @Func_Area, @Role, @KeySkills)"          63
Dc = New SqlCommand(Str_sql, SqlCnn)                                    64
EmpId = New SqlParameter("@EmpId", SqlDbType.VarChar, 4)                65
EmpName = New SqlParameter("@EmpName", SqlDbType.NVarChar, 50)          66
Gender = New SqlParameter("@Gender", SqlDbType.VarChar, 6)              67
BirthDate = New SqlParameter("@BirthDate", SqlDbType.DateTime)          68
Resd_Country = New SqlParameter("@Resd_Country", SqlDbType.VarChar, 80) 69
Location = New SqlParameter("@Location", SqlDbType.NVarChar, 80)        70
Std_Code = New SqlParameter("@Std_Code", SqlDbType.VarChar, 5)          71
Phone = New SqlParameter("@Phone", SqlDbType.VarChar, 10)               72
Mobile = New SqlParameter("@Mobile", SqlDbType.VarChar, 10)             73
Email = New SqlParameter("@Email", SqlDbType.VarChar, 80)               74
Photo = New SqlParameter("@Photo", SqlDbType.VarChar, 200)              75
Qualification = New SqlParameter("@Qualification", SqlDbType.NVarChar, 80) 76
Higher_Qual = New SqlParameter("@Higher_Qual", SqlDbType.VarChar, 50)   77
Specialization = New SqlParameter("@Specialization", SqlDbType.VarChar, 50) 78
Yr_Exp = New SqlParameter("@Yr_Exp", SqlDbType.NVarChar, 10)            79
Mon_Exp = New SqlParameter("@Mon_Exp", SqlDbType.NVarChar, 10)          80
Industry = New SqlParameter("@Industry", SqlDbType.VarChar, 80)         81
Func_Area = New SqlParameter("@Func_Area", SqlDbType.VarChar, 80)       82
Role = New SqlParameter("@Role", SqlDbType.NVarChar, 80)                83
KeySkills = New SqlParameter("@KeySkills", SqlDbType.VarChar, 200)      84
EmpId.Value = TxtEmpId.Text                                             85
EmpName.Value = TxtName.Text                                            86
If RbFemale.Checked Then                                                87
Gender.Value = RbFemale.Text                                            88
Else                                                                    89
Gender.Value = RbMale.Text                                              90
```

```
End If                                                          91
BirthDate.Value = TxtDateB.Text                                92
Resd_Country.Value = CmbCountry.Text                           93
Location.Value = TxtCurrLocation.Text                          94
Std_Code.Value = TxtCode.Text                                  95
Phone.Value = TxtPhone.Text                                    96
Mobile.Value = TxtMobile.Text                                  97
Email.Value = TxtEmail.Text                                    98
Photo.Value = Upload_file                                      99
Qualification.Value = TxtQualF.Text                           100
Higher_Qual.Value = TxtHQualf.Text                            101
Specialization.Value = TxtSpecl.Text                          102
Yr_Exp.Value = CmbYrs.Text                                    103
Mon_Exp.Value = CmbMonth.Text                                 104
Industry.Value = TxtIndustry.Text                             105
Func_Area.Value = TxtCfuncArea.Text                           106
Role.Value = TxtRole.Text                                     107
KeySkills.Value = TxtKeySkills.Text                           108
Dc.Parameters.Add(EmpId)                                      109
Dc.Parameters.Add(EmpName)                                    110
Dc.Parameters.Add(Gender)                                     111
Dc.Parameters.Add(BirthDate)                                  112
Dc.Parameters.Add(Resd_Country)                               113
Dc.Parameters.Add(Location)                                   114
Dc.Parameters.Add(Std_Code)                                   115
Dc.Parameters.Add(Phone)                                      116
Dc.Parameters.Add(Mobile)                                     117
Dc.Parameters.Add(Email)                                      118
Dc.Parameters.Add(Photo)                                      119
Dc.Parameters.Add(Qualification)                              120
Dc.Parameters.Add(Higher_Qual)                                121
Dc.Parameters.Add(Specialization)                             122
Dc.Parameters.Add(Yr_Exp)                                     123
Dc.Parameters.Add(Mon_Exp)                                    124
Dc.Parameters.Add(Industry)                                   125
Dc.Parameters.Add(Func_Area)                                  126
Dc.Parameters.Add(Role)                                       127
Dc.Parameters.Add(KeySkills)                                  128
Dc.ExecuteNonQuery()                                          129
MessageBox.Show("Data added", "Employee Data")                130
Btn_New.Enabled = True                                        131
Btn_Add.Enabled = False                                       132
End Sub                                                       133

Private Sub Btn_New_Click(ByVal sender As System.Object, _
ByVal e As System.EventArgs) Handles Btn_New.Click            134
Dim Emp_id As String                                          135
```

```
Dim Ctrl As String                                                      136
Dim Ctrls As Control                                                    137
For Each Ctrls In GroupBox1.Controls                                    138
If TypeOf Ctrls Is TextBox Then                                         139
Ctrls.Text = ""                                                         140
End If                                                                  141
Next                                                                    142
For Each Ctrls In GroupBox2.Controls                                    143
If TypeOf Ctrls Is TextBox Then                                         144
Ctrls.Text = ""                                                         145
End If                                                                  146
Next                                                                    147
For Each Ctrls In GroupBox3.Controls                                    148
If TypeOf Ctrls Is TextBox Then                                         149
Ctrls.Text = ""                                                         150
End If                                                                  151
Next                                                                    152
CmbCountry.SelectedIndex = 0                                            153
RbFemale.Checked = False                                                154
RbMale.Checked = False                                                  155
Dc = New SqlCommand("Select max(EmpId) from EmpData", SqlCnn)           156
Dr = Dc.ExecuteReader                                                   157
Dr.Read()                                                               158
If Not IsDBNull(Dr(0)) Then                                             159
Ctrl = Val(Mid(Dr(0), 2, 3)) + 1                                        160
Else                                                                    161
Ctrl = 1                                                                162
End If                                                                  163
Emp_id = ""                                                             164
If Len(Ctrl) = 1 Then                                                   165
Emp_id = "P" & "00" & Ctrl                                              166
ElseIf Len(Ctrl) = 2 Then                                               167
Emp_id = "P" & "0" & Ctrl                                               168
ElseIf Len(Ctrl) = 3 Then                                               169
Emp_id = "P" & Ctrl                                                     170
End If                                                                  171
TxtEmpId.Text = Emp_id                                                  172
TxtEmpId.Enabled = True                                                 173
PictureBox1.Image = Nothing                                             174
TxtName.Clear()                                                         175
TxtName.Focus()                                                         176
Dr.Close()                                                              177
LoadData()                                                              178
Btn_Add.Enabled = True                                                  179
Btn_New.Enabled = False                                                 180
End Sub                                                                 181
```

```
Private Sub Btn_Upload_Click(ByVal sender As System.Object, _
ByVal e As System.EventArgs) Handles Btn_Upload.Click                    182
PictureBox1.Image = Nothing                                              183
OpenFileDialog1.Title = "CADCIM - Open File"                             184
OpenFileDialog1.DefaultExt = "bmp"                                       185
OpenFileDialog1.Filter = "BMP-Windows Bitmap|*.bmp| _
JPG-JPEG|*.JPG|GIF-CompuServe|*.GIF|All Files|*.*"                       186
OpenFileDialog1.FilterIndex = 1                                          187
OpenFileDialog1.FileName = String.Empty                                  188
OpenFileDialog1.ShowDialog()                                             189
Upload_file = OpenFileDialog1.FileName                                   190
If Upload_file = "" Or Upload_file = "OpenFileDialog" Then               191
MessageBox.Show("Please upload your photo", _
"CADCIM - ERROR", MessageBoxButtons.OK)                                  192
Exit Sub                                                                 193
End If                                                                   194
PictureBox1.Load(OpenFileDialog1.FileName)                               195
End Sub                                                                  196


Private Sub TxtKeySkills_TextChanged(ByVal sender As Object, _
ByVal e As System.EventArgs) Handles TxtKeySkills.TextChanged            197
Lbl_Keys.Text = Len(TxtKeySkills.Text)                                   198
End Sub                                                                  199


Private Sub TxtCode_GotFocus(ByVal sender As Object, _
ByVal e As System.EventArgs) Handles TxtCode.GotFocus                    200
TxtCode.Clear()                                                          201
End Sub                                                                  202


Private Sub TxtCode_LostFocus(ByVal sender As Object, _
ByVal e As System.EventArgs) Handles TxtCode.LostFocus                   203
If TxtCode.Text = "" Then                                                204
TxtCode.Text = "Area Code"                                               205
End If                                                                   206
End Sub                                                                  207


Private Sub TxtPhone_GotFocus(ByVal sender As Object, _
ByVal e As System.EventArgs) Handles TxtPhone.GotFocus                   208
TxtPhone.Clear()                                                         209
End Sub                                                                  210


Private Sub TxtPhone_LostFocus(ByVal sender As Object, _
ByVal e As System.EventArgs) Handles TxtPhone.LostFocus                  211
If TxtPhone.Text = "" Then                                               212
TxtPhone.Text = "Telephone"                                              213
End If                                                                   214
End Sub                                                                  215
```

```
Private Sub TxtMobile_GotFocus(ByVal sender As Object, _
ByVal e As System.EventArgs) Handles TxtMobile.GotFocus          216
TxtMobile.Clear()                                                217
End Sub                                                          218

Private Sub TxtMobile_LostFocus(ByVal sender As Object, _
ByVal e As System.EventArgs) Handles TxtMobile.LostFocus         219
If TxtMobile.Text = "" Then                                      220
TxtMobile.Text = "Mobile Number"                                 221
End If                                                           222
End Sub                                                          223

Private Sub TxtName_Validating(ByVal sender As Object, _
ByVal e As System.ComponentModel.CancelEventArgs) _
Handles TxtName.Validating                                       224
If TxtName.Text = "" Then TxtName.Focus()                        225
End Sub                                                          226

Private Sub RbFemale_CheckedChanged(ByVal sender As Object, _
ByVal e As System.EventArgs) _
Handles RbFemale.CheckedChanged, RbMale.CheckedChanged           227
If RbFemale.Checked = False Then                                 228
If RbMale.Checked = False Then                                   229
RbMale.Focus()                                                   230
End If                                                           231
End If                                                           232
End Sub                                                          233

Private Sub Btn_Search_Click(ByVal sender As System.Object,
ByVal e As System.EventArgs) Handles Btn_Search.Click            234
Dim EmpId As String                                             235
Dim Sql_Str As String                                           236
EmpId = InputBox("Enter the Employee ID", "Search employee data") 237
If EmpId = "" Then Exit Sub                                      238
Sql_Str = "Select * from EmpData where Empid= '"& EmpId & "' "  239
Dc = New SqlCommand(Sql_Str, SqlCnn)                            240
Dr = Dc.ExecuteReader                                           241
If Not Dr.Read() Then                                           242
MessageBox.Show("Employee ID does not exist", _
"CADCIM - Information", MessageBoxButtons.OK)                   243
Dr.Close()                                                     244
Exit Sub                                                       245
End If                                                         246

If IsDBNull(Dr(0)) Then                                        247
MessageBox.Show("Employee ID does not exist", _
"CADCIM - Information", MessageBoxButtons.OK)                   248
```

```
Exit Sub                                                         249
End If                                                           250
TxtEmpId.Text = Dr(0)                                            251
TxtName.Text = Dr(1)                                             252
If Dr(2) = "Male" Then                                           253
RbMale.Checked = True                                            254
RbFemale.Checked = False                                         255
Else                                                             256
RbMale.Checked = False                                           257
RbFemale.Checked = True                                          258
End If                                                           259

TxtDateB.Text = Dr(3)                                            260
CmbCountry.Text = Dr(4)                                          261
TxtCurrLocation.Text = Dr(5)                                     262
TxtCode.Text = Dr(6)                                             263
TxtPhone.Text = Dr(7)                                            264
TxtMobile.Text = Dr(8)                                           265
TxtEmail.Text = Dr(9)                                            266
PictureBox1.Image = Nothing                                      267
PictureBox1.Load(Dr(10))                                         268
TxtQualF.Text = Dr(11)                                           269
TxtHQualf.Text = Dr(12)                                          270
TxtSpecl.Text = Dr(13)                                           271
CmbYrs.Text = Dr(14)                                             272
CmbMonth.Text = Dr(15)                                           273
TxtIndustry.Text = Dr(16)                                        274
TxtCfuncArea.Text = Dr(17)                                       275
TxtRole.Text = Dr(18)                                            276
TxtKeySkills.Text = Dr(19)                                       277
Dr.Close()                                                       278
End Sub                                                          279
End Class                                                        280
```

Explanation
The brief explanation of the source code is given below:

Line 1
Imports System.Data.SqlClient
In this line, the namespace **SqlClient** is imported and then it is used to establish the connection with the SQL server.

Lines 2-7
In these lines, the variables **Dr**, **Da**, **Dc**, **Ds**, and **Upload_file** are declared.

Lines 8-10
In these lines, the **FormClosing** event is raised, as a result of which the database connection will be terminated, when you close the form.

Lines 11-17

In these lines, the status of the database connection is checked. If the connection is closed, then it will be opened. Also, the value **False** is assigned to the **Enabled** property of the **Btn_Add** button, the value **True** is assigned to the **ReadOnly** property of the textbox **TxtEmpId**, and focus is set to the textbox **TxtName**.

Lines 18-39

In these lines, the procedure **LoadData()** is declared. Next, the variable **Dt** is declared as the **DataTable** data type and the new instance of the **SqlDataAdapter** object is created with two arguments. The first argument includes the sql command string and the second argument includes the sql data connection object. The **Fill** method of **SqlDataAdapter** object is used to fill the data in the **DataTable**. Also, the value **Country** is assigned to both the **DisplayMember** and **ValueMember** properties of the **CmbCountry** combo box. In lines 31-36, two **For-Next** loops are executed. The first loop will execute for 40 values and the second loop will execute for 11 values.

Lines 40-42

In these lines, the **ValueChanged** event of the **DateTimePicker** control is raised. Therefore, the value selected from the **DateTimePicker** control is assigned to the **Text** property of the **TxtDateB** textbox.

Lines 43-45

In these lines, the **Click** event of the **Btn_Update** button is raised. Therefore, when the user chooses the **Update** button, the form **FrmEmpReport** will be displayed.

Lines 46-55

In these lines, the **Click** event of the **Btn_Delete** button is raised. Therefore, when the user chooses the **Delete** button, an input box will be displayed prompting the user to enter the employee id. Next, the new instance of the **SqlCommand** is created with two arguments. The first argument includes the delete query and the second argument includes the object of the data connection. The **ExecuteNonQuery()** function will execute the SQL statement against the data connection and return the number of rows affected. Once the execution is over, the message **Record Deleted** will be displayed in the message box.

Lines 56-61

In these lines, the **Click** event of the **Btn_Add** button is coded. Therefore, if the user chooses the **Add** button without uploading any photograph, then an error message will be displayed on the form.

Line 62

In this line, the variables **EmpId**, **EmpName**, **Gender**, **BirthDate**, **Resd_Country**, **Location**, **Std_Code**, **Mobile**, **Email**, **Photo**, **Qualification**, **Higher_Qual**, **Specialization**, **Yr_Exp**, **Mon_Exp**, **Industry**, **Func_Area**, **Role**, and **KeySkills** are declared as **SqlParameter**. These sql parameters represent the parameter of the **SqlCommand**. The Sql parameters are passed to the SQL Server as named parameters and must map to parameter names in the SQL query or store procedures.

Line 63
In this line, a parameterized T-SQL query (**INSERT**) is created by adding more than one parameter to the query. Also, these parameters will be added to the command's parameters collection. This T-SQL query is assigned to the variable **Str_sql** as a string.

Line 64
In this line, the new instance of the **SqlCommand** object is created. The SQL query as a string (**Str_sql**) and a connection object **SqlCnn** are passed as arguments to the **SqlCommand**.

Lines 65-84
In these lines, the new instance of the **SqlParameter** object is created. The parameter name, the data type of the parameter, and the size of the parameter are passed as arguments to the **SqlParameter** object. The data types are defined using any values of **SqlDbType**. Also, note that the size and the data type of the parameter should match with the database object such as table, store procedure, and so on.

Lines 85-108
In these lines, the values will be assigned to the parameters.

Lines 109-128
In these lines, the **Parameters** method of the **SqlCommand** object will be used to add the parameters to the command's parameter collection.

Lines 129-130
In these lines, the **ExecuteNonQuery** method of the **SqlCommand** object will be used to execute the query associated with the **SqlCommand**. Also, a message box with the message **Data added** will be displayed.

Lines 134-181
In these lines, the **Text** properties of the **TextBox** controls are set to null. Also, the new employee id is generated and the **LoadData** method is called.

Lines 182-196
In these lines, the values are assigned to **Title**, **DefaultExt**, **Filter**, and **FilterIndex** methods of the **OpenFileDialog1**. The **OpenFileDialog1** prompts the user to select the image file from the dialog box. If the user does not choose any image file, then a message box with the message **Please upload your photo** will be displayed.

Lines 197-199
In these lines, the **TextChanged** event of the textbox **TxtKeySkills** will be coded. The value of length of the text entered into the textbox **TxtKeySkills** is assigned to the **Text** property of the label **Lbl_Keys**.

Lines 224-226
In these lines, the **Validating** event of the textbox **TxtName** is coded. Here, the value of the textbox **TxtName** is checked. If the user does not enter any value in the textbox **TxtName**, then it prompts the user to enter the value again.

Lines 234-280
In these lines, the **Click** event of the button **Btn_Search** is coded. Here, the input box with the message **Enter the Employee ID** prompts the user to enter the employee id. If the employee id entered by the user exists, then the details of that employee will be displayed on the form. Otherwise, a message box with the message **Employee ID does not exist** will be displayed.

Step 6
Execute the application; the output form will be displayed, as shown in the Figure 10-29.

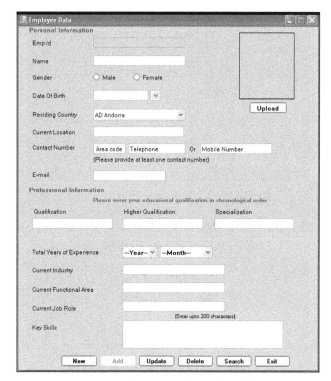

Figure 10-29 *The output form of Application 1*

Step 7
Choose the **New** button from the form; the new employee id will be automatically generated, as shown in Figure 10-30.
Step 8
Enter the other details in the form. After entering all the details, choose the **Upload** button from the form; the **Open File** dialog box will be displayed. Select the desired image file from the dialog box and choose the **Open** button, the image will be added to the form.

Step 9
Next, choose the **Add** button from the form; the employee details will be added to the database. Also, a message box with the message **Data added** will be displayed, as shown in Figure 10-31.
Step 10

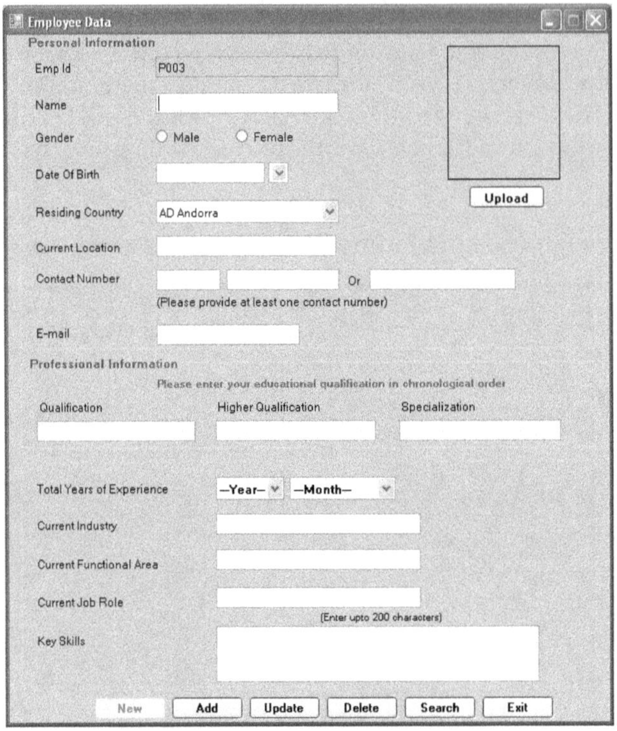

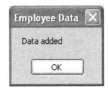

Figure 10-30 The new **Emp Id** generated

Figure 10-31 The message box

Next, to view the current record, choose the **Update** button from the form; the details of all employees will be displayed in a grid, as shown in the Figure 10-32.

Step 11

To search an employee's details, choose the **Search** button from the form; the **Search employee data** input box will be displayed, as shown in Figure 10-33. Enter the employee id in the input box. If the employee id exists in the database object, then all the details of the specified employee will be displayed on the form. Otherwise, a message box with the message **Employee ID does not exist** will be displayed, as shown in Figure 10-34.

Step 12

To delete the details of any specific employee, choose the **Delete** button from the form; the **Delete employee data** input box with the message **Enter the Emp ID** will be displayed, as shown in the Figure 10-35. Enter the employee id and choose the **OK** button in the input box; the **Employee Data** message box with the message **Record Deleted** will be displayed, as shown in the Figure 10-36.

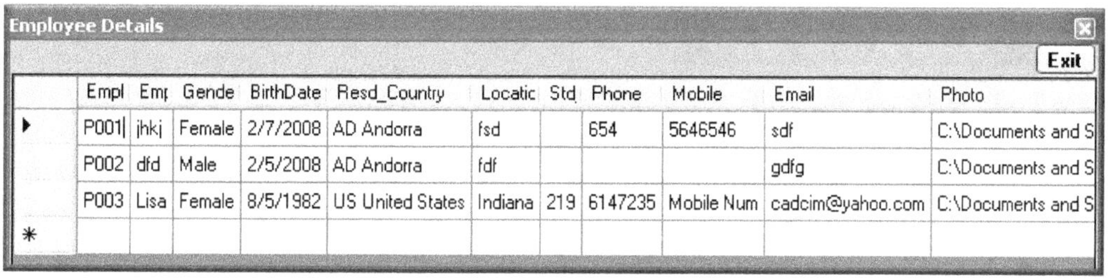

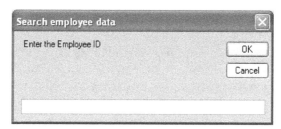

*Figure 10-32 The **Employee Details** grid*

*Figure 10-33 The **Search employee data** input box*

*Figure 10-34 The message box with the message **Employee ID does not exist***

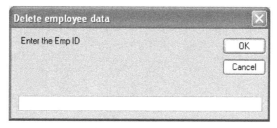

*Figure 10-35 The **Delete employee data** input box*

*Figure 10-36 The message box with the message **Record Deleted***

Self-Evaluation Test

Answer the following questions and then compare them to those given at the end of this chapter:

1. A _____ is a collection of tables that contain the related data.

2. In a database, every column is known as a _____.

3. The _____ key is a particular field or combination of fields that can identify each row in a table uniquely.

4. The _____ command is used to retrieve the fields from the table.

5. The _____ command is used to specify the criteria to retrieve the required records from a database.

Review Questions

Answer the following questions:

1. The _____ command is used to specify a range of values according to your requirement.

2. The _____ command uses partial string matching.

3. The _____ command is used to set the order of records in the dataset.

4. The _____ command is used to select the data that matches with the constant values in a table.

5. The _____ command is used to delete the rows from a table.

Exercises

Exercise 1

Create a table named **student_details** with the fields given next. Also, display the table on a web form.

1. Name
2. Rank
3. Subject

Exercise 2

Create a table named **employee_details** using the **DataGridView** control with the fields given below:

1. Emp_id
2. Designation
3. Address
4. Email_id
5. Contact number

Answers to Self-Evaluation Test
1. database, **2.** field, **3.** primary, **4. SELECT**, **5. WHERE**

Chapter 11

Introduction to Web Forms

Learning Objectives

After completing this chapter, you will be able to:
- *Create web forms.*
- *Add controls to web forms.*
- *Learn about web controls.*
- *Create HTML controls.*

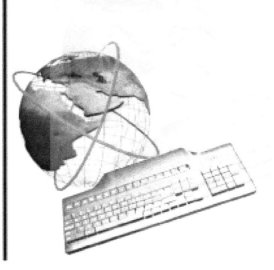

INTRODUCTION

In this chapter, you will learn to create the web applications by using the web forms.

WEB FORMS

The web forms are similar to the windows forms except that these can be accessed by any internet or intranet browser. These are based on ASP.NET (Active Server Pages) and the extension given to these web pages is *.aspx*. For executing the web forms, you need to configure IIS (Internet Information Services) on your computer. Web form is the visual component of the user interface programming. The extension for the coding part of this programming is *.aspx.vb*. For example, if the web page is saved as **Trial.aspx**, the coding will be saved as **Trial.aspx.vb**.

Creating a Web Application

The following steps are required to create a web application:

Step 1
Launch the Microsoft Visual Studio 2008; the **Start Page** will be displayed. Choose **Create Project** from the **Start Page**; the **New Project** dialog box will be displayed.

Step 2
Select the **Web** node from the **Project Types** list box and **ASP.NET Web Application** from the **Templates** area.

Step 3
You will notice that the default name of the web application is **WebApplication1**. You can change the name according to your requirement. Next, choose the **OK** button; a form will be displayed, as shown in Figure 11-1.

If you choose the **Source** tab, which is at the bottom of the web form, the HTML code window will be displayed, as shown in Figure 11-2. You can edit the code in this window. The IIS executes this HTML code and creates a standard HTML code from it. This standard HTML code is then sent to the browser. To make both the design window and the code window visible, choose the **Split** tab, as shown in Figure 11-3.

Adding Controls to a Web Form

You can add controls to the web forms in the same way as you did to the windows forms. The only difference between the windows and the web forms controls is that if you click on the web control, you will notice the **asp** code attached to the control, refer to Figure 11-4.

To enter the source code for a control, such as the **Button** control, double-click on it; the code window will be displayed. To execute the application, press the F5 key. If your application is not executing, then browse the internet explorer and choose **Tools > Internet Options** from the menu bar; the **Internet Options** dialog box will be displayed, as shown in Figure 11-5. Choose the **Advanced** tab and then in the **Browsing** area, clear the **Disable Script Debugging (Internet Explorer)** check box, as shown in Figure 11-6. Next, choose the **OK** button from the **Internet Options** dialog box.

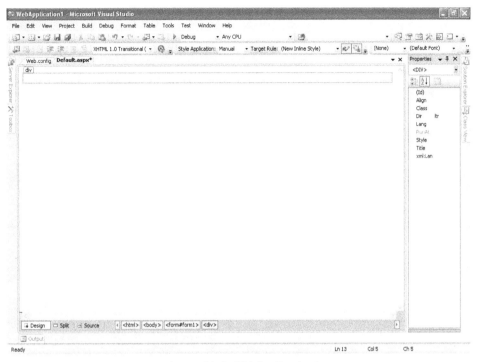

Figure 11-1   *WebApplication1*

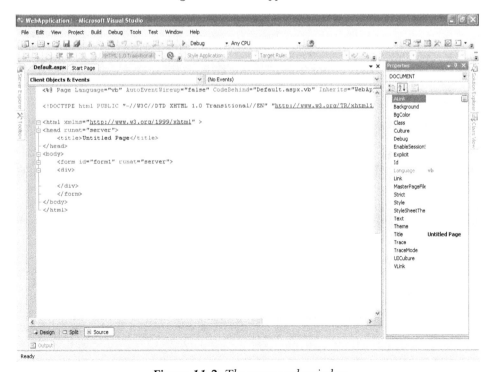

Figure 11-2   *The source code window*

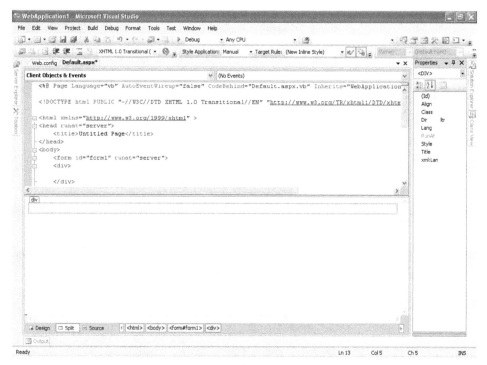

*Figure 11-3 The **Split** window*

*Figure 11-4 The **Button** control*

WEB CONTROLS

There are various types of web controls and some of the important ones are discussed next.

Literal Control

This control is used to display the text on the web page without adding any additional HTML tags.

Adding Literal Control to a Web Page

Double-click on the **Literal** control in the toolbox; it will be added at the upper left corner of the form. Edit the text that you want to display on the web page; the text will be directly added to the web page and therefore, there will be no need to modify its **HTML** page.

LinkButton Control

A **LinkButton** control looks similar to a **HyperLink** control but functions like a **Button** control. So, you can add the code for the **LinkButton** control in the same way as you did for the **Button** control.

*Figure 11-5 The **Internet Options** dialog box*

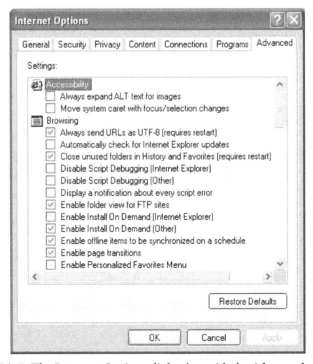

*Figure 11-6 The **Internet Options** dialog box with the **Advanced** tab chosen*

MultiView Control

The **MultiView** control acts as a container for other controls and allows you to view the multiple views alternatively. It is used to provide alternate set of controls according to the user's choice. To add a **MultiView** control to the form, double-click on it. To understand the use of the **MultiView** control, consider the following example:

Add a **Multiview** control to the web form. Within this **MultiView** control, add two **View** controls, **View1** and **View2**. In **View1**, add two **Label** controls, two **TextBox** controls, and a **Button** control. In **View2**, add a **Label** control and a **Button** control. The form should appear similar to Figure 11-7. Next, set the value 0 in the **ActiveViewIndex** property of the **MultiView** control. Execute the application; you will notice that the contents of only **View1** control are displayed, as shown in Figure 11-8. Now, set the value 1 in the **ActiveViewIndex** property of the **MultiView** control. Execute the application; you will notice that now the contents of **View2** control are displayed, as shown in Figure 11-9.

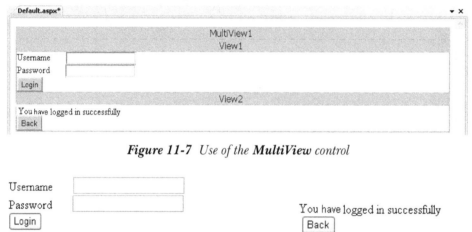

Figure 11-7 Use of the **MultiView** control

Figure 11-8 Contents of the **View1** control   *Figure 11-9* Contents of the **View2** control

RequiredFieldValidator Control

This control is used to ensure that the users have entered some values in the data entry control. In other words, using the **RequiredFieldValidator** control, you can make a field mandatory. For example, refer to the Figure 11-8, if you want to be sure that the user enters a value in the **Username** textbox, you need to use the **RequiredFieldValidator** control. To use the **Required-FieldValidator** control, move the cursor to the location where you want to add the control. Next, double-click on the **RequiredFieldValidator** control in the toolbox; it will be added to the form, as shown in Figure 11-10. Set the value of the **Text** property of the control to **Please enter a valid username**. Also, set the value of the **ControlToValidate** property to **TextBox1** (Username). Execute the application; the resultant form will be displayed, as shown in Figure 11-11. If the user forgets to enter the username, then an error message, **Please enter a valid username** will be displayed, as shown in Figure 11-12.

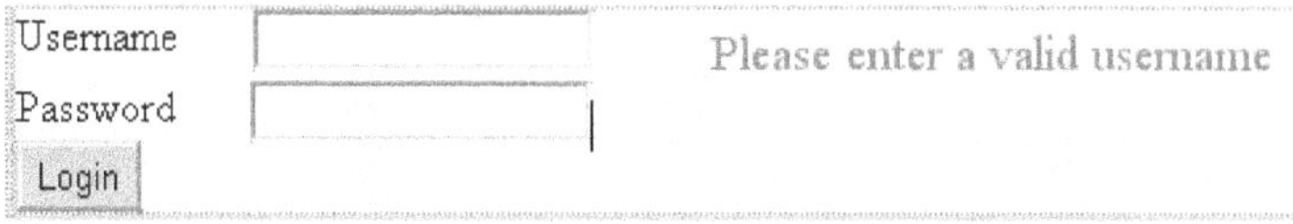

Username [ ] Please enter a valid username
Password [ ]
Login

*Figure 11-10 The **RequiredFieldValidator** control*

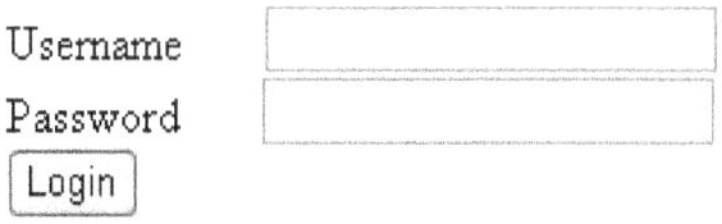

Username [ ]
Password [ ]
Login

Figure 11-11 *The resultant web form*

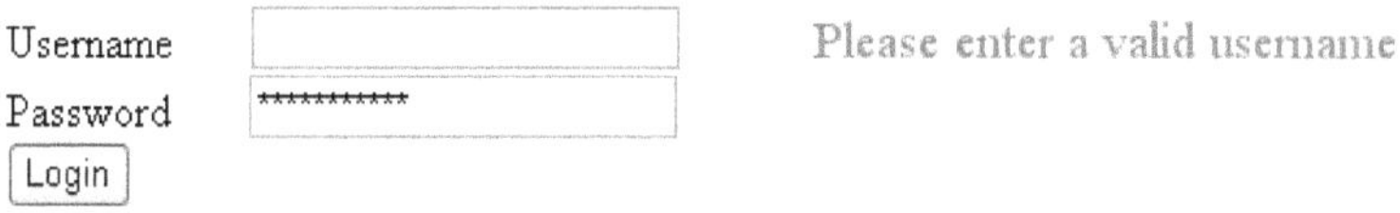

Username [ ] Please enter a valid username
Password [***********]
Login

Figure 11-12 *Output with the error message displayed*

CompareValidator Control

This control is used to compare the values of two textboxes and to ensure that both have the same value. For example, add one more **TextBox** control to the previous example and then name it as **Confirm Password**. If you execute this application now, the user will be prompted to retype the password in the **Confirm Password** textbox. Next, this value will be compared with the **Password** textbox using the **CompareValidator** control. And, if there is a discrepancy between the two values, an error message will be displayed, as shown in Figure 11-13. Note that you should specify the error message, **You have entered a wrong password**, in the **Text** property of the **CompareValidator** control. Also, you need to set the values for the **ControlToCompare** property and the **ControlToValidate** property. In this case, it is **TextBox2** (Password) and **TextBox3** (Confirm Password), respectively.

Figure 11-13 *The **CompareValidator** control*

RangeValidator Control

This control is used to check whether the value entered in the specified **TextBox** control or any other data entry control is within the specified range. For example, add a **Label** control and a **Textbox** control to the previous example. Move the cursor to the location where you want to add the **RangeValidator** control. Double-click on the **RangeValidator** control in the toolbox; it will be added to the form. Set the value of the **ErrorMessage** property to **You should be above 18 years**. Set the value of the **ControlToValidate** property to **TextBox4** (Age). You can also set the values for the **MinimumValue** and **MaximumValue** properties. Execute the application. Now, enter a value less than 18 in the **Age** textbox, for example 8; you will get an error message, as shown in Figure 11-14.

Username	Sam
Password	
Confirm Password	
Age	8 You should be above 18 years
Login	

*Figure 11-14 The **RangeValidator** control*

RegularExpressionValidator Control

This control is used to check whether the value entered by the user matches the pattern defined by the regular expressions. For example, the **Validation Expression** for **Internet E-mail Address** is \w+([-+.]\w+)*@\w+([-.]\w+)*\.\w+([-.]\w+)*, where \w, is used for the word characters, such as numbers, letters, and so on. To use this control, add a **Label** control and a **TextBox** control to the previous example. Next, double-click on it in the toolbox; it will be added to the form. Set the value of the **ControlToValidate** property of the **Regular-ExpressionValidator** control to **TextBox5** (Email). Next, select the **Validation Expression** property; an ellipses button will be displayed. Choose the button; the **Regular Expression Editor** dialog box will be displayed, as shown in Figure 11-15. Select the **Internet e-mail address** option from the **Standard expressions** area; the expression will be displayed in the **Validation expression** edit box. Execute the application.Now, if you enter an invalid email address in the **Email** textbox, an error message will be displayed, as shown in Figure 11-16.

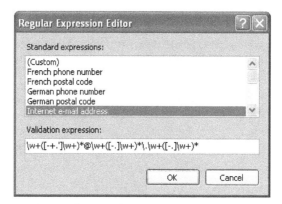

*Figure 11-15 The **Regular Expression Editor** dialog box*

Calendar Control

This control is used to display a single month of a calendar at a time. You can select the required dates from the displayed month in the calendar and also switch to the next or the previous month.

Properties of the Calendar Control

The following are some important properties of the **Calendar** control:

*Figure 11-16 The **RegularExpressionValidator** control*

DayNameFormat

This option is used to set the format of the name of the days in a week. It has four members. These members are discussed next.

Full

If you assign the value **Full** to the **DayNameFormat** property of the **Calendar** control, full names of the days will be displayed on the **Calendar** control, as shown in Figure 11-17.

| asp:calendar#Calendar1 |
| February 2008 |

Sunday	Monday	Tuesday	Wednesday	Thursday	Friday	Saturday
27	28	29	30	31	1	2
3	4	5	6	7	8	9
10	11	12	13	14	15	16
17	18	19	20	21	22	23
24	25	26	27	28	29	1
2	3	4	5	6	7	8

*Figure 11-17 The **Full** view of the **Calendar** control*

Short

If you assign the value **Short** to the **DayNameFormat** property of the **Calendar** control, the name of the days will be displayed in the short form on the **Calendar** control, as shown in Figure 11-18.

| asp:calendar#Calendar1 |
| February 2008 |

Sun	Mon	Tue	Wed	Thu	Fri	Sat
27	28	29	30	31	1	2
3	4	5	6	7	8	9
10	11	12	13	14	15	16
17	18	19	20	21	22	23
24	25	26	27	28	29	1
2	3	4	5	6	7	8

*Figure 11-18 The **Short** view of the **Calendar** control*

FirstLetter
If you assign the value **FirstLetter** to the **DayNameFormat** property of the **Calendar** control, only the first letter of the names of the days will be displayed on the **Calendar** control, as shown in Figure 11-19.

FirstTwoLetters
If you assign the value **FirstTwoLetters** to the **DayNameFormat** property of the **Calendar** control, the first two letters of the names of the days will be displayed on the **Calendar** control, as shown in Figure 11-20.

*Figure 11-19 The **FirstLetter** view of the **Calendar** control*

*Figure 11-20 The **FirstTwoLetters** view of the **Calendar** control*

FirstDayOfWeek
This option is used to set the first day of the week in the first column of the **Calendar** control. It has eight options, out of which seven are the names of the days in a week and the remaining one is the **Default** option.

NextMonthText
Its default value is **>**, that means only one forward arrow will be displayed on the **Calendar** control. If you change its value to **>>** then two forward arrows will be displayed at the upper right corner of the **Calendar** control.

PreMonthText
Its default value is **<**, that means only one backward arrow will be displayed on the **Calendar** control. If you change its value to **<<**, then two backward arrows will be displayed at the upper left corner of the **Calendar** control.

ShowDayHeader
The default value of this property is true. Therefore, the header on which the names of the days are mentioned will be displayed on the **Calendar** control. If you change its value to false, then the header will disappear.

ShowGridLines
This option is used to determine whether the grid lines should appear between the days or not. The default value of this option is false. If you change its value to true, then the grid lines will be displayed between the days.

ShowNextPreMonth

The default value of this property is true. Therefore, the forward and backward arrows will be displayed on the **Calendar** control. If you change its value to false, then the arrows will not be displayed.

ShowTitle

This option is used to determine whether the title should be displayed on the **Calendar** control or not.

TitleFormat

This option is used to set the format of the title that will be displayed on the **Calendar** control.

SelectionMode

This property has three options. The default value of this property is **Day**. If you change this value to **DayWeek**, then the forward arrows will be added to the left of the **Calendar** control. If you choose any of the forward arrows, then the whole row of the days associated with it will be selected. If you set the value to **DayWeekMonth**, then a forward arrow will be displayed in front of the header, on which the name of the days are mentioned. If you choose the arrow in front of the header, then all the dates of the displayed month will be selected.

CellPadding

This option is used to set the space used for cell padding in the **Calendar** control. Its default value is 2.

CellSpacing

This option is used to set the space among the cells in the **Calendar** control.

SelectedDate

This option is used to set the selected date in the **Calendar** control.

DayHeaderStyle

This option is used to set the style of the names of the days in a week on the **Calendar** control.

DayStyle

This option is used to set the style of the dates on the **Calendar** control.

NextPreStyle

This property is used to set the color and style of the forward and backward arrows on the **Calendar** control.

OtherMonthDayStyle

This option is used to set the style of the days of the other months, which are displayed along with the selected month.

SelectedDayStyle
This option is used to set the style of the selected date.

SelectorStyle
This option is used to set the style for the week and month selector. This property can be set only if the property **SelectionMode** is assigned to one of the following values, **DayWeek** and **DayWeekMonth**.

TitleStyle
This option is used to set the style for the title of the **Calendar** control.

TodayDayStyle
This option is used to set the style for today's date on the **Calendar** control.

WeekendDayStyle
This option is used to set the style for the weekend dates.

Table Control

This control is used to display the data in a tabular form on the web form.

Adding a Table Control to a Web Form

The following steps are required to add a **Table** control to a web form:

Step 1
Double-click on the **Table** control in the toolbar; it will be added to the form.

Step 2
Change the value of the **CellPadding** property to 15.

Step 3
Select the **Rows** property from the **Properties** window. Choose the button on its right; the **TableRow Collection Editor** dialog box will be displayed, as shown in Figure 11-21.

Step 4
Choose the **Add** button in the **TableRow Collection Editor** dialog box; a **TableRow** will be added to the **Members** area, indexed 0.

Step 5
Select the **Cells** property from the **TableRow Collection Editor** dialog box and choose the button on its right; the **TableCell Collection Editor** dialog box will be displayed.

Step 6
Choose the **Add** button thrice in the **TableCell Collection Editor** dialog box, three members will be added to the **Members** area of the **TableCell Collection Editor** dialog box. Select the first member. Enter the value **Name** in its **Text** property. Similarly, enter the values **Address** and **Contact** for the second and third members, respectively. Now, choose the **OK** button in the **TableCell Collection Editor** dialog box and then in the **TableRow Collection Editor** dialog box.

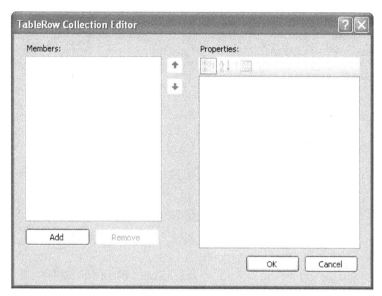

*Figure 11-21 The **TableRow Collection Editor** dialog box*

Step 7
Similarly, add the following values to the **Table** control:

Adim   Washington   0543768
Joe   New York   0786546

Step 8
Select the **GridLines** property of the **Table** control from the **Properties** window. Select the value **Both** from the drop-down list; the grid lines will be added to the **Table** control.

Step 9
Select the **BorderColor** property from the **Properties** window and set any color, for example, **Blue** for the border of the **Table** control.

Step 10
You can set the font and color for the text written in the **Table** control by selecting the **Font** and **ForeColor** properties. You can also set the background color of the control by selecting its **BackColor** property.

Step 11
If you want to set a color for **TableCells**, which is different from the one that you have set for **TableRows**, you can change it in the **TableCell Collection Editor** dialog box.

The values of the various properties in this application are given in the Table 11-1.

Properties	Values	Locations
BackColor	#FFFFC0	**Properties** window
BorderColor	Blue	**Properties** window
CellPadding	15	**Properties** window
Font	Arial, Medium	**Properties** window
ForeColor	Maroon	**Properties** window
GridLines	Both	**Properties** window
ForeColor	OrangeRed	**TableRow Collection Editor** dialog box

Table11-1 *The properties of **Table** control with their values*

Step 12
Execute the application; the **Table** control will be displayed, as shown in Figure 11-22.

Name	Address	Contact
Adim	Washington	0543768
Joe	New York	0786546

Figure 11-22 *The **Table** control*

HTML CONTROLS

In this section, you will learn to work with the HTML controls. These controls are derived from the browser controls.

The following are the HTML controls supported by VB.NET:

TextArea Control

This control is similar to the **Text Field** control, except that in this case, multiple lines of text can be added. To insert the **TextArea** control in a form, choose the **Source** tag and enter the following source code:

```
<textarea name= "area" rows="5" cols="20">This is the textarea example
</textarea>
```

In the above source code, the **textarea** tag is used to allow the user to enter multiple lines of text. The values assigned to the **rows** and **cols** properties specify the dimensions of the **TextArea** control on the form.

After the execution, the **TextArea** control will appear, as shown in Figure 11-23.

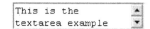

Figure 11-23 *The TextArea control*

Alternatively, you can add the **TextArea** control from the toolbox. To add the control, double-click on the **TextArea** control in the toolbox.

Checkbox Control
As you already know, a checkbox is a field that can have any one of the following two values, check or clear. In this control, a box is displayed on the left of the field title, which may or may not contain a cross-mark (**X**). It is used when a user wants to select one or more options from a list. To add a **Checkbox** control to a form, choose the **HTML** tag and enter the following source code:

```
<input id="checkbox" name="Chk" type= checkbox>
```

In the above source code, the **type** property indicates the type of control that you want to add to the form. If you want the checkbox to be selected, then set the **checked** property of the **Checkbox** control to the value **True** (between the input tags). Alternatively, you can add the **Checkbox** control to the web form from the toolbox.

Radio Button Control
The **Radio Button** control is a small circle. When a user selects the control, a black dot appears in the center of the circle. When the user clears it, the black dot disappears. To add the **Radio Button** control to a form, choose the **HTML** tag and enter the following source code:

```
<input id="radiobutton" name="Rdb" type= radio>
```

HTML Table Control
Tables are used in the HTML documents for the same purpose as they are used in the other documents. An HTML **Table** control can be used to:

1. Align the elements on a page.
2. Add images, text, and hyperlinks to the cells of a table.
3. Create borderless tables.

Creating a Table Control
To create a table, you need to use the **<table>** tag to begin and the **</table>** tag to end. For marking the rows of a table, use the **<TR>** tags and for marking the cells, use the **<TD>** tags. Insert the coding within the **<HTML>** tags. The following are the lines of the HTML source code for creating a table with three rows and three columns:

```
<table>
<TR>
<TD>Name</TD>
<TD>Address</TD>
<TD>Contact Number</TD>
</TR>
<TR>
<TD>Adim</TD>
<TD>Washington</TD>
<TD>0876768</TD>
</TR>
<TR>
<TD>
Albert</TD>
<TD>
Holland</TD>
<TD>
0932435</TD>
</TR>
</table>
```

Once these lines are executed, a borderless table will be displayed on the form, as shown in Figure 11-24.

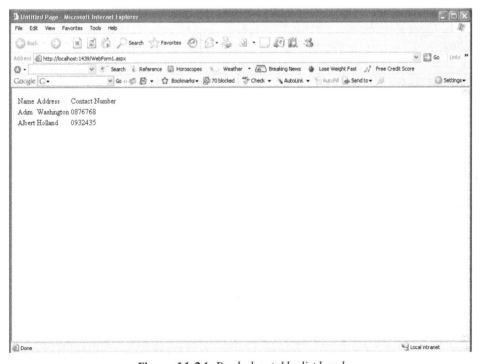

Figure 11-24 Borderless table displayed

Command Button Control

Buttons are generally used to trigger certain actions. The **Submit Button** control is used to transfer the contents of all controls on the page to the server. The **Reset Button** is used to reset the values of the other controls on the form to their initial values. To add a **Button** control to a form, enter the following source code within the **<form>** tags:

> <input type= submit name="Submit" value= Click id="sbt"
> style="FONT-WEIGHT: "FONT-SIZE: 12pt; COLOR: red">

On using the given source code, the **Click** button will be added to the web form.

The following application illustrates the use of the web controls.

Application 1

Create an application for requesting an evaluation copy of a book.

This application will prompt the user to enter his email address and then submit the request for an evaluation copy. This application will contain two web forms, one for confirming the email address and the other for registration.

The following steps are required to create this application:

Step 1
Start a new project; the **New Project** dialog box will be displayed, as shown in Figure 11-25.

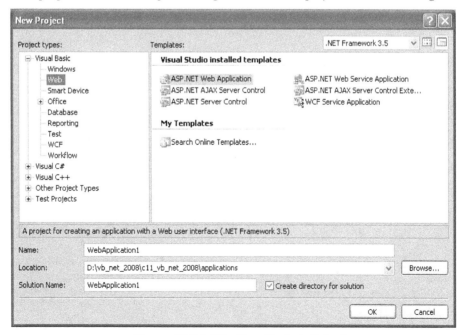

Figure 11-25   *The **New Project** dialog box*

Select the **Web** node from the **Project types** area and choose the **ASP.NET Web Application** option from the **Templates** area. Then, save the project as **c11_VB_NET_2008_01**.

Step 2

Add an HTML **Table** control to the form. To add the table, double-click on the **Table** control from the HTML tag of the toolbar.

Step 3

Add two **TextBox** controls, an HTML **TextArea** control, two **RadioButton** controls, and a **Button** control. Also, add the required text to the **Table** control. The resultant web form will appear, as shown in Figure 11-26.

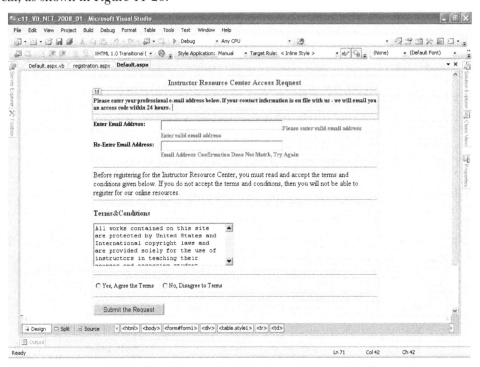

Figure 11-26   The design mode of the first web form of Application 1

Step 4

Add another web form to the project. To add the web form, choose **Project > Add New Item**; the **Add New Item** dialog box will be displayed, as shown in Figure 11-27. Select the **Web** node from the **Categories** area.

Step 5

Right-click on the form and choose the **View Code** option; the code window will be displayed. Next, enter the following source code in the code window. The line numbers on the right are not a part of the program and are for reference only.

Partial Public Class _Default   1
Inherits System.Web.UI.Page   2

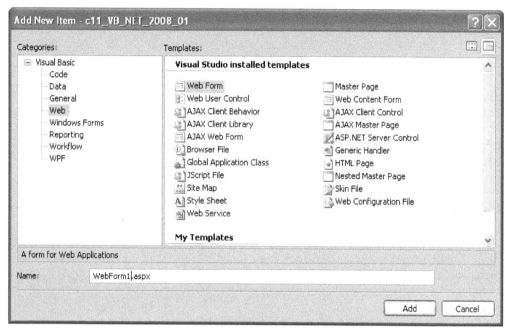

Figure 11-27 The **Add New Item** *dialog box*

```
Protected Sub Page_Load(ByVal sender As Object, _
ByVal e As EventArgs) Handles Me.Load                                    3
Btn_Submit.Visible = False                                               4
End Sub                                                                  5


Private Sub Btn_Submit_Click(ByVal sender As Object, _
ByVal e As System.EventArgs) Handles Btn_Submit.Click                    6
Session("Email") = Txt_Email.Text                                        7
Response.Redirect("registration.aspx")                                   8
End Sub                                                                  9


Private Sub RbYes_CheckedChanged(ByVal sender As Object, _
ByVal e As System.EventArgs) Handles RbYes.CheckedChanged                10
If RbYes.Checked = True Then                                             11
Btn_Submit.Visible = True                                                12
Else                                                                     13
Btn_Submit.Visible = False                                               14
End If                                                                   15
End Sub                                                                  16


Private Sub RbNo_CheckedChanged(ByVal sender As Object, _
ByVal e As System.EventArgs) Handles RbNo.CheckedChanged                 17
If RbNo.Checked = True Then                                              18
Btn_Submit.Visible = False                                               19
Else                                                                     20
```

```
Btn_Submit.Visible = True                                              21
End If                                                                 22
End Sub                                                                23
End Class                                                              24
```

Explanation
The line-by-line explanation of the above given source code is as follows:

Line 1
Partial Public Class _Default
In this line, the **Default** class is a partial restore operation.

Line 7
Session("Email") = Txt_Email.Text
In the above line, the value of the **Text** property of the **Txt_Email** textbox is assigned to the variable **Email** stored in the current **Session** (Variables stored in a session object hold the information about a single user and are available to all the pages in one application. The server creates a new session object for each new user and destroys the session object once the session expires).

Line 8
Response.Redirect("registration.aspx")
In the above line, the function **Response.Redirect** sends the message to the browser to move to another web page.

Step 6
Add an HTML **Table** control to the form.

Step 7
Add twelve **TextBox** controls, a **DropDownList** control, two **RequiredField** controls, a **CompareValidator** control, and two **Button** controls to the **Table** control. The form will appear as shown in Figure 11-28.

Step 8
Right-click on the web form and choose the **View Code** option; the code window will be displayed. Enter the following source code in the code window:

```
Public Partial Class registration                                      1
Inherits System.Web.UI.Page                                            2

Protected Sub Page_Load(ByVal sender As Object, _
ByVal e As System.EventArgs) Handles Me.Load                           3
Txt_Email.Text = Session("Email")                                      4
End Sub                                                                5

Protected Sub Btn_Submit_Click(ByVal sender As Object, _
ByVal e As EventArgs) Handles Btn_Submit.Click                         6
If Validate_Text() = False Then Exit Sub                               7
```

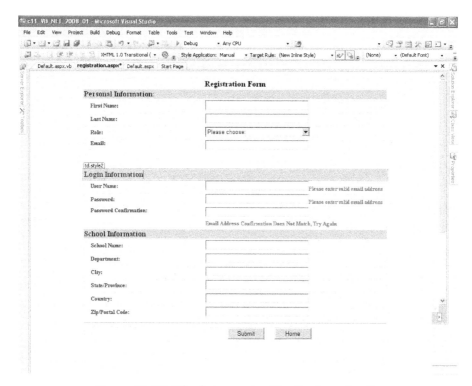

Figure 11-28 *The design mode of the **Registration Form***

```
MsgBox("Registered successfully")                                        8
End Sub                                                                  9


Public Function Validate_Text() As Boolean                             10
If TxtFname.Text = "" Or TxtLname.Text = "" Or TxtState.Text = "" Or _
TxtCountry.Text = "" Or Txtschool.Text = "" Or TxtZip.Text = "" Or _
DdRole.SelectedIndex < 0 Then                                          11
Validate_Text = False                                                  12
Else                                                                   13
Validate_Text = True                                                   14
End If                                                                 15
End Function                                                           16


Protected Sub Btn_Home_Click(ByVal sender As Object, _
ByVal e As EventArgs) Handles Btn_Home.Click                           17
Response.Redirect("Default.aspx")                                      18
End Sub                                                                19
End Class                                                              20
```

Step 9

Execute the application; the web form will be displayed, as shown in Figure 11-29. Enter the email address in the **Enter Email Address** textbox and then again enter the email address in

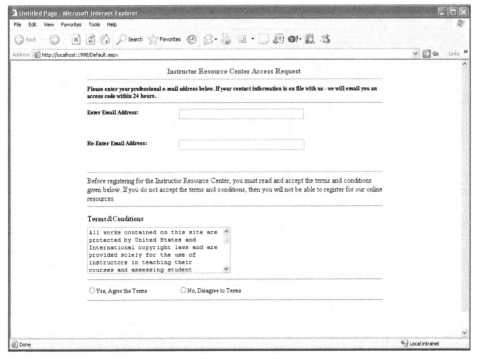

Figure 11-29   *The output of the first web form*

the **Re-Enter Email Address** textbox to confirm the email address. Next, select the **Yes, Agree to Terms** radio button. Next, choose the **Submit The Request** button; the **Registration Form** will be displayed, as shown in Figure 11-30.

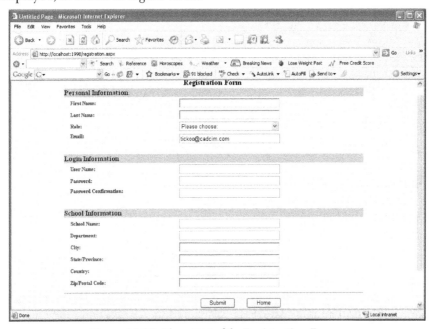

Figure 11-30   *The output of the* **Registration Form**

Step 10
Enter the required information in the **Registration Form** and then choose the **Submit** button; a message box with the message **Registered successfully** will be displayed.

Self-Evaluation Test

Answer the following questions and then compare them to those given at the end of this chapter:

1. Web forms are based on _____.

2. IIS stands for _____.

3. The visual components have an extension _____.

4. The _____ control is used to directly add text to the web page.

5. The _____ control is used to compare the values of one textbox with another.

Review Questions

Answer the following questions:

1. The _____ control is used to check whether the value entered in the specified control is within the specified range or not.

2. The _____ control is used to display a single month of a calendar.

3. The _____ property is used to set the first day of the week in the first column of the **Calendar** control.

4. The _____ property is used to set the text for the week selection element.

5. The _____ is used to set the style for the dates of the week on the **Calendar** control.

Exercises

Exercise 1

Create an application to display a form for placing an order for books. The output of your application should be similar to Figure 11-31.

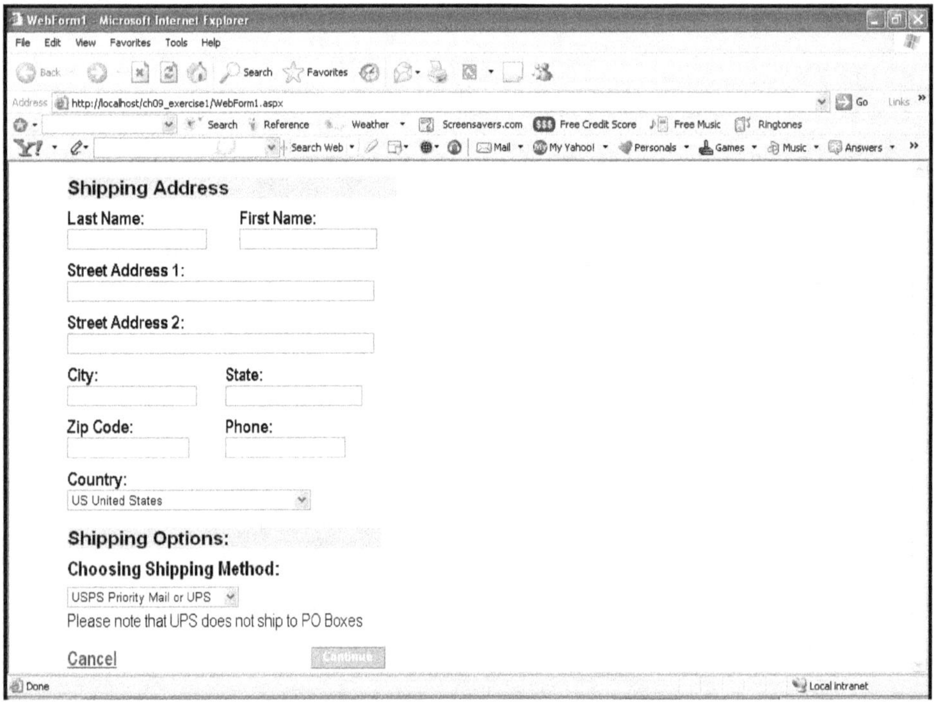

Figure 11-31 Output of Exercise 1

Exercise 2

Create an application to display a table. The output of your application should be similar to Figure 11-32.

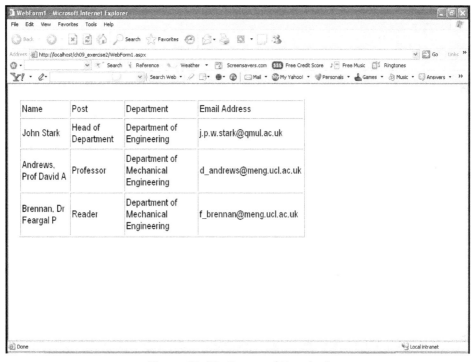

Figure 11-32 *Output of Exercise 2*

Answers to Self-Evaluation Test
1. ASP.NET, **2.** Internet Information Services, **3.** *.aspx*, **4. Literal**, **5. CompareValidator**

Student Projects

Student Project 1

Create an application to display a calculator. The output of your application should be similar to Figure 1.

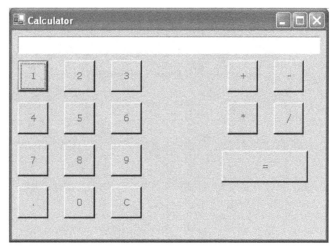

Figure 1 *Calculator*

Student Project 2

Create an application to display a loan calculator. The output of your application should be similar to Figure 2.

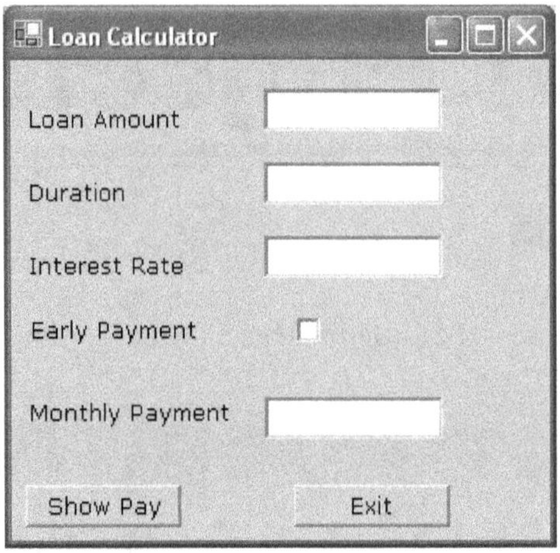

Figure 2 *The **Loan Calculator** form*

Student Project 3

Create an application that will display an order form for a bookstore. The application should include a MDI form with four menu items, as shown in Figure 3. The forms associated with the menu items should be similar to Figures 4, 5, and 6, respectively.

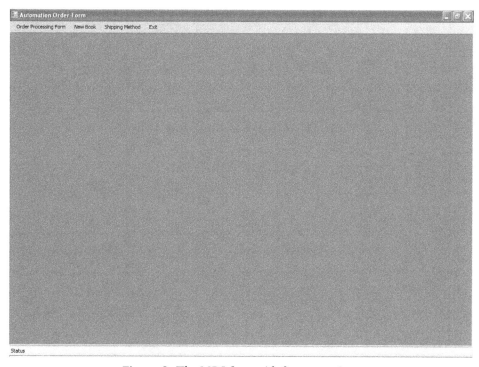

Figure 3 *The MDI form with four menu items*

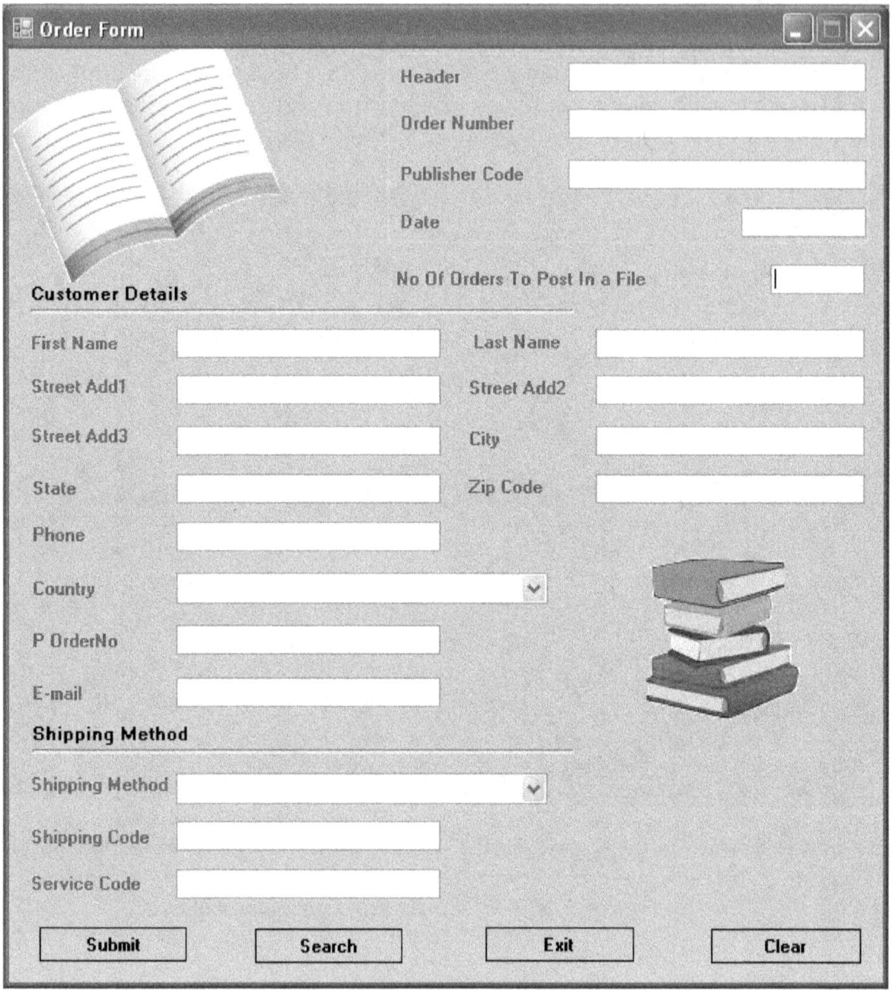

Figure 4 The ***Order Form***

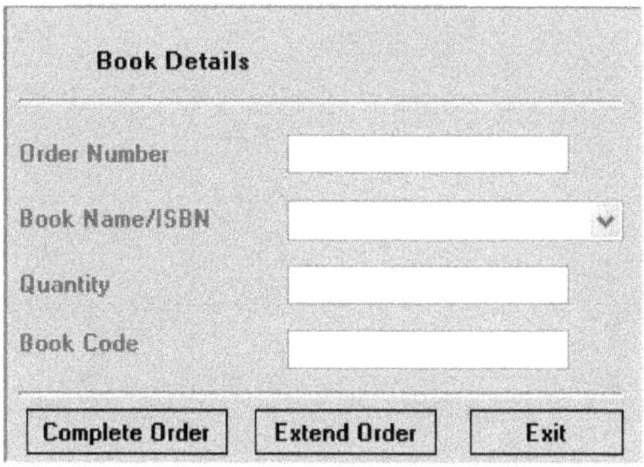

*Figure 5 The **Book Details** form*

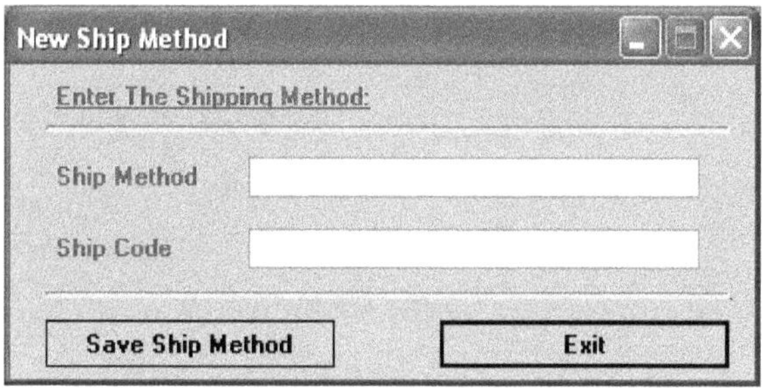

*Figure 6 The **New Ship Method** form*

Index

Other Publications by CADCIM Technologies

The following is the list of some of the publications by CADCIM Technologies. Please visit *www.cadcim.com* for the complete listing.

3ds Max Textbooks
- Autodesk 3ds Max 2016: A Comprehensive Guide, 16th Edition
- Autodesk 3ds Max 2015: A Comprehensive Guide, 15th Edition
- Autodesk 3ds Max 2014: A Comprehensive Guide
- Autodesk 3ds Max 2013: A Comprehensive Guide
- Autodesk 3ds Max 2012: A Comprehensive Guide

Autodesk Maya Textbooks
- Autodesk Maya 2016: A Comprehensive Guide, 8th Edition
- Autodesk Maya 2015: A Comprehensive Guide, 7th Edition
- Character Animation: A Tutorial Approach
- Autodesk Maya 2014: A Comprehensive Guide
- Autodesk Maya 2013: A Comprehensive Guide
- Autodesk Maya 2012: A Comprehensive Guide

ZBrush Textbook
- Pixologic ZBrush 4R6: A Comprehensive Guide

CINEMA 4D Textbooks
- MAXON CINEMA 4D Studio R16: A Tutorial Approach, 3rd Edition
- MAXON CINEMA 4D Studio R15: A Tutorial Approach
- MAXON CINEMA 4D Studio R14: A Tutorial Approach

Fusion Textbooks
- The eyeon Fusion 6.3: A Tutorial Approach
- Black Magic Design Fusion 7 Studio: A Tutorial Approach

Flash Textbooks
- Adobe Flash Professional CC: A Tutorial Approach
- Adobe Flash Professional CS6: A Tutorial Approach

Premiere Textbooks
- Adobe Premiere Pro CC: A Tutorial Approach, 3rd Edition
- Adobe Premiere Pro CS6: A Tutorial Approach
- Adobe Premiere Pro CS5.5: A Tutorial Approach

3ds Max Design Textbooks
• Autodesk 3ds Max Design 2015: A Tutorial Approach, 15th Edition
• Autodesk 3ds Max Design 2014: A Tutorial Approach
• Autodesk 3ds Max Design 2013: A Tutorial Approach
• Autodesk 3ds Max Design 2012: A Tutorial Approach
• Autodesk 3ds Max Design 2011: A Tutorial Approach

Softimage Textbook
• Autodesk Softimage 2014: A Tutorial Approach
• Autodesk Softimage 2013: A Tutorial Approach

AutoCAD Textbooks
• AutoCAD 2016: A Problem-Solving Approach, Basic and Intermediate, 22nd Edition
• AutoCAD 2016: A Problem-Solving Approach, 3D and Advanced, 22nd Edition
• AutoCAD 2015: A Problem-Solving Approach, Basic and Intermediate, 21st Edition
• AutoCAD 2015: A Problem-Solving Approach, 3D and Advanced, 21st Edition
• AutoCAD 2014: A Problem-Solving Approach

Autodesk Inventor Textbooks
• Autodesk Inventor 2016 for Designers, 16th Edition
• Autodesk Inventor 2015 for Designers, 15th Edition
• Autodesk Inventor 2014 for Designers
• Autodesk Inventor 2013 for Designers
• Autodesk Inventor 2012 for Designers
• Autodesk Inventor 2011 for Designers

AutoCAD MEP Textbooks
• AutoCAD MEP 2016 for Designers, 3rd Edition
• AutoCAD MEP 2015 for Designers
• AutoCAD MEP 2014 for Designers

Solid Edge Textbooks
• Solid Edge ST7 for Designers, 12th Edition
• Solid Edge ST6 for Designers
• Solid Edge ST5 for Designers
• Solid Edge ST4 for Designers
• Solid Edge ST3 for Designers
• Solid Edge ST2 for Designers

NX Textbooks
• NX 9.0 for Designers, 8th Edition
• NX 8.5 for Designers
• NX 8 for Designers
• NX 7 for Designers

SolidWorks Textbooks
- SOLIDWORS 2015 for Designers, 13th Edition
- SolidWorks 2014 for Designers
- SolidWorks 2013 for Designers
- SolidWorks 2012 for Designers
- SolidWorks 2014: A Tutorial Approach
- SolidWorks 2012: A Tutorial Approach
- Learning SolidWorks 2011: A Project Based Approach
- SolidWorks 2011 for Designers

CATIA Textbooks
- CATIA V5-6R2014 for Designers, 12th Edition
- CATIA V5-6R2013 for Designers
- CATIA V5-6R2012 for Designers
- CATIA V5R21 for Designers
- CATIA V5R20 for Designers
- CATIA V5R19 for Designers

Creo Parametric and Pro/ENGINEER Textbooks
- PTC Creo Parametric 3.0 for Designers, 3rd Edition
- Creo Parametric 2.0 for Designers
- Creo Parametric 1.0 for Designers
- Pro/Engineer Wildfire 5.0 for Designers
- Pro/ENGINEER Wildfire 4.0 for Designers
- Pro/ENGINEER Wildfire 3.0 for Designers

ANSYS Textbooks
- ANSYS Workbench 14.0: A Tutorial Approach
- ANSYS 11.0 for Designers

Creo Direct Textbook
- Creo Direct 2.0 and Beyond for Designers

Autodesk Alias Textbooks
- Learning Autodesk Alias Design 2016, 5th Edition
- Learning Autodesk Alias Design 2015, 4th Edition
- Learning Autodesk Alias Design 2012
- Learning Autodesk Alias Design 2010
- AliasStudio 2009 for Designers

AutoCAD LT Textbooks
- AutoCAD LT 2015 for Designers, 10th Edition
- AutoCAD LT 2014 for Designers
- AutoCAD LT 2013 for Designers
- AutoCAD LT 2012 for Designers
- AutoCAD LT 2011 for Designers

EdgeCAM Textbooks
• EdgeCAM 11.0 for Manufacturers
• EdgeCAM 10.0 for Manufacturers

AutoCAD Electrical Textbooks
• AutoCAD Electrical 2015 for Electrical Control Designers, 6th Edition
• AutoCAD Electrical 2014 for Electrical Control Designers
• AutoCAD Electrical 2013 for Electrical Control Designers
• AutoCAD Electrical 2012 for Electrical Control Designers
• AutoCAD Electrical 2011 for Electrical Control Designers
• AutoCAD Electrical 2010 for Electrical Control Designers

Autodesk Revit Architecture Textbooks
• Autodesk Revit Architecture 2016 for Architects and Designers, 12th Edition
• Autodesk Revit Architecture 2015 for Architects and Designers, 11th Edition
• Autodesk Revit Architecture 2014 for Architects and Designers
• Autodesk Revit Architecture 2013 for Architects and Designers
• Autodesk Revit Architecture 2012 for Architects and Designers

Autodesk Revit Structure Textbooks
• Exploring Autodesk Revit Structure 2016, 6th Edition
• Exploring Autodesk Revit Structure 2015, 5th Edition
• Exploring Autodesk Revit Structure 2014
• Exploring Autodesk Revit Structure 2013
• Exploring Autodesk Revit Structure 2012

AutoCAD Civil 3D Textbooks
• Exploring AutoCAD Civil 3D 2016, 6th Edition
• Exploring AutoCAD Civil 3D 2015, 5th Edition
• Exploring AutoCAD Civil 3D 2014
• Exploring AutoCAD Civil 3D 2013

AutoCAD Map 3D Textbooks
• Exploring AutoCAD Map 3D 2016, 6th Edition
• Exploring AutoCAD Map 3D 2015, 5th Edition
• Exploring AutoCAD Map 3D 2014
• Exploring AutoCAD Map 3D 2013
• Exploring AutoCAD Map 3D 2012

Revit MEP Textbooks
• Exploring Autodesk Revit MEP 2016, 3rd Edition
• Exploring Autodesk Revit MEP 2015
• Exploring Autodesk Revit MEP 2014

STAAD Pro Textbook
• Exploring Bentley STAAD.Pro V8i

Navisworks Textbooks
• Exploring Autodesk Navisworks 2015, 3rd Edition
• Exploring Autodesk Navisworks 2015
• Exploring Autodesk Navisworks 2014

Computer Programming Textbooks
• Learning Oracle 11g
• Learning ASP.NET AJAX
• Learning Java Programming
• Learning Visual Basic.NET 2008
• Learning C++ Programming Concepts
• Learning VB.NET Programming Concepts

AutoCAD Textbooks Authored by Prof. Sham Tickoo and Published by Autodesk Press
• AutoCAD: A Problem-Solving Approach: 2013 and Beyond
• AutoCAD 2012: A Problem-Solving Approach
• AutoCAD 2011: A Problem-Solving Approach
• AutoCAD 2010: A Problem-Solving Approach
• Customizing AutoCAD 2010
• AutoCAD 2009: A Problem-Solving Approach

Textbooks Authored by CADCIM Technologies and Published by Other Publishers

3D Studio MAX and VIZ Textbooks
• Learning 3DS Max: A Tutorial Approach, Release 4
  Goodheart-Wilcox Publishers (USA)
• Learning 3D Studio VIZ: A Tutorial Approach
  Goodheart-Wilcox Publishers (USA)

CADCIM Technologies Textbooks Translated in Other Languages

SolidWorks Textbooks
• SolidWorks 2008 for Designers (Serbian Edition)
  Mikro Knjiga Publishing Company, Serbia
• SolidWorks 2006 for Designers (Russian Edition)
  Piter Publishing Press, Russia
• SolidWorks 2006 for Designers (Serbian Edition)
  Mikro Knjiga Publishing Company, Serbia

NX Textbooks

- NX 6 for Designers (Korean Edition)
  Onsolutions, South Korea
- NX 5 for Designers (Korean Edition)
  Onsolutions, South Korea

Pro/ENGINEER Textbooks

- Pro/ENGINEER Wildfire 4.0 for Designers (Korean Edition)
  HongReung Science Publishing Company, South Korea
- Pro/ENGINEER Wildfire 3.0 for Designers (Korean Edition)
  HongReung Science Publishing Company, South Korea

Autodesk 3ds Max Textbook

- 3ds Max 2008: A Comprehensive Guide (Serbian Edition)
  Mikro Knjiga Publishing Company, Serbia

AutoCAD Textbooks

- AutoCAD 2006 (Russian Edition)
  Piter Publishing Press, Russia
- AutoCAD 2005 (Russian Edition)
  Piter Publishing Press, Russia
- AutoCAD 2000 Fondamenti (Italian Edition)

Coming Soon from CADCIM Technologies

- Solid Edge ST8 for Designers
- NX 10.0 for Designers
- NX Nastran 9.0 for Designers
- SOLIDWORKS Simulation 2015 for Designers
- Exploring Primavera P6 V8
- Exploring Risa 3D 12.0
- Exploring Autodesk Raster Design 2016 for Image Processing

Online Training Program Offered by CADCIM Technologies

CADCIM Technologies provides effective and affordable virtual online training on animation, architecture, and GIS softwares, computer programming languages, and Computer Aided Design and Manufacturing (CAD/CAM) software packages. The training will be delivered 'live' via Internet at any time, any place, and at any pace to individuals, students of colleges, universities, and CAD/CAM training centers. For more information, please visit the following link: *www.cadcim.com*

www.ingramcontent.com/pod-product-compliance
Lightning Source LLC
LaVergne TN
LVHW062301060326
832902LV00013B/1992